OIL AND FISCAL FEDERALISM IN NIGERIA

Oil and Fiscal Federalism in Nigeria

The political economy of resource allocation in a developing country

AUGUSTINE A. IKEIN
COMFORT BRIGGS-ANIGBOH

Ashgate

Aldershot • Brookfield USA • Singapore • Sydney

Published by
Ashgate Publishing Limited
Gower House
Croft Road
Aldershot
Hants GU11 3HR
England

Ashgate Publishing Company
Old Post Road
Brookfield
Vermont 05036
USA

H J

1501

.Z7

I37

1998

British Library Cataloguing in Publication Data
Ikein, Augustine A.
    Oil and fiscal federalism in Nigeria : the political
    economy of resource allocation in a developing country. -
    (The making of modern Africa)
    1. Fiscal policy - Nigeria 2. Revenue sharing - Nigeria
    I Title II. Briggs-Anigboh, Comfort
    351.7'25'09669

Library of Congress Catalog Card Number: 96-86363

ISBN 1 85628 848 X

Printed in Great Britain by The Ipswich Book Company, Suffolk

Table of contents

vii

List of tables

List of figures

Preface

A 'federal solution' has often been sought as a way to integrate diverse groups in a pluralistic and heterogeneous society into a single polity, while maintaining their independent identities at the same time. This attempt at bringing about a sort of equilibrium between the pressures for unity and diversity is being made by political leaders in such countries with diverse elements as in the United States, India, and a host of former British and other European colonies in the Developing World.

Even in the most successful federal systems, the power boundaries between the separate political units are never clearly delineated. Since these units share functions and responsibilities, the struggle for influence over crucial policy areas is a regular source of friction in any federation. And one is where the struggle is intensified is the financial arena where the ultimate goals of fiscal policy are decided, particularly the system of revenue allocation.

When Nigeria emerged as an independent nation in 1960, its economy was largely dependent on Agrarian produce, the national revenue allocation system was based on derivation principle and it was constitutionally guaranteed but the upsurge of oil that displaced cash crops as the major source of national wealth, the revenue allocation system was revised to a non-derivation based system of national wealth distribution.

In Nigeria, financing the federation had been very controversial and thorny issue, demonstrated by the desire for power by each region. There were two theoretical alternatives to explaining the drive for power by each regional government: To budget for the regions response to their needs or according to the total revenues which they provided from the sale of Agrarian produce. The policy makers from the then richer Western and Northern regions advocated the greater use of the Derivation Principle. The then Eastern Region policy makers resisted the derivation principle. However, only with the large discoveries of oil in the Eastern part of the country that the Eastern region policy makers began to prefer the Derivation Principle. But, irrespective of any regional government position, the Central government always allocated a major portion of the revenues to itself because the Federal government is considered the repository of the National interest and therefore all efforts should be made to strengthen its finances. That the financial stability of the Central government must be the main guarantor of the financial stability of Nigeria as a whole. By its strength and solvency the credit worthiness of the country will be appraised.

Despite this worthy desire to maintain a strong center, there has been apparent misapplication of this form of fiscal federalism in Nigeria, for policy makers tend to identify more strongly with their localities or parochial interest than with the federal government especially when the revenue allocation principles for inter state sharing are applied.

In the developing federations, due to a mixture of historical, economic and political circumstances, the bulk of the nation's revenues is usually collected centrally and then shared among and between the different governmental levels. The process of carrying out this intergovernmental transfer of revenues in a society that is still undergoing rapid and complex political and economic changes forms the crux of this work. Nigeria offers an interesting case for analysis because of gross disparities in its constituent parts, the ethno-cultural particularism that persists and the need to satisfy all interested parties, and at the same time, engage in economic growth and development. However, policy makers in a developing federation like Nigeria have a daunting task to perform when they set out to formulate fiscal policies and a system of revenue allocation.

Nigeria provides an excellent case for examining how the various issues involved in fiscal federalism in a developing economy are handled. The country has maintained a federal type of government despite several changes in government and leadership since independence. Its States are more or less ethnically defined and are locked in a fierce competition over the sharing of national revenues and other resources. Each successor government has tried and failed to establish regular and institutionalized mode of resource allocation, as practiced in older federations. Moreover, the bulk of the national revenue, which is obtained from crude oil, is derived from parts of the country populated by ethnic minorities who bemoan what they perceive as a lack of access to the federal policy making apparatus.

Thus, in Nigeria and other developing federations, the cardinal principles of fiscal federalism, equity and efficiency — are seen, not only in economic terms, but more so overtly in political terms. The goal of fiscal policy then, is to ensure there is a reasonable balance in power and resources between the various ethnic groups (or States) and translate that balance into fiscal equity that fosters regional and national development.

About the authors

Augustine A. Ikein, Ph.D. (Atlanta University), also holds a BSC.(Economics) degree from the City University of New York and an MBA (finance/management) from Adelphi University, New York and received the FulBright Scholar award in 1998 from the Council of International Exchange of Scholars. He has been a professor of economics, finance, and policy studies in several U.S. institutions and is a recipient of the UNCF and Lily Foundation Fellowship Awards. He is 1994 recipient of Nissan Fellowship [Nissan Fellows Institute, Graduate School of Business; University of Chicago] He is the author of such articles as "Barriers to Balanced Growth in Developing Countries"; Agrarian Women and the development of the indigenous textile industry in Nigeria. The Conflicting Choice Between Environmental Quality, Development and Human Welfare in Africa: Socio-economic, Environmental and Legal Aspect of Gas Flaring in the Nigerian Oil Industry in Developing Nations Environmental Dilemmas: Africa by the year 2000 and beyond. "The Socioeconomic Impact of European Reforms on Gender and Development in Africa". [Greenwood Press]; "World Oil Dynamics: A Consumer Producer Behavioral Order " , Nigeria: Oil,Nation Building and Foreign Policy. The Political Economy of Black Gold and Black Power in Africa .[Forthcoming Books]; "The Impact of Oil on A Developing Country. [Praegar Publishers, New York.] "Energy Self Sufficiency Versus Global Security: A Contending Perspective"; The Politics of Energy, God and Man"; "Should Human Reserves Take Precedence Over Oil Reserves? An Alternative to the OPEC Quota Allocation System"; Still Oloibiri: A Profile of Nigeria's Pioneer Oil Community". Dr. Ikein is also a coauthor of *Moral Equivalent of War?* A study of Nonmilitary Service in Nine Nations (Greenwood Press.) An International Comparative study on national service policy and programs. The author has special interest on the relationship between natural resource endowment and Development in the Third World.

Comfort Briggs Anigboh Ph.D. George Washington University, also holds B.A. and M. Phil degrees from the same university. Before her inception into academia, Dr. Briggs-Anigboh worked as a Journalist in Nigeria. She was a graduate teaching assistant at George Washington University. She was a lecturer in Public Policy at the University of Ibadan during her National Service years at Ibadan, Oyo state of Nigeria.

She was a special correspondent for a major Daily Newspaper at the National Assembly in 1980. She is currently a consultant with a private policy agency in Washington, D.C.

DEDICATION

This book is dedicated to our beloved parents, and uncle who toiled so hard for our education. They are all called back to be with the Lord and to the children the promise of our future.

Pa Ernest Briggs
Madam Darling Briggs
Parents of Dr. Comfort Briggs Anigboh
Chief Asangwua Ikein
Madam Bomopregha Ikein
Luke A. Sokoromo
Parents and Uncle of Dr. Augustine A. Ikein

And to the Children
Asangwua Abidi Ikein
Bomo Pregha Ikein
Esweni A. Ikein
Zenaeby Austin Ikein
Atosemy Fendougha Ikein
Uche Chukwu Anigboh
Ifeanyi Chukwu Angiboh

Acknowledgments

The full realization of this work was made possible through the support of our families, friends and the valuable contributions of many scholars and policy makers on the subject of oil revenues and fiscal federalism.

Our deep Gratitude to our family members and special friends: Senyi Briggs, Alaba Briggs, Adiledi, Charles Sokoromo, Victoria Eppie, Bara, Timi, Stella Ikein, Mrs. Ebiboere Yaye James Ebikoro, Abadere Sokoromo, Walter Ikein, Crowther Ikein, The Ikoloms, Dr. Ibiba Sasime, Dr. S. A. Agoro, Dr. Frank Ekanem, Prof. U. Akeh, Dr. Uzobeyi Anigboh, Onimi Briggs, Gloria Nwogu (Ikein), Dr. Tee, Dorothy Tee, Akpuruku, Ebi and Ibeni Iwollo and Chief Johnson Nwogu and Rev. Mrs. Esther Nwogu, Chief F.K. Tebepina, and Chief Bobai. The authors are particularly grateful to all previous researchers on the subject and the inspiration and enlightenment we have gathered from their work. The scholars whose works are cited herein or given permission for the use of their work in this book are highly commended for their effort. The authors are grateful to the following Nigerian associations and individuals who have contributed to various occasions to render constructive exchange of ideas that are pertinent to Nation Building in Nigeria. They are: Rivers Foundation, USA, Kalabari Association, Egbe Omo Oduduwa, Urhobo North America, Izon Association of California, Ijaw National Alliance and the Ijaw Associations in America and Europe, Zumunta Association, USA, Okrika Union, Ogoni Union, Tiv and Middle Belt Association Tai Eleme, Ikwerre, Andoni, Edo, Cross Rivers and Akwa Bom States Associations and Igbo National Organizations. We would like to express our special gratitude to the following persons: Dr. Ebiware, Dr. Chukwunta, Dr. Sikpi, Dr. Reuben Jaja, Dr. Amiso George, Raphael Okoroh, Robert Ellah, Dr. Didia, Dr. Briggs, Macaulay Osaisai, Bobojama Sovimi, Tari and Fakumoh Dick, Dawari Long John, Tony Eyenghe, Dr.Kpakol, Dr. Eneyo. Yabo MD, Dr. Onah Pellah, G.M. Odumgba, Mondy Gold, E. Onadowuan, Akpevi Ogbuigwe, LLB, LLM, John

xvii

Odusote, Allswell Muzan, JD, Professor Bedford Fubara, Eric Amaso and Allen Spiff. Also, Judge Karibi Whyte, Late-Tai Solarin, Dr. Monina Briggs, Dr. R. Lukman, Ambassador Joseph Garba, Dr. J.K. Onoh, and Dr. Gambari, for their scholarly and practical contribution to Nigerian development. Dr. Charles Wolfe and Dr Letha See for their interest in peace and development in Nigeria.

We would like to thank Dr. Jan Christopher, Dr. Winston Awadzi and Dr. Titi Oladunjoye for their editorial interest and input in meeting Ashgate publishers' guidelines and Dr. Sam Hoff for the exchange of ideas on comparative fiscal federalism.

Our special thanks to Elaine Ackerman, Miaka Roland, Kim Sudler, Patricia Harvey-Wiest, Debra Fisher, Sandra Haynes, Anita Williams, Korkoene Awadzi, and Ken White for their input of numerous auxiliary materials during the Manuscript preparation.

We would like to express our gratitude to Dr. Oriaku Nwosu, Dr. Olagunju, Ms. Yu Rose M. Durk and Mrs. Rosa Panda for their helpful service while we were researching and writing this book.

Finally, the authors are grateful to Ashgate Publishers for bringing this work into fruition and special gratitude to the Nigerian policy makers, scholars and citizens who have contributed to keep the nation intact irrespective of their differences.

We salute them for their effort in building Unity in Diversity.

Motivational words of inspiration and wisdom

"We must recognize our diversity as a source of great strength, and we must do all in our power to see that this Federal System of Government is strengthened and maintained".

Alhaji Sir Abubakar Tafawa Balewa
First-Prime Minister of Nigeria.

Oil is the modern world's heroin. The pleasure it provides fuels a way of life no other energy source can satisfy so plentifully and so cheaply. Today the trade in petroleum, like the traffic in drugs is so much in the veins of nations that most countries whether rich or poor find their economies held hostage to this remarkable substance.

Miller, J. and Mylroie, L. (1990)
Black Gold in Saddam Hussein and the Crisis in the Gulf.

On Oil Wealth and Distributive inequities, a notable Islamic scholar M. Ali Fekrat points to a pattern of pervasive underdevelopment side by side with extreme and highly concentrated wealth which resulted from the oil boom. Such a disparity between the rich and poor is in his view, diametrically opposed to the fundamental precepts of Islam and thus leads to a widening gap between the Islamic socioeconomic ideals on the one hand and the actual state of economic affairs on the other...

M. Ali Fekrat "Stress in the Islamic world." *Journal of South Asian and Middle Eastern Studies 4* (1981) p.7.

There are enough resources on this earth to meet the needs of all but not enough to satisfy the greedy, Mathma Ghandi stated. This may apply to Nigeria in that the nation has enough resources to meet the needs of all its citizens but not enough to satisfy the greedy. The presence of unscrupulous interest groups and mismanagement put serious strain on national development.

Dr. A. A. Ikein
Newark, Delaware, USA 1993

Compromise is the art of symbiotic living; hence the most successful politicians are those who compromise for the common good whilst not sacrificing fundamental principles.

Dr. Nnamdi Azikiwe
Daily Times
June 23, 1979

Without an individual, there can be no community; without communities, there can be no tribe, without tribe, there can be no nation. It takes individuals to form a tribe; it takes tribes to form a nation. Let us make the atmosphere of our nation conducive so the maintenance of law, order and good government and tribalism will be harnessed to become an instrument for forging our national unity.

Dr. Nnamdi Azikiwe
Speech at University of Nigeria
Nsukka, May 15, 1994

Christian Social Creed

In Affirmation of care, love, equitable distribution of resources and justice for all people, the Christian United Methodist church social creed reads: ------

We believe in God, creator of the world and all people and in Jesus, Incarnate among us------ and in the holy spirit present with us to guide, strengthen and comfort-----

We rejoice in every sign of God's kingdom in the upholding of human dignity and community in every expression of love, justice and reconciliation in each act of self-giving on behalf of others in the abundance of Gods gifts entrusted to us that all may have enough; in all responsible use of earth's resources, Glory be to God on high and on earth peace---

We confess our sins, individual and collective by silence or actions through the violation of human dignity based on race, class, sex, nation or faith; through the misuse of power in personal, communal, national and international life; through the search for security by those military and economic forces that threaten human existence (pollution of mineral areas) through the abuse of technology which endangers the earth and all life upon it-

We commit ourselves to take up the cross--- To seek abundantly for all humanity struggles for peace with justice and freedom----
The search for responsible social, political and economic behavior without a threat to any unit of mankind; God's creation or species of the ecosystem.

United Methodist Church Social Creed

According to (M.O. Junaid, 1994), the need for evolving a viable political system and the administration to move forward was earnestly felt when the State was founded in Medinah. The state itself was diverse and complex judging from the heterogenous nature of its component parts. This brought into prominence the institution of Brotherhood among the Emigrants(Muhajirun) and their hosts (Ansars)------

This constitution promulgated more than fourteen hundred years ago, was not only of great importance but also a relevant document of recent times. This is because of its application to the prevailing condition as well as the ever changing circumstances which its authors had in mind. Thus, the constitution was indeed a vital document in the development of constitutional and legal freedom in the contemporary world.

What was said to have been guaranteed to the modern world by the American Declaration of Independence (1776), the French Revolution (1789), and the Universal Declarations of Human Rights of the United Nations were already embodied in the constitution of Medinah. It is regarded as the first written constitution of the world which has been preserved by the Muslims intact.

A cursory look at the various articles of the said constitution would reveal that it was not merely a Treaty of Alliance, but a constitution designed to regulate the relationship between the various components of the society. The various changes by the constitution on the life of the people were quite profound. By its application, the constitution dealt a serious blow to tribalism and individualism which has been preserved by the Muslims intact.

It introduced a new system of life where nationality was based on neither common race, language nor tribe----
The center of gravity was no longer the tribal system but the new Ummah which consisted of tribes as political units and individuals as its members. The Ummah worked through the newly established state under the leadership of the prophet who used to consult the members on important issues.

The promulgation of the constitution of Medinah by the prophet was indeed a pointer to the fact that any state or country should have a written constitution outlining the broad principles of the structure of government as well as its checks and balances. The constitution should guarantee not only the fundamental rights and duties of the citizen but protect the rights and interests of the minorities with meticulous care.

Daily Champion, July 1, 1994. page 5

Wealth and Charity

The love of desired objects, like women and children and stored up reserves of gold and silver, and pastured horses and cattle and crops, appear attractive to people. All this is the provision of the hither life; and it is Allah with whom is an excellent abode. (3:15)

The purpose of the Islamic economic system is that wealth should be in constant circulation, should be widely distributed and should be employed as to yield the maximum beneficence for the largest number of people. It should not circulate only among the well-to-do. (59:8)

Sir Muhammed Zafrulla Khan
The Review of Religions vol. LXXXI no.5 May 1986

Everywhere there must be freedom.
Freedom for you
Freedom for me
Everywhere, there must be freedom.
Freedom! Freedom!
Everywhere there must be freedom.

Sang *Mbonu Ojike* and *Dr. Nnamdi Azikwe*
Nigeria Nationalists, 1951

The object of government is the welfare of the people. The material progress and prosperity of a nation are desirable chiefly so far as they lead to the moral and material welfare of all good citizens.

President Theodore Roosevelt
United States of America

Words of the Prophet Joel

The word of the Lord that came
to Joel, the son of Penthuel
Hear this, you aged men,
give ear, all inhabitants of the land!
Has such a thing happened in your days,
Tell your children of it,
and let your children tell their children,
and their children another generation.
What the cutting locust left,
the swarming locust has eaten ...
For a nation has come up against my land,
powerful and without number;
its teeth are lions' teeth,
and it has the fangs of a lioness.
It has laid waste my vines,
and splintered my fig trees;
it has stripped off their bark and
thrown it down; ...
the wine fails,
the OIL LANGUISHES ...
because the harvest of the field has perished ...

The Bible - Book of Joel

Nigeria needs an improved socioeconomic and political order that cares for all its citizens with equity and fairness... That the minority and majority groups are bond into one sense of National Consciousness and Nationhood.

That, parochialism in national politics and tribalism [the African Equivalent of racism] needs to be eliminated ...

It behooves us to care for all our resource producing areas with socially responsible economic and political behavior. That, our National interest should supersede parochial interest in seeking the common good of the greatest number for all Nigerians.

Dr. Augustine A. Ikein
Excerpts from Keynote Address at Nigeria's 33rd Independence Anniversary Newark, Delaware U.S.A.

In a true Federation, each ethnic group no matter how small , is entitled to the same treatment as any other ethnic group, no matter how large...

Chief Obafemi Awolowo

Foreword

Professor Toyin Falola

It is difficult for me at this moment to think of any other scholar who is more qualified than Dr. Augustine A. Ikein to write on this important theme. His reputation for provocative and original thinking is widely recognized and acknowledged not just by those in his field, but by many others engaged in the study of Third World political economy. His talents are broad, covering such diverse fields as human services, management, business and economics. His previous study on *The Impact of Oil on a Developing Country* has been well received. I found *Oil Revenues and Fiscal Federalism in a Developing Country* a worthy successor.

His coauthor, Dr. Comfort Briggs is noted for her brilliant work on fiscal federalism in Nigeria and the study of political influence on Revenue Allocation in a developing Federal System. The combinations of the two scholarly talents in the various areas of expertise have produced this new remarkable volume on *Oil and Federalism* in a developing economic and political system.

This new book will further enhance Dr. Ikein's reputation and bring credit to his publisher. Timely, well-conceived, and thoughtfully presented, the book offers an interesting overview of the Nigerian economy. It is striking for the depth and freshness of its insights, with a lot to offer regional experts and students from a wide range of disciplines. To the African policy makers, one can only wish that the strictures expressed would be taken to heart and the sound recommendations will command serious attention.

Designed partly to prevent the debilitating impact of centrifugal pulls in a multi-plural society, federalism as a political model has been adopted in several new nations. However, in the case of Nigeria, there has been a slide towards a powerful unitary government, and more disturbingly, towards authoritarianism. This slide is a negation of federalism and democracy, in large part a consequence of a parasitic, self-seeking military oligarchy bent on perpetuating itself in power sometime acting as custodial is the nations constitution when merchandising democracy fails. It is the *problematique* of distributing the so-called common resources in a federal system in a country as chaotic and wild as Nigeria that Dr. Ikein and his coauthor has brilliantly drawn attention to. Those who are familiar with the muddy water of Nigerian politics will appreciate the very difficulty of this enterprise. It is to the credit of our distinguished author that he shows an outstanding competence and wisdom in navigating this tortuous terrain, and exposing the difficulties that Nigerians face and the complexity of distributing scarce resources.

The complexity derives from the need to balance ethnic and class interests, but in recent time compounded by the greed and mismanagement of a tiny cabal. Dr. Ikein rightly focuses on oil which contributes the bulk of the country's revenues. Oil resources are located in a small corner of the country, populated by minority ethnic groups. Power resides in the hands of the majority ethnic groups who use their privileged position to dominate. In resource allocation, the oil producing areas get a marginal share because of a fiscal arrangement that de-emphasizes the principle of derivation. The authors are able to clarify many of the difficult aspects of the politics of allocation. I agree with their profound remark that federalism in Nigeria will suffer if the dividends derived from oil or any resources are constantly distributed in favor of a small class or of the majority ethnic groups without sensitivity to minority interests and concerns for justice, fairness and better balance.

Other novel ideas emerge from this book. Rather, than rely on the center for their resources, Drs. Ikein and Briggs call for a "competitive fiscal federalism" which will compensate those states that are able to generate internal revenues to run their administrations. The federal government needs to diversify to be able to withstand the unpredictability of the international market. In addition, poor people must benefit from oil revenues through judicious management and the provision of basic necessities.

This book is a literate rendering of what is supposedly a highly complex and technical subject, a lived reality and not one of those imaginary model constructions in political strategy or economic theory. It shows a genuine concern for the stability of Nigeria and the welfare of its impoverished population. Here is a book that will offer profit to scholars, pleasure to the general readers, and excellent ideas to those who are interested in seeking rapid change in the Third World. For combining such a high academic standard with clear pragmatic policy recommendations, Drs. Ikein and Briggs deserve both our gratitude and respect.

Professor Toyin Falola
University of Texas at Austin

1 Introduction to fiscal federalism, experts and policy making

This work is primarily concerned with Revenue Allocation in Nigeria. Its basic assumption in this study is that all revenue allocation policies in Nigeria have been politically shaped. The resulting policy, the study will try to prove, has been more a product of political bargains and compromises than a solution obtained from scientifically derived formulas. This is to say that, the decision to choose among the different alternatives available during the revenue allocation exercises, was more politically than economically determined. Therefore, despite all its economic and other technical trappings and trimmings, and in spite all of the efforts made to make it look apolitical, deriving revenue allocation formulas in Nigeria has been basically a process influenced by political factors.

In summary, the inquiry seeks to determine those political factors that influenced fiscal policy in Nigeria, especially as it involved oil and statutory revenue sharing. Thus, it will focus on the types and sources of influence that operated on the experts commissioned to formulate the various Revenue Systems in Nigeria since 1946, and the role of oil in fiscal federalism in the post-independent Nigeria.

The writers have employed a mixture of theoretical conceptualizations and empirical references in the course of investigations into fiscal federalism in Nigeria and the extent to which oil revenues influenced revenue allocation in the post-Colonial era.

This particular way of looking at Revenue Allocation is significant in that it tends to go beyond studying the structure of the different systems. Some excellent attempts, especially by economists, have been made to analyze, in detail, fiscal federalism in Nigeria. But the majority of them focus on the mechanics of federal finances. The emphasis had been on the different formulas, how they were derived, their uses and their effects on the national

1

and regional finances.[1] This study will however, look at the issues, perspectives, and problems, which were common to all the allocation formulas ever derived; concentrating on the derivation of the formulas and the principles involved. In other words, in addition to finding out the outcomes of the deliberations of the fiscal review boards, this work gives in-depth analysis of the plausible rationales behind the recommendation of each empirical revenue allocation alternatives in federalism and fiscal policy [with special emphasis on the role of Oil Revenues on Fiscal Federalism and the interest of minorities in the oil mineral producing areas of the country]. And in doing so, it examines the use of experts by policy-makers in formulating public policies of the State.

Federalism and fiscal policy

"There is and can be no final solution to the allocation of financial resources in a federal setting"[2] so said Kenneth Wheare, the noted theorist on federalism; and no where is the saying more apt than in Nigeria which has had limited success in dealing with its intergovernmental fiscal policies. From 1946, when the country was first administered as one political and economic entity, to 1982, when a new modified formula was adopted, Nigeria has utilized eight different formulations (excluding military decrees dealing with the issue) to determine how to share its financial resources among and between the different tiers of government.

Though the country started its existence as a British colony with a unitary system of government, Nigeria can be said to have always possessed the characteristics that are usually associated with federal societies. The Group of Provinces (or Regions or States, as they came to be known) which makes up the country are not merely geographical configurations, but represent clusters of cultural and ethnic groups that different between and among themselves. With such pluralistic and heterogeneous society, the federal solution' has often been seen as a way to integrate the diverse groups into a single polity,[3] and at the same time, maintain their independent identities -- a sort of equilibrium between pressures for unity and diversity.

Several political analysts have expounded theories on how this equilibrium is brought about. Kenneth Wheare proposed that it can be determined by legal and constitutional means, while William Livingston and R. L. Watts attributed it to the articulation of interests by the diverse social groups or forces. William Riker and Aaron Wildavsky argued that the equilibrium is the result of a bargaining process between the political leaders and/or political parties representing the various interest groups in the society. Carl Friedrich and Michael Reagan, on the other hand, de-emphasized the bargaining aspect of the process and insisted that the equilibrium is maintained through a dynamic process of constantly adjusting power patterns in response to political, social, and economic forces in the society.[4]

However the elusive concept of Federalism is formulated, the issue of power and control is and underlying theme. When separate politial units decide to enter into an arrangement whereby they adopt joint policies and make decisions on join issues in a federal setting,[5] there is always the problem of allocating influence (the exercise of power) over policy issues. The power relationship between the disparate communities which have united into one nation and the central government which symbolizes that unity is usually an uneasy one; most often it is a flux. Even in the most successful federal systems, the power boundaries are never clearly delineated. And since the governmental units share functions and responsibilities, the struggle for influence over crucial policy areas is a regular source of friction in any federation. Advocates of Federal Might often clash with those of State Right, transforming the simple joint decision-making into a heavily politicized battle ground.

One area where the struggle is intensified is the financial arena, where the ultimate goals of fiscal policy are decided. Since money is the life blood of anybody politic, the politics of who controls the financial resources and, therefore, exerts influence over the fiscal policies of the country, is ever present and crucial. More complications set in when, as in the newer federations, due to a mix of historical, economic and political circumstances, the bulk of the nation's revenues is collected and then shared among and between government levels. This tendency to integrate and even centralize various policy areas, especially functional and financial ones, is rooted in the belief that such a system is needed to evolve a national fiscal and developmental strategy in planning the economy.[6] If every unit of the government were left to plan its own economic and fiscal course, a haphazard economy would result, to the detriment of fledgling federation.

The country under study, Nigeria, is a new federation with gross disparities in economic development and fiscal capacities among the regions (or present States) that make up the country If all the parts of the country were equal in every imaginable way, then Revenue Allocation, as the process of sharing of central revenues is termed, would be child's play -- divide the revenues into equal parts. But since Nature is not so obliging, intergovernmental transfer of revenue is inevitable, and the process of allocating it to satisfy all interested parties becomes a nightmarish act.

Due to the unequal status of the constituent parts in terms of size, population, and resource endowment, various criteria must be used in allocating the central revenue, and the decision to use one set of criteria or another has not come easily. The struggle for influence over choice of criteria to be used in the revenue allocation scheme and the weights to be attached to them is often exacerbated in a political setting where ethno-cultural particularism still persists. Policy making thus becomes a multifaceted undertaking when such volatile issues as ethnicity and partisanship come into play; such is the case with Nigeria. Unlike older federations like the United States, Canada, and Australia, which have more settled constitutional histories and have developed regular, rational, and institutionalized bases of deciding revenue policies, Nigeria is still undergoing a series of rapid changes, both politically and economically. The country increased, in terms of financial units, from three regions by independence in 1960, to nineteen States in 1976 and thirty states in 1989. Also, it has experienced various types of government since its inception as a nation in 1914. Starting as a colony with a unitary government, it changed to an independent federation with a Westminster parliamentary style. It then came under thirteen years of military rule, returned to a civilian but presidential system and again passed under another military rule after the annulment of the June 12 Presidential Elections in 1993. This uneasy and rough political journey has meant that Nigeria's fiscal policy making, especially as it concerns revenue sharing, has also remained controversial and unstable.

Decision-makers in Nigeria, be they colonial administrators, indigenous politicians, or military leaders, have tried to portray the making of revenue allocation policy as an economic undertaking. They have appointed eight revenue allocation commissions, comprised of experts schooled in economics and finance, to carry out serious and lengthy analysis of the revenue problem and advise the government of the best course to take. Nevertheless, as stated above, the formulation of the policy has remained a political activity which involved bargaining and struggle among the different interested stakeholder in the federation.

The inextricable link between fiscal policy and politics can be further demonstrated by the schematic diagram below. It shows, in general, the stages involved in the formulation and adoption of a revenue allocation formula.

P	=	Political Party (relevant interests during military era)
C	=	Constitution (includes Edicts and Decrees)
TR	=	Terms of reference
CG	=	Central government
RAC	=	Fiscal experts (Revenue Allocation Commissions)
RF	=	Revenue allocation formula

Figure 1.1 Formulation and adoption of revenue allocation policy

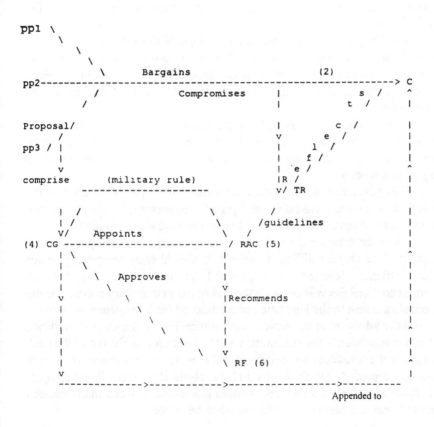

Formulation and adoption of revenue allocation policy explanation

During constitutional conventions, delegates representing the various political parties and regions (1) meet and deliberate on the writing of a new constitution. Several proposals are submitted, and after a series of debates bargaining and compromises, a draft constitution is produced and later adopted. (2) The constitution, among other things, provides the structural framework of the political system.

Another product of the conventions is a list of directives about the fiscal arrangements in the system, and a mandate to the central government to set up the machinery for the division of the fiscal resources. These terms of reference (3), as the directives are referred to, are based on the settlements in the Constitution.

The central government (4) then appoints a body of experts (usually people knowledgeable in the fields of economics, finance and public administration) (5) and instructs them to devise a formula to be used in sharing the nation's revenues.

Using the terms of references as guidelines, the expert body, after sifting through data obtained via public and private testimonies, devises a revenue formula (6) and send its recommendation to the central government.

These proposed solutions then undergo a process of approval and adoption. The process differs; sometimes a special body comprising senior public officials (elected or appointed) is set up to consider the recommendations (as was done up the end of the first military regime) or the proposals are sent to the legislature to be debated (as it happened in 1980).

After adoption of the Revenue Allocation Policy, the usually modified formula is appended to the constitution and becomes part of the law of the land. Whenever the constitution is reviewed and a new one is proposed, the whole process is repeated. Dr. O. Teriba, in his analysis of revenue allocation aptly portrayed the rather complex relationship that exists between the fiscal and constitutional arrangements in Nigeria when he wrote:

> Developments and innovations in fiscal arrangements have, in general, been dictated by the tenor and pace of constitutional change and transformation, but the latter is also, in turn, occasionally influenced by the former.[7]

Though Nigeria has had only ten years of constitutional rule since gaining independence in 1960, the federal arrangements which were established by the constitutional settlements have persisted through all the regimes. Even during the military periods when edicts and decrees replaced formal constitutions as the articles of governance, the basic structure of the political system remained intact, and the same political problem of power relationship in the system still overarched fiscal policy making and underwrote the technical issues of federal finance. From the diagram and its explanation, the major difference in the allocation process during the non-constitutional rule was that the Federal Military Government usurped the role of the political parties and set its own agenda without benefit of a constitutional convention. In other words stages (1) and (2) are absorbed into stage (4) [see broken arrow]. The role of the central government as a channel of transmission of tax revenues to the regions (or states) was constantly examined and readjusted during both periods. (What combinations of historical, political, economic, and oil conditions led to the assumption of that role by the center will be analyzed later).

Thus what determines the type of allocation system or formula adopted is mainly the interplay of the various competing influences which operated, directly or indirectly, on the expert commissions that were set up to resolve this complicated political issue, sometimes in conjunction with the actors responsible for interpreting the commissions' recommendations and deciding whether and how they should be translated into law and into practice.

It is pertinent at this point to examine the concept of expert involvement in policy making. This is relevant because, as indicated above, Nigerian policy-makers rely on expert advice in formulating the revenue policies under review here.

Experts and policy making experts and expertise

The use of pertinent knowledge to produce a format for policy decisions (the laying out of Alternative choices) and of determining future needs for policy-relevant information[8] is widely seen as a prudent undertaking by decision-makers.[9] However, in some cases, the policy problems may be too complex, new or unexpected, and the information about them too sophisticated for the policy-maker may feel 'direction less', full of conflict and uncertain about the knowledge he possesses.[10] He then usually turns to people who are perceived as having superior skill, information or experience -- the experts.[11]

These specialists or experts in the fields of social, economic and political knowledge -- intellectuals, as they are often referred to -- [12] have traditionally performed several functions in the policy arena. As researchers, they produce and implement knowledge through educating the public. Experts go further, in their roles as advisors, to facilitate utilization of the knowledge in decision-making.[13] As George A. Kelly reminds us: "The expert as policy counselor has been available to societies from earliest times, wearing among other transitory costumes those of magician, tax collector, confessor, constitutional-writer, strategist, and economic planner. The form has changed with convenience, values on the scale of knowledge, morale and culture, but the function has stayed rather constant."[14]

It is in this advisory role that expertise becomes a co-determining factor in social and political policy process.[15] Experts, whether employed on an individual basis or recruited as a group into commissions and committees, have become indispensable in many political systems. This is very evident in Great Britain where it is an established procedure to derive policies from reports submitted by expert bodies. As Herman Finer observed:

> It is probably true to say that since the early part of the 19th Century hardly a social, economic, or political statute of any importance has been drafted and introduced into Parliament otherwise than as a result of recommendation of a Royal Commission.[16]

In Nigeria, the use of experts in policy-making is also pervasive. They have been recruited to study and analyze policy problems, and recommend solutions for them. The resulting suggestions have often served as a basis for government policy.[17]

In the United States, most of the experts involved in policy-making are employed in the bureaucracy as regular staff. Their tenure may be permanent or temporary depending on the type of skill they possess and the purposes for which they were recruited. These professional, often called policy analysts, perform a dual role in policy-making. They help in defining the policy problems as well as in formulating their solutions through the search for policy alternatives.[18]

The situation is a little different in Great Britain and most of its former colonies such as Nigeria, which have adopted of its former colonies such as Nigeria, which have adopted some form of the Westminster model of government. In this group of countries, commissions composed of experts are set up to perform similar roles -- inquire into policy problems and advise decision-makers on solution. But the expert advisory bodies are often *ad hoc* and independent of any other institution, deriving their power from the central government that appointed them. The Prime Minister, with his Cabinet, assesses the issues, that is to say, defines the problems, and then decides whether expert advice is needed or not. If a need is perceived, and expert commission, often referred to as a Royal Commission, consisting of people deemed competent, is created.[19] Their role and function could be said to

8

parallel that of a Congressional Committee in the United States; both can summon witnesses, examine evidence and elicit information which can be used as an aid in the preparation of legislation.[20] However, congressional committees, as distinct from commissions, are usually partisan and biased in membership and they do not pretend to be impartial or expert in the pursuit of information.[21]

Rationale for using experts

The decision to use experts as an instrument in policy-making is based on two basic assumptions: (1) they possess and have the ability to apply knowledge which is exclusive, relevant and acceptable; and (2) they have the ability to discern and observe the right actions in the source of their work.[22]

One attribute of experts that is widely recognized is their possession of specialized technical knowledge. They are looked upon bring that special competence or skill to the problem that the client public sees as a mystery which is not given the ordinary man to acquire.[23] Thus it is expected that the expert, who by virtue of his training has access to new knowledge or new ways of putting the old,' and sees combinations we do not see' will help the decision-maker translate them into action.[24]

However, mere possession of cognitive competence is not enough. What is even more crucial in policy making is the rational application of the relevant knowledge and information by these persons credited with the special knowledge or expertise.[25] Experts, it is assumed, will undertake a careful professional study' of the problem and recommend the most reasonable course of action,[26] based on the findings about objective data gathered through rational procedures.[27] This belief is fostered by the fact that most intellectuals in government see the maintenance of objectivity and neutrality as a source of their strength. They are concerned that portraying a different image will undermine the basis of their expertise and influence.[28] Since the policy issues with which the experts are usually involved are highly conflicting and of major national importance, it becomes imperative that these issues be resolved by trained minds, impartial judgements and disinterested study.[29] The advisory bodies are neither judicial nor administrative, therefore they are, outside the field of party political controversy[30] and in addition to the scientific knowledge possessed, they are a means of depoliticizing such issues. It is this belief in the scientific rationality of experts coupled with their objectivity and neutrality that has led to a growth of highly differentiated network of expert commissions and committees[31] set up by policy-makers to advise them on policy issues. "Like most other policy-makers faced with complicated policy issues, Nigerian political authorities rely on expert advice to help them solve the problem of fiscal adjustment. Taking the cue from the British whose Royal Commissions have been described as a typical English device for bringing the best in the country to bear on great legislative tasks,"[32] a total of eight *ad hoc* fiscal review commissions have been established since 1946, the year the country became a unified political unit. The expressed function of the commissions was to devise a rational means of distributing the proceeds of the various central taxes between the different units of governments and among the lower tiers themselves. Accordingly, the advisory boards comprised of experts specially competent in the fields of knowledge relevant to the issue[33] --economics, finance and public administration -- are well recognized. The people most apt to serve on the commissions are not usually linked to the formal political structure, with the view and hope that being removed from the arena of active political debate, only economic and fiscal considerations will be the foundations to base their recommendations.

It is pertinent to note that it was not until the military era, in 1968, eight years after independence, that a non-European was appointed to head a team of fiscal experts. It may be that political leaders in Nigeria's First Republic could not agree on a Nigerian panel that would be impartial. Alternatively, the retention of expatriate panels could have been a function of the policy making process in newly independent countries where the policy practices and structure of the write are adopted with little modification until a major crisis, such as a military coup, disrupts the system and demands autonomous policy-making.[34]

Using mostly economic variables, the fiscal experts have tried to show that the formulas they recommend represented a balance between the two broad-based objectives of Equity and Efficiency usually pursued by fiscal experts dealing with public finance. Equity here implies fairness and equality in sharing revenues. They can be divided on the basis of need, leading to equal results, or shares can approximate contributions -- a sort of proportional equality. The Efficiency objective, on the other hand, aims at designing a system that will obtain the maximum benefit relative to cost, thus demanding both administrative conveyance and fiscal prudence.[35]

These formulations, which are quantitative are also very complex. How the panelists arrived at the figures was not usually disclosed; where they attempted to show the process, certain important variables were left out; therefore, the non-expert would find the procedure difficult to decipher. Nevertheless, the completed reports of the various commissions had been accepted by the parties concerned, and once they were adopted, they automatically became a part of the law of the land, incorporated into the existing constitution. To date, only two reports have been rejected, and only one has undergone a protracted legislative debate before being adopted.

The ease with which these formulas were consented to, albeit, with minor modifications, gives the observer the impression that the technical bases (which have never been questioned) on which they rested were objective and rational, satisfying all parties involved. Given the high professional status and personal integrity of the experts one would expect them to be able to determine a more valid accommodation of all interests and thus to approximate 'objective justice'.[36] However, as is argued in the following paragraphs, that has not been the case.

Constraints and pressures on experts

There is abundant evidence in the literature which shows that experts involved in policy-making come under severe constraints that are often times concealed behind a neutral facade. Studies on the use of experts do point out the elusiveness of the objective technical advice and assessment. As Harold Margolis bluntly stated:

> There is no such thing as objective technical advise in the sense of as assessment of the technical issues in a policy controversy which will be acceptable to all parties as fair and adequate statement.[37]

During almost all of Nigeria's fiscal adjustment exercises, there have been loud protests from the interested parties expressing dissatisfaction with the technical advice, in terms of the allocation formulas, given the policy-makers. This is largely due to the fact that experts present their recommendations as technical in nature and tend to understate the extent to which they are involved in making normative judgement.[38] Given that government authorities usually refer matters which are politically controversial but lacking in consensus, to experts,[39] these professionals who utilize their expertise to resolve such matters are inevitably drawn into situations where they may choose positions,[40] and that could have far reaching political consequences beyond their expectations. They are thus caught between recommending alternatives which may be effective but are beyond the range of political viability and those which may not be so efficient but are within the boundaries of political reality.[41] Political interference in the expertise community is a widely known occurrence, with its most extreme effects observed in Nazi Germany and Stalinist Russia.[42] The dynamics of the policy

11

arena usually impact on the knowledge of the experts where their expertise is shaped, manipulated, and often distorted.[43] There is seldom any issue to which expert knowledge is applied that has been resolved without some admixture of politics.'[44] The need to satisfy some, if not all, of the parties interested in the issue often means that experts are required to produce what could be termed, 'acceptable' and 'not necessarily sound' judgment.[45] That they sometimes have to resort to this, shows how much expertise can be compromised.

It has been found that there is a tendency for experts to show a certain degree of comradeship with the decision-maker and thus share his point of view.[46] This often leads to a situation where so-called technical decisions become based on political grounds such that the way experts select data and interpret their findings are related to the policy goals of the decision-maker.[47] The whole activity of the professional becomes geared towards contributing to formulating and justifying the client's policy objectives.[48] These experts perform what is normally referred to as a Legitimation Function, where the political system incorporates scientific authority, sometimes in subtle ways, and uses it to defend the legitimacy of specific decisions.[49] An author described the phenomenon as follows:

> This form of intellectual collusion is a strategy of discursive incorporation through which legitimacy crises are repaired and the reforms they engender are publicly presented.[50]

In other words, decisions taken for political motives are presented as having been taken for rational technical reasons.[51]

It is not difficult for policy-makers to exploit expertise to justify their political vies and thus legitimate their decisions because the expert is in a quandary. In the first place, the organizational setting in which the professional or advisor carries out his tasks provides a view or vantage point which orders and makes salient various policy problems and solutions.[52] Whether the analyst works as an in-house or outside expert, the social and political environment in which he operates places some restrictions on him. He is constrained by bureaucratic pressures from having the largest scope for carrying out his work,[53] being dependent on the resources and other amenities provided by the policy-maker. Even the course of action to follow is often imposed on him, limiting the expert in making use of his knowledge fully in searching for alternatives.[54] As he is not free to make his choices, and can only analyze those given him by the policy-maker, the expert cannot bring to the problem, creative and novel alternatives.[55] Those who attempt to go beyond their given parameters by either adding further values or choices of their own or ignoring the ones given to them, are often charged with impertinence and dereliction of duty, and dismissed, their findings rejected.[56] Thus the policy-maker is able to control the output of the expert and manipulate it in such a way as to fit the policy goals -- a legitimating procedure.

Secondly, since most policy areas are grey, there is right or wrong. This gives rise to many options and room for interpretation, making it relatively easy for the decision-maker to select the advice he wants to hear and discard the rest.[57] The chosen one usually fits into a policy model already in place, the expert having been used to provide a rationale for a previously decided option. Sometimes, advice not immediately used is not discarded, but filed away for use at a more auspicious time when the political conditions have changed and become more conducive.[58] The policy-maker, thus, not only controls the output of the expert, but also the utility of the advice by engaging in selective usage.

The need for an expert to be sensitive to the political environment of the policy-maker and act accordingly is emphasized throughout the literature.[59] Though experts do not expect to play any political role, they sometimes find that they have to, given the fact that decision-makers often disregard to even attack experts whose findings violate their political interests and sentiments.[60] Consequently, some professionals recognize the trend of prevailing opinion and present recommendations which are likely to be accepted.[61] Thus they listen to the advice that though analysts should not ignore practical political constraints.[62] By being aware of political reality, in terms of knowing who is in charge and his behavior, experts can keep whatever influence they may have acquired. As Guy Beneveniste, who has studied experts and their roles both abroad and at home, put it:

> Experts are concerned with goals, or more exactly, with intended outcomes and functions. The concern for outcomes, functions, and goals is logical: since experts are supposed to help politicians choose between various courses of action, and since experts are not supposed to be political actors, they need to know where the politicians want to go. Once they know the destination, they can specify the road to follow.[63]

However, for the politician, it is not easy to state exactly where that destination is. It takes a 'high level of political consensus' to arrive at any well defined goals that can satisfy all the divergent and contending factions that are interested in the same goals.[64] Since most issues with high political stakes are dominated by politics,[65] it requires that experts who deal with them possess not only the substantive technical expertise, but also enough political knowledge to assess the climate of the environment they are working in.[66] A failure to do that adequately often results in both the advisor and his advice being dispensed with.

The situation with the Revenue Allocation Commissions in Nigeria has not been much different. All eight commissions were set up in response to impending political and constitutional changes, instead of economic and fiscal considerations. Every constitutional conference had been convened to debate the power relationship between the central and the regional (State) governments; and it has led to a review of the existing fiscal and financial relations between them too. Thus, Nigeria had as many fiscal review panels as constitutions. Even during the military era when the constitutions were suspended, but a change of regime took place, two revenue panels sat, in addition to a plethora of revenue decrees.

Delegates to the constitutional conferences, who represented different political interests, usually decided among themselves how the revenue commissions should go about their business. They established guidelines, decided terms of reference, which were results of political compromises and imposed them on the experts. It was s if they told the experts: We have decided to do this and that. Now go and crank out some figures to justify this course of action.[67] The terms of reference, having been determined through political processes, reflected the objectives of the politicians who were responsible for setting up the commissions. The professionals recruited to advise the politicians on the issues thus found themselves working within a rigid system comprised of constitutionally prescribed structural arrangements."[68] Though some of them tried to stretch the limits of the system, most of them, by and large, worked within their given terms of reference. Dr. Pius Okigbo, chairman of the last review body exemplified this when he stated that an expert commission should keep its terms of references constantly in front of it, to ensure that it does wander too far afield and that it is expected to solve.[69] Those experts who did venture out of the set boundaries had their recommendations soundly rejected for either exceeding their powers or ignoring their terms of reference.

The fact that only two out of the eight revenue allocation commissions had their expert advice not taken suggests that, in general, the expert bodies that reviewed fiscal policy in Nigeria reflected the prevailing philosophy or way of thinking of the policy-makers; in other words, selector and the selected agree in their bias.[70] (It is significant to note that the two sets of recommendations rejected were done so by people other than those who appointed the panels. The Dina Interim Revenue Allocation Review Committee of 1968 was set up by the then new military government, but its report went to a group of civilian administrators (Commissioners of Finance in the Federation) who strongly advised against adopting it. The other one, the Aboyade Technical Committee on Revenue Allocation, in 1977, also established by the then departing military and again submitted to aspiring politicians in the Constituent Assembly for approval, was promptly rejected. In both cases, however, the military regimes that set up the commissions approved their recommendations. As will be shown in later chapters, some specific proposals put out by the rejected Reports found themselves transformed into policy).

The convergence of thought between the experts and the policy-maker did not come about by accident. Generally, the government usually takes care to make sure that experts appointed to appointed panels were willing to give it what it wants, be that valid directives or relief from political pressure.[71] Thus, the composition of the expert commissions often portrayed the political foundations on which they were based. As Charles Hanser saw it, a decision-maker who sets up a panel,

> ...can almost determine the course that it is going to take, since he will have a pretty good knowledge beforehand of the minds of the experts whom he puts on it, while of course, avoiding any appearance of packing his team.[72]

This view is not shared by all, especially the experts involved. It makes them look like 'castrated intellectuals' who do not have much discretion in either defining policy problems and/or selecting suitable alternatives.[73] Dr. Akinola Aguda, an eminent jurist, who chaired an expert panel set up by the Nigerian government to advise it on selecting the site for a new capital, strongly rejected the characterization, insisting that experts involved in policy-making are not 'yes men'; rather they are men of distinction in politics, business or scholarship who can be trusted to use their collective strengths to deliver appropriate judgments on complicated and important public problems. He denied any agreement or collusion between him as chairman, and the Head of State who appointed him, as to what the result should be. Instead, he and his team were given general directions, mostly procedural, and instructed to analyze the issue and come up with the best solution.[74] In this respect, he would seem to agree with Don K. Price who wrote that:

> The process of responsible policy-making is not something that begins with the definition of a political ideal according to some partisan political doctrine and concludes by using administrative and scientific means to attain that goals.[75]

and argued that instead policy-making is a process of interaction among scientists, professional leaders, administrators and politicians.[76]

Though the image of the 'castrated intellectual' is too extreme, nevertheless, no expert is allowed to roam about in the policy arena without any directives. As one former top Nigerian politician categorically stated, the government usually makes its preferences well known to expert panels, and if the problem is very controversial, it might insist that a certain criteria be adopted.[77] In this way, the decision maker can fortify his position vis-a-vis that of his opponents by including his choices in any new policy being formulated.[78] For instance, former President Shagari communicated to the Okigbo Commission, both formally and privately, his desire to include the 'derivation' principle in the revenue allocation formula it was working on. He was thus able to score some points especially among the oil producing States by reviving this long-abandoned principle.[79]

If one can assume that the advice given by the experts is impartial, objective and value-free, the utilization of the knowledge is usually political. Despite the tendency to portray political questions as technical ones, and use experts to solve them, the value differences that are frequently the real origins of the conflict can only be addressed by the politicians.[80] One can agree with the conclusion that:

> On all questions of policy the final decisions rest in the hands of politicians, whose determination will often be dictated by political considerations which bear little or no relation to expertness or impartiality.[81]

This is not to belittle the enormous contributions made by experts to the policy-making process, but it is to assert and try to prove in the next chapters in this paper that the formulation of crucial policies like revenue allocation policy Nigeria is basically a political affair. The fact is further brought home when on e examines the process by which the expert report is adopted and implemented. Onn submission to the government, the report usually undergoes what one author terms a civil service filter. This is the process whereby top civil servants comment on policy proposals and decisions are taken after a serious of correspondence within the governmental hierarchy, at the apex of which is the Head of State.[82] The resulting decision is then issued in the form of statement called 'White Paper' or 'Command Paper', which sets out the advisory bodies.[83] It is the contents of the White Paper that are sent to the Legislature to be debated upon, or any other body giving the necessary approval. The government's White Paper is published at the same time as the expert report, and usually there are no major significant differences between them. However, sometimes an errant expert panel may decide to ignore some specific instructions given to it by the government or will take it upon itself to include some terms or measures that were not explicitly forbidden. When that happens, policy makers often rectify the situation by either adding the necessary or deleting the offensive paragraphs in the White Paper before it is published. For instance, though the Presidential Commission on Revenue Allocation was advised to include the principle of derivation in its formula, the review board decided otherwise. Since that was the only major flaw in the Report, instead of rejecting the whole work, the government, in its White Paper, rewrote the revenue formula to include the derivation principle. In this way, it is emphasized that the government has the final responsibility in making policy. Experts are useful in providing necessary technical advice on complex issues to a policy-maker when he or she may be either too inexpert or too preoccupied with transient political consideration to undertake the serious and lengthy analysis that such problems require,[84] play a subordinate role. After he completes his project and hands over the report to his client, the expert does not have much more input in the final outcome. However, since the recommendations provide the foundation on which the final decision is based, parties interested in the policy always try to exert influence on the professionals when they were engaged in the process of sifting through the policy alternatives.

Experts and policy makers in Nigeria

The penchant for Nigeria's political leaders to appoint expert bodies to study and recommend on policy issues is well known. Almost every public policy issue, especially a controversial one, ranging from States' creation, siting of a new federal capital, salary increases, IMF loans, to revenue allocation, has been initially analyzed by an expert commission whose suggestions often has formed the basis of the final decision. The proliferation of experts on the Nigerian policy-making scene can be attributed to many factors. First, it is an accepted practice on Britain to set up Royal Commissions to look into complex policy areas and advise the Cabinet, and ex-colonies usually imitate the write in many administrative ways. Added to this is the cultural belief that Western education holds the answer to most, if not all, problems -- another legacy of the colonial heritage. Given the low literacy rate, and the emphasis placed on education by both government and individuals, it is no wonder that individuals with proven academic expertise are rated very highly in the society. What more prestigious and talented body can be set up to handle difficult policy issues and give intelligent solutions than one comprised of academics?

In surveys conducted among Nigerians, people possessing technical and administrative skills, otherwise known as the educated elite, have consistently

17

scored highest in 'esteem order' rankings. They are usually seen as a group which contributes the most to the country and to development.[85] Being the successors to the colonizers, they have assumed control of the institutions of the State,[86] and view themselves as the class around whom history has been revolving in modern Nigeria, and who would build and integrate Nigeria into the developed zone of the world.[87] And Nigeria's political leaders seem to share that same vision, and have allowed them to play a significant role in setting the main patterns of continuity and change in the post-colonial society[88] of Nigeria.

By deferring policy issues to the educated elite for them to deliberate upon before arriving at final decisions, the federal government utilizes the knowledge and expertise of this reputable group. In addition, and equally important, the government also benefits from the non-political milieu which the expert commissions carry out their tasks. In a country like Nigeria which has deep schisms running through almost every imaginable social and political stratum, giving some aspect of policy-making, a veneer of non-partisanship of the general make up of the various revenue allocation commissions will illustrate the effort made by Nigerian policy makers to maintain this nonpartisan environment in which the experts operated.

Composition and selection of fiscal commissions in Nigeria

Policy makers in Nigeria, realizing not only the salience but also the highly volatile nature of the revenue issue had ben selective in their choice of members to the fiscal commissions. As stated above, the major rationale for appointing experts to deal with the special knowledge and the reputed scientific rationality and objectivity possessed by experts, that they would be able to devise a solution that would be acceptable to the interested parties. Thus, looking at the composition of the several commissions, one sees this commitment to competence and a high level of impartiality.

In terms of their academic and professional status, members of their academic and professional status, members of commissions can be grouped into three categories within which they usually represented the top echelon, in other words, the *creme de la creme* of the group. The first category consisted of university professors and other high ranking faculties in the social sciences, with emphasis on economics. They include professors O. Aboyade and Tijani M. Yesufu (former vice-chancellors [presidents] of Universities of Ife and Benin respectively). G.O. Nwankwwo, O. Teriba and A.O. Phillips (former heads of Department of Economics); Drs. J.S. Odama, mo Omoruyi, Ibrahim Tahir, and John Hicks, together with his wife Dr. Ursulla Hicks, of Oxford University. Senior public administrators who were either career civil servants

18

like Chief I.O. Dina, Mr. Ahmed and Sir Sidney Phillipson (former financial secretary of the colony of Nigeria), or people appointed to ministerial positions in the public service such as Mr. K.J. Binns (former treasurer and state's commissioner of Taxes, Tasmania, Australia) and Dr. G. Leton, a former federal minister, made up the second group. The last category comprised of top management individuals in public or private enterprises like Dr. Pius Okigbo, a well known economic consultant, and Alhaji Mannan Daura, former managing director of a national daily newspaper.

None of the fiscal commissioners, at the time of appointment, were active in politics. Where some of them had been indirectly connected with partisan politics, it was usually in the role of advisors to elected officials. Moreover, in Nigeria, civil servants and university personnel (academic or administrative) were forbidden by law to engage in partisan politics. So a group consisting mostly of such individuals carried with it the reputation of being non-political.

In addition to being competent and non-political, the composition of the review boards satisfied another important criterion -- that of being represented. Commissions set up before the military were non-indigenous so the problem did not arise. When the first all Nigerian body was inaugurated in 1968, it became necessary to take such issue into consideration. Accordingly, the last three Revenue Allocation Commissions had as members, experts from the major ethnic/regional groups in the country, in other words, there had always been an Ibo, Hausa and Yoruba on the principle of federal character (that is, balanced member from one of the minority States. It was important that ethnic balance be maintained if the recommendations of the commissions were to remain credible. Though the details of the actual selection process are not open to the public, it is known that a short list of possible candidates, compiled by staff of the Cabinet Office, is usually presented to the Head of State who makes the final selection.

Looking through the lists of people who had been appointed to serve on the expert commissions, one notices that they were individuals with whom the ruling government would be comfortable. There was always a certain degree of camaraderie between the selector and selected, leading to a meeting of minds over most issues. Thus one finds only 'status quo' or 'mainstream' experts, and not 'fire-brand' or 'radical' ones. An intellectual who served on several expert bodies once commented: "Why would the government appoint anybody who espouses anti-government sentiments to any of its commissions?" He continued, "it will be like appointing well-known Marxists to a panel dealing with economic issues when the country operates a capitalist economy."[89] Not only were the experts of the same political persuasion with the ruling government, but they were people willing and proud to serve on the panels.

Being appointed a member of any commission was regarded as prestigious and a recognition of one's scholarly achievement. That is why despite the lack of any monetary compensation for the arduous task (the last Revenue Commission took six months to collect, collate, sift, analyze data, and write its report), there had never been any difficulty in securing the eminent professionals needed to sit on the panels.

Though some individual members of commissions had issued Minority Reports in which they disagreed with some areas of the final Report, basically there has been a high degree of compromise and compatibility among the commissioners, and this rapport usually extends to the government.

Unfortunately, there are no empirical studies on which an objective assessment can be made of the public perception of experts in Nigeria. However, given the results of the Beckett and O'Connell survey cited above, together with the high academic and professional standing of individuals appointed to expert bodies, one can say impressionistically that there appears to be widespread trust in the competence and integrity of those experts. In addition, there had not been any outright criticism of the membership of the various panels; or any questioning of their credibility; thus one can safely assume that the public, in deference to the experts accepts their selection in good faith.

Talking informally with various people, one gets the feeling that the Nigerian public usually yields to the judgment or opinion of the experts. If a government White Paper differs significantly from an expert Report on an issue, there is the tendency to accuse the government of tampering or 'playing politics' with the policy issue. It is this atmosphere of trust and respect that the Nigerian public has for experts that have allowed them to carry out their legitimating function.

However, in spite of the government's apparent dependence on experts to aid in resolving policy issues, final decisions, especially on the revenue issue, usually result from the balance of political forces at a particular point in time, making it a subject for political not scientific solution.[90] Thus, interested parties attempt to exert influences on the policy process. Where these influences originate from and how they are manifested during the decision making process of revenue allocation policy in Nigeria is the theme of our study.

Organization of study

In order to discover the sources and effects of the influences on the expert involved in revenue allocation policy-making, one has to examine the overall political configuration of the country. Revenue Allocation in Nigeria, as indicated above, can be described as an expression of the political system as it operates. Thus, a study of the structure and working of the political machinery will be useful.

There are many factors in the Nigerian politics environment that have exerted some influence on the revenue sharing policy formulation process. For reasons of brevity and simplicity, they can be grouped into three general areas: those arising from formal authority as evidenced in the various constitutions; those brought about by the prevailing political party systems; and those resulting from the military regime that ruled the country for thirteen years and, thereafter, the brief Civil Administration 1979-1983 and re-emergence of military rule from [Gen. Buhari through Gen. Babangida to Gen. Abacha] except the interim government Chief Shenakan.

The Constitution provides a systematic way of distributing formal power to the different units that make the government by assigning functions, responsibilities and resources to them. This legitimate blueprint of the political structure of the country is usually arrived at through political compromises forged during a constitutional convention. Agreements reached at the bargaining sessions that bear on fiscal relations are manifested in the types of revenue policies were given guidelines drawn up at the constitutional conventions during the non-military years.

As important as knowledge of the distribution of fiscal and constitutional powers may be in understanding influences on a country's revenue sharing policy-making, it is even more significant to have an idea of the political processes that underlie the system. The effectiveness of these influences is usually determined by the structure of the political parties or factions, where genuine political parties do not operate, and the role they play.[91] In Nigeria, during its constitutional periods, genuine political parties have operated; it is , therefore, necessary to study the growth and evolution of these institutions of interest aggregation. In Nigeria during the two constitutional periods, 1946-1966 and 1979-1983, when political parties were coterminous with government, what a people wanted from their rulers was directed toward the parties which struggled for shares of the national resources [especially revenues derived from oil]. Thus, the making of revenue allocation policy reflected one arena of this struggle, who should have control over the 'oil pot' and what manner the oil wealth is apportioned between the various competing constituencies.

Military rule in Nigeria lasted thirteen years, 1966-79, during which certain changes which bear significant consequences for revenue allocation policy-making took place. The most important changes were, in the words of Sam Oyovbaire, the removal of open competitive elections; the multiplication

21

and reduction in size of the component parts of the Federation; the emergence of a national consciousness on the part of the country's rulers; and the overwhelming importance of the oil industry as a source of revenue.[92] How these factors, combined with military-style government, transformed revenue allocation policy-making is crucial to this study. Some of the practices and institutions introduced during that era continued to influence expert commissions that analyzed fiscal policies in Nigeria after military rule.

Revenue sharing in Nigeria is carried out in two steps or stages: one is between the Federal and State governments, and the second among the States themselves and the Local Governments. As decisions on these stages are made simultaneously, we shall assume that they are influenced by the same type of political pressures. So both types of allocation will be analyzed together.

Several kinds of evidence will be explored to assess and evaluate the sources and effects of these influences. The terms of references given the expert commissions will provide clues to the political bargaining which took place during the constitutional conventions. So also will examination of the actual proposals of the commissions enable us to study the effect of political influences. Since interstate allocations are more controversial and volatile, a critical look at the various revenue allocation principles will yield wealth of relevant information for our analysis. This is because it is at this level that all political weapons are drawn and used. While all States may act in unison when fighting against the Center, the accord usually breaks down as the debate shifts to allocating the States' share among themselves.

There are several difficulties and problems involved with a study of this nature. The writers were not privy to the intimate and delicate political 'horse-trading' that went on during the constitutional conferences and other high-level meetings which led to the establishment of the expert commissions. Also absent from our data base are the deliberations within the fiscal review boards themselves, since the sessions were held in secret. All that is available are publications put out by the government stating the results of such clandestine meetings.

In addition to the lack of primary data described above, there is a general dearth of reliable data and information of almost any kind; individuals involved in policy-making -- politicians, civil servants, and experts -- are usually very reluctant to divulge information which they perceive as sensitive, and that seems to cover almost all information. One is often advised to refer to the government reports, which may contain sanitized views.

However, pertinent and valuable information and data are gleaned from the following sources:

22

(1) Government documents.
(2) Relevant books and journals.
(3) Newspapers and magazines.
(4) Informal conversations and interviews with government officials, members of commissions (experts), politicians, and other individuals with knowledge about the subject matter.

Using all the available data, we have been able to carry out the study of revenue allocation from a socioeconomic and political perspective. The authors have combined their interdisciplinary expertise in public policy, economics, oil and development in analyzing wealth distribution and fiscal federalism in Nigeria. In certain instances, the authors have repeated specific statements or citations previously quoted in the text with view to reemphasize a point that is deemed relevant to the analysis of the subject at hand.

Organizational structure of the book

In order to facilitate the analysis of the types and sources of political influences which acted on the various expert commissions set up to formulate revenue allocation policies in Nigeria, the book has eleven chapters. A brief summary of the main theme of each chapter is given below.

Chapters 1 and 2 deal with the theoretical and historical foundations of the issue under study. After a brief introduction which includes an analysis of experts in policy-making and the purpose of the inquiry, the first chapter presents a conceptual framework of public policy-making, drawing on the relevant literature. Highlighted is the policy process in newly independent states. Where possible, comparisons with Western democracies are made. The focus of Chapter 2, is on political environment in which both the experts and policy makers carried out their duties in the constitutional periods. Starting with a short historical overview of political parties in Nigeria, the party system of the country is critically analyzed by examining the roles and performances of these groups.

Chapter 3 presents the historical growth of federalism in Nigeria, from its unitary roots in 1914 to the end of the Second Republic in 1983. The bargains and compromises that led to the drafting and adopting of the various constitutions are discussed here in conjunction with the numerous military edicts and decrees that superseded the constitutions during the military eras.

Chapter 3 and 4 look at the effects of the political factors on revenue allocation policy during the three stages of Nigeria's short political life.

Chapter 4 begins with a brief overview of the literature dealing with fiscal federalism, interspersed with examination of revenue allocation in Nigeria. Emphasis is laid on the origins and rationale for centralization of the nation's revenues. Chapter 4 examines these factors during the colonial period and before the military coup, that is, from 1946 to 1966. To be considered in detail is the changing emphasis on revenue allocation principles as the nation's political and constitutional structures metamorphosed. The military years also make up Chapter 4. Emphasis is on the change in political system and style. The effect of the growth of oil as the most important revenue generating source, how this fact played a role in the preparation and execution of the civil war by both protagonists, and also in the creation of new States, is examined here.

Chapter 5 details of revenue allocation commissions which operated during each historical period, their terms of references, recommendations and composition will be given. Also, an analysis of political influence on revenue allocation and the rationale for fiscal centralization and fiscal adjustments in the Nigerian Federal system is explained.

Chapter 6 examines the return of Civil Rule in 1979, and with it, partisan politics. What difference this had on revenue allocation, in the light of post-military politics. The long drawn out legislative battle concerning the 1980 Revenue Allocation Act is highlighted.

Chapters 7 through 8 deal with policy implications for the forthcoming Republic and beyond. It will attempt to look back at the mistakes of previous regimes in the resource allocation area, and offer alternatives for the future that may be less dependent on oil as a sole source of national revenues. The analysis will be extended to include implications and lessons to be learned by other developing areas of the world, as these countries drive toward democratic ideals, political stability, and growth and development.

Chapter 8 discusses summary of revenue allocation in retrospect.

Chapter 9 contains a special contribution by Tony Furro with an in-depth discussion on the historical development of Nigerian revenue sharing problems, perspectives, and choices for the country.

Chapter 10 examines the origin of inter-ethnic politics, oil and socio-political development in the country. The discussion in this chapter is extended to cover the evolution of oil industry in Nigeria with particular reference to oil discovery, production and oil producing areas. The chapter offers additional insights to the role of oil in nation building in Nigeria.

Chapter 11, the final chapter, examines oil, Fiscal Federalism and the future of Federalism in Nigeria. This chapter discusses obstacles to effective Federalism in Nigeria, with particular emphasis on inter-ethnic politics, oil, distributive imbalances, ethnic nationalism, the minority question, and the implications for the future of Federalism in Nigeria. The discussion is extended

24

to cover alternatives for building better Federalism in Nigeria (with fiscal equity). Furthermore, the chapter reliance on oil-based economy, such that the states of the federation could become less dependent on the Federal government for its funding sources. There are recommendations for the states and the Federal government to encourage enhancement of the fiscal capacity initiative by state governments through the development of alternative economic resources. Chapter 11 also covers policy alternatives for the care of mineral producing areas through appropriate development planning and compensation for the oil communities. The discussion has emphasized some mechanisms for compensation and restitution in which the writers have drawn both Christian, Islamic, and Secular enlightenments on the subject of compensation planning and restitution in the quest for social and economic justice. The book concludes with analysis of socio-economic and environmental concerns for the nation's well-being and its succeeding generation.

Notes

1.   The major works done on Nigerian federal fiscal relations are:
      Adebayo, Adedeji, *Nigerian Federal Finance*. (New York: Africana
      Publishing Corporation, 1969); and
      Okigbo, Pius N.C., *Nigerian Public Finance*. (Harlow, Essex:
      Longmans, Ltd., 1965).
      There are several articles written about specific periods during which
      revenue allocation was analyzed. They include:
      Phillips, Adedobun, Nigeria's Federal Financial Experience, ' *Journal of
      African Studies*, Vol. 9, No. 3, (September 1971).
      Phillips, Adedobun, Three Decades of Inter-Governmental Financial
      Inter-Governmental Fiscal and Financial Relations , *Nigerian Journal
      of Public Affairs*, Vol. 6, No. 1, (May 1976).
      Teriba, Nigerian Revenue Allocation Experience, 1952-1965: A Study
      in Inter-Governmental Fiscal and Financial Relations,' *Nigerian Journal
      of Economic and Social Studies*, Vol. 8, No. 3, (July 1966).
      Rupley, Lawrence A., Revenue Sharing in the Nigerian Federation,
      Journal of Modern African Studies, Vol. 19. No. 2, (June 1981).
      Oyediran, Oyeleye and Olatunji Olagunju, The Military and the Politics
      of Revenue Allocation, in Oyeleye Oyediran, (ed.) *Nigerian
      Government and Politics Under Military Rule, 1966-1979*.
      Oyovbaire, Samuel E., The Politics of Revenue Allocation,' in S.K.
      Panter-Brick, (ed.), *Soldiers and Oil: The Political Transformation of
      Nigeria*. (London: Frank Cass, 1978).

2.   Wheare, Kenneth C., *Federal Government*. (London: Oxford Press,
      1968), p. 117.

3.   Omoruyi, Omo, 'Representative in Federal (Plural Systems: A
      Comparative View,' in Akinyemi, A.B., P.D. Cole and Walter
      Ofonagoro (eds.) Readings on Federalism. (Lagos: Nigerian Institute
      of Inter-national Affairs, 1979), pp. 372-73.

4.   For a detailed analysis of the theories of Federalism, see: Kenneth C.
      Wheare, *Federal Government*, op. cit. Livingston, William, A Note on
      the nature of Federalism, in J. P. Meekinson (ed.), *Canadian
      Federalism: Myth or Reality*. (Toronto: Methuen Publications, 1968).
      Watts, R.L., *New Federations: Experiments in the Commonwealth*.
      (Oxford: Oxford   University Press, 1966).
      Riker, William, *Federalism: Origins, Operations, Significance*.
      (Boston: Little, Brown & Company, 1964).

Friedrich, Carl, *Trends of Federalism in Theory and Practice.* (New York: Frederick Praeger, 1968).
Reagan, Michael, *The New Federalism.* (New York: Oxford University Press, 1972).

5. Friedrich, Carl, *Federalism: National and International.* (Oxford: Oxford University Press, 1963), p. 9.

6. Watson, M. M., Federalism and Finance in the Modern Commonwealth, *Journal of Commonwealth Political Studies,* Vol. 3 (1965), p. 119.

7. Teriba, O., Nigerian Revenue Allocation Experience, 1952-65; A Study in Inter-governmental Fiscal Relations,' *Nigerian Journal of Economic and Social Studies.* Vol. 8, No. 3, (November 1966), p. 380.

8. Williams, Walter, *Social Policy Research and Analysis: The Experience in the Federal Social Agencies.* (New York: American Elsevier Publishing Company, 1977), p. xi.

9. Laswell, Harold D. And Daniel Lerner, in Preface, Albert H. Teich (ed.) *Scientists and Public Affairs.* (Cambridge, MA: MIT Press, 1974), p. ix.

10. Meltsner, Arnold J., *Policy Analysts in the Bureaucracy.* Berkeley, CA: University of California Press, 1976), p. 50.

11. Lerner, Allan W., *The Politics of Decision Making.* (Beverly Hills, CA: Sage Publications, 1976), p. 19.

12. Merton, Robert K., *Social Theory and Social Structure.* (New York: The Free Press, 1968), p. 256.

13. Nowotny, Helga, 'Experts and Their Expertise: On The Changing Relationship Between Experts and Their Public,' *Bulletin of Science, Technology and Society,* Vols. 1, No. 3 (1981), p. 236.

14. Kelly, George A., The Expert As Historical Actor,' *Daedalus,* Vol. 92, No. 3, (Summer 1963), p. 529.

15. Helga Nowotny, p. 236.

16. Finer, Herman, The British Style,' *University of Chicago Law Review.* (Spring 1951), p. 554.

17. Adamolekun, Lapido, *Politics and Administration in Nigeria.* (Ibadan, Nigeria: Spectrum Books, Ltd., 1986), p. 123.

18. Arnold J. Meltsner in his *Policy Analysis in the Bureaucracy,* op. cit. provides a detailed analysis of this phenomenon.

19. Hanser, Charles J., *Guide to Decision: The Royal Commission.* (Totowa, N.J.: The Bedminster Press, Inc., 1965), pp. 37-38.

20. Clokie, Hugh M. And J. William Robinson, *Royal Commissions of Inquiry: The Significance of Investigations in British Politics.* (Stanford: Stanford University Press, 1977), p. 22. This book gives the best historical analysis of Royal Commissions.

21. Ibid., pp. 15-22.

22. Laffin, Martin, *Professional and Policy: The Role of the Professional in the Center-Local Government Relationship.* (Aldershot, England: Gower Publishing Co., Ltd., 1986), pp. 26-28.

23. Wilensky, H., The Professionalization of Everyone? *American Journal of Socioogy.* Vol. 70, (1964), pp. 148-9.

24. George Kelly, op. cit., p. 529.

25. Van Dyke, Vernon, Process and Policy as Focal Concepts in Political Research,' in Austin Ranney, (ed.), *Political Science and Public Policy.* (Chicago: Markham Publishing Company, 1968), pp. 33-34.

26. Benveniste, Guy, *The Politics of Expertise.* (2nd ed.) , (San Francisco: Boyd & Fraser Publishing Co., 1977), p. 59.

27. Nelkin, Dorothy, The Political Impact of Technical Expertise,' *Social Studies of Science.* Vol. 15, No. 1, (February 1975), p. 36.

28. Arnold Meltsner, op. cit., pp. 11 & 52.

29. Clokie & Robinson, op. cit., p. 3.

30. Chapman, Richard (ed.), *The Role of Commissions in Policy Making.* (London: George Allen & Unwin, Ltd., 1973), p. 174.

31. Helga Nowotny, op. cit., p. 236.

32. Dibelius, Wilhelm, *England.* (New York: Harper Bros., 1930), p. 253.

33. Burton, Frank and Pat Carlen, *Official Discourse*. (London: Routledge & Egan Paul, Ltd., 1979), p. 1.

34. Ballard, J.A., *Policy Making in a New State*. (St. Lucia, Australia: University of Queensland Press, 1981), p. 6.

35. *Report of the Presidential Commission on Revenue Allocation*. Vol. 1, (Lagos: The Federal Government Press, 1980, p. 25).

36. Charles J. Hanser, op. cit., p. 151.

37. Margolis, Harold, *Technical Advice on Policy Issues*. (Beverly Hills, CA: Sage Publications, 1973) p. 13.

38. Martin Laffin, op. cit., p. 29.

39. Richard Chapman, op. cit., p. 184.

40. Helga Nowotny, op. cit., p. 235.

41. Schultze, Charles L., *The Politics and Economics of Public Spending*. (Washington, D.C.: Brookings Institution, 1968), p. 82.

42. Blume, Stuart S., *Towards A Political Sociology of Science*. (New York: The Free Press, 1974), pp. 26027.

43. Helga Nowotny, op. cit., p. 235.

44. Charles J. Janser, op. cit., p. 49.

45. Clokie & Robinson, op. cit. p. 166.

46. Harold Margolis, op, cit., p. 25.

47. Mazur, Allan 'Dispute Between Experts,' *Minerva*. (April 1973), pp. 243-62.

48. Arnold Metsner, op. cit., p. 80.

49. Nelkin, Dorothy (ed.), *Controversy: Politics of Technical Decisions*. (Beverly Hills, CA: Sage Publications, 1979), p. 15.

50. Burton & Carlen, op. cit., p. 8.

51. Guy Benveniste, op. cit., p. 55.

52. Arnold Meltsner, op. cit., pp. 6-7.

53. Robert Merton, op. cit., pp. 268-69.

54. Guy Benveniste, op. cit., pp. 59-61.

55. Arnold Meltsner, op. cit., pp. 134-35.

56. Richard Chapman, op. cit., p. 111.

57. Guy Benveniste, op. cit., p. 61.

58. Ibid., p. 61.

59. Arnold Meltsner, op. cit., p. 136.

60. Robert Merton, op, cit., p. 256.

61. Clokie & Robinson, op. cit., p. 137.

62. Charles Schultze, op. cit., p. 82.

63. Guy Benveniste, op.cit., p. 84.

64. Ibid.p. 85.

65. Lapido Adamolekun, op. cit., p. 162.

66. Arnold Meltsner, op. cit., p. 153.

67. Guy Benveniste, op. cit., p. 60.

68. Ladipo Adamokekun, op. cit., p. 164.

69. *Report of the Presidential Commission on Revenue Allocation*, op. cit. p. 9.

70. Clokie & Robinson, op. cit., p. 165.

71. Charles Hanser, op. cit., p. 173.

72. Ibid., p. 49.

73. Arnold Meltsner, op. cit., p. 83.

74. Conversations with Dr. Akinola Aguda. (June-July 1986).

75. Price, Don K., *The Scientific Estate.* (Cambridge, MA: Harvard University Press, 1965), p. 67.

76. Ibid., p. 68.

77. Informal interview with Dr. Chuba Okadigbo, former Special Advisor on Political Affairs to former President Shehe Shagari. (March 1987).

78. Guy Benveniste, op. cit., p. 62.

79. See note 71 above.

80. Brooks, Harvard. The Federal Government and the Autonomy of Scholarship,' in Charles Frankel (ed.), *Controversies and Decisions.* (New York: Russell Sage Foundation, 1976), p. 244.

81. Clokie & Robinson, op. cit., p. 166.

82. Ladipo Adamolekun, op. cit., p. 123.

83. Wilson, Harold, *The Government of Britain.* (New York: Harper & Row, 1976), pp. 140-54.

84. Clokie & Robinson, op. cit., p. 3.

85. Beckett, Paul and James O'Connell, *Education and Power in Nigeria.* (New York: Africana Publishing Co., 1977), pp. 145-46.

86. Ibid., p. 7.

87. Ayandele, E.A., *The Educated Elite in the Nigerian Society.* (Ibadan: University of Ibadan Press, 1974), p. 3 as quoted in Beckett & O'Connell, op.cit.

88. Beckett and O'Connell, op. cit. p. 146.

89. Conversations with Dr. Ibidayo Ajayi, an Economics professor, University of Ibadan, Nigeria. (March-April 1987).

90. Adamolekun, Lapido, *Public Administration: A Nigerian and Comparative Perspective.* (New York: Longman, Inc. 1983), p. 99.

91. Aluko, Sam, Nigerian Federal Finance: A General Overview,' *Quarterly Journal of Administration,* Vol. iv, No. 2, (January 1070), pp. 81-82.

92. Oyovbaire, Samuel E., The Politics of Revenue Allocation,' in S. K. Panter-Brick (ed.), *Soldiers and Oil: The Political Transformation of Nigeria.* (London: Frank Cass, 1978), p. 225.

2 Theoretical and historical foundations to fiscal federalism

When a condition or situation in a society precipitates a need or dissatisfaction among the people whose relief cannot be met privately,[1] a public problem is said to have occurred. Usually, actors who are recognized by most members of the political system as having responsibilities over certain matters, "and whose actions are accepted as binding most of the time by these members, so long as they act within the limits of their roles,"[2] follow a purposeful course of action in dealing with the problem.[3] This selected line of action adopted and implemented, with the intention of affecting a particular object or sets of objects (goals, purposes, objectives or commitments) in the political environment is referred to as Public Policy.[4] As distinct from other actions, it is carried out by authoritative government actors.[5] In short, public policy consists of sanctioned decisions by authorities in a political system designed to affect outputs in the system.[6]

Public policies are not formed in a vacuum; they are formulated when issues, arising from conflicts among and between objectives, goals, customs, plans, activities or stakeholders'' need to be resolved.[7] These issues are far from simple, one-dimensional matters; they are usually interlocked or mingled with other sub-issues.[8] Therefore, a resolution of any policy question involves some kind of settlement among the various interested parties whose values and preferences are different.[9] The resulting choice as such is usually not to the absolute advantage of any one of the groups, instead, it satisfies some more than others.[10] Hence, the observation that public policy problems are never solved but resolved — resolved' being defined as a process in which policy problems undergo change.[11]

In the process of deciding how to strike a balance between the conflicting parties or forces involved in a public policy issue, policy-makers have to choose among a variety of possible alternatives.[12] Several factors come into play in determining the ultimate choice of the contents of a particular policy. One important consideration is the environment, that is, the dynamic social world into which government programs are introduced,[13] and the other involves the values that serve to guide the decision-maker.

An aspect of the environment which makes a significant contribution to the how and why of a policy is the political culture. As Gabriel Almond and Sidney Verba illustrated in their seminal work, *The Civic Culture*, the beliefs, values and attitudes held by a people toward their government help to shape the relationship between the citizens and the rulers.[14] And since public policy, as defined above, involves goal-oriented actions by governmental institutions and officials through the political process,[15] what people think a government should do and how it should do it, makes a significant difference in what kinds of policies are formulated, adopted and implemented.

Another environmental factor that bears on public is the set of socio-economic conditions that operate in a society, A prime source of conflict in any society is the economic activity of the people, as well as the social changes it endangers. All these tend to provoke demands for government action leading to policies designed to resolve the conflict.[16] As public policy decisions are made in response to conflicts arising out of differences between the interests of the various groups in the society, the nature of the conflict as well as the circumstances surrounding it, often influence the particular policy pursued.

In his analysis of public policy, James Anderson recognized five sets of values which act to serve as guidelines for the decision-maker. These are:

(1) Political Values — decisions made for the advancement and political advantage of a political interest group;
(2) Organizational Values — decisions based on enhancing organization or its survivability;
(3) Personal Values — decisions arrived at promoting or protecting the individual decision-maker's well being, reputation or position;
(4) Policy Values — decisions based on perception of public interest on what is proper to do; and
(5) Ideological Values — decisions aimed at preserving the ideology of the people.[17]

These values thus set the parameters within which the policy-maker makes his choice from the alternatives. What policy eventually emerges will depend on the value hierarchy and its salience to him.

Public policy approaches and process theoretical approaches

There is no grand unified theory of public policy. However, several theoretical approaches, each of which contributes to the understanding of the subject matter, have been proposed. One of them is the *Political Systems Theory*, championed by David Easton in his trilogy.[18] In Easton's work, policy is seen as a response of a political system to demands or claims made on it by individuals or groups in the system. The *Group Theory* approach views public policy as a product of group struggles in the system; 'group' here referring to a collection of individuals of shared attitude who "makes a claim through or upon any of the institutions of government."[19] According to Earl Latham, "what may be called public policy is the equilibrium reached in this group struggle at any given moment and it represents a balance which the contending factions or groups constantly strive to weight in their favor."[20] Akin to this is the *Elite Theory* which proposes that public policy reflects the values and preferences of the ruling elite, and it is implemented by public officials and agencies.[21] Instead of describing what public policy is, other analysts try to understand it by focusing on the activities which are involved in the policy-making process; this approach is referred to as the *Functional Process Theory*.[22] Still others study the structural aspects of governmental institutions, that is, "the set of regularized patterns of human behavior that persists over time."[23] This approach is described as *Institutionalism*.

Public Policy can be viewed as an analytical category or strictly a theoretical construct whose contents are "inferred from the patterns of relevant behavior."[24] These patterns constitute the conceptual framework that can be used to analyze the policy-making process. The process can be broken into several stages, each later stage presupposing and earlier one. They are:

(1) Problem Formation — setting up a public agenda, that is, deciding the general salience of a public problem and formulating it as an issue that demands public action.
(2) Policy Formulation — developing alternatives or acceptable courses of action for dealing with the problem or resolving the issues.
(3) Policy Adoption — choosing among the pertinent proposals or alternatives.
(4) Policy Implementation — carrying out or applying the chosen alternative.
(5) Policy Evaluation — finding out how effective the policy is or its impact, desired or undesired.[25]

No agreement has emerged among scholars, in the literature, on how the policy process, from Problem Formation through Policy Evaluation is actually carried out. Some of them in the *Rational Choice* school propose that policy-makers clearly define the problems, and carefully elaborate and analyze the different choices of solution according to their costs and benefits. The selected alternative is usually the one which maximizes utility, that is, one which has the highest ratio of achieved goals to sacrificed values.[26] However, others, like Herbert Simon, contend that real world conditions do not always allow maximization of utility. This *Organization Process* group states that decision-makers make efforts to select the option which 'satisfies' or sets minimum standards.[27] There are still other scholars, chief among whom is Charles Lindblom, who maintain that problems and/or policy goals are not always well defined. Therefore, they argue, there is no comprehensive evaluation of all the options; instead decisions are made through small moves on particular aspects of the problem, building upon existing decisions.[28] This approach is often referred to as the *Incremental Process*.

Thus, for the policy-maker faced with the task of making new policies or old ones with new dimensions, the making new policies or old ones with new dimensions, the process is usually carried out in several ways and in various organizational settings that can be understood by applying any or all of the above competing paradigms. These alternatives represent different strategies for resolving issues, but policy makers know that there is the basic need to identify the problem as well as the options available. And that usually requires the application of relevant knowledge and information — an arena where experts play a crucial role.

The policy process in developing states

In many developed countries of the world like the United States and Great Britain, decision-making is carried out through stable institutions and established organizational processes which grew out of internal necessities of the state and have endured over time. However, this is not the case in many of the newly independent nations. Here, political and administrative institutions geared toward policy-making were set up by the metropolitan government to fit its needs during the colonial period. After independence, the indigenous politicians and public officials who took over control, often opted to maintain those colonial structures without much substantial change. They were usually too preoccupied with the transfer of formal power as well as replacing the old legal policy-making authority, and dealing with issues paramount to regime maintenance like building up popular support.[29] Therefore, they were least likely to uproot the established order. This is especially evidenced in states like Nigeria, which negotiated their independence through peaceful means. (Even in the so-called revolutionary states, the colonial administrative apparatus was usually left intact.) When the need arose to build new institutions, they were often modeled after those in the metropole.

It was not only structures that were inherited, but also the style and form of policy-making processes were holdovers from pre-independence days. Political leaders in new states were often recruited from among the crop of persons who received their education and experience from the expatriates. They were thus politically socialized in the mores and customs of the colonial government and were often "less willing to exploit by radical reform, the temporary vulnerability of the institutions and broader policy dispositions of the colonial state."[30] For instance, in Nigeria, expert commissions fashioned after the Royal Commissions of Great Britain, in composition, style and function, were routinely set up to study controversial public issues and advise policy-makers. Even the process leading to the adoption of the expert recommendations by the Cabinet or Executive were remarkably similar. While the intricacies of the bureaucracies may differ, the same civil service procedures were followed in both the ex-colony and the metropole. (For details on expert bodies, see Introduction.)

What this portends is that policy-makers often go through the decision-making process without much innovation, just improvising as they go along. However, as Albert Hirschman observed in Latin America, and this is true in many Third World countries, 'autonomous policy-making' results "when control weakens and the existing social and political structures are under serious attack."[31] The state, facing new challenges to "adapt the old order to new circumstances or to build a new order,"[32] has to search for novel alternatives and this process is often intense because of the lack of policy precedents.[33] Thus, in Nigeria, during military rule, the policy-making process, especially in the revenue allocation area, was upturned. The old process was set aside, and new ways involving the use of decrees and edicts, were used to establish new allocation systems.

The demand for fresh ideas or policies usually emanates from the need for national integration and development — problems which are linked to the fundamental issues of legitimacy and transfer and distribution of power. These conflict areas are regime elaboration, economic development and resource allocation.[34] Because of their urgency and significance to the important task of nation-building, a task with high political content and a tendency to generate socio-political tensions, policy-making in these areas is usually concentrated at the center. The paucity of both material and manpower, and the dictates for expediency often require that the executive play a much larger role in policy formulation than is otherwise observed in most developed countries.[35]

In addition, while legislatures, interested groups and individuals in most Western democracies have established roles in the policy-making process, these institutionalized support systems may not exist in a developing nation. Where they do not exist, they may be either too weak to offer any appreciable support or too antagonistic to be of any help. Western legislatures exert formal influence on policies, especially when the executive has to legitimate (seek approval or authorization of) his policies; and this is done through majority coalition building among them.[36]

On the other hand, the influences from such groups that bear on a decision-maker in a new state are usually personalized.[37] Therefore, more effort is spent on manipulating or recruiting these groups to achieve the degree of support needed for the policy programs.[38] Because of this, extra rational components creep into the policy formulation process, making the selection of alternatives a highly politicized undertaking with high stakes. The explosive nature of the policy formulation process is further exacerbated when the political activity involved takes place in a developing federation which has pronounced and deep cleavages, both among and within the different levels of government as well as the people. The country of study, Nigeria, and the policy area looked into, Revenue Allocation, provide excellent examples of this phenomenon.

In the next chapter, we will take a brief historical tour of Nigeria, see how these schisms developed and how they were expressed and managed. This will lead us to understand the theme of this paper, which is the role of politics in revenue allocation policy formulation.

Notes

1. Anderson, James E., *Public Policy Making*, 2nd ed. (New York: Holt, Rinehart & Winston, 1979), p. 52.

2. Easton, David, *A System Analysis of Political Life*. (New York: John Wiley & Sons, 1965), p. 212.

3. James Anderson, op. cit., p. 3.

4. Ranney, Austin, 'The Study of Political Content: A Framework For Choice' in Austin Ranney (ed.) *Political Science and Public Policy*. (Chicago: Markham Publishing Co., 1968), pp. 7-8.

5. Salisbury, Robert H., 'The Analysis of Public Policy: A Search For Theories and Roles,' in Austin Ranney, op. cit., pp. 152-53.

6. Kash, Don E. and Robert W. Roycroft, *U.S. Energy Policy: Crisis and Complacency*. (Norman, Oklahoma: University of Oklahoma Press, 1984), p. 23.

7. Coates, Joseph, 'What is a Public Policy Issue?' in Kenneth R. Hammond (ed.) *Judgment and Decision in Public Policy Formation*. (Boulder, Colorado: Westview Press, 1978), p. 37.

8. Ibid., p. 37.

9. Eyestone, Robert, *Political Economy*. (Chicago: Markham Publishing Company, 1972), p. 80.

10. Ibid., p. 80.

11. Jones, Charles O., *An Introduction to the Study of Public Policy*, 2nd ed. (North Scituate, MA: Duxbury Press, 1977), p. 212.

12. Austin Ranney, op. cit., p. 8.

13. Charles Jones, op. cit., p. 212.

14. For details, see Gabriel Almond and Sidney Verba, *The Civic Culture*. (Boston: Little, Brown & Company, 1965).

15. Anderson, James E., David W. Brady and Charles Bullock, III, *Public Policy and Politics in America*. (North Scituate, MA: Duxbury Press, 1978), p. 5.

16. James Anderson, op. cit., pp. 31-32.

17. Ibid., p. 14.

18. Easton, David, *The Political System*. (New York: Knopf, 1953); *A Framework for Political Analysis*. (Englewood, New Jersey: Prentice Hall, 1965); and *A System Analysis of Political Life*. (New York: John Wiley & Sons, 1965).

19. Truman, David, *The Governmental Process*. (New York: Knopf, 1965), p. 37.

20. Latham, Earl, *The Group Basis of Politics*. (New York: Octagon Books, 1965), p. 36.

21. Dye, Thomas and Harman Zeigler, *The Irony of Democracy*. (Belmont, CA: Wadsworth, 1970), p. 6.

22. Laswell, Harold, *The Decision Process*. (College Park, MD: Bureau of Governmental Research, University of Maryland, 1956).

23. James Anderson, op. cit., p. 22.

24. Eulau, Heinz and Kenneth Prewitt, *Labyrinths of Democracy*. (Indianapolis: Bobbs-Merrill, 1973), p. 465.

25. For details of these stages, see among others, Anderson, op. cit; Charles Jones, op. cit., pp. 15-55; and Rose, Douglas D., 'Power, Salience and Public Policy,' in Robert Eyestone (ed.) *Public Policy Formation Public Policy Studies*, Vol. 2 (Greenwich, CT: JAI Press, Inc., 1984).

26. Zeckhauser, Richard and Elmer Schaefer, 'Public Policy and Normative Economic Theory,' in Baeur, Raymond A. and Kenneth J. Gergen (Eds). *The Study of Policy Formation*. (New York: The Free Press, 1968), pp. 27-101.

27. Simon, Herbert, *Administrative Behavior*, 2nd ed. (New York: The Free Press, 1957), pp. xxiii-xxvii.

28. Lindblom, Charles E., *The Policy Making Process*. (Englewood Cliffs, New Jersey: Prentice Hall, 1968).

29. This paragraph is culled from Ballard, J. A., *Policy Making in a New State*. (St. Lucia, Australia: University of Queensland Press, 1981), Chapter 1.

30. Ibid., p. 6.

31. Hirschman, Albert, 'Policy Making and Policy Analysis in Latin America—A Return Journey,' *Policy Sciences*, Vol. 6, (1975), p. 389.

32. Ibid., p. 390.

33. Dror, Yehezkel, *Public Policy Making Re-examined.* (Scranton, PA: Chandler Publishing Company, 1968), p. 108.

34. J.A. Ballard, op. cit., p. 9.

35. Yehezkel Dror, op. cit., p. 113.

36. Charles Jones, op. cit., p. 92.

37. Yehezkel Dror, op. cit., p. 114.

38. Ibid., pp. 111-112.

3 Evolution of federalism in Nigeria

Introduction

There are two distinct schools of thought as to how Nigeria came to adopt a federal type of government. Some analysts believe that the British colonial government deliberately imposed federalism on Nigeria in order to perpetuate neo-colonial control after independence. They argue that the British, had they wished, could have created a strong unified and unitary system instead of exploiting the 'particularistic tendencies' on the different ethnic groups that make up the entity. Thus they left behind, at the wake of their departure in 1960, an economically weak and politically under-developed nation which would depend on the mother-country for some time to come.[1]

The other school holds that given Nigeria's geographical cultural, historical, and ethnic diversity, a federal system of government was inevitable. It would have been impossible for such a variegated and unwieldily country to be governed from one center for a long time.

Moreover, there is the notion that the views of Nigeria's western educated nationalist elite contributed a major part to federalizing the country.[2] These interests were said to have 'colluded' with the British to carve out exclusive territories, in the form of autonomous regions, which they could exploit without checks and balances from competitors.

A cursory look at the history of the country suggests that Nigerian federalism was as much a creation of Britain as Nigeria herself. Instead of actually imposing federalism upon Nigeria, the colonial masters inadvertently governed Nigeria into a federal system with active aid from Nigerians themselves.

The first organized attempt to unify the British acquisitions of the Royal Niger Company, which later came to be known as Nigeria, was made in 1898, when Secretary of the Colonies, Joseph Chamberlain, set up the Selbourne

42

Committee to deliberate on the future of these holdings. Though the committee did not recommend immediate consolidation, it did suggest that once communication networks had been established, it would be desirable to unite the three different British administrations. It also advised the use of existing African political institutions, so as to keep British expenses down to a minimum.[3] Nevertheless, the separate administrations continued until 1906, when the three groupings were reduced to two, viz: a Northern and Southern Group of Provinces, and placed under Sir. Frederick Lugard, who was mandated to unite them into a single political entity.[4]

Many reasons have been given as to why the British sought amalgamation. One is that what was to become Nigeria formed a continuous and contiguous stretch of British authority, and it made no sense to operate different economic, especially railroad policies. Moreover, it was practically impossible to maintain the artificial barrier between the North and the South. However, most observers contend that the main rationale behind the amalgamation move was to relieve the British Treasury of the bonus of financing the impoverished Northern Group of Provinces (or Protectorate, as they were called later). Unification meant that the enormous revenue which the self-supporting South obtained from customs receipts could be shared with an almost bankrupt North. Thus the 1914 amalgamation was seen as a face and Lugard's intention, not so much for unity as for uniformity in administrative processes.[5]

The separate development of the North and the South which had started long before amalgamation continued in spite of it. As each area came under British rule and influence at different means, they were administered differently, depending on the particular local ruler and the political culture of the community.[6]

British colonial policy in the North could be described as one of "minimal interference with the indigenous political system."[7] That system was rooted in the hierarchical structure of the emirate North. Administration was based on a chain of command from the Resident British Agent and Emir down to the village head and to the people. This policy of indirect rule (the British masters were never in direct contact with the ruled) was very convenient for the British because the entrenched local aristocracy cooperated in keeping the status quo.[8]

In the South, various types of administrative systems evolved due to the varying political cultures of the peoples. In areas where there were strong traditional rulers, as in Yorubaland in the West, and in the Niger Delta, indirect rule flourished; in the other areas, some form of direct administration took place.[9]

That Nigeria developed into a country with a "deep schism in tradition, character and orientation" has been seen by some analysts as a deliberate effort by the British to carry out what is usually referred to as 'Divide and Rule' policy.[10] This is a policy whereby all efforts are made by the rulers to accentuate and reinforce the differences between the Regions or States and proceed to govern them like antagonists. That the British adopted this policy cannot be disputed. In 1922 when the opportunity came to include some elected African representatives in the Legislative Council, the North was conspicuously left out and only Southern legislatures were elected. The only link established by the 1922 Constitution between the North and the South was financial; all other important political departments remained separate.[11] The Legislative Council so created was to legislate for Lagos and the Southern Region alone, its only function in the North was to sanction expenditure of funds there. The Governor alone had any say in legislative and political matters in the Northern Provinces.[12]

This policy of shielding one region from the other and developing differential institutional structures in the regions continued until it was realized that the establishment of a common political framework for Nigeria could not be further delayed.[13] However, before acquiescing to a single administration, the Southern Protectorate was further divided into two distinct regions: Eastern and Western regions in 1939; an act that has been described as a set back to the "fragile structure produced by amalgamation."[14]

According to the Governor, Sir Arthur Richards, Nigeria fell naturally into three regions, the North, the West, and the East; each region differing widely in race, custom, outlook, and traditional systems of government. So by administrative pronouncement and fiat, Nigeria was divided into three distinct regions, and each endowed with a political life of its own and governed as such.[15] Also the Governor argued that the sub-division of the South would bring administration nearer to the people in the West (the capital of the Southern Provinces had been Enugu in the East).[16]

Before going on to examine the growth and nature of federalism in Nigeria, we shall take a brief detour look at the foundations of the various constitutions which had guided the establishment of the political system.

The constitutional background

From 1946, when the first formal constitutional arrangement for the whole country was drawn up, to 1979, the year of the latest experiment, six different documents of fundamental principles relating to the governance of the country have been issued. Each of which was conceived in response to political demands,

44

reflecting the convoluted history of the nation, as will be discussed below. According to Kenneth Wheare, new constitutions are usually drafted and eventually adopted because "people wished to make a fresh start, so far as the statement of their system of government was concerned."[17] And in H.C. McIlwaine's words, a constitution can be safely described as the "assemblage of laws, institutions and customs derived from certain fixed principles of reason...that compose the general system, according to which the community has agreed to be governed."[18] But if this be so, it should come as no surprise that the constitutional foundations of Nigeria have undergone, so many discussions, reviews and sometimes outright revisions. Unlike some countries like the United States and Great Britain, whose home-grown constitutions may easily fit into the above definition, all but the last two of Nigeria's constitutions were drafted and enforced by a suzerain power that jealously guarded its prerogative to dictate the political and constitutional advancement of its colony.[19]

The constitutions, actually legal documents called 'Orders-in-Council', were drafted under British legal criteria with little or no input from the community governed. They owed their legitimacy to the fact that the resident British sovereign and/or the British Parliament sanctioned the enactment or promulgation.[20] Hence what resulted was a technical document which detailed the structures, functions and procedures of the colony's administrative set up.[21] In this way, the constitution never functioned as a "charter for the affirmation of fundamental objectives or directive principles of government, and as a source of inspiration for enlightened governmental action."[22] In other words, it was a far cry from being a manifesto, a confession of faith or statement of ideals,[23] that a constitution is usually thought to be.

From the above, one might make the case that the British documents (the Orders-in-Council) were not constitutions at all; nevertheless, however removed they may be from our concept of traditional constitutions, they still reflected, to some degree, the broad political configuration of the people,[24] both the indigenous population and the alien rulers. After earlier attempts to exclude all input from the colonized populace, the framers of Nigeria's constitutions were pressured into acknowledging certain demands made by an emerging but forceful Nigerian political elite and incorporating these demands into the formal documents. Thus as the constitutional development of the country progressed, though still largely determined by the colonial powers, the resulting collection of legal and extra legal rules that define and prescribe the "relationships of the various organs of government inter se and with the citizen",[25] tended to embody the compromises between the conflicting beliefs and interests in the country. It can thus be reasonably argued that the later constitutions of Nigeria were "indeed the resultant of parallelogram of forces — political, economic, and social,"[26] that operated when these constitutions were drafted and adopted.

The early years of Nigerian federalism

As stated earlier, the isolationist policy of the British colonial authority in which the Northern Region was politically quarantined, proved to be ineffective. The cultural, economic and social barriers between the North and the South were very permeable, thus making the policy anachronistic and obsolete. In 1946, the first constitution applicable to the whole country was adopted. It provided a central legislature with veto power over the regional bodies.

It was during the discussion and criticism of the 1946 Richards Constitution (named after the Governor) that opinions of federalism took definite shape. The Constitution was faced with the task of integrating the North and the South into a centralized political structure.[27] The systems to be created, however, would allow the diverse elements which had been grouped into three sections, to progress at varying speeds. Yet, they were supposed to amicably and smoothly evolve towards a closely integrated economic, social and political unit.[28]

It can be seen that the very nature of the Richards Constitution was based on the premise that the integration of the different parts of each region into a regional unity and the subsequent integration of the regions was a necessary prerequisite for national political unity.[29] Based on that conviction, Sir Arthur Richards created a tripartite Nigeria constitutionally.[30]

The educated African elite themselves became the vanguard for a federal style of government. Dr. Nnamdi Azikiwe, the foremost Nigerian nationalist who later became its first president, suggested that Nigeria be divided into eight nationalities and be federated into a commonwealth. To him, federalism was a means of breaking up a massive country in the interest of more efficient administration.[31] Agreeing with Dr. Azikiwe that federalism might be the best approach to Nigeria's political advancement was the late Chief Obafemi Awolowo, who was Opposition Leader in the first Republic. However, to Chief Awolowo, the country should be divided up into ten regions representing the main ethnic groups, each progressing at its own rate.[32] Also concurring with them was the late Sir Abubakar Tafawa Balewa, Nigeria's first Prime Minister. He opined that the country's future did indeed lie in federalism because the rate of regional progress and development was not equal and each region ought to be allowed to develop on its own.[33]

With such a preference for federal type of government, it was not surprising that the 1946 unitary constitution came under heavy attack and was

46

condemned bitterly by every Nigerian politician. Though some Nigerian political scientists like the late Dr. Kalu Ezera concluded that, but largely for the arbitrary manner in which it was introduced, and not necessarily for its defects, the Richards Constitution embittered and alienated the nationalists elements of the country;[34] this author contends that it was the unitary nature of the constitution that fueled the agitations. The newly created regions which contained within them the major ethnic groups had acquired personalities of their own and were growing separately. Various interest groups based on cultural/linguistic affinity had emerged in the regions, expressly to promote cultural and political awareness among its members. Each of these groups was led by a group of upcoming Nigerian bourgeois elite who wanted 'a piece of the action.' With the knowledge that the colony would eventually become independent, they needed to carve out spheres of influence for themselves. But with the constitutional provisions as they were, such dreams might never be fulfilled. It was these cultural organizations that later metamorphosed into political parties. Twenty-one years later, in 1967, when General Aguyi-Ironsi introduced another unitary system in Nigeria, he encountered the same bitter reactions.

The MacPherson Constitution that followed in 1951 dealt with the question of whether Nigeria was to be a fully centralized political system with all the legislative powers concentrated at the center, or a federal system where different regions would exercise some measure of autonomy. The overwhelming conclusion was that Nigeria should go the federal way.[35] Each region had its reason for demanding a federal system. The North's rationale was due to its educational and social backwardness, it needed its own regional government to catch up to the others. The West, following Chief Awolowo's cue, wanted a federation of States whose boundaries would reflect the homogenous ethnic and/or linguistic groupings and in which each region was left to seek its own means of improving its social and political status depending on its resources.[36] This instance was particularly favored because at that time, the West being the richest region, believed its advancement and march to progress would be retarded if it mixed with a slow North and a poor East.[37]

Leaders of the East, however, had a different view. Though they wanted a federal system, their model was actually more unitary in nature. The type of federation recommended was one in which the central legislature had a veto power over any regional legislation.[38] The reason behind this volte-face was the realization that only under a unitary arrangement could the Eastern-based political party, The National Council of Nigeria and the Cameroons (NCNC) have a chance of winning a national majority.[39] Thus it can be seen that each region's recipe for government was based on the need to advance its cultural, political and economic system.

The resulting constitution was, according to Awolowo, a "wretched compromise between federalism and unitarianism." It marked the embryonic stage of federalism, by providing for Regional Assemblies with not only deliberate but legislative powers within the regions. Also there was a Central House of Representatives with both legislative and executive powers. Its membership was open to members of the Regional Assemblies, whose leaders carried out the recruitment. That has been described as the beginning of "consolidation and primacy of regional interests in the affairs"[40] of the central legislature.

Regional political leaders who were not satisfied with the 'wretched compromise' worked hard towards the failure of the MacPherson Constitution. Given this its inherent structural defects, it was finally abandoned, and a new constitution proposed in its stead.

The federal era

With the adoption of the Lyttelton Constitution in 1954, federalism became firmly and constitutionally established in Nigeria, with 'Unity in Diversity' as the watchword. The constitution has been referred to as a 'Regionalist' constitution which canalized and entrenched regional autarchy forces.[41] It transformed the structure of Nigerian "government from its unitary foundations to the existing bases of federalists."[42] This was so because the former constitution having proved unworkable, the colonial rulers decided that it should be revised "to provide for greater autonomy and for the removal of powers of intervention by the Center in matters which can, without detriment to other regions, be placed entirely within regional competence."[43]

Therefore, it was agreed that Nigeria would become a federation made up of a central legislature and three self-governing regions. These regions had residual powers invested in them, that is to say, they were endowed with full legislative and executive powers in all matters except for a specified list of Exclusive Subjects which were left for the central government.[44] Thus political power devolved from the regions to the center, making for politically and financially autonomous regions.

Under the 1954 Constitution, the residual list (matters to be dealt by the regions alone) covered a wide range of issues, but more importantly, these issues were those that affected the daily lives of Nigerians; they included a host of social services such as health, primary and secondary education, town planning, agriculture and public works. These regional responsibilities had the effect of making the average Nigerian think of government largely in terms of regional government which had control over every aspect of his everyday life;

48

to him it was the regional level that mattered and since it provided his needs, he owed loyalty to it.[45] The central government was an almost mystical institution ran by a decreasing number of expatriate officials who would soon leave when the country achieved independence in the not so distant future.

Almost every public institution — the civil service, police, government-owned corporations and parastatals, marketing boards — was regionalized. According to some sources, if the colonial administrators had not restrained the Nigerian leaders, regionalization would have been extended to the railways and post and telecommunications.[46] The breaking up of the Central Marketing Board and the sharing of its proceeds is of great significance to fiscal policy formulation, and hence to this study, so its consequences would be examined in due course.

The basis for the mutual settlement that produced the constitution lay in the desire of majority of the interested parties at the conferences to reduce the powers of the central government and make it a mere agency of the regional governments.[47] The claim for greater regional autonomy at the expense of the central government based on the notion that original sovereignty lay with the regions, prevailed during the deliberation. With a 'regionalist version of anti-colonialism'[48] prevalent among the Nigerian delegation, the federal cause was overwhelmed and the regions emerged as the centers of power.[49] Each region had something to gain form the compromise; the North had now been safeguarded to domination;[50] the East and West, on the other hand, could go ahead and "make further constitutional advance without being hampered by the reservations of the North, and without forcing their ideas on the North." Each region, now considered a separate entity could develop and progress at its own pace[51] and that was what the leaders wanted. The situation was aptly described by an analyst who wrote:

It was on October 1, 1954, that the new federation was officially launched. But the first toast alas, did not go to the country; it went to the newly created Premiers. Alhaji Ahmadu Bello in the North, Azikiwe in the East, and Awolowo in the West, became counterparts in a self-created Nigeria.[52]

After the elections in 1954, the new Premiers, who were heads of the regional governments and also the party bosses, decided to stay in their respective regional capitals and instead sent their lieutenants to Lagos to run the Federal Government.[53]

Included in the constitution was a provision which granted full internal self-government to any region which wanted it. This was another compromise reached to find a middle ground between the NCNC-Action Group (AG) demand that self-government be granted in 1956 and the Northern Peoples' Congress (NPC) which wanted to delay it, citing their lack of experience in Western style government. In 1957, Eastern and Western Regions became self-governing, and two years later, in 1959, the Northern Region followed suit.

Having consolidated their hold in the regions that had become fully institutionalized as the primary focus of political power, Nigerian politicians decided to devote themselves to making the 1954 constitution suitable for an independent country. The political and economic stakes had been bartered and shared among them during the last constitutional convention. With independence coming, the need for a genuine national government became apparent and there was a noticeable change in the attitude of the political leaders as they gathered again in London to debate the future of their country which was about to gain freedom. The Constitutional Conferences of 1957-58 showed a high degree of cooperation between the Nigerian delegates, who, in spite of their differences, "put up a good show of determined, even if superficial, unity of purpose."[54]

The most important recommendation was the provision for creation of the position of a Prime Minister who would fill the vacuum at the center left by the departing colonial authority. The leader of whichever party won a majority of seats in the House of Representatives was to occupy the post.[55] The 1959 federal election which was fought by all the parties 'with unprecedented vigor and resources'[56] showed how important the center had become to Nigerians. Many regional politicians, notably Awolowo, Premier of the Western Region and leader of the Action Group party, left their comfortable seats at home and vied for a place at the center. That willingness to participate in the central government grew out of the realization that as the colonial administration, which had become anonymous with the central government, was finally leaving the stage for good, it was left to those politicians to assume that role. Since they were the ones to inherit and sit on the center throne, it was to their advantage that its formal position be improved. Consequently, the Independence Constitution which they bargained for provided such provisions that made the center enviable.

One of the exclusive powers given the Federal Government was the 'state of emergency' provision which empowered it to exercise control over any region in the case of war, public emergency (defined by the federal government) or subversion.[57] That prerogative which was later incorporated into the Emergency Powers Act of 1961 was used to successfully subjugate the Western Region and its party the Action Group which was the Opposition Party in the federal legislature, during the 1962 leadership crisis in the region.[58] In addition to the security powers, the Federal Government also acquired greater roles in the planning of economic and foreign policies. Since

50

independence was in sight, attention was being focused on defense and foreign affairs, and the status of these offices increased. Before 1960, the political parties were not interested in such issues so they were left on the federal 'Exclusive List'.[59]

What really made control of the central government such a priceless trophy was the economy. In 1954, under the 'separatist' constitution, the regions decided to adopt a fiscal policy which put the bulk of the revenue from export of commodities in their hands. Unfortunately, even before the policy was fully implemented, world market prices of these produce declined, plunging the regions into severe budgetary strains.[60] Meanwhile, the central government was experiencing budgetary surpluses, political parties battled hard to gain control of the government machinery at the center.[61] Moreover, inter-regional trade had grown and the main means of transportation — railroads and major roads — were under federal jurisdiction.[62] Thus all policies concerning economic planning and development lay in the hands of the federal government. As time went on, that function became more and more important and Nigerians became increasingly cognizant of the role of the central government in the economic development of the country.[63]

The 1963 (Republic) Constitution which was adopted after a one-day meeting between the Prime Minister and regional premiers, did not present much change in the realities of political power.[64] The political leaders decided and agreed among themselves that Nigeria should become a Republic and the 1960 Constitution was amended to show that new status.[65] The Governor-General who was acting as surrogate head of state on behalf of the Queen of England, became the President, and the ability of the Legislature to vote out any member of the Cabinet was greatly reduced.[66]

Throughout the First Republic, 1960-1966, there was a gradual shift of political activity from the regions to the Center, which helped the federal government to establish a "definite, if limited, supremacy over the regions."[67] However, despite the tilt in balance on the side of central empowerment, Nigerian politics was still run by powerful regional party barons. The elections of 1959 and 1961 showed that the "triangular pattern of identification continued to crystallize" in the country.[68] During the elections, each political party won in its region and sent to Lagos representatives who would argue the region's cause. That made an observer comment that:

> Indeed a reading of the debates of the House of Representatives might lead one to conclude that the primary concern of many of the legislators was to take claim to a share of the development services for their constituency.[69]

And indeed it was. The regionalization of interests and loyalties on the part of federal legislators and the consequent weakening of their commitment to the center which made the federal government a "very weak institution manipulated by over-mighty regions,"[70] continued after independence. With the withdrawal of the alien over-arching authority of the British, the federal center became a battle ground for regional interests who fought over how many shares of the nation's resources they could extract and repatriate home. As a result, the political game of who gets what, how, why, and by how much,[71] was played twice in Nigeria. Once at the federal level, by regional leaders, and then replayed at the regional front by all other interests.

It was the pattern of parochial behavior, aided and abetted by the needs to satisfy the terms of colonial withdrawal,[72] that resulted in the type of federal systems described above. The articles of governance which, over time, placed regional governments in a "decisive position over tremendous range of functions,"[73] were a natural outgrowth of the ethno-clientistic political party system that flourished in Nigeria.

The very dominant regional-based political parties which negotiated the type of federalism Nigeria was to have in the post-independence era, sealed the decision against a strong federation. The linguistic, cultural, religious, and economic divisions which those parties exploited, all dictated, as one author put it, "the adoption of the federal system in order to minimize conflict and to provide for unity in diversity."[74] However, conflict was not minimized, instead, discord and antipathy, coupled with mutual distrust and fear riddled the system and led to its eventual collapse only six years after independence.

Military federalism

The heydays of superior regional power came to a halt with the first military coup d'etat on January 16, 1966, led by a group of young army officers. Several of the leading politicians, including the Prime Minister, Sir Abubakar Tafawa Balewa, the Premiers of both the North and the West, Sir Ahmadu Bello and Chief Samuel Akintola, and many high ranking military officers were killed. The 1963 Constitution was suspended and decrees became the source of law. The first decree — The Constitution (Suspension and Modification) Decree 1966, Decree No. 1 — suspended all parliamentary institutions and gave the Federal Military Government, "power to make laws for the peace, order and good government" of the whole country.

In addition, the Decree established a Supreme Military Council (SMC) consisting of the Head of the Armed Forces and the four Military Governors. Also established was a Federal Executive Council (FEC) comprised of the same personalities plus the Inspector-General of Police and the Attorney-General. The SMC was not vested with any particular functions, but was given the responsibility for "the maintenance of the law and order and good government" throughout the federation. On the other hand, the FEC acted to "perform the functions exercised by the former Council of Ministers."[75] Each region had its own Executive Council but these Councils were subordinate to the Federal Executive Council.

With the setting up of the military government, 'Federalism' ceased to exist in Nigeria, at least in theory. The very hierarchical nature of the military regime and command is inconsistent with federal division of constitutional powers. However, the fact that the new government decided to call itself the FEDERAL MILITARY GOVERNMENT has some significance. The federal structure of the political system was left intact. Regions still existed and functioned in the same semi-autonomous fashion as before, except that Military Governors had inherited the legislative and executive powers of the former civilian premiers, albeit in a modified form. Thus the quasi-federal character of the country remained in place.[76]

It was not to last long. General Thomas Aguyi-Ironsi, the man chosen to head the new government after the dust had settled down, decided to put into action the mechanisms of a unitary government. The groundwork of the new system came to light in a speech by the Head of State in which he diagnosed the root cause of Nigeria's problems as corruption, nepotism, inefficiency, and regionalism. He went on to declare that Nigerians all "want an end to regionalism," and that "tribal loyalties and activities which promote tribal consciousness and sectional interests must give way to the urgent task of national reconstruction."[77]

Right after the speech, the Military Governor of the Mid-Western Region, Lt. Col. David Ejoor, was reported as saying that the 'National Government' set up by the Army was the prelude to the re-introduction of a unitary form of government.[78] Furthermore, a senior government official, Mr. Francis Nwokedi, was appointed to consider and report to the Supreme Military Council on the establishment of 'an administrative grid' for a united Nigeria, and the "unification of the Public Services and Judicial Services." Another public official was to help in the review of "statutory corporations, State-owned companies, and related organizations throughout the federation."[79] Later, in a press conference, General Ironsi defended the proposed unitary government on the grounds that:

> It has become apparent to all Nigerians that rigid adherence to regionalism was the bane of the last regime and one of the main factors which contributed to its downfall. No doubt, the country would

53

welcome a clean break with the deficiencies of the system of government to which the country has been subjected in the recent past. The existing borders of governmental control will be re-adjusted to make for less cumbersome administration.[80]

He went on to add that, "the country needs a sort of nerve center which will give the necessary direction and control in all major areas of national activities, so that we will be in a position to plot a uniform pattern of development for the whole country."[81] It is the lack of such a 'nerve center' that has been blamed for the failure of the federal government in the First Republic.

The type of government from 1960-66 could best be described as regionalist, where regions "in their corporate or collective capacities and as contra-distinguished from the individuals of whom they consist,"[82] controlled the sources of power, values and interests of the whole society. These constitutionally established regions which contained within their boundaries, the major ethnic groups, could have worked together if there had been a political and administrative 'grid' "superimposed on these different groups with sufficient force at its disposal to coerce them if necessary."[83] But as General Ironsi observed, the 'grid' was missing.

Though the 1960 and 1963 constitutions established a federal government with emergency powers which could be used to coerce the regions, the politicians who made up the central government owed their positions and allegiance to the regions and were thus reluctant to invoke them. The pervasive power of the regions grew to encompass the individual's interests, rights and values.[84] When regional loyalty overrides or prevails over general loyalty, the possibility of the union breaking apart as a result of interregional conflict is greatly increased. It is even more so when regional boundaries coincide with ethnic enclaves, as was true in Nigeria. And the new military government was determined to break the backs of the powerful regions.

On May 24, 1966, despite loud and bitter opposing voices, General Ironsi promulgated Decree No. 34. Nigeria ceased to be a federation. The Federal Military Government was re-designated the 'National Military Government'; all former regions were abolished and the country divided into 'Groups of Provinces'. Furthermore, the Federal and Regional Civil Services were unified into a National Public Service.[85]

This unilateral attempt to bring about a unitary form of government by decree met with an opposition so serious that some analysts believe it precipitated the second coup. Though federalism had not been working well, the sudden decision to turn the country into a unitary system was not welcome. Interested sub-national groups which flourished under the federal type of government, and which ultimately regained political power, refused to follow the move. General Ironsi, in spite of all the committees set up to study the issue, including the Constitution Review Committee, held little consultation with important political groups before embarking on such a radical move.[86] The military leaders found to their dismay that without negotiated compromise with, and regard for, the interested sub-national groups, any imposition from the top was bound to fall through. Instead of creating a strong center as they envisioned, what actually took place was an unstable center which was pulled down by the centrifugal forces of the regions. The Army which had been an integrative force practically disintegrated as a national entity, and that unleashed a widespread demand for regional autonomy.[87] Thus Ironsi's prescription for the disease of 'regionalism' was never tried, another illustration of the strong hold regions still had on the Nigerian political scene.

That the second military coup was organized and executed mainly by officers of Northern origin is significant. It had been argued, rather persuasively, that the underlying cause of the breakdown of Ironsi's regime was the move to unify the public services. Already the first coup, in eliminating only Northern and Western political leaders and leaving unharmed their counterparts in the East, had been viewed with suspicion. Most people in the North interpreted it as an attempt by the Ibos of the East to dominate the country.[88] The final straw was the unification attempts. Ibos, at least numerically, dominated the Federal Public Service, and to put all public services under one command meant to many Northerners, a deliberate attempt to combine 'bureaucratic and executive political dominance' by the Ibos.[89] They felt such plans were part of the "final solution to the 'Northern menace'."[90]

Thus, one of the first acts of the new regime, headed by Lt. Col. (later General) Yakubu Gowon, was to do away with the unitary form of government, and "its centralization of political authority."[91] In a nationwide address on August 1, 1966, General Gowon proposed another constitutional about-turn, reversed the unitary government and restored the federal system.[92] He declared that the "basis of confidence in our unitary system of government had been unable to stand the test of time,"[93] and therefore by Decree No. 59 of September 1, 1966 (Constitution [Suspension and Modification] Decree) formally reinstated the federation. The previous names were restored, the former regions got their identities as well as their separate public services back. In that way, Decree No. 1 was reenacted with minor amendments.[94]

One of the heaviest casualties of the two coups was the Nigerian Army. It ceased to be a cohesive force and practically disintegrated into regional armies. Surviving Ibo soldiers (there had been a massacre of them in the North just before and after the July coup) trooped back home, while a reverse flow of Northern soldiers also took place. Since the Army was in such disarray, the

Regions re-created, started to move even further apart. Decision-making shifted from Lagos (which now had only a tenuous hold on the government) to the regions, and as one might add, from the military to politicians.[95] Old politicians reared their heads again, the most visible being Chief Obafemi Awolowo, former Premier of the Western Region an ex-leader of the old Action Group Party. He had been imprisoned in 1963 for treasonable felony, having been found guilty by the Balewa government for plotting to overthrow it through violent means. After his release by General Gowon, he was hailed as 'Leader of the Yorubas' and enjoyed authority rivaling that of the Military Governor. The shift in the balance of political power is aptly described by S.K. Panter-Brick when he wrote:

> The Supreme Commander was reduced to the status of a convener; decisions affecting the country as a whole were made dependent upon negotiations between regional delegates, and regional opinion itself tended to be much more openly discussed and formulated in consultative assemblies, composed partly of traditional leaders and partly of 'leaders of thought'; that is people recognized to have a political following.[96]

One such 'consultative assembly' was the Ad-Hoc Constitutional Committee set up in September 1966, to manage and direct the political affairs of the country. As expected, it consisted of civilian representatives from the Regions and Lagos. Most of the delegates were politicians, no military personnel attended, and the Federal Military Government was not represented.[97] As one newspaper editorial put it, the Conference proceedings had been like 'Hamlet' without the Prince.[98] Four alternatives about the future of Nigeria, not one of which was the unitary system, were discussed. That showed the unequivocal distaste for the system shared by the country's new leaders.

During the deliberations, the older regions, North, East, and West, all expressed opposition to Nigeria retaining the status quo; they wanted a break-up of the country into constituent parts bound together in what could be termed a confederation. The loose association of autonomous regions would give these regions the right to secede unilaterally completely at any time of their choice.[99] Only the Mid-West Region prodded by its Military Governor, insisted that the Federal Government remain as a united whole and that in any new constitution, "there shall be no right of secession by any Region."[100]

The apparent consensus among the Big Three on several issues broke down when the issue of creating more States was raised. Nigerians, especially those from the minority ethnic groups within the respective regions, had been agitating for separate States since pre-independence days. One reason for the request to divide Nigeria was the need for government to be more effective administratively. However, the most voiced rationale for the creation of more States was to minimize or eliminate conflict between the different States and within each State.[101] It was believed by many Nigerians that fear of domination of one region or ethnic group over another would be reduced if more States were created. Several Commissions had been agreed upon.[102]

When the same question came up during the Ad-Hoc Conference, the regions split ranks. The East and North were very opposed to the idea of creating more States because most of the proponents for new States came from those regions; the West, on the other hand, wanted more States based on ethnic and linguistic affinities.[103] How and where those proposed new States would be carved out became the bone of contention. Before the discussions got very far, severe communal riots broke out in the North from May through September 1966, in which many Easterners living there were murdered. The political stability of the nation deteriorated to such a degree that the East boycotted the second meeting of the Conference. It was subsequently adjourned *sine die* in November 1966, but the vexing issue of States creation was later settled, rather dramatically.

Following the disturbances (the killings and lootings) in the country, General Gowon, who had assumed full powers under a declared state of emergency, summed up the problem thus:

> The main obstacle to the future stability in this country is the present structural imbalance in the Nigerian Federalism. Even Decree No. 8 or Confederation or Loose Association will never survive if any one section of the country is in a position to hold others to ransom.[104]

So in order to preempt any secessionist moves (already in the air) and correct the 'structural imbalance', twelve States out of the four regions were created by decree on May 27, 1967; six in the North and six in the South.

A critical look at the States created shows that the recasting of Nigeria reflected not only structural-constitutional motives but also those of political advantage. Though the move was an emergency measure, a last-ditch effort that failed to offset an eventual secession attempt, it achieved the purpose of cutting down those giant regions to size, such that none would be in a position to challenge single-handedly the central government as the Eastern Region came to do.[105]

More significant however, was the pattern of division. The Eastern Region, the source of the secessionist threat, was cut up into three States, concentrating all the Ibos in one, the East-Central State; two other States were carved out to cater to the major minority groups in the area, Rivers and South-Eastern States. The West, on the other hand, which was almost as big and populous as the East, was left intact. So in the South, the only really new States were those in the East. It had been argued that concentrating all the Ibos in one State made it easier for the Federal Government to prosecute the civil war that ensued. Moreover, the Federal Government scored a political goal with the non-Ibos in the Eastern Region for removing them from a perceived Ibo domination. The States they had been clamoring for since 1958 had now seen the light of day, thanks to General Gowon. The political goodwill reaped by the Federal Government was manifested by the whole-hearted support to the Federal war effort given by these people who saw a federal victory as a fulfillment of their dreams.[106]

Meanwhile, before the States were created, the Military Governor of the then Eastern Region, Lt. Col. Odumegu Ojukwu had refused to recognize the authority of the new regime. His objective was based on two grounds: (1) Lt. Col. Gowon was not the most superior army officer after General Ironsi, therefore, Gowon was violating or ignoring the order of seniority, a vital principle in any military organization; and (2) Gowon took over the reins of power through 'force of conquest' and therefore, he, Ojukwu, and the East were not ready to accept blindly any leadership from Lagos.[107]

A series of negotiations took place between Ojukwu and Gowon about the plight of the Ibos and their safety in the country. The question gained prominence with the events of the now infamous September 29 pogrom described by Ojukwu as follows:

Another wave of violence was unleashed in the Northern Region against men, women and children of Eastern Nigeria origin. The mass slaughter of our people which started that day, has been far greater in magnitude and callousness than what shocked the world in May.[108]

As the violence continued, so did the threat of secession gain credence. Ibos, especially those forced to return to the East from other parts of the country, questioned the survivability of the Ibos in a united Nigeria.

Further attempts at reconciliation through personal contacts on the telephone between the two protagonists failed. Gowon accused Ojukwu of not 'behaving like an officer and a gentleman'; while Ojukwu berated Gowon for being a well meaning but weak officer "in the grips of forces more powerful than himself."[109] Pressured by several sources, they decided to meet under the auspices of the Ghanaian government at Aburi, near Accra. Between January 4 and 5, 1967, the Supreme Military Council of Nigeria, consisting of General Gowon, the four Military Governors, representatives from the Navy, Lagos and the Police, deliberated on the future of the country. Certain agreements were reached on the situation of things. They included among others, a regionalization of the Army, a renouncing of the use of force, and the granting of sovereign authority in all legislative and executive matters to the Supreme Military Council. If the Council could not meet to decide on any issue, "such a matter must be referred to Military Governors for comment and concurrence";[110] a move that amounted to a veto-power by the regional governors.

On their return to Nigeria, the Federal government and the Eastern regional government interpreted the Aburi Agreements very differently. To Ojukwu, Aburi meant extreme decentralization which would give the East an almost semi-sovereign status within a federal system. During a press conference given on his return from Aburi, Ojukwu stated that the "East believes in confederation, and I believe that is the only answer."[111] Ojukwu then refused to attend any other SMC meetings until the agreements had been implemented. 'On Aburi We Stand' became the slogan and was heard throughout the length and breadth of Ibo land,[112] and at the end of February 1967, Ojukwu declared that: "If the Aburi agreements are not fully implemented by 31 March, I shall have no alternative but to feel free to take whatever measures may be necessary to give effect in this Region to those agreements."[113]

The Aburi agreements got a very different reception in Lagos. After conferring with senior civil servants, Gowon realized that the Federal Government had given away too much. They pointed out to him the "inconsistencies of the Aburi document and the destructive effect of its implications on the maintenance of effective federal power."[114] Thereupon, during a press conference, on January 26, 1967, Gowon back-tracked on most of the agreements. According to Frederick Forsyth (1969):

> By the time he had finished with the small print there appeared to be little of Aburi left. He may well have disagreed with what he signed; that might well have been a good case for reconsidering Aburi; but the fact remains that he and his fellow colonels had all voluntarily signed the document, after two days of talks, without any coercion, and the unilateral rescinding of so many of the important paragraphs, particularly the ones most vitally sought after in the East, effectively dealt a blow to Nigeria from which it never recovered.[115]

It had been said in the literature dealing with the Nigerian civil war that Ojukwu outsmarted the federal delegation both with his intellect (he was the most educated of them, having been a product of the English public schools, and Oxford University where he got a M.A. degree) and his preparedness. He had gone to Aburi ready to finalize and sign a 'firm constitutional document' on the relationship between the central and the regional governments.[116] Gowon and his group, on the other hand, saw the meetings as the first steps toward re-establishing old ties, and the agreements as bases for further discussions. They felt that with the different views expressed at Aburi, many matters still required further clarification and might need qualification. Thus the 'spirit of Aburi' quickly disappeared when accusations and counter-accusations of bad faith arose in the aftermath of the conflicting interpretations.[117]

Later, on March 17, 1967, General Gowon issued Decree No. 8 of 1967 to implement the decisions as he understood them. The provisions of this Decree made "maximum possible concessions to Eastern demands for confederation"; the regional military governors were given all the legislative and executive powers they had before the coup; the SMC could not legislate on some specific vital matters without the concurrence of the Head of State and at least three of the four governors. (At Aburi, unanimity was required). Those provisions made the central government virtually dependent on the regional governments. Nigeria then became more confederal than it had ever been since 1954.[118]

Nevertheless, Ojukwu rejected the decree and its provisions, seeing it as a "Northern instrument for political power over the South."[119] As far as Ojukwu was concerned, Gowon had reneged on the Aburi deals, so he had to implement them unilaterally. As he threatened, on March 31, 1967, he started 'regionalizing' federal property in the East and his relationship with Gowon deteriorated further. Several peace-making attempts, notably those of the National Reconciliation Committee, were made to bridge the gap between the two adversaries; all to no avail. Meanwhile, pressures from important sectors of the Ibo community were being put on Ojukwu to secede. On May 27, 1967, the Eastern Region's Consultative Assembly called on him to declare "at an early practicable date Eastern Nigeria as a free, sovereign, and independent state by the name and title of the Republic of Biafra."[120] Eventually, Eastern Nigeria, on May 30, 1967, seceded from the federation and proclaimed itself the independent Republic of Biafra. Thereupon, the Federal Military Government initiated what it called a 'Police Action' to stem the rebellion, but it intensified and grew into a major conflict that took three years to quell.

Throughout the Civil War, which started in July 1967 and ended in January 1970, and the entire military rule of thirteen years, 1966-79, there existed in Nigeria, a style of government termed 'Military Federalism.'[121] It was characterized by a gradual erosion of States' power by a dominant military superstructure at the center. In addition to the command style of government, the new States which proliferated to nineteen were geographically too small and financially too weak to challenge the authority of the central government. Therefore, the Federal Government grew at the expense of the States and rolled back most of their independence and freedom gained before the civil war.

Decrees were enacted to limit the legislative and executive powers of the States. An early one, Decree No. 27, of 1967, restricted the authority of States to only residual matters; everything else was to be decided by the Federal Government. Certain constitutional functions which were directly under regional control, like taxation, marketing boards, education, and health, were taken over by the center. Military Governors, appointed by the Head of State, and owing allegiance to him, were given full powers over all constitutional responsibilities in the States.[122] The third coup in July 1975 in which Gowon was overthrown, did not drastically change the political picture of the country. Rather, further centralization took place. The creation of seven additional States following a flood of demands, making a grand total of nineteen States, reduced whatever powers the States had. That development was captured in a poignant editorial by the *New Nigeria*, which wrote that, "it is a piece of constitutional fiction to pretend that States are successors to Regions, for the more States there are, the more powers are aggregated to the center."[123]

General Murtala Mohammed, who took over the reins of power, ruled effectively form Lagos. It had been said that Military Governors in the Gowon era, got 'too big for their boots'. Some of them created 'fiefdoms' in their respective areas of operation, and that had been blamed on the personal style of leadership Gowon exhibited. To arrest that situation and prevent any 'chumminess' with the new Governors, General Mohammed excluded them from the Supreme Military Council and made them subject to its authority. However, there was frequent changing of the guard at the State level, leaving the States as no more than puppets, controlled and directed from the Center.[124]

When the mantle of leadership fell on General Olusegun Obasanjo after Mohammed was killed in an abortive coup attempt in February 1976, the emasculating trend did not cease. The new regime declared that it would carry out the policies of the last government and it did. The central military administration, without much help from the States, proceeded to run the country as it deemed fit. One major event in which the States did not have much, if any, input was the conducting of the civilian elections, in which political parties that did not have what the military rulers described as a national base were disqualified. That was a means of preventing a return to the regional-based political orientation of the last civilian period, a situation that left the central government at the mercy of the Regions.

Federalism and post-military politics

After thirteen years of military rule (1966-1979) the Army finally went back to the barracks, leaving behind established political parties, elected officials, and a new Constitution. The 1979 Constitution was drafted by a Constitution Drafting Committee, debated extensively by the public and a Constituent Assembly, and finally promulgated into law by General Obasanjo after adding seventeen amendments.[125] The new civilian government which came into office on October 1, 1979, under President Shehu Shagari of the National Party of Nigeria (NPN), was modeled after the American federal system. It had an executive leadership, separation of powers between and within the different levels of government, and concomitant checks and balances.

The centralization tendency which began with military rule in 1966 was very much evident in the civilian government of 1979. The Constitution consolidated the "transfer of national jurisdiction of many important functions and powers that were requisitioned by military decrees,"[126] especially the "economic and regulatory activities" of the country.[127] The effect this had on federalism in Nigeria was that States became relatively weaker and dependant on the center. Unlike at the beginning of post-independence politics, when the regions came together to form a federation, now the Federation was "reconstituting itself in its own sovereign fashion."[128] The States were being created by the center.

Nothing buttressed this fact more than the mode of election into the National Assembly. Instead of representing States, as do Senators in the United States, Nigerian Senators represented senatorial districts within the States, thereby diluting any State or regional base on which any of them could attack the Federal Government. Added to this was the creation of yet another system, which received funding directly from the Federal Government.

One significant feature about the second attempt at partisan politics was the sincere effort made by political parties to garner national following. Each of the five major parties that survived the scrutiny of the Federal Election Commission had its core support in a particular ethnic area, leading one to surmise that "the pre-military pattern of political alignment apparently triumphed."[129] Nevertheless, there were integrative elements present in the dynamics of the parties, and they showed up in their composition and election strategy employed. The new electoral laws demanded, and party leaders realized, that ethnic or regional-based political vehicles had no place in the presidential system. So in order to counter-balance the lingering ethnic roots of the parties, party offices were dispersed among the various peoples of the nation and membership was open to all.

During the 1979 elections, Nigerian political parties tried to break out of their ethnic molds, and took pains to venture into other parts of the country. And as the election results indicated, they achieved some success. The Yoruba-led Unity Party of Nigeria (UPN), was able to score an impressive 22 percent of the votes in Gongola State in the far North; Plateau State, situated in the middle belt of the country, fell to the Ibo-dominated Nigerian People's Party (NPP); while the two minority States in the East, Rivers and Cross River States were captured by the Northern-based National Party of Nigeria (NPN), which eventually won the general elections.

That cross-regional voting, though not spectacular and far-reaching enough to destroy the pattern of ethnic allegiance of political parties, was, at least effective in breaking up the hegemony of the largest ethnic groups. Minority States within the old regions rebelled and became 'king-makers' in that no political party could win any national election without their support and votes. Each of the parties carried the votes in its ethnic enclave; what gave NPN the winning edge was its ability to win impressive victories in many of the minority States. Thus the base of political power shifted away from the majority ethnic groups that dominated Nigeria's politics in the First Republic. However, since the minority States were too small, both in size and population, and did not possess the political clout commensurate with their newly acquired potential, they were unable to exploit the political situation. That resulted in the federal center becoming the premier arena for politics in Nigeria. Unlike the pre-military days when powerful regional leaders reigned supreme and practically dictated what went on at the center, State party leaders usually deferred to the national headquarters in Lagos for directives. Party discipline, especially in the national legislatures, was weakened by cross-cutting cleavages. For instance, during the debate on the Revenue Allocation Bill, legislators crossed party lines and voted according to State's interests.

Not only were political parties federalized, almost every national institution was encouraged to reflect what was referred to as 'federal character'. That requirement which an author called "a dimension in which the

Second Republic achieved decided progress over the first,"[130] meant that all appointments to, and resources of, a public institution should be distributed evenly and fairly across the nineteen States. Somehow akin to the Equal Opportunity laws (voting, housing, employment, etc.) of the United States, the provision for federal character was applied in almost every political, social and economic undertaking. Employment into the federal civil service, admission into universities, awarding of scholarships and federal contracts, appointment to statutory boards and commissions, all came under the 'federal character' stipulation. Even the President's Cabinet was composed of Ministers from all the States. Though it had been criticized for promoting mediocrity, an arguable proposition, the federal character requirement had produced and fostered a national feeling strong enough to contain the "powerful centrifugal forces inherent in Nigeria's ethnic composition."[131]

The return of the military at the end of 1983 was necessitated by a failure of the civilian government to arrest massive corruption and its inability to lift the country out of the economic depression it fell into after oil prices plummeted. As Major-General Sani Abacha, who announced the coup disclosed, the main rationale for the takeover was to rescue the country from "the grave economic predicament and uncertainty that an inept and corrupt leadership has imposed on our beloved nation for the past four years."[132] This was in stark contrast to the first coup in 1966 in which the soldiers intervened to save the nation from political disintegration. While intense ethnic rivalry and conflict precipitated the demise of the old civilian government, there had been a considerable reduction of internecine passion since after the civil war, and the feeling was carried over to the Second Republic.[133] The charges of corruption and economic mismanagement were levied at all the politicians, regardless of party or ethnic affiliation, though the ruling NPN bore the brunt of the blame.

Thus, during the life of the second civilian government in Nigeria, 1979-1983, the executive presidency, non-regional political parties, and the concerted effort to instill a feeling of belongingness in all Nigerians, all combined to make sub-national tendencies much less feasible than was obtained before 1966.

The Federal State power position became that of super-ordinate — subordinate, reflected in the relatively weak National Assembly and the financially dependent and geographically small States. With the military once more at the helm of things in the country, the position of the States, vis-a-vis the central government is not likely to be any better. Instead there will be further aggrandizement of central power at the expense of the States.

Below is the chronology of significant events in the evolution of Nigeria as a federation, from its colonial roots to the Annulment of June 12 Elections 1993, the Return of the Military and the Promise of Democracy in the 1994-5 Constitutional Conference.

Periods and characteristics of federalism in Nigeria

1898: Selbourne Committee deliberates future of British acquisitions of the Royal Niger Company.

1914: Amalgamation of North and South Protectorates. Nigeria as a unified British colony born.

1922: First Constitution. Legislative Council (with some African members) set up, but limited to South.

1944: NCNC (first national political party) inaugurated.

1946: Richards Constitution. (first constitution to cover the whole colony). Three regions created by fiat. Central Legislative Council composed of delegates from three Regions. Regional Councils established with some administrative but no legislative authority. Decentralized Unitary System.

1951: Macphearson Constitution. At Center, a House of Representatives and Council of Ministers set up. Regional Assemblies given some legislative and executive powers. Two new political parties, Action Group and NPC, born to contest first general elections. Partisan politics begins in earnest. Beginnings of Federalism.

1954: Lyttleton Constitution. Regions become self-governing with full executive and legislative powers in all matters. Central government's authority limited to specified list of Exclusive Subjects only. Full Regionalism.

1960: Independence granted. Further accentuation of regional powers. Tafawa Balewa elected first Nigerian Prime Minister.

1962: A fourth Region created Mid West.

1963: Nigeria becomes a Republic. Azikiwe appointed first Nigerian President.

1966: January 19 — First military coup. Constitution suspended. General Ironsi abolishes Regions, and sets up 'National Government.'. All public services united. Nigeria ceases to be a Federation. Unitary System.

July 29 — Second military coup. General Gowon reestablishes federalism. Regions re-created with new Military Governors.

1967: January 4-5. Negotiations between General Gowon and Lt. Col. Ojukwu (Military Governor of the East) on the future of Nigeria at Aburi, Ghana.

May 27 — Twelve States created out of four Regions.

May 30 — Eastern Region secedes and declares itself the 'Republic of Biafra'.

July 6 — Civil war ensues.

1970: January — End of civil war after surrender of rebel forces. During civil war, new States stripped of power, authority restricted only to residual matters. Military Governors appointed form Center given full legislative and executive powers. Supreme Military Council, SMC, becomes law-making body for the whole country. Military Federalism.

1975: Third military coup. General Mohammed takes control. Military Governors excluded from SMC, and subject to its authority. Seven more States created, making a total of nineteen. Further eroding of States' responsibilities and authority.

1976: Attempted coup. Mohammed assassinated. General Obasanjo assumes office. Preparation for return to civilian rule put into motion. Constitution Drafting Committee; re-organization of Local Government System (LG's became independent third tier of government) and non-partisan elections.

1977: Draft Constitution sent to Constituent Assembly.

1978: Ban on political parties lifted; five new parties ready to contest elections.

1979: New Constitution promulgated into law. Elections to State and Federal legislatures and Executive offices held.

> October 1 — End of military era; second Republic established under President Shagari. American style federal model replaces old Westminster system. Provision for executive leadership, separation of powers, checks and balances. Central government given exclusive jurisdiction in most matters; States become increasingly weaker and dependent.

1983: December 30 — End of second Republic, fourth military coup. President Shagari was succeeded by General Buhari.

1985: August 27 — Fifth military coup. General Babangida succeeded General Buhari.

1993: General Abacha took over from the Interim Government headed by Chief Shonekan (after the step down of General Babangida, culminating from the June 12 Federal Presidential Elections controversy).

1993-1995: Nation in Search of Democracy in a constitutional Conference in Abuja. The promise of lasting democracy in Nigeria may be hinged on Abacha's statement on Nigeria's 35th national anniversary in which he stated that "some of our political controversies, which have almost become part of our national way of life, are transient in nature, but others have to be faced and tackled. The Council, in its deliberation, understood the origins of the sympathy for the principle of rotation, which we all recognize as a way of satisfying the fears of marginalization. At the end of careful study of the issue, the PRC decided that, in the higher and long-term national interest, the proposal of rotational power sharing should be accepted. This option will apply to all levels of government. The PRC has also endorsed a modified presidential system in which six key executive and legislative offices will be zoned and rotated between six identifiable geographical groupings."[134] In this regard, writing for the TSM Sunday Magazine of August 20, 1995 captioned "Attention: Afenifere and younger generation of Yorubas" Tola Adebayo stated that:

> ... a pity we have short memory - always going for quick, short, term advantages. To some of our respected elders and leaders, every thing must happen in their life time. They must either be the kings or the king makers. No thought for the younger generations, nothing, absolutely nothing should be left for them.

We employ members of Afeniefere to fume back to memory lane and recall that (a) most of them were the most vocal claimants that Papa Awolowo won the 1979 democratically conducted presidential election but was denied victory by the now historic 12 2/3 per cent wonder judgment (b) the very bright chance of Chief Adisa Akinloye, Chief Richard Akinjide and of course, Chief M.K.O Abiola under the N.P. N Party's democratic presidential zoning arrangements were thwarted with the now equally historic. "THE PRESIDENCY IS NOT FOR SALE." We now know the full import of the presidency not for sale - Not for Southerners. (c) The open day denial (ANNULMENT) of Chief MKO Abiola's electoral victory in a peaceful democratically conducted election in June 1993 is super historic.

Under Chief Bola Ige's democracy, both chiefs Awolowo, Abiola and others have been denied access to the presidency. And of course, the story will continue until our interests and rights as citizens are guaranteed. This is why a whole lot of us- the younger grassroots politicians- are insisting on the inclusion of the Rotational Presidency in the Constitution.

We believe that the presidential zoning arrangement between North and South as recommended in the draft constitution by the conference is perfectly okay. This is because, both the defunct NPN, SDP, NRC and in fact virtually all the new emerging political associations have accepted six zones in the country as follows: Western zone, Eastern zone, Southern zone, North

Eastern zone, North Western zone, North central zone. With Rotational Presidency between North and South enshrined in our national constitution and zoning accepted by the parties, it will be left for the political parties to decide from which zone to start the presidential rotation. Assuming that for purposes of illustration, the rotation starts from the South, then all the eligible candidates fro all the three Southern Zones should contest and the whole country including the North will choose and elect the best candidate who becomes the president for the first 5 years. In the second 5 years, the presidency automatically moves to the North and similarly all the eligible candidates from the 3 Northern zones should contest and the best candidate elected.

In the third 5 years, that is, from the 11th year, the presidency returns to the south, this time around, all eligible candidates from the two other zones (other than the zone that produced the president in the first 5 years) will contest and the best emerges. This process will be carried on until the six accepted zones including the minority South/south zone and the minority North central zone must have had their chances of producing presidents within the next 30 years. What is undemocratic about this?

Nigeria is 35 years old as an independent nation. What is democratic with the fact that for 35 years, this country has been ruled for 57 percent of the period by one tribe, Hausa/Fulani (including Babangida from North Western and North Eastern zones), while the minority North central zone has ruled for 31 percent of the period and the whole of the South for only 12 percent of the period?"

Notes

1. Osuntokun, Jide, 'The Historical Background of Nigerian Federalism,' in Akinyemi, A.B., P.D. Cole and Walter Ofonagoro, (eds.) *Readings in Federalism*. (Lagos: Nigerian Institute of International Affairs, 1979), p. 91.

2. Eleazu, Uma, *Federalism and Nation-Building: The Nigerian Experience, 1954-1964.* (Great Britain: Arthur Stokwell, Ltd., 1977), pp. 85-90.

3. Ballard, J.A., 'Administrative Origins of Nigerian Federalism,' *African Affairs*, Vol. 70, No. 281, (October 1971), p. 334.

4. J. Osuntokun, op. cit., pp. 92-93.

5. Ibid., pp. 93-94.

6. Uma Eleazu, op. cit., p. 75.

7. Okoli, Ekwueme F., *Institutional Structure and Conflict in Nigeria*. (Washington, D.C.: University Press of America, Inc., 1980), p. 16.

8. J. Osuntokun, op. cit., p. 94.

9. Ibid., p. 95.

10. Ekwueme Okoli, op. cit., pp. 15-17.

11. Ibid., p. 16.

12. Awa, Eme O., *Federal Government in Nigeria*. (Berkeley, CA: University of California Press, 1964), p. 11.

13. Ekwueme Okoli, op. cit., p. 19.

14. Ayoade, J.A., 'Inter-governmental Relations in Nigeria' *Quarterly Journal of Administration* (Ife, Nigeria). Vol. 14, No. 2 (January 1980), p. 126.

15. Uma Eleazu, op. cit., pp. 83-84.

16. Adejuyigbe, Omalade, 'Rationale and Effects of State Creation in Nigeria with Reference to the 19 States,' in Akinyemi, et al., op. cit., p. 191.

17. Wheare, Kenneth C., *Modern Constitutions*. (London: Oxford University Press, 1956), p. 9.

18. McIlwain, Charles H., *Constitutionalism: Ancient and Modern*. (Ithaca, NY: Cornell University Press, 1947), p. 3.

19. Nwabueze, Benjamin O., *The Presidential Constitution of Nigeria*. (New York: St. Martins Press, 1982), p. 6.

20. Kenneth C. Wheare, op. cit., p. 76.

21. B. Nwabueze, op. cit., p. 10.

22. Ibid., p. 10.

23. Kenneth C. Wheare, op. cit., p. 46.

24. Greenstein, Fred and Nelson W. Polsby, (eds.) *Government Institutions and Processes*. (Reading, MA: Addison-Wesley Publications, 1975), p. 5.

25. B. Nwabueze, op. cit., p. 8.

26. Kenneth C. Wheare, op. cit., p. 98.

27. Ekwueme Okoli, op. cit., pp. 19-20.

28. Eme Awa, op. cit., p. 17.

29. Okwudiba, Nnoli, *Ethnic Politics in Nigeria*. (Enugu, Nigeria: Fourth Dimension Publishers, 1978), p. 154.

30. Ibid., p. 154.

31. Eme Awa, op. cit., p. 27.

32. Ibid., p. 27.

33. Uma Eleazu, op. cit., p. 86.

34. Ezera, Kalu, *Constitutional Development in Nigeria.* (Cambridge: Cambridge University Press, 1964), p. 81.

35. Uma Eleazu, op. cit., p. 87.

36. Eme Awa, op. cit., p. 28.

37. Uma Eleazu, op. cit., p. 89.

38. Ibid., p. 90.

39. Coleman, James, *Nigeria: Background to Nationalism.* (Berkeley & Los Angeles: University of California Press, 1958), p. 324.

40. Eme Awa, op. cit. p. 39.

41. Ekwueme Okoli, op. cit., p. 26.

42. Sklar, Richard, *Nigerian Political Parties.* (Princeton, NJ: Princeton University Press, 1963), p. 133.

43. Parliamentary Debates, 5th Session, Vol. 515, House of Commons, Official Report, (May 4-22, 1953), pp. 2263-68 as quoted in Richard Sklar, op. cit., p. 132.

44. Ekwueme Okoli, op. cit., p. 32.

45. B. Nwabueze, op. cit., p. 123.

46. Billy Dudley, op. cit., pp. 52-57.

47. E. Awa, op. cit., p. 51.

48. J. Ostheimer, op. cit., p. 27.

49. Ademoyega, Wole, *The Federation of Nigeria: From Earliest Times to Independence.* (London: George G. Harrap & Co., Ltd., 1962), p. 152.

50. *Royal Institute of International Affairs, Nigeria: The Political and Economic Background.* (London: Oxford University Press, 1960), p. 49.

51. O. Arikpo, op. cit., p. 96.

52. W. Ademoyega, op. cit., p. 152.

53. O. Arikpo, op. cit., p. 82.

54. K. Ezera, op. cit., p. 232.

55. *Report of the Nigerian Constitutional Conference, cmnd 207.* (London: HMSO, 1957), pp. 17-18.

56. Royal Institute, op. cit., p. 60.

57. *Report of the Resumed Nigerian Constitutional Conference.* (Lagos: Federal Government Printer, 1958), pp. 30-31.

58. For details of this crisis, see Post, K.W.J. and M. Vickers, *Structure and Conflict in Nigeria, 1960-1965.* (London: Heinemann, 1973).

59. Mackintosh, J.P., 'Federalism in Nigeria,' *Political Studies.* Vol. IX, No. 3 (October 1962), p. 238.

60. E. Okoli, op. cit., p. 85.

61. Billy Dudley, op. cit., p. 56.

62. Cole, Taylor, 'Emergent Federalism in Nigeria,' in Tilman, Robert O. and Taylor Cole, (eds.) *The Nigerian Political Scene.* (Durham, NC: Duke University Press, 1962), p. 52.

63. Ibid., p. 54.

64. Nicolson, I., 'The Structure of Government at Federal Level' in L. Franklin Blitz, (ed.) *The Politics and Administration of Nigeria.* (London: Sweet & Maxwell, 1965, p. 56.

65. B. Nwabueze, op. cit., p. 6.

66. J. Ostheimer, op. cit., p. 51.

67. John Mackintosh, op. cit., p. 86.

68. C. Goertz, op. cit., p. 151.

69. I. Nicolson, op. cit., p. 60.

70. Ekwueme Okoli, op. cit., p. 3.

71. Olorunsola, Victor (ed.), *The Politics of Cultural Sub-Nationalism in Africa*. (New York: Anchor Books, Doubleday & Company, Inc., 1972), p.20.

72. C.S. Whitaker, op. cit., p. 3.

73. Ibid.

74. J. Osuntokun, op. cit., p. 102.

75. Panter-Brick, S.K. (ed.), *Nigerian Politics and Military Rule: Prelude to the Civil War*. (London: University of London, Althone Press, 1970), Appendix B, pp. 177-79.

76. Panter-Brick, S.K., 'From Military Coup to Civil War, January 1966 to May 1967,' in S.K. Panter-Brick, op. cit., pp. 15-16.

77. Daily Times (Nigeria January 29, 1966.

78. *Morning Post* (Nigeria), January 31, 1966.

79. *Sunday Times* (Nigeria), February 13, 1966.

80. *New Nigeria* (Nigeria), February 23, 1966.

81. Ibid.

82. Alexander Hamilton, *Federalist Papers*. No. XV.

83. Post, Kenneth, and Michael Vickers, *Structure and Conflict in Nigeria, 1960-1966*. (Madison, WI: The University of Wisconsin Press, 1973), pp. 6-7.

84. Ekwueme Okoli, op. cit., pp. 6-8.

85. Ijalaye, D.A., 'The Civil War and Nigerian Federalism' in Akinyemi, et al., op. cit., p. 145.

86. Benneth, Valeria P. and A.H. Kirk-Greene, 'Back to Barracks: A Decade of Marking Time,' in S. Keith Panter-Brick (ed.) *Soldiers and Oil: The Political Transfiguration of Nigeria*. (London: Frank Cass & Company, Ltd., 1978), p. 15.

87.   D. Ijalaye, op. cit., p. 146.

88.   Ojigbo, Okion, *Nigeria Returns to Civilian Rule*. (Lagos: Tokion (Nigeria) Company, 1980), pp. 28-29.

89.   Onum, Nduka, 'And Who Expected Any Change?' *The Punch* (Nigeria), July 17, 1979, as quoted in O. Ojigbo, op. cit., p. 28.

90.   Kurfi, Ahmadu, *The Nigerian General Elections, 1959 and 1979 and the Aftermath*. (Lagos: Macmillan Nigeria Ltd., 1981), pp. 31-32.

91.   Eliagwu, J.I., 'The Military and State Building: Federal-State Relations in Nigeria's 'Military Federalism', 1966-1978,' in Akinyemi, et al., op. cit., p. 164.

92.   Benneth and Kirk-Greene, op. cit., p. 16.

93.   *Federal Republic of Nigeria: The Struggle For One Nigeria*. (Lagos: Federal Ministry of Information, 1967), pp. 38-39.

94.   S. Keith Panter-Brick, op. cit., Appendix B, p. 180.

95.   S.K. Panter-Brick, in S.K. Panter-Brick, op. cit., pp. 27-28.

96.   Ibid., p. 28.

97.   D. Ijalaye, op. cit., p. 147.

98.   *New Nigeria* (Nigeria), April 24, 1967.

99.   Okoin Ojigbo, op. cit., pp. 39-40.

100. Kirk-Greene, A.H., (ed.), *Crisis and Conflict in Nigeria: A Documentary Source Book, 1966-1967*, Vol. 1, (London: Oxford University Press, 1967), pp. 272-77.

101. O. Adejuyigbe, op. cit., pp. 195-96.

102. For a full treatment of the States Creation issue, see Tamuno, T.N.T., 'Separatist Agitations in Nigeria since 1914,' *The Journal of Modern African Studies*, Vol. 8, No. 4, (1970).

103. S.K. Panter-Brick, in S.K. Panter-Brick, op. cit., p. 39.

104. Federal Republic of Nigeria, *The Struggle....*, op. cit., pp. 45-46.

105. J. Eliagwu, op. cit., p. 169.

106. This author was in one of the Minority Areas (Rivers State) during the civil war and personally witnessed the resistance to the 'Biafran Cause' put up by the people and the hearty ovation and sigh of relief that greeted the Federal troops when those areas were 'liberated'. In fact, 'Liberation Day' celebrations were held for years after the civil war.

107. S.K. Panter-Brick, in S.K. Panter-Brick, op. cit., pp. 27-28.

108. Ojukwu, C. Odumegwu, *Biafra: Selected Speeches and Random Thoughts*. (New York: Harper & Row, Publishers, 1969), p. 50.

109. Dent, M.J., 'The Military and the Politicians,' in S.K. Panter-Brick, op. cit., p. 88.

110. S.K. Panter-Brick, op. cit., Appendix D, p. 245.

111. *West Africa*. (January 21, 1967), p. 93.

112. Whiteman, K., Enugu: The Psychology of Secession, 20 July, 1966 to May 1967, in S.K. Panter-Brick, op. cit., p. 122.

113. As quoted in Frederick Forsyth, *The Biafra Story*. (Hammondsworth, Great Britain: Penquin Books, 1969), p. 91.

114. M. Dent, op. cit., p. 89.

115. F. Forsyth, op. cit., pp. 90-91.

116. M. Dent, op. cit., p. 88.

117. S.K. Panter-Brick, in S.K. Panter-Brick, op. cit., p. 39.

118. Ibid., p. 45.

119. S. Keith Panter-Brick, op. cit., Appendix C, p. 220.

120. Luckham, Robin, *The Nigerian Military: A Sociological Analysis of Authority and Revolt, 1960-67*. (Cambridge: Cambridge University Press, 1971), pp. 319-22.

121. J. Eliagwu, op. cit., p. 177.

122. Ibid., pp. 170-74.

123. *New Nigeria* (Nigeria), May 21, 1974.

124. J. Eliagwu, op. cit., p. 179.

125. Kraus, Jon, 'Return of Civil Rule in Nigeria and Ghana,' *Current History*. (March 1980), p. 118.

126. C.S. Whitaker, op. cit., p. 10.

127. Jon Kraus, op. cit., p. 118.

128. S.K. Panter-Brick, in S.K. Panter-Brick, op. cit., p. 334.

129. Joseph, Richard A., 'The Overthrow of Nigeria's Second Republic,' *Current History*, Vol. 83, (March 1984), p. 122.

130. Diamond, Larry, 'Nigeria in Search of Democracy,' *Foreign Affairs*, Vol. 62, (Spring 1983), p. 121.

131. Ibid., p. 121.

132. Major-General Sani Abacha, *Radio Broadcast to the Nation*. December 30, 1983.

133. Richard Joseph, op. cit., p. 122.

134. Abacha, General Sani. "Abacha's Anniversary Broadcast". West Africa. October 9-15, 1995. p. 1556.

4 Nigeria's quest for federalism

Introduction

Experts involved in formulating Revenue Allocation policy in Nigeria often found themselves functioning in an environment which was highly charged with political currents. In a society described as 'intoxicated with politics' and "channels its energy into the struggle for power to the detriment of economically productive effort," it is inevitable that political solutions would be sought to virtually every problem.[1] And when that problem pertained to distribution of fiscal resources, political forces set the stage for its resolution. So that whatever knowledge or expertise these experts brought with them to aid the policy-makers was shaped, manipulated and often distorted by the political dynamics of the policy arena.[2]

Since Revenue Allocation represented a system of sharing the fiscal aspects of political power, the struggle over control of the system has been one of the most enduring and controversial battles fought on the Nigerian political scene. Given such a situation, fiscal experts have been usually sensitive to the prevailing political atmosphere and took into account, various important political considerations when choosing among policy alternatives. It is very important to highlight the characteristics of the political party system in a study of revenue allocation because the conflict over which formula was adopted reflected to a large degree the desperate struggle for control over the nation's resources. The ability to participate in and influence the sharing of the national cake (as centralized revenue is often referred to) was the basis of competitive politics in Nigeria. As stated in the last chapter, the state had become the main distributor of goods and services in the society, and one direct access to it was via political party channels. Since parties could only sustain the patron-client relationship (described in detail later) through the provision of benefits to their local constituencies, they had to make sure that they were not excluded from the arena of policy-making. That is why parties place a high premium on winning and maintaining political power.[3]

The various constitutions (as well as the decrees and edicts) were all results of bargains and compromises between contending interests. From the 1940s when the first political movements were established until the military take-over in 1966, and then again between 1979 and 1983, political parties were the sole institutions of interest articulation and aggregation and thus gained a near monopoly of political power. Other centers of interest such as commercial or social groups were either coopted or eliminated, leaving the parties as the major source of political association and venue for exerting political influence on policy formulation.[4] The patterns of associations forged during those periods set the tone for future aggregations. Even during the military days when parties were effectively banned and there were no formal outlets for articulating interests, informal and often clandestine associations, based on the models established by the parties, were formed.

Before looking at the origins and performance of the political parties in Nigeria, we shall attempt to define what a political party is, especially in the context of a non-Western country such as Nigeria. This is important because there abounds in the literature, several taxonomies of political parties which often leave the researcher confused as to what type of association constitutes a political party. The following paragraphs will point out how the term is used in this study.

Definition of a political party

Political parties, usually regarded as the means by which the 'chaotic mass public will'[5] is organized in a society, exist in all types of political climates, ranging from the most liberal democracy to the most authoritarian dictatorship. And the organizing task is carried out in a variety of ways; via competitive multi-party systems, one-party cliques, or some denomination in between. With all the different manifestations, it is not easy to define exactly what constitutes a political organizations that are outside the familiar European or American setting about which a lot has been written.[6] Therefore, attempting a precise definition of the term 'party' may not be very useful when considering non-Western, especially African political parties. Instead, as Thomas Hodgkin insisted:

> ...For the moment it is probably most convenient to consider as 'parties' all political organizations which regard themselves as parties and which are generally so regarded.[7]

A definition that comes close to following Hodgkin's prescription is provided by Giovanni Sartori who sees a political party as "any political group identified by an official label that presents at elections, and is capable of placing through elections (free or non-free) candidates for public office."[8] However, the emphasis on the election prerequisite would exclude many nationalist movements or congresses that performed party roles "before any electoral possibilities were opened to them."[9]

Under the system of dyarchy practiced by the British in some of their African colonies, these 'proto-parties', as they are sometimes referred to, were allowed to participate in some governmental activity prior to their full blossoming into vehicles for elections.[10] They had programs and platforms which reflected a "fundamental disagreement with the mode of governing and the general direction of existing policies,"[11] and the main interest around which they aggregated and whose "value they generalized into an ideal,"[12] was the dismantling of the whole colonial administrative and political structure. By and large, these organizations provided the only instruments with which the arduous task was to be carried out; and to that end, they were effectively and successively utilized.[13] Thus, even in situations where they could not officially translate the preferences of the mass public will into public policy,[14] they were able to articulate the public interest or will and channel them to the appropriate official quarters. Insofar as the popular demand, which in the colonial days, centered on political freedom, was articulated, communicated to, and eventually implemented by the ruling body, these political movements ought to be, and they are in this paper, properly described as political parties, even though they might or might not have partaken in elections. We shall now take a general overview at the roles these parties perform in Africa.

Political parties in Africa: A general overview

The roles political parties play and the functions they perform vary from nation to nation. However, there are enough commonalities among the emergent parties of Africa to allow one to make general observations. Political parties in Africa, especially those that participated in the government before independence assumed greater roles than their counterparts in Western democracies. As the demands of the citizens expanded, so did the roles. There was the newly politicized populace that needed to be organized into getting involved in their own political affairs;[15] and the party provided the instrument to carry out this act of political socialization. Thus, in addition to the usual functions of representing people, expressing their demands and supplying channels for articulating, communicating, and implementing these demands,[16]

80

African political parties, particularly in pre-independence days, and immediately after, had to "perform the functions of fostering and establishing a national consciousness and providing a set of national symbols;"[17] in short, they had to establish the very legitimacy of their regimes. It is this added responsibility that differentiates them from most Western political parties; and points to their primacy and centrality in the politics of their countries.

Given the close identification with the nation in one-party states like Nkrumah's Ghana and Ivory Coast or with the ethnic/regional enclave as in Nigeria, political parties in Africa have been analyzed in terms of 'clientele' or 'political machine' models.[18] In describing political parties in the one-party states of West Africa, Aristide Zolberg surmised that:

> With some variation from country to country, the party was initially a loose movement which naturally incorporated the characteristics of the society in which it grew; it was eventually transformed into a political machine but continued to reflect the state of incomplete integration of the territorial society.[19]

(This description can be extended to include multiple party states if 'region' or 'ethnic group' is substituted for 'state' in the extract.) What led to the transformation was the same set of societal factors that promoted the political machines which flourished among the immigrant communities in large urban areas [at the turn-of-the-century] in the United States — "poor newly urbanized people with particularistic loyalties, easily swayed by concrete material incentives,"[20] yearning to participate and benefit from their new government.

The African political party machine, however, was more expansive in that its outreach was not confined to specific population areas but it covered the whole state, region, or in some cases, the entire country. Because the party usually controlled the government, it was able to establish a network of reward systems through which it distributed material benefits and favors to its supporters.[21] The ability to manipulate effectively technical and political resources made it possible for the party to become the principal reservoir of patronage, economic security and protection that were traded for personal loyalty and obedience of the people.[22] The exchange mechanism was carried out "either directly and formally or indirectly and informally through the medium of the party or ex-party men who dominated the public boards, corporations and commissions,"[23] and hence controlled the source of the rewards.

The 'personalized and reciprocal relationship'[24] between the party and the people was stable and popular because the party machine was flexible enough to adjust to the demands of its clientele.[25] In the rapidly changing society of a new nation, it was important to have an institution that would respond to the changes, and the party machine, through various informal channels by which political power was funneled into the system, performed this essential task.

To illustrate the political ramifications beyond the "immediate sphere of dyadic relationships"[26] between the party and the people in Nigeria, we shall look at the beginnings of the political parties in Nigeria and then analyze their performance, with particular reference to the machine-like qualities enumerated above.

Nigeria has had two distinct phases in its political history when partisan politics flourished. The first period commenced after the First World War when nationalistic movements swept across the old British West Africa. Those movements late evolved into different territorial parties and continued to function in the colonies even after independence. Political participation ended in 1966 when the Nigerian Army overthrew the parliamentary government in a coup d'etat. After twelve years of military rule, political parties were given the chance to re-emerge in 1978. But their presence on the political scene of the country was short-lived; just after five years, the soldiers decided to come back, and on December 30, 1983, political parties were once again banished and the military re-emerged in 1993 with an identical ban on political parties.

A look at how they began and the roles they performed will be the subject of the next paragraphs.

Genesis of political parties in Nigeria

The beginnings

In 1922, the British colonial government set up a Legislative Council to which some African representatives were to be elected. Herbert Macaulay, one of the pre-eminent leaders of the anti-colonial movement, decided to organize a political party to contest the elections. That party, the National Democratic Party, an offshoot of the sub-continent wide nationalistic political movement, became the first formal political party in the country.[27] About fifteen years later, several socio-political groupings, notable, the Nigerian Youth Movement founded by H.O. Davies, and the Zikist Movement, organized by Nnamdi Azikiwe, sprang up mobilizing the indigenous people against the colonial status quo.[28] Both Davies and Azikiwe were leaders in the protest movement which initially demanded participation in, and later, total control of, their government.[29]

These early parties had several things in common. They were broad-based in membership and multi-ethnic in composition, and wore nationalistic outlooks, both in their manifestos and behavior. Particularist tendencies like ethnic, religious allegiances played no obviously significant part in the set up of the parties. Their expressed aim was to secure some sort of representation, if not total independence, for Nigerians in the colonial government. The anti-colonial orientation guided the functioning and provided that basis for their survival, and they operated along such lines until their demise or transformation.[30]

However, the political parties that emerged after these fore-runners, succumbed to the lure of ethnic and regional chauvinism. One reason could be that the unifying anti-colonial stand was becoming obsolete, since independence was in the offing. People started thinking in post-independence terms, and worried about securing whatever political benefits they could get. The regions, having been created, cried out for indigenous leaders, and what better way to solidify one's political stronghold than preaching and playing on ethnic differences.

Three major parties dominated the political spectrum of the country in its first phase of party activity. They were the National Council of Nigeria and the Cameroons (NCNC) the Action Group (AG) and the Northern Peoples Congress (NPC).

The National Council of Nigeria and the Cameroons, NCNC

This party was a result of the decision of several early political movements to coalesce into a single political party. Nnamdi Azikiwe, who later became the leader of the party, summoned all the different groups and reminded them that "time was ripe for artisans of independence to create a unified national front."[31] A clarion call was made, and on August 26, 1944, over forty organizations came together to "work in unity for the realization of our ultimate goal of self-government within the British Empire."[32] That 'ultimate goal' was to be attained under an umbrella political organization, the NCNC.

Membership in the party was not open to individuals but to unions, associations, clubs, and societies. Thus, one found in the NCNC, a melange of different peoples and groups from all over Nigeria except the far North (there were not many of them from that area in Lagos in the 1940s and political activity was centered in Lagos). The ambition of the party was to extend democratic principles to all Nigerians and educate them politically so as to be prepared for self-government and eventually total independence.[33] To further enhance its nationalistic image, the NCNC later evolved into a mass party whose campaign was designed largely to increase its membership numerically.[34] That it accomplished by associating with various interest groups from all parts of the country. In the North, it was affiliated with a minority party, the Northern Elements Progressive Union (NEPU); in the West, its association was with several cultural unions especially in the old Benin and Delta provinces, and in the city of Ibadan; the Ibo State Union was its ally in the East; and non-regional interests like workers' unions were also linked to it. With this wide array of support systems, the NCNC could be referred to as a national party.[35]

It was the NCNC's liaison with the Ibo State Union, a socio-cultural pan-Ibo organization set up to promote the advancement of its members, that tainted its otherwise national image. Nevertheless, unlike the other parties, it had its support, both electoral and popular, from other parts of the country besides the East, home of the Ibos and Azikiwe, the leader. For example, both in the 1951 and 1954 legislative elections, the NCNC won a sizable number of seats in the West. Though there were many Ibos and other non-Yorubas in the old Delta and Benin Provinces of the Western Region that voted for the NCNC, what is significant is that the party also carried the city of Ibadan — seat of the Western government and the largest Yoruba city. No other political party ever succeeded in penetrating the domain of another party as the NCNC did.

What finally forced the NCNC to become a culturally and ethnically bound political party, beholden to the Ibos in the East and fighting for their political survival, can be attributed to the springing up of a rival political party in the West — the Action Group. The ethnic and regional origin of the Action Group (more below) and its parochial behavior pushed the NCNC into an ethnic shell from which it never emerged.[36] The 1951 elections and its aftermath saw the beginning of a non-national NCNC.

The MacPherson Constitution of 1951 had provided for an election of Federal legislators by members of the regional bodies. The Action Group won and controlled the Western House to which Nnamdi Azikiwe, leader of the NCNC, was also elected as a member from the Lagos constituency. However, efforts by Azikiwe to get elected to the Federal House of Representatives were foiled by the Action Group majority. Those elected refused to step down for him, and the NCNC leader was stuck in the Western House pigeon-holed into obscurity as the leader of the opposition against his wishes. Two years later, in 1953, he resigned his position, contested and won a seat in the Eastern House, from where he became the leader of the Eastern Regional Government.[37] As one author put it:

> By this last act, the NCNC capitulated to the vastly growing forces of ethnic chauvinism and regionalism generated in the parliamentary political arena by the Action Group.[38]

84

Thus, all the important members of the NCNC, including their leader, were domiciled in the Eastern legislature.

When Azikiwe moved across the Niger River (the boundary between the Eastern and Western Regions) and went back East, the NCNC became increasingly the political arm of and for the Ibos, an image the party could not shake off till its demise in 1966.

The Action Group, AG

Unlike the NCNC, the Action Group never pretended to be a national political movement. From its very foundation, it had always existed as a political vehicle for the upliftment of the Yorubas and their culture. Its roots are found in the cultural nationalism espoused by the Yoruba cultural group called the Egbe Omo Oduduwa — The Association of Descendants of Oduduwa, the mythical ancestor of the Yoruba people.[39] As founder of the Egbe, established in London in 1945, the late Chief Obafemi Awolowo put into practice his belief that all the people of an ethnic group should form a single political entity. He felt that it was only through such homogenous entities that the cultural heritage of the various groups that make up Nigeria could be protected; in other words, he advocated ethnically constituted regions.[40]

The metamorphosis of Egbe Omo Oduduwa into Action Group was quickened by the provisions of the MacPherson Constitution of 1951 to cater essentially and entirely to Yorubas. Its membership, however, included some non-Yorubas because it was necessary to have wider support base if control of central power was ever to be had.[41]

To gain acceptance from the masses, the Action Group relied on "ethnic sentiments, sensibilities and interests."[42] During its campaigns, the party asserted the dissimilarities of culture between the East and West, insisting that the NCNC with its Ibo majority would not "show respect for elders or protect the chieftaincy," a tradition much revered by the Yorubas. The party further pointed to the alleged aggressiveness and drive of the Ibos and alluded to possible "encroachment of the more populous and land hungry Ibos from the East."[43] Therefore, the party leaders argued that the economic and political security of the Yorubas, as well as non-Ibo minorities in the Western region would be better protected within the Action Group and not the alien NCNC.[44]

Compared with the NCNC, the Action Group could not be labeled a mass party. Rather, it was essentially a 'caucus' party, securing its support by appealing to people of influence in each locality such as traditional rulers, the business class of large-scale merchants, transporters, and contractors, and the educated elite.[45]

Another political party that was an offshoot of a cultural organization was the Northern People's Congress, NPC. Like the Action Group, the NPC was formed in 1951 as a response to the MacPherson Constitutional provisions. With the NCNC already in position, and the Action Group established earlier in the year, political leaders in the North decided to convert the cultural organization, Jamiyyar Mutanen Arewa (Congress of the Northern Peoples) into a political party. The main stimulant was the threat, real or imagined, of southern domination,[46] and the party was thus formed as a "protective shield against the political and intellectual assault"[47] of the already established southern parties. However, one of the founding members of the Congress, Malam Aminu Kano, had fallen out of favor with the organization, and with a group of other dissidents formed a rival Northern party — the Northern Elements Progressive Union — which was radical and allied itself with the NCNC. To the leaders of the NPC, that was a "symbol of potential southern domination"[48] that should be resisted.

From its inception, the NPC was a party formed by Northerners for Northerners. Its motto was "One North, One People, Irrespective of Religion, Rank or Tribe", and the objectives were limited to the North. Unlike the Action Group, it was not an ethnic party; rather it could be termed a regional party. Its membership was restricted to people of Northern Nigerian descent — the only political party to declare a regional limitation in its constitution.[49] Though the North was ethnically more heterogenous than the South, the two institutions of Islam and Emirates had an integrative effect over the people, and when the political cry of "Join or be dominated by the educationally more advanced peoples of the South" went out, Northerners answered positively in large numbers.[50] All through the first republic, the NPC won a vast majority of votes in the North especially among the Hausa-Fulani people which formed the bulk of both the membership and the leadership of the party. In regional elections to the House of Assembly and federal elections, NPC consistently scored more than 80 percent in Hausa-Fulani constituencies.

Though support from the non-Hausa speaking and/or non-Moslem peoples of the Middle Belt area was not as strong as that of the Hausa-Fulani group, the party still succeeded in gaining the majority of votes in those areas. In the 1959 federal, NPC won votes ranging from 43 percent to 60 percent.[51]

Thus as a regional party, the NPC was well entrenched in the North and had support from most Northerners, irrespective of ethnic origin or religion.

There were other, smaller parties that dotted the Nigerian political scene between 1951 and 1966. These minority parties were localized and arose as vehicles for particular ethnic and/or sub-regional interest groups. They were mostly in opposition to the major party in their areas and were usually allied to parties in other regions. Those small parties provided avenues for parties dominant in its region to infiltrate and extend influence into other parts of the country.[52] Without them, Nigeria's first attempt at partisan politics would have been a completely closed affair, with each party operating only within its own region. Some of the regional minority parties included the aforementioned NEPU, the Niger Delta Congress, the Middle Belt Congress, the Mid-West Democratic Front, the Kano Peoples Party, and the United Nigerian Independent Party.

Political parties in the 2nd republic

Second beginnings

The second coming of political parties and partisan politics in Nigeria was made possible by General Murtala Mohammed who promised in 1975 to return the country to civilian rule after accomplishing certain tasks that included conducting nationwide elections.

As a preparatory move towards that goal, a Constitution Drafting Committee (CDC) was set up in October 1975 to draft a new constitution for the country, which would ensure, among other things, the elimination of cut-throat political competition based on a system of winner-takes-all, the discouragement of institutionalized opposition to government in power, and the evolution of a free and fair electoral system which would provide for adequate representation of all the peoples of the nation at the Center.[53] A series of deliberations took place, mainly in camera, and produced a draft constitution in August 1976. The draft constitution was then subjected to an animated public debate for about a year and later submitted to a Constituent Assembly (CA) in October 1977, for adoption.[54]

However, General Murtala was greatly displeased with the performance of the old political parties, which he described as "little more than armies organized for fighting elections in the regions for the Regional and Federal Legislations."[55] While addressing the Constitution Drafting Committee, at its inaugural meeting, the Head of State even went further, adding that:

The SMC (Supreme Military Council) is of the opinion that if during the course of your deliberations and having regard to our disillusion with

87

political parties in the past, you should discover some means by which Government can be formed without the involvement of political parties, you should feel free to recommend.[56]

But fortunately for the Nigerian politicians the CDC recommended a multi-party system. Thus, on September 21, 1978, the Military Government lifted the ban on political activities and Nigerians could once again form associations to aggregate their political interests.

That the military government wanted parties that were truly national, and not merely ethnic vehicles, was not lost on the CA members. They, like those in the CDC, recommended political parties competing for elections to fulfill specific conditions which "removed them from geographical, ethnic or religious connotation;" in other words, prospective parties should be national both in outlook and composition.[57] The provisions incorporated in the Electoral Decree No. 73 of 1977 insisted that for the Federal Electoral Commission, FEDECO, (established under Decree No. 14 of 1977 to conduct and supervise elections) to register any political association, the grouping must fulfill the following requirements:

(1)   register the names and addresses of its national officers with FEDECO;

(2)   membership open to every Nigerian citizen irrespective of his/her place of origin, religion, ethnic group or sex. (This precludes parties of the old NPC which was limited to people of Northern descent);

(3)   the name, emblem or motto has no ethnic or religious connotation;

(4)   no appearance that the activities are confined to only a part of the geographical area of Nigeria;

(5)   headquarters is situated in the Federal Capital;

(6)   establish office in each of at least two-thirds of the States in the Federation, with officers duly elected or appointed to run these branches;

(7)   aims and objectives confirm with relevant provisions of Constitution dealing with Fundamental Objectives and Directive Principles of States Policy, Chapter II.[58]

Despite all these admonishments, some critics have argued that:

> In the end only experienced politicians of the First Republic emerged to lead more affluent new parties with roots stretching deeper into the past in linkage to pre-military parties, liabilities, antagonisms and organizational structures and assets.[59]

We shall see whether the new parties that vied for the 1979 elections really were reincarnations of parties past.

Though Decree No. 31 of 1969 banned all organizations, cultural or ethnic, with political overtones, Nigerians met clandestinely and prepared themselves for some future political activity. Those meetings held under various guises such as 'leaders of thought' conferences, religious charity meetings, development associations, and so on, are alleged to have started in the early 1970s or even before.[60] Certain factors affected the emergence of those associations during the 12-year ban on political parties. They included (a) breaking up the regions into States; (b) the civil war; (c) various promises (kept and unkept) to return the country to civilian rule; (d) meeting of the Constitution Drafting Committee; (e) Local Government reorganizations and elections; and (f) elections to the Constituent Assembly, which gave politicians, old and new, an opportunity to meet and discuss issues.[61] Thus, Nigerians had ample time to organize themselves and get ready for the 1979 elections. Little wonder that when the ban on political activities was lifted on September 21, 1978, a total of fifty-two "associations of persons whose activities include canvassing for votes in support of a candidate to the office of the President, Governor, or membership of the Legislative House or a Local Government Council,"[62] came forward to be registered by FEDECO. Out of the lot, only five satisfied the commission enough to be registered as political parties, and allowed to contest the 1979 elections.[63] They were the Unity Party of Nigeria (UPN), the National Party of Nigeria (NPN), the Nigerian Peoples' Party (NPP), the Great Nigerian Peoples' Party (GNPP), and the Peoples Redemption Party (PRP) and formed from the various combinations of the several nocturnal politician associations which appeared on the political scene during the ban.

The Unity Party of Nigeria

In March 1966, political admirers and cronies of the late Chief Obafemi Awolowo, former leader of the banned Action Group, met ostensibly to celebrate his 57th birthday, and organized a Committee of Friends to do so. This association, consisting mainly of ex-Action Group stalwarts who felt persecuted in the last civilian administration and had come to regard Awolowo as their leader and hope for a brighter future, had political undertones. According to one analyst, since Awolowo's exit from the forefront of politics (he was jailed by the Federal government for treason in 1963), there had been nobody to provide a focal point for unity in the Western Region.[64] With his release by the military in late 1966 and involvement in military government itself, the point for rallying around was re-born.

Meanwhile, several 'Committee of Friends' groups were being organized, and later, they coalesced and formed the National Committee of Friends, with Awolowo as chairman. It is to his credit that the old Action Group leader held discussions with many other politicians, especially his former opponents, in order to form alliance for future political activities. However, Awolowo did not venture too far out to seek any new faces; and by the time he understood the nature of the 1979 electoral system, it was too late. He would not get enough political heavyweights from the East or North needed to penetrate those areas. Moreover, some of his old lieutenants, notably S.G. Ikoku (Secretary-General of AG) and Anthony Enahoro (Vice President of AG) left him. Nevertheless, less than 24 hours after the ban was lifted, the National Committee of Friends was dissolved and transformed publicly into the Unity Party of Nigeria (UPN),[65] with Awolowo as its presidential candidate.

From the origins of the UPN, one is tempted to conclude that it was the re-incarnation of the banned Action Group. In terms of leadership, organizational style, and manifestos, the parties could be two peas in a pod. However, perhaps due to FEDECO directives, UPN membership was more diversified, and, though Yorubas still provided the bulwark of the party, non-Yorubas, especially in Bendel State, accepted Awolowo's leadership. Also, it is on record that the vice-presidency of the party was initially offered to Professor Iya Abubakar, a Northerner, who turned it down; later it was accepted by an Easterner. The apparent diversification of the membership base was born out by the fact that during the presidential elections, UPN, apart from winning majorities in the old Western Region (Lagos, Oyo, Ogun, Ondo and Bendel States), scored an impressive 21.67 percent in Gongola State, the most ethnically heterogeneous State in the North. Nevertheless, Awolowo, try as he might, was not able to shake off the image of himself as a Yoruba leader who personified Yoruba politics.[66]

The National Party of Nigeria

The nucleus of this party was said to have been formed when various Northern dignitaries got together in Sokoto at the 40th anniversary celebrations of Sir Abubakar as Sultan of Sokoto and Sarakin Mussulimi.[67] Thereupon a consolidation of separate poly-groups took place and that resulted in an association called The National Movement of Nigeria. The core of this new group consisted mainly of former NPC members and sympathizers. In addition, certain important leaders from the Northern minority States of Benue and Kwara were attracted; the most notable being Joseph Tarka who was champion of minority rights in the North. Later Southern groups made up of pre-civil war politicians like K.O. Mbadiwe, Nwafor Orizu (both ex-NCNC) and Anthony Enahoro (ex-AG) were allowed to join.[68] In 1978, after the ban was lifted, the different groups met and formally agreed to work together as a political party, to be named The National Party of Nigeria.

In its composition, NPN was a conglomerate of the surviving members of the old regime in the North, most of Nigeria's top qualified and educated elite, ex-army and police officers, some radicals and progressives.[69] This odd mixture, which looked like an honor roll of prominent Nigerian civilians, made the NPN a party of 'heavy weights' or 'dead weights' depending on one's preference.[70] It also gave it its national character, the party being the most widespread and broad-based.

Though described as the linear successor to the NPC because of the heavy Northern presence in the party, if Sir Ahmadu Bello, Sarduana of Sokoto, father of the NPC, were to wake up from his grave, he would not recognize his old party. Apart from spreading its tentacles into almost every State, its leadership cadre was drawn from all parts of the country. In the 1979 elections, the NPN presidential candidate had the most geographical spread in terms of electoral votes, winning a plurality of the votes in nine states, and coming second in nine of the remaining ten states, failing only in Lagos State. One can then conclude that the NPN was not really a chip off the old NPC block, but a relatively new party. To buttress this was the zoning principle of the party which stipulated that leadership be spread out to represent the federal character of the country. In other words, since the presidential candidacy went to a Northerner, an Ibo got the vice presidential nomination, and the chairmanship of the party was assigned to the Yorubas. In that way, the NPN, as its name implied, became the most national party of all the political parties that evolved in post-war Nigeria.

The Nigerian Peoples Party and the Great Nigerian Peoples Party

Three disparate groups formed during the era of underground politics in the military period got into an uneasy alliance to provide the nucleus of what came to be known as the Nigerian Peoples Party, NPP. They include the National Council for Understanding and Solidarity, NCUS; the Committee for National Unity, and Club 19. They are later joined by the Progressive Fronts of Lagos, and of the Eastern States.[71] The NCUS was a grassroots organization formed by Alhaji Waziri Ibrahim, a prominent and wealthy businessman from Borno State in the North, who was once a Federal Minister and an old member of the NPC. Alhaji Waziri started canvassing even before the ban on politics was lifted.[72]

The Committee for National Unity was a caucus of former supporters of Dr. Nnamdi Azikiwe, former leader of the NCNC, and it was led by Adeniran Ogunsanya, an ex-federal Minister; while Club 19 consisted of "young educated men aimed at bringing together minority elements from all the nineteen states (hence the name) as an insulation against domination of Nigerian politics by the major ethnic groups."[73] The Progressives was headed by Femi Okunnu, a former radical leader of the Young Zikist Movement and also an ex-federal minister. All these political associations fused in October 1978 to form the Nigerian Peoples Party, NPP.[74]

However, less than a month later, the alliance broke up. What led to the split is still debated, but most analysts believe it came about because Waziri Ibrahim insisted on being both the chairman of the party as well as its presidential candidate.[75] There are others who argue that the rationale for the break-up was indeed more Machiavellian than just a demand for a democratization of leadership. According to them, some leaders of the NPP realized that the party as it was unlikely to emerge as the winning coalition in the race for the presidency. Therefore, a smaller and tighter knit group would be in a more advantageous position to bargain with the larger parties.[76] The NPN-NPP accord which emerged after the elections seemed to confirm this view.

When the break-up did come, Alhaji Waziri left the group with his supporters and formed a new party, which he called the Great Nigerian Peoples Party, GNPP, and became its chairman and candidate for the presidency. The remaining members, mainly of the old NCNC stock, retained the original name of NPP and invited Dr. Azikiwe to be the party's presidential candidate. It can thus be seen that the NPP which started as a national party, degenerated into a clone of the old NCNC, made up of mostly Ibos, and won the elections only in the Ibo-dominated States of Anambra and Imo, and in Plateau State, a non-Hausa Northern State where the vote was probably due to anti-Hausa sentiment.

The Peoples Redemption Party

This party started as a group of young radical socialists in the North who were opposed to the National Movement of Nigeria, the precursor of NPN. Lacking a leader of national status, they invited Malam Aminu Kano to take over the reigns of leadership.[77] He was the founder of NEPU, an anti-establishment party of the first republic and a thorn in the flesh of the NPC and the ruling hierarchy in the North.[78] A dedicated socialist, he brought with him an Ibo intellectual and Marxist, S.G. Ikoku, who was a lieutenant of the late Chief Awolowo in the AG days, and Michael Imodu, the doyen of the Nigerian labor movement.[79]

It is interesting to note that Malam Aminu was one of the original founders of the NPN. He later left the party on ideological grounds, claiming that he could not "reconcile himself with the gradualist conservatism of the NPN."[80] With the coalition of radicals, socialists and labor leaders, the PRP became the most left wing party in Nigeria. However, its election victory was limited to Kano and Kaduna States in the North, the home base and stronghold of the leader, and that made many analysts doubt the national spread of the party.

From the above, the original assertion that the parties of the second republic were reincarnations of those in the first is not entirely wrong. The old ethnic loyalties still lingered on, evolving around the tried and true political figures of the past. Though ethnic voting could be said to have somehow diminished, it still dominated the Nigerian political scene, and so the performances and roles of the new parties were not quite different from those of the old ones.

Roles and performance of political parties in Nigeria

Political parties in Nigeria, just as in any other society with an active party system, played several roles. However, it was when they were performing what Kenneth Post termed the 'interpretative function' that the 'clientelistic' characteristics described earlier were largely manifested. Acting as intermediaries between the old traditional society and the relatively new modern one, political party functionaries interpreted and explained the myriad of demands government made on the people and helped to meet them.[81]

This function was very vital, especially at the local level because the society was, and still remains, basically illiterate and traditional. Many people did not understand the intricacies of modern westernized governmental processes. So it was left for the parties to serve as the bridge between the new, somewhat frightening and confusing outer-world of politics and the insecure selves of the people.[82] While interpreting the world to the citizens, party leaders worked through customary institutions based on cultural foundations and realized that they gained not only their respect but also support[83] which could be translated into votes in an election — an informal way of 'deenfranchisement'. The process proved so successful that many Nigerians felt morally obligated to support the political party which provided them with avenues through which they could participate in the government.

As government and party politics became more salient, the "need to feel in close proximity to the developing world of politics"[84] increased. The customary institutions, many of them in the form of ethnic associations, through which the interpretative function was carried out, gradually got politicized. Instead of just being the link between the party leaders and the people, they strove to maximize their presence on the political scene by aligning themselves with the political parties, in order to gain influence and patronage.[85] Eventually, following the lead of the cultural organizations, almost every noteworthy interest group in the country was either co-opted into the political party and became an appendage to it or was eliminated.[86]

Having eradicated all other sources of interest aggregation in the society, political parties in Nigeria gained control not only over the government machinery, but also the significant positions in the dominant institutions of the country. In this way, the party became the primary force and played decisive roles in the lives and destinies of people and institutions;[87] and thus determined both the social and economic stratification in the society.[88] Leaders of the parties thus constituted what Gaetano Mosca would call the Political or Ruling class.

Earlier, we have seen how political parties in Nigeria emerged and functioned as ethnic vehicles within the regions. The majority party in a particular region was in essence, an extension of the regional government[89] and its leadership exercised full and absolute executive power within the region.[90] That led to a situation where the distinction between party in power and government was so blurred that the two institutions became coterminous. Thus, the ruling party, in any region or state "monopolized the coercive machinery of the state" and alone decided who got what, and how much.[91] In a society like Nigeria where government permeates directly or indirectly into all aspects of a citizen's life, an institution like the political party which had a monopolistic control of the regional or state government would 'wax fat in its house of patronage' and they all did. The governor (or premier as he was called in pre-war days) who was the head of the state government personified the leadership cadre of the party and had the power of patronage. Like a political machine boss, he had within his sphere of activity, the appointment of people to boards of public corporations, banks and other avenues of commerce.[92]

Since the party had "the money, favors, jobs and honors to distribute among those who would support it," anybody who wished to receive anything, be it a bank loan, scholarship, or a government contract, was induced to support it.[93] As one author put it,

> the coincidence of personalities, power and patronage at regional centers made them very visible in the mind of the average voter and thus became the new foci of political demands.[94]

Political parties in power did not become only the new but sometimes the only focus of power in a region or state such that "the consequences of not belonging to them is sufficiently unattractive to provoke a 'band-wagon' or 'wave of the future'."[95] Party leaders had been known to threaten (and some did carry out the threat) "with impunity to deny social amenities to any constituency which fails to return the government party's candidate at election."[96] During the 1983 elections, party leaders, especially at the state level, were observed issuing slightly disguised warnings against constituencies which might think about voting against the party in power; and offering enticements to those who would climb on board.[97] Such blatant use of patronage either positively to reward supporters or negatively to punish non-supporters, was accepted practice and the resulting spoils systems of government was condoned by generality of Nigerians.[98] There was thus a "powerful nexus of political patronage, influence, discipline and allegiance — all at the disposal of regional regimes"[99] which were run by political parties.

The dual role of interpreters and bestower of benefits combined to make Nigerian political parties very 'representative' in the full sense of the term; that is they were expected to know their constituencies, to understand their needs and be prepared to secure for them as many benefits as they could.[100] This meant that party competition revolved around struggle for obtaining the political power necessary to control and extract resources which would be used to "satisfy elite demands and to buy political support."[101] When a party failed to 'deliver the goods' through its inability to control the 'instrumentalities of government,'[102] it usually lost favor with the electorate. The results of the 1983 elections, though fraught with charges of massive riggings and other corrupt electioneering practices, still demonstrated this phenomenon. Parties like the People Redemption Party, PRP, and the Great Nigerian Peoples Party, GNPP, which could not secure any substantial foothold on the national scene, saw their share of the electorate greatly reduced; the Unity Party of Nigeria, UPN, lost its only non-Yoruba State, Bendel; all to the benefit of the ruling National Party of Nigeria, NPN. What the erstwhile supporters of the losing parties perceived that made them switch was their parties' inaccessibility to resources and hence a reduction in extracting capabilities.[103] If the political party could not fulfill its election promises to the people (in terms of benefits), then it was not worth supporting.[104]

There thus existed among the political parties in Nigeria, a haunting fear of the loss of political power,[105] since the end result of politics was "not so much winner-take-all as loser-forfeit-all."[106] That realization precipitated an intensive and desperate struggle to win control of state power and made politics a matter of life and death,[107] prompting Billy Dudley to equate the Nigerian political scene to the Hobbesian 'state of nature'.[108] This, he said, was possible because,

> for most Nigerians, 'power' is not a relation, as it would generally be construed to be, but a 'property' (or put differently, a predicate), and as such something to be valued not only for its own sake, but because its possession is what makes everything else possible.[109]

Nigerian politicians thus heeded the advice given by Kwame Nkrumah that they "seek ye first the political kingdom and everything else shall be added unto you."[110]

Given the intricate and expanding network of patron-client ties which permeated the Nigerian political society, and the enduring ethnic cleavages, politics in Nigeria has been described as 'ethno-clientelism'.[111] Party leaders, serving as 'political patrons' performed strategic brokering roles by seeking out their constituencies (consisting mainly of their kinfolk) for patronage and/or support.[112] These ethno-clientelistic linkages provided the bases on which the parties were formed. In the First Republic there was a "virtual synergistic combination of party competition, regionalism and ethnic nationalism"[113] sustained by longstanding networks and reciprocal ties of patronage. This basic pattern persisted despite efforts to introduce structural changes that might mitigate the effects of ethno-regional politics. One of the consociational devices designed to arrest the regrowth of closed party systems (parties formed solely for the purpose of advancing a particular ethnic/regional group, as did the pre-military parties) was the requirement that the new parties reflect the 'federal character'[114] of the country in order to qualify for registration.[115] However, what took place was that parties, even those with national pretensions (which they all claimed to be in 1978) fought over the "recruitment of men and women whose affiliation can mean the inclusion of a community of followers varying from a handful of villages to the block vote of an ethno-linguistic group," leading to a "formation of sectional caucuses within parties."[116] The NPN, which claimed to be a pan-Nigerian party (compared with the others, the claim could be substantiated) was a loose coalition of many diverse ethnic groups, all jockeying for positions and power,[117] within the party.

Thus the integrative function — that of "inculcating national values in place of communal or parochial values"[118] that the writers of the 1979 Constitution had hoped the new political parties would perform, was circumscribed by the ethno-clientelistic nature of the Nigerian political society.[119]

In the next four chapters, we shall examine the subject of fiscal federalism and how the experts dealt with it in the various political climates. These had ranged from a colonial autocratic administration running a unitary government through an authoritarian military regime to a democratically elected federal government. Whatever the system, interests forged during the party periods had remained intact and acted as the chief stakeholders in the revenue allocation debates.

Notes

1. Ake, Claude, 'Presidential Address to the 1981 Conference of the Nigerian Political Science Association,' West Africa. (May 26, 1981), pp. 1162-63.

2. Nowotny, Helga, 'Experts and Their Expertise: On the Changing Relationship Between Experts and Their Public,' *Bulletin of Science, Technology and Society*. Vol. 1, No. 3, (1981), p. 235.

3. Claude Ake, op. cit., p. 116.

4. Dudley, Billy, *An Introduction to Nigerian Government and Politics*. (Bloomington, IN: Indiana University Press, 1982), pp. 51-52.

5. Neumann, Sigmund, 'Toward a Comparative Study of Political Parties', Andrew J. Milnor (ed.), *Comparative Political parties: Selected Readings*. (New York: Thomas Y. Crowell Co., 1969), p. 27.

6. There are several seminal works about Political Parties in Europe and North America.

7. Hodgkin, Thomas, *African Parties*. (London: Penguin African Series, 1961), pp. 15-16.

8. Sartori, Giovanni, *Parties and Party Systems*. (Cambridge: Cambridge University Press, 1976), p. 63.

9. Emerson, Rupert, 'Parties and National Integration in Africa', in LaPalombara, Joseph and Myron Weiner (eds.) *Political Parties and Political Development*. (Princeton, NJ: Princeton University Press, 1969), p. 270.

10. LaPalombara, Joseph and Myron Weiner, 'The Origin and Development of Political Parties,' in Lapalombara and Weiner, op. cit., p.31.

11. 'Introduction' in Andrew Milner, op. cit., p. 3.

12. MacDonald, Neil A., *The Study of Political Parties*. (New York: Random House, 1961), p. 5.

13. Rosberg, Carl G. Jr., 'Democracy and New African States', in Kirkwood, Kenneth (ed.), *African Affairs*. No. 2, St. Andrews Papers, No. 15, (London: Chatto & Windus, 1963), p. 30.

14. Key, V.O. Jr., *Public Opinion and American Democracy*. (New York: Knopf, 1961), p. 433.

15. 'Introduction' in Andrew Milner, op. cit., p. 2.

16. G. Sartori, op. cit., pp. 27-28.

17. Carl Roseberg, op. cit., p. 31.

18. G. Sartori, op. cit., p. 254.

19. A. Zolberg, op. cit., p. 123.

20. Scott, James C., 'Corruption, Machine Politics and Political Change,' *American Political Science Review*. Vol. 63, No. 4 (December 1969), p. 1145.

21. Ibid., p. 1144.

22. LeMarchand, Rene, 'Political Clientelism and Ethnicity in Tropical Africa: Competing Solidarities in Nation-Building.' *American Political Science Review*. Vol. 66, No. 1 (March 1972), pp. 71-9.

23. Whitaker, C.S., *The Politics of Tradition*. (Princeton, NJ: Princeton University Press, 1970), p. 375.

24. LeMarchand, Rene and Keith Legg, 'Political Clientelism and Development,' *Comparative Politics*. Vol. 14, No. 2 (January 1972), p. 151.

25. James Scott, op. cit., p. 1145.

26. LeMarchand and Legg, op. cit., pp. 151-2.

27. Elias, Taslimi O., *Government and Politics in Africa*. (New York: Asia Publishing House, 1963), pp. 95-96).

28. Mackenzie, W.J.M. and Kenneth E. Robinson (eds.), *Five Elections in Africa*. (Oxford: Clarendon Press, 1960), p. 12.

29. Wallerstein, Immanuel, 'The Decline of the Party System in Single Party African States', in LaPalombara and Weiner, op. cit., p. 201.

30. Mackenzie and Robinson, op. cit., p. 12.

31. Coleman, James, *Nigeria: Background in Nationalism*. (Berkeley & Los Angeles: University of California Press, 1958), p. 324.

32. Sklar, Richard, *Nigerian Political Parties*. (Princeton, NJ: Princeton University Press, 1963), p. 57.

33. Olorunsola, Victor (ed.), *The Politics of Cultural Sub-Nationalism in Africa*. (New York: Anchor Books, Doubleday & Company, Inc., 1972), p. 17.

34. Mackenzie and Robinson, op. cit., p. 123.

35. Dudley, Billy, *An Introduction to Nigerian Government and Politics*. Bloomington, IN: Indiana University Press, 1982), p. 46.

36. Okwudiba, Nnoli, *Ethnic Politics in Nigeria*. (Enugu: Fourth Dimension Publishers, 1978), pp. 154-55.

37. Ibid., p. 155.

38. Ibid., p. 156.

39. Mackenzie and Robinson, op. cit., p. 14.

40. Billy Dudley, op. cit., p. 14.

41. Kurfi, Amadu, *The Nigerian General Elections, 1959 and 1979, and the Aftermath*. (Lagos: MacMillian Nigeria, Ltd., 1981), p. 7.

42. N. Okwudiba, op. cit., p. 155.

43. T. Elias, op. cit., p. 96.

44. V. Olorunsola, op. cit., p. 17.

45. Mackenzie and Robinson, op. cit., p. 123.

46. J. Coleman, op. cit., pp. 361-63.

47. T. Elias, op. cit., p. 97.

48. J. Coleman, op. cit., p. 359

49. Billy Dudley, op. cit., p. 49.

50. N. Okwudiba, op. cit., p. 157.

51. For details, see Richard Sklar, op. cit., p. 324.

52. Billy Dudley, op. cit., p. 50.

53. Oyediran, Oyeleye, 'The Road to the 1979 Elections', in Oyediran, Oyeleye (ed.), *Nigerian 1979 Elections*. (Lagos: MacMillan Nigeria, Ltd., 1981), p.12.

54. Kraus, Jon, 'Return to Civilian Rule in Nigeria and Ghana,' *Current History*. (March 1980), p. 118.

55. O. Oyediran, op. cit., p. 11.

56. *Report of the Constitution Drafting Committee Containing the Draft Constitution*. Vol. 1, (Lagos: Federal Ministry of Information, 1976), p. xiiii.

57. O. Oyediran, op. cit., p. 14.

58. A. Krufi, op. cit., pp. 92-93.

59. Anise, Ladun, 'Political Parties and Election Manifestos', in O. Oyediran, op. cit., p. 91.

60. A. Kurfi, op. cit., p. 91.

61. Oyediran, Oyeleye, 'Political Parties: Formation and Candidate Selection', in O. Oyediran, op. cit., p. 45.

62. That was the definition of a political party given by Section 76 of the Electoral Decree No. 73 of 1977.

63. A. Urfi, op. cit., pp. 93-94.

64. O. Oyediran, op. cit., pp. 45-60.

65. Ibid.

66. Herskovits, Jean, 'Democracy in Nigeria,' *Foreign Affairs*. (Winter 1979-80), p. 319.

67. Billy Dudley, op. cit., p. 189.

68. O. Oyediran, op. cit., pp. 51-57.

69. *African Research Bulletin (Political, Social and Cultural Series).* Vol. 16, No. 1 (January 1979), p. 5125.

70. Legum, Colin (ed.), *African Contemporary Record.* Vol. xi (1978/79), p.B731.

71. Ibid., pp. B730-31. (See also *African Research Bulletin*, op. cit., Vol. 15, No. 9 (September 1978), p. 490.

72. *African Research Bulletin*, op. cit., p. 5126.

73. Billy Dudley, op. cit., p. 193.

74. Colin Legum, op. cit., p. B731.

75. O. Oyediran, op. cit., p. 55.

76. Billy Dudley, op. cit., p. 194.

77. O. Oyediran, op. cit., p. 60.

78. *African Research Bulletin*, op. cit., p. 5126.

79. Colin Legum, op. cit., p. B732.

80. Billy Dudley, op. cit., p. 195.

81. Post, Kenneth, *The Nigerian Federal Election of 1959.* (London: Oxford University Press, 1963), p. 48.

82. Kenneth Post, op. cit., p. 48.

83. Sklar, Richard and C.S. Whitaker, Jr., 'Nigeria', in Coleman, James and Carl Roseberg (eds.), *Political Parties and National Integration.* (Berkeley, CA: University of California Press, 1970), p. 620.

84. Eleazu, Uma, *Federalism and Nation-Building: The Nigerian Experience, 1954-1964.* (Devon, Great Britain: Arthur Stockwell, Ltd., 1977), p. 154.

85. Ibid., pp. 154-57. A good description of the politicization of a cultural association is given here.

86. Billy Dudley, op. cit., p. 52.

87. Coleman, James, 'The Emergence of African Political Parties' in Haines, C. Grove (ed.), *Africa Today*. (Baltimore: The Johns Hopkins University Press, 1955), p. 238.

88. Sklar, Richard, 'Contradictions in the Nigerian Political System,' *Journal of Modern African Studies*. Vol. 3, No. 2 (August 1965), p. 204.

89. E. Okoli, op. cit., p. 113.

90. James Coleman, op. cit., p. 238.

91. Ake, Claude, *A Theory of Political Integration*. (Homewood, IL: The Dorsey Press, 1967), p. 63. Professor Ake was describing a one-party state but the same principles are applicable to the regional party system that operated in Nigeria.

92. Richard Sklar, op. cit., p. 203.

93. Ibid., p. 204.

94. U. Eleazu, op. cit., p. 149.

95. James Coleman, op. cit., p. 238.

96. Arikpo, Okoi, *Development of Modern Nigeria*. (Middlesex, England: Penguin Books, 1967), p. 113.

97. The author, Briggs, C., was working as a journalist in Nigeria and covered the 1983 elections.

98. O. Arikpo, op. cit., p. 113.

99. Whitaker, C.S. Jr., 'Second Beginnings: The New Political Framework,' *Issue*. Vol. xi, No. ½ (Spring/Summer, 1981), p. 4.

100. Kenneth Post, op. cit., p. 390.

101. Billy Dudley, op. cit., p. 63.

102. Ibid.

103. Tordoff, William, *Government and Politics in Africa*. (Bloomington, IN: Indiana University Press, 1984), p. 115.

104. It is important to add here that the switch in votes did not alter the basic ethno/regional pattern of voting in the country. Bendel is a minority State and thus was up for grabs. The other Yoruba States stood solidly behind UPN; also adherents of PRP and GNPP are found mostly in the Northern States, and the beneficiary of their votes was the Northern-based NPN which coincidentally was the party in power at the center.

105. Austin, Dennis, *Politics in Africa (2nd ed.).* (Hanover, R.I.: University Press of New England, 1984). p. 46.

106. C.S. Whitaker, op. cit., p. 5.

107. C. Ake, op. cit., p. 63.

108. Billy Dudley, op. cit., p. 22.

109. Ibid.

110. Quoted in ibid., p. 60.

111. Joseph, Richard, 'Class, State, and Prebendal Politics in Nigeria,' *Journal of Commonwealth and Comparative Studies.* Vol. 21, No. 3 (November 1983), pp. 28-29.

112. Ibid., p. 30.

113. C.S. Whitaker, op. cit., p. 4.

114. See Chapter 2 for an explanation of this term.

115. Sklar, Richard, 'Democracy in Africa', in Patrick Chaba (ed.), *Political Domination in Africa: Reflection on the Limits of Power.* (Cambridge: Cambridge University Press, 1968), p. 25.

116. R. Joseph, op. cit., pp. 29-30.

117. Diamond, Larry, 'Cleavage, Conflict and Anxiety in the Second Nigerian Republic,' *Journal of Modern African Studies.* Vol. 20 (December 1983), pp. 638-64.

118. W. Tordoff, op. cit., p. 109.

119. For fuller expansion of this theme, see Joseph, Richard A., *Democracy and Presidential Politics in Nigeria: The Rise and Fall of the Second Republic.* (Cambridgeshire, NY: Cambridge University Press, 1987);

Rimmer, Douglas, 'Development in Nigeria: An Overview', in Bienen, Henry and V.P. Diejomaoh (ed.), *The Political Economy of Income Distribution in Nigeria*. (New York: Holmes and Meier, 1981), pp. 29-88; and Williams, Gavin and Terisa Turner, 'Nigeria', in Dunn, John (ed.), *West African States: Failure and Promises*. (Cambridge: Cambridge University Press, 1978).

5 Fiscal federalism and evolution of revenue allocation policy in Nigeria

Introduction

In a federal system, where the making of important policies involves joint decisions by both the central government and the constituent units, the distribution of fiscal resources becomes the most common source of friction.[1] This is because how these resources, the possession and use of which translates into power, are allocated influences to a great degree the political and administrative relationship between the units of the government; in other words, it influences the political bargain that governs the existence of the federal system. Thus political considerations play a vital role in determining the fiscal policy of the federation,[2] even though it may appear to be a purely economic and administrative undertaking.

When demands on the government and the need to meet them adequately and promptly increase, a proper division of functions and corresponding financial powers between the different levels of government becomes imperative.[3] However, it is virtually impossible to obtain a division of revenue sources that corresponds exactly the division of governmental responsibilities. At any given time, the central government always gains the upper hand in its ability to exploit and control revenue-generating sources in the state.[4]

The situation usually leads to an uneasy struggle for power between the central and regional governments because the basis of autonomy or independence of a governmental unit in a federation lies, not only in the constitution, but also in its ability to carry out its functional responsibilities directly controlled by it. Where this ability is not possible, as in most cases, subordinate levels of government have to barter their freedom for the proverbial mess of pottage, and become dependent economically and politically on higher levels. Thus the politicization of fiscal policy-making in a federation is deeply rooted in the very nature of resource endowment.

As stated above, a strict demarcation of functions between central and regional/state governments, either constitutionally or otherwise, does not obtain in any federation. Moreover, there are usually gross disparities in economic, fiscal and developmental capacities between and among the different units of government. In many newer federations, especially the former colonies of Great Britain, the tendency has been to institute functional, and hence financial, integration in the planning of their national fiscal policies.[5]

They perceive a need to avoid or reduce to a minimum, the vagueness and overlapping of financial policies which often lead to unwanted competition between the Center and the units. This has paved the way to the establishment of central governments with strong fiscal powers, and economic doctrines which emphasize need for overall governmental regulation and control of the economy.

Fiscal centralization in Nigeria

Concentrating fiscal control at the Center has historical, political and economic bases. The colonial administration which most of these newer anglophonic federations experienced, tended to centralize both political and economic powers. After independence, the pattern persisted, on the premise that centralization was necessary to promote and maintain a balanced economic development, income redistribution and national stability.[6] Therefore, the huge and expanding sources of revenue, such as customs and excise duties and personal and corporate taxes usually have been centralized and the responsibility for collecting and managing them have been assigned to the central government.[7]

In Nigeria, the basic rationale for creating the political entity itself lay largely in the notion of unifying revenue sources. Before the country was amalgamated, two British possessions, each operating a different economic and fiscal system existed side by side. Whatever economic activity existed between them was hindered by burdensome surtaxes levied on traders as they crossed the borders. In addition, the development of duplicate and competitive customs stations and railroad systems further led to economic disparity. The Southern Protectorate prospered and had, by the time of amalgamation, over one million pounds sterling in reserves. The North, however, was in such financial straits that it had to depend on annual grants averaging 314,500 pounds sterling from the British Treasury for its survival.[8] The anomalous situation prompted Sir Frederick (later Lord) Lugard, the architect of amalgamation, to describe Nigeria as a country with an "aggregate revenue practically equal to its needs but divided by an arbitrary line of latitude,"[9] and suggested that for the country to be fiscally and economically viable, the separate and widely different systems must be integrated.[10] And he set about to do it in 1914.

In the fiscal field, certain departments such as Customs, Railroads, and Post & Telegraphs were centralized, and revenues from them put in one purse. Also centralized were Public Debts, the Military and Pensions.[11] In addition, all the revenues of the three governments — Central Northern and Southern and Lagos Colony — were deposited into a general fund.[12] Nevertheless, there was no attempt to develop a centralized budget. Rather, estimates of revenues and expenditures of the administrative units were prepared separately, and only the aggregate budget was required to be balanced.[13] So there was no relationship between revenue and expenditure of the individual governmental units.

This pattern continued until 1926 when separate budgets ended and were replaced by a unified fiscal system — in line with the political reality in the country. Thus began the institutionalization of the Center as the repository and regulator of the nation's financial resources, and it has continued so until the present, in spite of the various types of governmental systems the country has experienced.

The rationale behind the policy of centralizing revenues is both economic and political, and that is why it has endured so long. In a country where there is a shortage of "cadres, means and skilled labor," there is usually the proclivity towards streamlining all efforts of economic activity by concentrating control and direction at the Center.[14] This is seen as necessary in formulating a national fiscal policy that will promote economic growth and stability, while eliminating waste and minimizing costs.

The doctrine of fiscal centralization was also promoted to achieve some political goals. Given the multi-ethnic and diverse cultural setting in Nigeria, a federal center was needed to "create and strengthen the collective sentiment of belonging together irrespective of individual or sub-group differences."[15] And one of the most effective ways of upgrading that status of that center was to let it handle the purse strings. Since there was no great consensus about nationhood at the time of federation, creating and sustaining such a consensus becomes imperative. A federal center with substantial fiscal jurisdiction was considered to be one instrument that can be used to achieve the consensus. If the sub-national units were left alone to chart their own fiscal courses, centrifugal forces, which are present in any country, may overwhelm the whole political system, leading to a breakup of the federation.

The designation of central government as the chief tax collector in the federation has remained unchanged over the years. In fact, starting with the first military regime in 1966, the number and type of taxes placed under central jurisdiction have expanded. The table below shows the distribution.

Table 5.1
Tax jurisdiction in Nigeria

Federal	*Region*
(1) Import Duties	Personal Income Tax
(2) Export Duties	Sales and Purchase Taxes on Produce and other Commodities
(3) Excise Duties	Entertainment Tax
(4) Mining Rents and Royalties	Cattle Tax
(5) Petroleum Profit Tax	Football Pools and other Betting Taxes
(6) Companies Income Tax	Capitals Gains Tax (Administration)
(7) Non-Federal Jurisdiction	Motor Vehicle Tax and Drivers' License Fees

Source: 'Fiscal Centralization Tendencies in the Federal Republic of Nigeria Since 1966,' by Fajana, Oladunjoye (unpublished mimeograph, 1979). Table 1, p.4.

By 1979, at the end of the 13-year military rule, the following changes had taken place:

(1) Personal Income Tax federalized.
(2) Sales and Purchase Taxes on Produce and other Commodities abolished; Marketing Boards taken over by Federal Government.
(3) Football Pools Tax federalized; Taxes on Gaming and other Betting Taxes and Licenses abolished.[16]

With all the important revenue sources under the jurisdiction of the central government, a system of intergovernmental financial transfer becomes necessary.

Fiscal adjustment in federal states

Transfer of funds

Basically, two methods are used in federal systems to transfer funds from Center to the constituent parts; these are Grants and Revenue (tax receipts) Sharing.

Intergovernmental fiscal adjustments, in terms of revenue transfer are designed to achieve fiscal equity among the different levels of government. This is needed to correct the fiscal imbalance brought about by several factors.

Firstly, imbalance may arise from the pattern of revenue allocation. In most federations, the largest revenue-generating sources, such as customers and excise duties, are constitutionally allocated to the Center (see above).[17]
So the States start off from a financially disadvantageous position vis-a-vis the central government. This leads to an imbalance between revenue resources and expenditure responsibilities, making it imperative for the Center to rectify the situation by way of grants.[18]

Another reason why transfers are necessary in a federation is that different States have varying capacities for raising revenues, as they are not all equally endowed with resources. Nevertheless, all are expected to carry out the minimum responsibilities commensurate with their status as governing units. This often means that poorer States lag behind in the provision of public services and have to impose heavier tax burdens on their citizens.[19] If these differences become substantial, loud protests are heard about the lop-sided economic development that usually results from them. Thus the central government comes under severe pressure to give special aid to poor States. Even if the same revenue is given to every State, there will still be disparities in the level of social services provided, due to the differences in population and level of economic growth. This too, will eventually lead to pressures on the Center to balance the inequality.[20]

Sometimes, revenue transfers are needed to encourage or stimulate particular State activities. Such transfers usually act as incentives for localities to provide goods which may produce benefits that go beyond the limits of the localities, what economists refer to as positive externalities.[21]

All revenue transfers from the Center to the States fall into two categories — Conditional and Unconditional Grants — and all federal governments rely on a combination of the two. Depending on the motive behind the transfer, that is, whether the country is trying to maximize national welfare or enforce financial responsibility,[22] the proportion of the mix of the two types of grants differs from federation to federation.

Conditional Grants are payments of funds from one level of government (mostly higher) to the other for a specific purpose in accordance with certain prescribed standards or requirements.[23] They are used to achieve a national minimum standard in the level of services provided in the federation by correcting fiscal imbalances among the States. This is also a means of redistributing national wealth and it introduces a certain flexibility to the operation of the federal constitution. These grants are used to pragmatically realign financial powers to constitutional responsibilities between the central and State governments.[24] Also, they are needed to optimized resource allocation to local spending programs that have significant external benefits.[25] Alternatively, sometimes, Conditional Grants can be used by the government to stimulate innovation in a particular area or field as well as to further certain national goals, even at the cost of creating greater imbalances.

The drawback in using Conditional Grants lies in the fact that the transfer is generally left to the discretion of the central government, thereby strengthening its formidable position to the detriment of States which become financially dependent. This dependence often distorts decision-making at the State level due to uncertainties in budgetary planning.[26]

Unconditional Grants, on the other hand, are unrestricted and usually consist of balancing and equalizing transfers. They are used to offset or balance any general fiscal deficiency experienced by State or Local governments, which prevents them from financing internal programs at reasonable tax rates.[27] Thus their main purpose is to maximize the national welfare.

The argument against Unconditional Grants is that they encourage financial irresponsibility. If States know they will receive transfers funds, there may not be the incentive to maximize their tax generating efforts. There is also the tendency for States to misuse the resources, for example, embarking on uneconomic but prestigious and oftentimes politically expedient programs. However, Unconditional Grants usually strengthen the budgetary positions of State and local governments,[28] and help loosen the strings to the central government.

Revenue allocation in Nigeria

The other method of transferring resources is through Revenue (tax receipts) Sharing, and in Nigeria it is the dominant means to deal with fiscal disparities between and among the governmental levels. Unlike the non-statutory grants described above, revenue sharing is mandated by the constitution where provisions for financial adjustments, in terms of distributing central revenues, are usually made. Under a military regime, appropriate decrees and edicts dealing with the revenue policy are issued.

The need for a formal system of revenue allocation began with the adoption of the first unified constitution in 1946 under Governor Arthur Richards. The decentralized unitary government that resulted meant that the newly created regions, which were given some measure of administrative authority and responsibility, be allocated revenues to carry out their functions.[29] So the "first realistic attempt to create institutions and policies" to deal with inter-governmental and inter-regional fiscal equity was initiated.[30] An expert commission was set up under the auspices of the Financial Secretary of the colony, Sir Sidney Phillipson, to develop a revenue allocation formula that would be incorporated into the new constitution. The first Revenue Allocation Commission introduced certain basic principles which have formed the foundation of revenue allocation policy ever since. One of them is the decision allow the central government to retain jurisdiction over the major sources of revenue, be they customs duties or other taxes from agricultural produce in the 1950s and 1960s or proceeds from petroleum sales in the 1970s and 1980s. Concomitant with this is the policy of allocating a greater share of the national income to the Center. It is interesting to note that despite the changes in the governmental structure of the country, these principles have not been abandoned.

Over the years, the federal center has not only controlled the fiscal pulse of the country, but it also has been allocated the bulk of the nation's revenues. In all the allocation exercises, the Center has received between 60-70 percent of the revenue available for sharing. This division is based on the assumption that the federal government is the repository of the national interest; therefore, all efforts should be made to strengthen its finances. As one of the fiscal review boards put it:

> The financial stability of the Federal Center must be the main guarantee of the financial stability of Nigeria as a whole and.........by its strength and solvency, the credit-worthiness of the country will be appraised.[31]

112

In addition, provisions of the various constitutions have given the Center certain responsibilities and obligations that policy-makers have felt warranted huge allocations. Even during the heyday of regionalism, from 1965-1965, when residual powers were vested in the regions, adequate independent revenue sources could not be found for the regions, and they had to depend on revenues from federally collected taxes.[32] For instance, during that period, an average of 56 percent of percent of regional revenue came from statutory allocations.[33] By 1975, the share had increased to 81 percent, and hovered around that figure until the military went back to the barracks in 1979. After that, it has gone down, but not by much.

The fact that the central government not only collected most of the revenues, but also retained the bulk of it, has been criticized. Describing the system as 'rampant centralism,'[34] and as even more centralized in the world,[35] critics have questioned its validity and suitability in a federal Nigeria.[36] However, the trend has continued; it seems both civilian and military authorities in Nigeria want it that way. The political ramifications of such a system will be explored in later chapters.

The major problems of revenue allocation in Nigeria have been about issues involving inter-State sharing of statutory allocation. Since the establishment of regions in 1946, the emphasis has been on separate development and the devolution of power and resources from the Center to the regions. There was no corresponding stress on contribution of resources and surrender of powers by the regions to the federal government until 1966, when a military regime forcibly changed the system. The result was that each region has striven to maximize the resources for its own separate development.[37] Even after the regions were broken up into 12, then 19, States each with much reduced financial and political powers, inter-State allocation remained the 'hot bed of tropical intensity' in fiscal adjustment, because "people still identified more strongly with their own localities than with the Federal Government."[38]

Various principles and criteria, and the formula for using region/State has ever been satisfied with the type of system used or its share of the revenue.[39] Table 5.2 on the following pages lists revenue allocation principles and the Commissions that recommended their use.

Table 5.2
Revenue allocation principles for inter-state sharing

	Commission		Principle
(1)	Phillipson, 1946	i.	Derivation
		ii.	Even Progress
		(a)	population - proxy
(2)	Hicks-Phillipson, 1951	i.	Derivation
		ii.	Need
		iii.	National Interest
(3)	Chick, 1953	i.	Derivation
(4)	Raisman, 1958	i.	Derivation
		ii.	Need
		(a)	population
		(b)	continuity in government services
		(c)	minimum responsibilities
		(d)	balanced development
(5)	Binns, 1964	i.	Financial Comparability
		(a)	need
		(b)	even development
(6)	Dina, 1968	i.	Need
		ii.	Minimum National Standards
		iii.	Balanced Development
		iv.	Derivation
(7)	Various Revenue Allocation Decress, 1967-1977	i.	Equality of States
		ii.	Population
		iii.	Derivation (only 20% of on-shore mining royalties)

(Continued)

Table 5.2 (Continued)
Revenue allocation principles for inter-state sharing

	Commission		Principle
(8)	Aboyade, 1977	i.	Equality of Access to Development Opportunity
		ii.	National Minimum Standards
		iii.	Absorptive Capacity
		iv.	Independent Revenue and Tax Effort
		v.	Fiscal Efficiency
(9)	Okigbo, 1980	i.	Minimum Responsibility
		ii.	Population
		iii.	Internal Revenue Effort
		iv.	Social Development Factor
		(a)	primary school enrollment

Derivation was later added to the Okigbo recommendations.

Source: *Report of the Presidential Commission on Revenue Allocation, Vol. 1*, (Lagos: Federal Government Press, 1980), Chaps 2 & 9.

Which principles to use, in what combinations and how much weight should be assigned to them, in order to obtain some level of satisfaction from the interested stakeholders, had been a "most serious and intractable political issue"[40] in Nigeria. Examining the list shows that two principles featured prominently in the allocation formulas; they are 'Derivation' and 'Need', which appeared seven and six times respectively, more than any other principle. A note on each of them at this point would be helpful.

The derivation principle

This principle is based on the notion that when centrally collected revenues are being shared, a region/state ought to get "all revenues which can be identified as having come from or can be attributed to"[41] that particular region/state. This basis of allocating revenues is common in systems where "the regions have little sense of national unity or common citizenship"[42] — often referred to as loose federations. Since each region/state receives a share proportional to its

115

contributions to the total revenue, without subsidizing other regions/states, the principle can be seen as being equitable.

However, application of this principle has two major drawbacks. First, in order to accurately assess the amount of revenue contributed by a region/state, adequate and reliable data that can be analyzed precisely have to be available. And since consumption and production patterns of the regions/states tend to change overtime, the data collected have to be reviewed and updated on a continuing basis.[43] Secondly, fully applying the Derivation Principle is likely to bring about gross economic disparity among the regions/states. Those which have revenue-yielding resources will develop faster and provide more and better services than resources-poor regions/states. This will eventually result in a lopsided economic development pattern, leading to social and political instability in the country. Also, it limits the ability of a nation to compensate for cyclical or idionsycratic factors that harm the economies of specific regions/states at specific times.

In Nigeria, these defects have been applicable. A constant lamentation of the fiscal review boards had been the lack of accurate and reliable statistical data of any kind. That made it very difficult to quantify the principle to the satisfaction of the interested parties leading to charges of inequity. Moreover, since national integration is one of the political goals of the country's leaders, to allow a widening of the economic gap between the regions/states whereby the rich ones got richer, and the poor ones poorer, would defeat the purpose. But due to political expediency and other reasons to be explored throughout this section, the principle to Derivation has continued to be utilized to the present. The emphasis put on it has varied, but Derivation has almost become a constant in the revenue allocation equation.

The need principle

The definition of this principle differs depending on the type of allocation. With regards to vertical sharing, that is, among the tiers of government, Need refers to the constitutional functions and responsibilities assigned to each tier and the corresponding financial expenditures and obligations.[44] It implies that every level of government has certain duties to perform and therefore should be allocated enough revenues to carry them out. This is the basic argument by the central government for allocating the bulk of the revenues to itself.

In inter-regional sharing, two main indicators have been used to define the principle of Need. One indicator, labeled 'Minimum Responsibilities', or 'Minimum National Standards', or 'Equality of States' or 'Continuity of Government Services', by the different review boards, is based on the proposition that for each state/region, to function as a governing unit, it has to carry out a minimum number of responsibilities. Therefore, it requires each state/region to maintain its constitutionally allowable equivalent amount of revenues in order to effectively carry out its responsibilities as a governing unit with the Federation of Nigeria.

The other indicator for the principle of Need is Population. It is based on the premise that "government is about people, that development is about people, and that the end of government is the Welfare of its people."[45] Therefore, all citizens should have equal claim to the national revenue, regardless of whatever region they reside.[46] When Need is operationalized this way, it has the effect of levelling out economic and social disparities among the states. However, it can also bring about resentment on the part of richer states/regions[47] which may want to retain their resources for the benefit of their own population, large or small.

Moreover, there is no generally acceptable way of using Population as an indicator of Need. If raw figures are used, the different dimensions of population such as age, sex, and literacy rate are ignored; on the other hand, if the figures used are weighted, the issued of assigning weights come in.[48] The problem is even more complicated because in Nigeria there have never been any census figures which have not been manipulated, precisely for the reason that population will be used as an indicator for Need in sharing central revenues.[49]

Critics of the principle contend that applying it in the revenue allocation exercises often makes states/regions "lose incentive to increase tax effort to raise revenues on their own."[50] But proponents insist that using any of indicators for Need tempers the disengaging elements often brought about by the application of the Derivation Principle. In other words, Derivation separates, Need brings together.

The decision by experts to adopt one principle or other and the "degree to which it was given operational effect"[51] has often depended on how they assessed the political power play between the different levels of government as well as among the states/regions themselves. Since different states/regions benefitted from the application of different principles, the battle to indirectly influence the experts so that they utilize a particular set of principles has always been severe. The more powerful a state/region was perceived to be, relative to the others, the more it would be able to exert influence, either during the constitutional conventions when the background was laid, or during the adoption of the expert recommendations where an unfavorable proposal could be expunged from the Report.

One of the significant features in the evolution of revenue allocation policy is the connection between the constitutions and making of the policy.

117

That the system of sharing centrally collected revenues should be embodied in constitutional provisions indicates the inextricable bond between politics and finance. The expert panels set up to devise inter- and intra-governmental fiscal adjustments have produced arrangements that are politically sensitive. A cursory look at the division of formal powers and corresponding revenue allocation systems adopted shows this relationship.

During the early days of the colony, both financial and constitutional powers were vested almost entirely in the central government. As the policy of decolonization was being realized, the colonial government started to devolve political power to the indigenous political elite. In the same mood, fiscal commissioners suggested revenue formulas that led to a gradual decentralization of fiscal powers too. At independence in 1960, both political and fiscal systems had been regionalized, leaving behind a relatively weak Center politically and financially. The position was reversed by the onset of the military regime; the federal government became very powerful and the whole fiscal structure was altered, through the issuance of decrees and edicts, to reflect the new power relationship. By the time the military government gave way to a civilian one in 1979, the Center was firmly in control of almost every facet of the country's political, economic and social life. The existing fiscal system continued more or less in the same manner, increasing the political, and hence financial powers of the federal government at the expense of the constituent parts.

Each of the fiscal review panels had been able to reflect the changes in the revenue allocation system by its choice of principles used. When the political mood was swinging toward increased power for the regions, more weight was attached to those principles like 'Derivation' which promoted separate regional development; as the Center became more relevant and a feeling of national consciousness started emerging among the rulers,[52] principles which contributed to a more even development, like 'Population' and 'Equality of States' took center stage.

Prior to military rule, after a particular revenue allocation formula has been adopted, it became part of the existing constitution, and remained so until a new constitution was drawn up. This method of sharing the bulk of the nation's revenues by statutory means has often been attacked for being too rigid, with no room for flexibility. It is thus "difficult to modify the system in response to fluctuations in the economy and the fiscal condition of the various governments."[53] However, the fixed system prevented the federal government from capriciously changing the size of revenue available to the regions/States.[54] This insulation and predictability of revenues was shattered by the military government which altered the system at will. Even then, the changes in allocation formulas produced by revenue decrees did remain in place until a new decree replaced or altered them.

Conclusion

Unlike other federations like the Indian and the Australian, which have permanent fiscal commissions that meet at prescribed times (India's convenes every five years, while that of Australia is a Standing Commission), Nigeria's panels as described above, have been *ad hoc*. The chronic inter-governmental fiscal conflict can be largely attributed to this lack of permanence and durability of revenue systems. As long as revenue sharing was tied to constitutional reviews, each new attempt at fiscal adjustment would bring on either fresh agitations or renew old ones for imagined or real inequalities in the existing formula. The expert commissions would also be subjected to more political influence that would a permanent body. However, despite recommendations by experts, and promises by policy-makers to set up a permanent system with regular review schedules, revenue allocation system in Nigeria has remained *ad hoc*. It seems nobody wants to lose whatever influence he is exerting on the experts and the political benefits obtained by publicly advocating one set of allocation principles or the other.

The role of experts and policy-making changes in the political environment showed varying emphasis on the different principles of revenue allocation utilized by the experts. That showed an acute sensitivity, on the part of the experts, to the political realities of the system in which they were working.

Notes

1. Aluko, Sam, *Recent Trends in Federal Finance*, seminar paper. (Lagos: Nigerian Institute of International Affairs, 1979), pp. 4-5.
    See also, Daudu, P.C.A., 'Nigerian Draft Constitution: Analysis of the Division of Power in Relations to the Financial Provisions', in Kumo, Suleiman and Abubakar Aliyu (Eds.), *Issues in the Nigerian Draft Constitution*. (Zaria: Institute of Administration, 1977), p. 138.

2. Birch, A.H., 'Intergovernmental Financial Relations in New Federalisms,' in Hicks, U.H.K., et al. (eds.), *Federalism and Economic Growth in Underdeveloped Countries*. (London: George Allen & Unwin, Ltd., 1961), p. 113.

3. Sam Aluko, op. cit., p. 5.

4. Birch, A.H., *Federalism, Finance and Social Legislation*. (Oxford: Clarendon Press, 1957), p. 6.

5. Sastri, K.V., in U.H.K. Hicks, et. al., op. cit., pp. 129-30.

6. Offensend, Dennis G., 'Centralization and Fiscal Arrangement in Nigeria,' *Journal of Modern African Studies*. Vol. 14, No. 3, (September 1976, pp.307-13).

7. Ray, Amal, *Intergovernmental Relations in India*. (Bombay: Asia Publishing House, 1966), p. 60.

8. Adedeji, Adebayo, *Nigerian Federal Finance*. (New York: Africana Publishing Co., Inc., 1969), pp. 27-28.

9. Lugard, Lord Frederick, *Report of North and South Nigeria and Administration, 1912-1919*. Command Paper 468, p. 7, cited in Dudley, B.J., *Federalism in Nigeria*. M.A. Thesis, University of Leicester, 1959, (unpublished), pp. 25-26.

10. Adebayo Adedeji, op. cit., p. 28.

11. Awa, Eme, *Federal Government in Nigeria*. (Berkeley, CA: University of California Press, 1964), p. 189.

12. Adebayo Adedeji, op. cit., p. 29.

13. Ibid., p. 29.

14. Frankel, Max, 'Liability of the Federal Formula for New Nations', in Akinyemi, A.B., P.D. Cole and Walter Ofonagoro (eds.), *Readings on Federalism*. (Lagos: Nigerian Institute of International Affairs, 1979), p. 262.

15. 'Introduction' in Akinyemi, et al., op. cit., p. 5.

16. Fajana, Oladunjoye, 'Fiscal Centralization Tendencies in the Federal Republic of Nigeria since 1966.' (unpublished monograph, 1979), pp. 9-12.

17. A.H. Birch, *Federalism, Finance....*, op. cit., p. 115.

18. May, R.J., 'Intergovernmental Finance,' *Public Administration (Sidney)*. Vol. 28, No. 1, (March 1969), p. 42.

19. Olaloku, F.A., 'Nigerian Federal Finances: Issues and Choices', in Akinyemi, et al., op. cit., p. 110.

20. A.H. Birch, op. cit., pp. 17-18.

21. Maxwell, James, *Financing State and Local Governments*. (Washington, D.C.: The Brookings Institution, 1969), p. 67.

22. Scott, Anthony, 'The Evaluation of Federal Grants,' *Economica*. Vol. 14 (1947).

23. Wright, Deil S., *Federal Grants-In-Aid: Perspectives and Alternatives*. (Washington, D.C.: American Enterprise Institute for Public Policy, 1968), p. 34.

24. Smiley, D.V., *Conditional Grants and Canadian Federalism*. (Toronto: Canadian Tax Foundation, 1963), Chapter IV.

25. Break, George F., *Intergovernmental Fiscal Relations in the United States*. (Washington, D.C.: The Brookings Institution, 1967), p. 153.

26. May, R.J., *Federalism and Fiscal Adjustment*. (London: Clarendon Press, 1969), p. 42.

27. George Break, op. cit., p. 108.

28. Watson, M.M., 'Federalism and Finance in the Modern Commonwealth,' *Journal of Commonwealth Political Studies*. Vol. 3 (1966), pp. 118-21.

29. *Report of the Presidential Commission on Revenue Allocation.* (Lagos: Federal Government Press, 1980), Vol. 1, p. 16.

30. Okoli, Ekwueme F., *Institutional Structure and Conflict in Nigeria.* (Washington, D.C.: University Press of America, Inc., 1980), p. 73.

31. *Report of the Fiscal Commission.* cmd 481. (London: HMSO, 1958), paragraph 28.

32. Adebayo Adedeji, op. cit., p. 154.

33. Teriba, O., 'Nigerian Revenue Allocation Experience, 1952-65: A Study in Intergovernmental Fiscal and Financial Relations,' *Nigerian Journal of Economic and Social Studies.* (Ibadan: Vol. 8, No. 3, (July 1966), p. 375.

34. *Report of the Technical Committee on Revenue Allocation.* (Lagos: Federal Government Press, 1977), p. 14.

35. Aluko, Sam A., 'Trends in Public Expenditure in Nigeria Since 1960,' *The Economic Insight.* Vol. 2, No. 1, (June 1978), p. 25.

36. Oladunjoye Fajana, op. cit., p. 22.

37. Ekwueme Okoli, op. cit., p. 69.

38. Rupley, Lawrence A., 'Revenue Sharing in the Nigerian Federation,' *The Journal of Modern African Studies.* Vol. 19, No. 2 (June 1981), p. 259.

39. Fajana, Oladunjoye, 'Intergovernmental Fiscal Relations in the Report of the Technical Committee on Revenue Allocation,' *Quarterly Journal of Administration, (Ife, Nigeria).* Vol. 14, No. 2 (January 1980), p. 20.

40. Nicolson, I.F., *Administration of Nigeria, 1900-1960.* (Oxford University Press, 1969), p. 253.

41. Phillips, Adedotun, 'Nigeria's Federal Financial Experience,' *Journal of Modern African Studies.* Vol. 9, No. 3, (October 1971), p. 390.

42. Scott, Anthony, 'The Economic Goals of Federal Finance,' *Public Finance.* No. 3 (1964), p. 252.

43. Adedeji, Adebayo, *Nigerian Federal Finance.* (London: Hutchinson Educational, Ltd., 1969), pp. 64-65.

44. *Report of the Presidential Commission on Revenue Allocation*. (Lagos: Federal Government Press, 1980), Vol. 1, p. 27, (to be referred to as the *Okigbo Report*).

45. Ibid., p. 28.

46. *Report of the Commission on Revenue Allocation*. (Lagos: Government Printer, 1951), p. 77.

47. A. Phillips, op. cit., p. 391.

48. *Okigbo Report*, op. cit., p. 28.

49. The last 'reliable' census was taken in 1963.

50. A. Phillips, op. cit., p. 391.

51. Offensend, David, 'Centralization and Fiscal Arrangement in Nigeria,' *Journal of Modern African Studies*. Vol. 14, No. 3 (September 1976), p. 509.

52. Oyovbaire, S.E., 'The Politics of Revenue Allocation', in Panter-Brick, S.K. (ed)., *Soldiers and Oil: The Political Transformation of Nigeria*. (London: Frank Cass, 1978), p. 225.

53. Lawrence Rupley, op. cit., p. 258.

54. Lawrence Rupley, op. cit., p. 258.

6 Nigeria: Military government, secession, states creation, and revenue allocation system (1966-1979)

Introduction

With the intervention of the military in January 1966, the political system as it operated ceased to exist. Several parts of the constitution were suspended, and Decrees and Edicts became sources of law in the land. Some of the characteristics of the civilian government faded away as the central government took control of almost every aspect of the society. The regional based system of alliance was replaced by a more centrally coordinated structure. In addition to this was the then rapidly increasing oil revenues.

The overwhelming importance of the petroleum industry as the main source of revenue, especially in the 1970's has had significant political and financial implications for the country. It had been suggested that a desire to de-emphasize the use of the Derivation Principle in sharing the proceeds played a crucial role in forming events that eventually led to the succession attempt and civil war that followed in 1967.

The availability of a tremendous amount of revenue in the hands of a centralized military government altered the face of revenue allocation. As the country became balkanized into geographically small and financially dependent states, the center reigned supreme as the fulcrum around which all the states rotated. The command structure of the military tolerated no dissent, so state representatives could only gently acquiesce to central demands and federal influence in fiscal policy-making increased by leaps and bounds.

That was manifested by the government's resort to decrees and edicts in place of revenue commissions in the making of fiscal policies, after an earlier attempt at going the traditional way (via expert panels) failed. Thus, several far-reaching changes were made without benefit of political scrutiny, making that period, 1970-78, the most apolitical in revenue allocation policy-making in Nigeria. A final attempt by the military regime at the eve of its departure to 'legitimize' its fiscal policies in the eyes of the on-coming civilian government met a disastrous end.

Secession and states' creation - relation to revenue allocation

Background

The ethnic/regional hostility which characterized politics in the first Republic was resurrected soon after the dust settled on the military takeover on January 19, 1966. As the initial shock wore off and people began to look critically at the new military government headed by General Thomas Aguyi-Ironsi, events began to be interpreted in ethnic terms. It did not help matters that the young army officers who planned and executed the coup were mainly Ibos, and that every region in the country lost high ranking government officials, including some premiers and the Prime Minister himself, except the Eastern Region. In addition, an Ibo civil servant, Mr. Nwokedi, was put in charge of restructuring the government from a federal base to a centralized unitary set up. That policy provoked so much fear and outrage among the Northerners (who must have felt they were losing their grip at dominance of the country) that in May 1966, it sparked off the first wave of atrocities and massacres against Ibos living in the North.[1] As the ethnic tensions increased in the society, they interacted with internal divisions — themselves partially due to ethnicity in the Army, and a second coup, this time led by Northern soldiers, took place in July 1966.[2]

Revenue issue and secession

Eastern Nigerians, especially the Ibos, had always believed that no other group contributed more to the political and economic development of a united country than they. The only political party in the pre-military era to ever have a national base and win elections outside its regional enclave was the Ibo-dominated NCNC (it won the 1959 elections in the Western region and remained a force to reckon with thereafter). One could also recall the efforts made by both the NCNC and its leader, Dr. Azikiwe, in the fight for self-government and, later, total independence. Moreover, Azikiwe was the most reluctant among the three regional Premiers to agree with the extreme regionalism fostered by the 1954 Lyttleton Constitution. Partly due to their relatively infertile and over-crowded region, and partly due to their own aggressive and competitive lifestyles, Ibos are the most migratory ethnic groups in Nigeria, having established prosperous communities in all parts of the country. However, they felt that they had not been given their due shares of the national wealth "and had been deprived of the main prizes" in terms of federal projects in the region and adequate revenue to run the services.[3] Thus when the old system collapsed and the Ironsi government embarked on the journey to abolish the federal type of government and replace it with a unitary type, Ibos were elated. That was why "the reversal of power situation at the center was deeply traumatic"[4] to them. It was like a recurring nightmare, and coupled with the intense anti-Ibo feeling in the country manifested by the wanton slaughter of Ibos in the North and lack of sympathy from the others, leaders of the East decided it was high time they charted their own course, one that was different from the rest of the nation.

Scholars who have analyzed the events leading to the secession and civil war associate them with the development of oil in the Eastern Region. Colonel Chukwuemeka Ojukwu, the former Governor of the Eastern Region and leader of the secessionist regime remarked that "I have found it very difficult to get away from this Tshombe stigma...,"[5] referring to Moise Tshombe and the ill-fated attempt to carve out mineral-rich Katanga Province from Zaire with the help of the Belgian multinational mining company, Union Minere. There had been no factual evidence to prove that Shell-British Petroleum Development Company (Shell-BP), the Anglo-Dutch oil company that produced and exported the bulk of Nigeria's oil, had encouraged the secession, but the very presence of large deposits of crude oil in the region does seem to have emboldened the region's leadership to arrive at that decision.

When Nigerian military leaders convened at Aburi, near Accra in January 1967, under the auspices of the Ghanaian government, to discuss the political fate of the already crumbling federation, Ojukwu proposed a loose federal system in which each region would manage its own affairs including finances. From various reports, it seemed that, that and other proposals were accepted by the conferees. However, when they got back to Nigeria, the Aburi accords were interpreted differently due to pressures from interested parties, as explained in Chapter 3.

General Gowon, who emerged after the July coup to head the new government, issued Decree No. 8 of 1967 to implement the Aburi agreements as he understood them but the provisions of the Decree were not satisfactory to Ojukwu who insisted that "the East believes in confederation and I believe that this is the only answer."[6] Based on that belief, Ojukwu had earlier proposed financial relations which would require all fiscal and taxing powers to be vested in the Regions, with the Federal Government relying on equal contributions from the Regions to carry out its responsibilities. That demand for increased regional financial autonomy was made in the light of the huge influx of refugees to the Eastern Region from all parts of the country, especially the North.[7] The proposed system was like that sought by the Northern Region in its 8-point program introduced during the 1954 Constitutional Convention, and raised during discussions with Sir Louis Chick as he formulated the Revenue Allocation formula. However, despite tedious meetings between financial officers from both the Federal and Eastern Regional governments, there were no agreements, not even on how the East could obtain its usual statutory share of federally collected revenues.

As the debacle over the Aburi agreements and the insistence that the Federal Government pay the Eastern Region its debt of £11.8 million; (how he arrived at that figure was never stated). Ojukwu then issued an ultimatum that by March 31, 1967, if all his demands were not met, "He would consider it a duty to take appropriate actions to effect it through edicts."[8] The deadline came, and, as threatened, Ojukwu decided to implement unilaterally the Aburi decisions as he interpreted them. The edict, that is of relevance to us here, is the Revenue Collection Edict by which all federal revenues collected in the East were to be put into the Regional Government's treasury instead of the Federal Government's. Those included monies collected by the Customs, Railways, Airways, Post Office, Port Authority and other federal departments.[9] According to Ojukwu, the edict served three purposes:

(1) To make sure that what is statutorily due to us from the Federal Government comes to us promptly;
(2) to recover federal indebtedness to us;
(3) to prevent authorities in Lagos from further accumulating their debt to us.[10]

He argued that "there is nothing in the edict to show that I have unilaterally altered the existing formula for revenue allocation," but added that "the irreversible shift in population which had resulted in a population increase of 16 percent in this Region has rendered the present basis of revenue distribution illogical and untenable."[11] Therefore, Ojukwu concluded that "there must be a new basis for arranging our economic and financial affairs."[12]

The "existing formula for revenue allocation" he was referring to was the Binns' formula of 1964, a system that the Eastern Region perceived as biased and unjust. Despite his claims to the opposite, what Ojukwu did with that

Edict was to "nullify the constitutionally prescribed method" for revenue allocation,[13] thereby defying the federal authority in 'deliberate and systematic fashion.'[14] What followed was a series of blockades and embargoes imposed by both governments. The Federal Government suspended all flights to the East and put tight controls on foreign exchange transactions. The Eastern Region, on its own, took not only the revenues but complete control over all federal statutory bodies; authorized the Eastern Nigerian Marketing Board to stop selling its products via the Nigerian Produce Marketing Company; established an autonomous legal system; and requested all Easterners, especially those in the Armed Forces, and Police to return to the region.[15] By the end of April, Eastern Region "became, not only 'de factor', but also 'de jure', an independent state."[16]

Oil revenue was to become significant in the final decision to dismember Nigeria. What led to the final invasion of the East by the Federal Government was the destination of oil royalties. Having declared Eastern Region as the independent Republic of Biafra on May 27, 1967, Ojukwu proceeded to issue a decree on June 21, 1967, in which all companies prospecting for oil in the East were ordered to pay the rents, royalties and other affiliated taxes to his new government.[17] Viewing that decree as a threat to its sovereignty, the Federal Government warned the companies, especially Shell-BP, that if they complied with Ojukwu's request, it would invade the East.[18] On July 2, 1967, there were unconfirmed reports that Shell-BP had actually paid Ojukwu a token sum of about $700,000 out of an estimated $15-19 million total revenue. Thereupon, on July 4, a naval blockade was imposed on Bonny and Port Harcourt — the two oil terminals and ports in the region. And two days later, on July 6, 1967, Federal troops invaded Eastern Region; the civil war had started.[19] (Later investigations showed that Shell-BP did offer to pay Ojukwu the token amount with promises to pay the rest later; and Ojukwu was said to have found the amount insulting and rejected it.[20])

There is not enough evidence to ascertain whether Ojukwu would have stopped short of secession if he had not been buoyed by reports from economists that the Eastern Region would be financially secure and even prosperous from the proceeds of the rich oil wells in its delta areas and beyond. On the other hand, the proposition cannot be disproved either. At the beginning of the civil war, there was optimism in the region that whatever was spent on the war (which most people thought would be swift and short) would be supplemented by oil revenues.[21] Moreover, the rather intriguing rumor that Ojukwu had sold the "exclusive rights of exploitation and extraction" of mineral deposits in the region for ten years to the Rothschild Bank in France for a paltry sum of 6 million pounds,[22] which was circulated by the Federal Government but denied by everybody else, is seen by the author as an attempt to link the secession with both greed and desperation. Some reports did show though, that Ojukwu actually made the offer of monopoly of mineral exploitation to many foreign industrial giants but none was willing to take the offer and the risks involved in it[23] — the main one being the uncertainty of Ojukwu's success and fear of possible reprisals by Nigeria. However, even after Ojukwu lost control of the oil areas early in the war, he refused to surrender until almost the whole region was captured. That could be attributed to pride or to the fact that the war was really not about control of oil revenues but of people's right to secede from a political entity in which they no longer felt secure. Whatever might have been the basic motivation, the presence of oil was one of the driving forces behind the decision to secede.

Oil revenue and states' creation

The issue of states' creation had been festering since pre-independence days especially among minority ethnic groups who felt dominated and suppressed in the tripod structure of the country. Within each region, there were sizable minorities that agitated, though ineffectively, for their political and economic rights to self-determination. Several commissions had been established to study and recommend ways to deal with the problem but the hegemonic regions prevented any real and lasting solutions from emerging as no regional leader wanted to lose either territory or people. The minority political parties that tried to articulate the demands of their followers were no match for the regional giants. Given the fact that the majority party controlled the government in each region and therefore the source of patronage, it was no surprise when, during elections, the regional parties claimed huge victories, having manipulated the electoral systems to suit themselves. The only political leader who tried to support the aspirations of the minority groups was Chief Awolowo and his Action Group because he had always believed that Nigeria should be divided into states based on ethnic and linguistic affinities. Yet he resisted the carving out of the Mid-Western Region from his Western Region in 1963. Both the gigantic North and the East remained intact until 1967.

In 1964, due to the census, election, and revenue allocation crises, there were some movements by the Eastern Region which raised suspicions about possible secession. Dr. Azikiwe, then President of the country, revealed that, and Sir Ahmadu Bello, the Northern Premier, accused Eastern Regional leaders of planning to break away from the federation by the end of the year. Though the allegation was denied, the leading party in the North and at the Center, the NPC, threatened that if the East, because of the recent discovery of oil in its region, made any serious moves to secede, it would suffer the same consequences as did the Western Region during the 1962-63 crisis which included:

(1)   declaring a state of emergency in the Region and putting its leaders under restriction, with some of them including the party leader Chief Awolowo convicted of treasonable felony and jailed;
(2)   setting up a commission of inquiry to investigate financial dealing and sources of party finance;
(3)   breaking up the Region and removing the oil producing areas to form a new Region — Mid-West, thus depriving it of future benefits.[24]

Being in control of the federal machinery, the Northern Region had always hinted that it could dispense with the 'troublesome Ibos', but would hold on to the main structure and all its assets already swollen by oil.[25]

So, when on May 27, 1967, General Gowon, in what seemed like a preemptive move against secession, divided Nigeria into twelve states, observers noted that the pattern of breaking up the Eastern Region closely resembled the 1964 Northern Regional plan. Most of the oil facilities and the oil itself were in parts of the region that are inhabited by minority ethnic groups. Those minorities did not share Ojukwu's conviction that secession was the best solution to the brewing problems; in fact they saw themselves as persecuted by the dominant Ibos and wanted to obtain their own self-government. The Federal Government recognized that 'Achilles Heel' of the region and took advantage of it.[26] Three states were created, two of which belonged to minority but oil producing areas. One was Rivers State, where Nigeria got almost 70 percent of its on-shore oil and had its only oil terminals, refineries and second largest seaport. The other was South-Eastern State, where Mobil Oil Company had started showing excellent oil prospects, especially off-shore. The third State, East-Central, which came to be inhabited only by Ibos, was thus separated from the resource-rich portions of the old region which Ibos once controlled.

Early attempts at revenue sharing

During the entire military era, there were frequent changes in the revenue formula and composition of the Distributable Pool Account (DPA). Most of those changes were made without assistance from fiscal review commissions as had been the practice before the coup. That was possibly due to the "nature of military rule, with its greater command structure and cohesiveness."[27] The first of such changes occurred when the twelve states were created out of the four regions and the problem arose as to how the DPA would be shared and the principle of Derivation applied. Due to the exigencies of the civil war, there was no time to study and fully understand the fiscal implications of the situation.[28] In order to make it easy for the states to settle down and execute their responsibilities, the Federal Military Government made financial provisions in Decree No. 15 of 27 May 1967 (States Creation Decree) which provided for transitional payments to them. Using the same basis that was obtained under the old regional arrangements, the shares of the regions in the DPA were to be divided among the new states. Thus the 42 percent of the Northern Region was distributed equally among the new six states, each having 7 percent of the DPA; these new states were Kwara, Kano, Benue-Plateau, North-East, North-West and North-Central. The old Western Region was split into two: Lagos having 2 percent and Western State 18 percent. Of the East's 30 percent, the new state of East-Central got 17.5 percent; South-East had 7.5 percent and Rivers State took the remaining 5 percent. The mid-Western Region, then renamed Mid-West State retained its old 8 percent. Every other aspect of the fiscal system was left intact. From the above, it showed that the DPA was shared according to two principles — Population in the South, and Equality in the North.[29] No explanation was given why two different criteria were used.

The prevailing system was at best a temporary solution to the demands of the military coup and creation of states. Expectedly, the new fiscal system was accepted initially, but when the state of emergency was relaxed (in people's minds, that is), criticisms poured out. In the first place, its foundation was arbitrary and haphazard, for all the Decree did was subdivide the DPA shares of each of the four old regions among the new states that comprised them. This capricious way of allocating revenue did not take into account the need of the new states which inherited the constitutional powers and functions of the old regions. Both principles of revenue allocation used assumed that expenditure would either vary proportionately with population in the South, or that it was equal in all the Northern States. Moreover, the cost of setting up a new government machinery was not given any attention. In the new configuration, only two states were 'old' — the West and Mid-West; the rest had to start from scratch to build up administrative systems. That meant that most of them had insufficient revenue with which to perform their duties.[30] The situation was aggravated by the fact that those new political entities had much reduced revenue bases and could not supplement whatever revenue they received from the Federal Government.[31]

Another problem that arose from the new revenue allocation system created by Decree No. 15 of 1967 was the uneven development of the country as a whole. That was due to the disparity among the states in terms of their shares of the Distributable Pool Account. As stated earlier, the DPA was apportioned on the basis of population in the South and equality in the North. That raised considerable opposition and resentment from the very populous and large states in the North like Kano, North Central and North West; at the same time, smaller states in the South like Lagos felt they were unduly penalized for their size without regard for the responsibilities of a state, no matter how small.[32] Compounding the uneven development of the country was the fact that 50 percent of revenues from the oil industry was still being shared among the states (then regions) according to the Derivation principle. What that resulted in was that oil-rich states like Rivers and Mid-West saw their revenues sky-rocket while other states could not balance their budgets. That situation brought about further criticisms that the new formula dealt only with the DPA and neglected other vital elements of the fiscal system of the country.

The 1963 Constitution, which was still in effect, though amended by decrees and edicts, provided for a fiscal review commission to be appointed every five years to examine the state of revenue allocation. Since the Binns Commission was established in 1964, a review was due in 1969. However, the high level of dissatisfaction expressed, especially from the North (which more or less was still considered a block and the exigencies of the period — military rule, civil war, states creation — all demanded a thorough review and preferably a readjustment of the whole revenue allocation system. So in 1968, a year short of the recommended date, the Federal Military Government set up a new fiscal review panel consisting entirely of Nigerians for the first time.

The interim revenue allocation review committee, 1968

The review board, named the Interim Revenue Allocation Review Committee had as its chairman the late Chief I.O. Dina, an economist and senior public administrator and was given these terms of reference;

(a) Look into and suggest any change in the existing system of revenue allocation as a whole. This includes all forms of revenue going to each Government besides and including the Distributable Pool.

(b) Suggest new revenue resources both for the Federal and State Governments; and

(c) Report findings within four months.[33]

These were the first terms of reference since 1946 that were drawn up solely by the central authority without any input from any of the constituent states.

Though the Supreme Military Council, which was the major policy-making organ for the country, was composed of the state governors, they were appointed by and thus owed allegiance to the center. Moreover, being military men or members of the police force (with the exception of Mr. Ukpabi Asika, Administrator of East-Central State), they "were under an obligation to accept the ruling of their military superior" [34]

The Dina Commission (after its chairman), despite its narrow terms of reference and the obvious interim nature of the panel, took it upon itself to carry out a major overhaul of the entire fiscal system. It critically examined the past allocation systems and rejected them all on the basis that, previous fiscal arrangements seemed to have depended too much on political and constitutional developments. That had prevented them from utilizing operational allocation principles and had, therefore, made planning for national integration and fiscal administration problematic.[35] According to the panel, revenue allocation should be, the essence of an overall financial and economic settlement in which all the governments are motivated and geared to the integrated national economy within the context of a truly united Nigeria.[36]

Based on that conviction and viewing the uneven development of the country as an example of a non-integrated national economy brought about by politically motivated revenue allocation policies, the committee recommended certain measures that would "attempt to solve the problem of national integration through fiscal allocations and outside of politics."[37] Those measures included a uniform income tax rate; the harmonization of pricing and policies of the Marketing Boards; the assumption by the Federal Government of full responsibility for some matters on the Concurrent Legislative list, such as higher education and scientific and industrial research, and the making of conditional grants to the states for health and transport.[38]

Although the civil war was still going on, the Dina Committee felt that there was "a new spirit of unity to which the nation is dedicated,"[39] apparently referring to the united and concerted effort made by the rest of the country to defeat the goal of the secessionists. Therefore, the committee reasoned that, it is in the spirit of this new found unity that we have viewed all the sources of revenue of this country as the common funds of the country to be used for executing the kinds of programme which can maintain this unity.[40]

One of the major sources of revenue in the country was oil, and the states in which it was produced were entitled to 50 percent of the mining rents and royalties, to the resentment of other states. Since all sources of revenue were to be viewed as common funds, the Dina Committee put great emphasis on the redistribution of those oil revenues. For the first time, a distinction was made between off-shore and on-shore oil revenues. That could be attributed to the fact that the eruption of the civil war made on-shore oil drilling

133

precarious and forced oil companies to shift their operations off-shore. The oil revenues were to be allocated as follows:

(1) On-shore mining rents — still to be retained by states of origin.
(2) On-shore mining royalties —
     (a) 15% — Federal Government
     (b) 10% — States of Origin
     (c) 5%   — Special Grants Account, established to finance special emergency and contingency needs
     (d) 70% — States Joint Account (new name for DPA, designed to avoid divisive image of the word 'distributable' in DPA)
(3) Off-shore mining rents and royalties —
     (a) 60% — Federal Government
     (b) 30% — States Joint Account
     (c) 10% — Special Grants Account[41]

Committed to restructuring the imbalance among the States, the fiscal panel stressed the use of revenue principles that in its opinion addressed fiscal needs in the sharing of the States Joint Account (SJA). Those principles chosen were basic needs, minimum national standards, balanced development and derivation. The special Grants Account was to be distributed among the states, using tax effort, balanced development and national interest as criteria.[42]

The net effect of the formula wold have been to drastically reduce the revenues obtained by the oil producing states, whose shares received through derivation had already decreased from 50 percent to 10 percent.[43] However, proceeds from Marketing Boards, also allocated on the basis of derivation, was not included in the redistribution scheme. That was probably because, compared with oil revenues, the amount of income from agricultural products was insignificant.

The Dina Report was submitted in January 1969 and circulated to all the states for consideration. In April, Commissioners of Finance from all over the federation met and deliberated over the Report. According to them, the expert panel "exceeded its powers and in many respects, ignored its terms of reference."[44] Therefore, the recommendations were rejected. The Federal Military Government, on the other hand, made no official comment on the fate of the Report, and no White Paper was issued, as was usually the case.

The allegation by the Finance Commissioners had some validity, in that the fiscal board was warned, during its preliminary meeting with the Permanent Secretary, Federal Ministry of Finance, that the terms of reference were deliberately made restrictive because "the fundamental structure of the present revenue allocation system should not be changed until a Constituent Assembly had met."[45] Nevertheless, the Dina Commission reinterpreted and expanded those directives and examined the "larger question of federalism in Nigeria rather than merely that of revenue sharing."[46] Going through the objectives raised by some of the states, one finds that the 'new spirit of unity' on which the Committee based its suggestions was not shared by all interested parties. It was still fledgling and had not been assimilated by a nation being ravaged by an internecine civil war. The reference to 'common funds', 'uniform taxes' and the continued downgrading of the derivation principle was, to say the least, controversial, revolutionary and too far ahead of its time.[47]

In the early years of the military government, most of the ministerial positions were manned by civilians. The members of the finance panel who scrutinized the Dina Report and found it wanting were civilians, many of whom had been active politicians in the First Republic (the panel was headed by the late Chief Obafemi Awolowo, who was then Federal Minister of Finance). The attempt to determine a Revenue Allocation formula without resort to political and constitutional considerations was anathema to those politicians. They had hoped that the military regime would be short-lived and that a return to civilian rule could put them in a position to influence the next fiscal review board through selection of members and terms of reference.[48] That the regional politicians were able to exert enough pressure on the Federal Military Government to prevent the immediate adoption of the recommendations was basically due to the dependence of the military regime on those seasoned politicians. They played a crucial role in policy-making and thus were almost indispensable to the military leaders who needed able administrators to run the country while they concentrated on prosecuting the war.[49] Until the war ended in January 1970, deference was shown to those politicians in matters of public policy formation,[50] and revenue allocation was no exception.

Another reason often cited as having possibly contributed to the rejection of the Dina Report was that the all-Nigerian composition of the panel might have "raised suspicion of a partial and interested arbitrator."[51] Though the members were all men of high academic and professional standing (four were university teachers and five including the chairman, were able public administrators), and thus compared favorably with the all-European boards of pre-military days, Nigerians were not yet used to seeing indigenous experts tackling controversial issues. The image of the apolitical colonial administrator has been imprinted on the minds of many people, especially when it is reinforced by scholars who write that:

> They (colonial administrators) did not meddle in politics, and they kept up the ideal of a politically neutral civil service. They were also

apolitical in that they never participated in the indigenous political life of the countries in which they served.[52]

As far as Nigeria was concerned, and revenue allocation policy making in particular, those colonial and post-colonial European administrators were far from being politically neutral. Those who served in the colonial service were aptly described as political officers,[53] and they were subjected to various types of political influences — above from the British government and below from Nigerian political leaders. But the myth of the unbiased expatriate still persists. The only advantage he could have over the Nigerian expert might be his disinterestedness. Whatever the case may be, Nigerian politicians were so full of mutual mistrust that they never appointed an indigenous panel. It took a military government to break that mold, and all-Nigerian commissions flourished during the military era and have continued to this day.

As an expert body, the Dina Committee satisfied its client — the Federal Military Government. Though its recommendations were rejected by the civilian group, they were praised as being of "high quality and objective nature" and actively embraced by a select group of key Permanent Secretaries which emerged as members of a post-war inner caucus that enjoyed primacy in the formulation of public policy.[54] That group wanted it, and within the next five years the Dina proposals were adopted, albeit piecemeal, by the Federal Military Government.

Fiscal adjustments through decrees

General Gowon, upon assumption of office after the second coup in July 1966, stated categorically that for Nigeria to survive as a united polity it must remain a federal system but one with a strong central government[55] and issued decrees to that effect. The emergencies of the civil war further enhanced the formal power and prestige of the federal government, which relegated to itself several functions and responsibilities. The expanded federal role in the social and economic life of the country required higher and higher levels of central spending.[56] Having kept Nigeria one as it promised, the post-war military administration began to assert its powers. The "centralizing trend in the distribution of power and expenditure"[57] continued and the states which had hitherto retained some of the old regional ideas of autonomy (as evidenced by the rejection of the Dina Report), realized how much of that autonomy had eroded as power was delegated to them by a central army command. Thus, one had a political system which remained federal in form but with a preponderant, almost hegemonic central government. It was in such a system that the Dina Committee recommendations came to be implemented.

Policy-makers have been known sometimes to reject ostentatiously experts' findings because of unfavorable political conditions. Those suggestions are usually filed away until the situation becomes more conducive to their acceptance.[58] That was exactly what the Federal Government did as regards the Dina Report. Since it already had in mind what changes it wanted to introduce into the Nigerian fiscal system, the central authority did not want to deal with politicians again. Instead, it relied on the "military's directness, swiftness and assured lack of opposition" which often produced "an electrifying effect on operational efficiencies,"[59] by issuing various decrees to effect those changes it deemed necessary.

The first of such decrees in the after-war set up was the Constitution (Distributable Pool Account) Decree No. 13 of 1970, proclaimed soon after the civil war, and made retroactive to April 1, 1969. The Decree sought to shift the bulk of centrally collected revenues to the Federal Government. Table 6.1 shows the major changes in the distribution system.

Table 6.1
Highlights of decree no. 13 of 1970

	Source of Revenue	Old Formula (May '67)	New Formula (April '69)
(1)	Export duties	100% = States (derivation)	60% = States 40% = DPA
(2)	Excise duties (tobacco and fuel only)	100% = States	50% = FMG 50% = DPA
(3)	Mining rents and royalties	50% = States 35% = DPA 15% = FMG	45% = States 50% = DPA 5% = FMG
(4)	Petroleum tax	N/A	100% = FMG

FMG = Federal Military Government
DPA = Distributable Pool Account
N/A = Not Applicable

Source: *Federal Government of Nigeria*, Decree No. 13, 1970.

As can be seen, the Central Government had started to share in certain revenues such as excise duties on tobacco and fuel which were once limited to the states only. But more significant was the petroleum profits tax that had become the "single most important source of revenue," accounting for about 40 percent of the Federal Government recurrent revenue.[60] However, that huge source of revenue was denied to the states.

The other important effect of the Decree was the change of allocation formula in sharing the DPA among the states. Instead of using two criteria for different parts of the country, the principles of equality and population were to be applied uniformly. Half of the Pool would be shared equally and the other half would be allocated on the basis of population. That signified the end of the regional pattern of allocation; states now obtained their allocated shares based on their population, not dependent on which region they were originally part of.[61] The principle of derivation had been relegated to the bottom, while those of Need (population) and Even Development (equality of states) had become prominent.

Perhaps due to the military nature of the government and the need of the Central Government to increase its financial resources to reconstruct and rehabilitate a war-torn country, the various states did not offer any loud objections to that or subsequent Decrees.[62]

The next one was Off-Shore Revenues Decree No. 9 of 1971 in which an even more critical change was made. The Decree stated that the "ownership of Nigeria's continental shelf was vested in the Federal Military Government"; therefore, it would collect all the rents and royalties of all off-shore oil mines.[63] Since off-shore production had increased greatly due to the civil war, that Decree deprived oil-producing states of the substantive revenue that accrued to them. With those two decrees, the Dina recommendation of transferring huge revenues from the states to the center had been fulfilled.[64]

By 1976, ten years after the military takeover, the whole structure of inter-governmental fiscal relationship had been transformed. Through the promulgation of Constitution (Financial Provision, etc.) Decree No. 6 of 1975, the Distributable Pool Account became the major channel of sharing revenues among the states. Into it were paid all the revenues to be allocated to the states, except 20 percent of on-shore mining rents and royalties which was allowed to still be shared via the derivation principle. Thus, the DPA was fattened by 80 percent of on-shore mining rents and royalties; 35 percent of import duties on all goods except fuel, tobacco and liquor; 100 percent of duties on fuel, liquor and tobacco; 50 percent of all excise duties; and 100 percent of export duties on produce, hides and skin.[65] The Federal Government also decided to "surrender its entire share of both on-shore and off-shore royalties into the DPA."[66] Once again, the Pool was to be shared on the same basis equally — Population and Equality of States.

With that Decree, the principle of derivation was virtually eliminated from the revenue allocation system. (No reason was given for retaining the principle to share 20 percent of on-shore oil rents and royalties. Maybe the Federal Government felt that being the sources of the national wealth, those states deserved a little more of the revenue than others; also, they did suffer tremendously from environmental hazards associated with oil production. At that time, there was no national policy dealing with such matters as oil spills, population displacements, etc.) Decree No. 6 of 1975 also had the effect of increasing the amount of statutory revenue to the state governments, but their proportion of federal revenue actually declined. That was because the most productive and fastest growing source of federal revenue — the petroleum profit tax — was excluded from the allocation system. By 1975, the tax made up almost 66 percent of federal revenue.[67] The tremendous growth in oil revenues during the period meant that the Federal Government was able to run surplus and in order to aid the state governments who were not sharing in the boom, it instituted a system of conditional grants.

In addition to the decrees affecting the revenue allocation system directly, the Federal Military Government embarked on policies that affected on the fiscal system as a whole. It issued the Income Tax Management (Uniform Taxation Provisions, etc.) Decree No. 7 of 1975, by which income tax rates and allowances were centralized and standardized, thus removing state governments from tax jurisdiction. Another change in the fiscal structure was the reform of the Marketing Board system. Earlier in 1968, the Central Bank of Nigeria had taken over the financing of the Boards from commercial banks.[68] Then in 1973, the Federal government arrogated to itself the power to fix producer prices and later abolished export duties, and sales taxes on produce handled by the Boards;[69] thus eliminating the surpluses usually kept by Regional (state) governments and used for a variety of purposes. Later in 1977, the regionalized Marketing Boards, the source of independent revenue for states, were federalized and reconstituted into seven national Commodity Boards.[70] So, as Douglas Rimmer put it,

> The importance in the economic life of the country of those great regional institutions, the Marketing Boards, has lessened and they have been placed under federal control.[71]

It was not only the Marketing Boards that came under federal control; other state functions also did, such as education, where the Federal Government introduced and largely financed the Universal Primary Education scheme and also began to run the university system as well, health, roads, even sports, were all taken over by the Federal Government.

The effects of all those changes in the fiscal system was to strengthen the financial position of the Federal Government. The government at the federal level became the Center, "the fountain of unprecedented public wealth far in excess of any local resources."[72] That was largely due to the explosion in the price of petroleum and the position it occupied in the economy. While oil was only 58 percent of the exports and accounted for only 26.3 percent of total revenue in 1970, six years later, in 1976, oil dominated the export sector—a whopping 94 percent of all exports, and contributed almost 80 percent of total national revenues. As Table 6.2 shows, all through the post-war period, oil revenue was the most important source of income for the Federal Government. And since it kept the Petroleum Profit Tax (80 percent of oil revenues) to itself, the Central Government increasingly dominated the fiscal relations of the country.

Table 6.2

Federal government revenue from crude oil, 1969-80
(in millions)

Year	Total Federal Revenue	Revenue From Oil*	Oil Revenue As % of Total Revenue
1969	378.4	33.4	8.8
1970	633.2	166.4	26.3
1971	1,169.0	510.2	43.6
1972	1,404.8	764.3	54.4
1973	1,695.3	1,016.0	59.9
1974	4,537.0	3,726.7	82.1
1975	5,514.7	4,271.5	77.5
1976	6,765.9	5,365.2	79.3
1977	8,042.4	6,080.6	75.6
1978	7,371.1	4,654.1	63.1
1979	10,913.1	8,880.8	81.4
1980	15,523.4	12,353.8	79.6

* Oil Revenue = Petroleum Profit Tax and Mining Rent, Royalties, Fees

Source: Central Bank of Nigeria, *Economic and Financial Review*. Vol. 13 (Dec. 1975), p. 81, Vol. 20, (June 1982), p. 74.

Another result of the new fiscal system was that state governments became less dependent on export duty revenues but more so on statutory allocations from the Center. Being shielded from the uncertainties of the produce world and assured financial stability by the Federal Government,[73] states had to lose the financial autonomy they so jealously guarded.[74] The grants system that was established tied the states to the apron strings of the Federal Government. In addition, the centralization of income taxes and Marketing Boards eroded the independent sources of revenue of the states, reducing them to little more than fiscal vassals of the Center.

The Military Government was able to issue far-reaching decrees and proposal that in effect emasculated the states and that could be attributed to three causes. First was the tremendous growth in oil revenues and its effects as explained above. Secondly, the command structure of the government gave the states little opportunity to complain. By that time, there had obtained what might be referred to as a 'subordinate-superordinate relationship' between the states and the Federal Government.[75] Even military governors who felt dissatisfied with the fiscal arrangements could not muster enough courage to speak out for fear of being branded 'enemy of unity'. Whether "unity actually existed or not, at least, there was a growing feeling of national identity. Thirdly, most of the old regional political leaders who were part of the Gowon regime at its onset, had withdrawn from public office having realized that military rule was not a temporary situation."[76]

The new civilian administrators in the military government were largely not linked to the old regional order and together with the 'super permanent secretaries' that run the civil service,[77] expressions of regional sentiments were not welcome in Lagos. When, at a conference of Permanent Secretaries of Finance, the issue of oil revenue and its allocation was being debated and the oil-producing States of Mid-West and Rivers asked for larger retention of mining royalties, they were reminded that soldiers from all over the country died to liberate those states from the clutches of Ojukwu; therefore, the revenue from oil produced in those states should become common revenue and be shared among all the states.[78] A similar* type of response was given by the Military Governor of the Mid-West State to placate his citizens whose share of revenue was greatly reduced by Decree No. 6 of 1975. He said:

The new allocation formula was agreed upon by Nigerian rulers in the overall interest of the country...the nation's interest should take precedence over that of the State.[79]

Thus, the Federal Military Government "asserted itself as a unifying force"[80] and either coerced or cajoled the states into accepting a centralized fiscal system.

The development of an integrated economy was the main purpose of the Dina Committee when it made what then seemed like controversial recommendations. By gradually adopting and implementing those suggestions, the Federal Military Government could be said to have succeeded in integrating the governmental machinery, especially in the fiscal area. That achievement was explicitly manifested in the statement by the federal government;

> The country as a whole constitutes a single economic system and so long as this system is viable, the viability of the component units can be assured through the normal process of exchanges and the redistributive actions of the Federal Government.[81]

After the implementation of Decree No. 6 of 1975, critical constitutional and administrative developments with bearing on the fiscal system of the country took place. At the top of the list was the establishment of a new military regime in July 1975 after another successful coup d'etat. The political structure of the country was altered as nineteen states were created out of the original twelve; further reducing both the economic and political power and resources from the individual states. With the recognition of local governments as the "third tier of governmental activity" in 1976 vesting in them the authority to govern at the local level,[82] the Federal Government further diminished any political or economic leverage the states might have. As independent units of government, those local governments needed autonomous sources of revenue, different from the states, to carry out their responsibilities. By their very recognition, the Military Government introduced a new variable into the revenue allocation system. Instead of dividing revenues between two levels of governments, now the scheme involved a third level.

Meanwhile, a Constitutional Drafting Committee set up in 1976, had included in its Draft Constitution a suggestion that a permanent fiscal review commission be established to "keep the federal fiscal system and the financial relations between the federation and the states under constant review and to propose from time to time a formula for the allocation of revenue among the states and between the Federal Government and the states."[83] Moreover, since the Dina Report was officially rejected, there had not been a written set of proposals beyond the decrees, to guide the government in forging a new fiscal policy in view of the changes mentioned above. Therefore, as part of its political program, the Federal Military Government decided to appoint a fiscal review panel. The government hoped that the political environment in which the controversial Dina Report was discarded, had improved, since civilian rule was already in the air. Also the military authority wanted to use the opportunity to hand over to the new anticipated civilian administration, not only a constitution, but also a working revenue allocation system that would incorporate and, therefore, legitimize all the fiscal edicts and decrees issued over the thirteen years of military rule.

The Technical Committee on revenue allocation, 1977

The new fiscal review board, seventh in the line of revenue allocation commissions, and once again composed entirely of Nigerians, was inaugurated in July 1977. Its six-man panel consisted of four economists, one political scientists, and the managing director of one of Nigeria's leading daily newspapers. The chairman was Professor O. Aboyade, a former head of the Economics Department at the University of Ibadan and one-time Vice-Chancellor (President) of the University of Ife. Given the politicized nature of revenue allocation, the Military Government believed that gathering a group of such highly skilled, ostensibly apolitical experts into a 'technical committee' would depoliticize the issue and reduce it to an "exercise in statistical projection and quantification."[84] A formula wrought by objective technical experts who presumably were free of political prejudices would, it was hoped, appeal to the public at large. With that as the background, the Committee was given the following terms of reference:

> Taking into consideration the need to ensure that each government of the federation has adequate revenue to enable it to discharge its responsibilities and having regard to the factors of population, equality of states, geographical peculiarities, even development, the national interest and any other factors bearing on the problem, the Committee should:
>
> (a)   examine the present revenue allocation formula with a formula with a view to determining its adequacy in light of the factors mentioned above and representations from the Federal Government and the State Governments and other interested parties;
>
> (b)   following the findings in (a) recommend new proposals as necessary for the allocation of revenue as between the Federal, State, as well as the Local Governments;

(c)   make whatever recommendations are considered necessary for the effective collection and distribution of Federal and State revenues.[85]

Examining those terms of references reveals that, despite its technical nature, the Committee came under certain pressures. First, several specific principles of allocation, all previously used at one time or another were named, signifying a special preference for them by the military authority. That those criteria were not novel suggests a reluctance on the part of the government to break entirely with past civilian experiences. After all, the new Report was to be debated and adopted by a civilian Constituent Assembly, and non-military rule was imminent. The military wished those principles to be included in any new formula, but in such a sophisticated and scientific way that they would not evoke as much criticism as before. Once again, experts were being asked to utilize their knowledge for the support and promotion of particular policy goals of decision-makers,[86] just as almost all the other fiscal review panels had been requested to do, directly or indirectly. The very imposition of those restricted and value-laden terms of reference could be interpreted as an attempt to justify political motives in rational technical terms.[87]

One rather interesting observation about the terms of reference was the request to ensure that each government of the Federation has adequate revenue to enable it to discharge its responsibilities. That was the first time a fiscal review panel had been mandated specifically to correlate constitutional functions with resource allocation. The allocation of distinct functions and corresponding adequate sources of revenue to the different levels of government is one of the factors theoretically essential to financial arrangements in a federation.[88] The Nigerian military government had been operating a de facto unitary government in a federal setting; for it to suggest allocating revenues on the basis of constitutional responsibilities[89] — one of the basic tenets of orthodox fiscal federalism — was significant and pointed to their foresight. They were actually proposing a new fiscal system for the incoming civilian government which they hoped would change the unitary status of the political system to a genuine federal one. Tied to that was the request that the newly created local governments be given fiscal autonomy, to enable them to carry out their responsibilities. So, instead of dealing with two levels of government as the previous commissions had, the Technical Committee had to grapple with three seemingly autonomous governmental units with varying political and financial status and power.

The Aboyade Committee, as it was called, realized that its recommendations would be utilized, not by the military government that appointed it, but by a future civilian government. Therefore, it decided to go beyond its limiting terms of reference and examine the whole military system, especially its allocation of formal responsibilities. The Committee indicted the Federal Government for its "seemingly inexorable march to centralism"[90] and recommended that it give up and transfer back to the state and local governments, those functions like agriculture, housing, education, and health that the central government had appropriated over the years. In fact, it was suggested that the system should return to the 1963 constitutional position, in terms of division of function between the levels of government, with suitable amendments to accommodate the new local government set up.[91] The state and local governments were advised to make greater effort to generate internal revenue through more efficient taxation. By that time, states were dependent on statutory allocations from the Federal Government for up to 80 percent of their aggregate recurrent revenue.[92]

It is rather unusual for a fiscal review body composed of mainly academic economists to recommend a redistribution of constitutional functions and responsibilities in the political system; more so when a Constitutional Assembly was about to debate a Draft Constitution. This showed an independence of thought by those experts. However, the Aboyade Committee felt that for it to assign adequate revenue to the different levels of government, it had to examine the delineation of functions between them because that serves as a basis for tax jurisdiction and independent revenue sources. As an author put it, "If the distribution of functions does not generate adequate independent revenue, a principal canon of federalism, i.e., fiscal independence, is in jeopardy."[93] And so the Committee decided, in the name of fiscal efficiency and economy, to carry out its brand of constitution making.[94]

Having re-assigned functions and responsibilities to the different tiers of government, the Committee set out to devise an inter-governmental allocation system. It was with regards to the formula that the Committee differed from its predecessors. Two major innovations were established; first was the suggestion that all federally collected revenues (with the exception of income tax of the Armed Forces, External Affairs personnel and the new Federal Capital Territory which would be retained by the Center) be consolidated into one account. That was a departure from the earlier formulas where "specific revenue sources had been earmarked for different governments."[95] The account, titled the Nigerian General Revenue Fund, was to be shared among the three tiers of government on the basis of budget needs (recurrent and capital) and national interest. The reason behind the consolidated account was to allow all levels of government to "share in the rapidly expanding revenue sources...the conditions for which collection they all helped to create."[96] Thus, states could share in the proceeds of the petroleum profits tax — once a monopoly of the Federal Government. Based on the newly assigned

145

constitutional functions and tax jurisdictions, and without any explanation as to how those functions could be quantified, the Committee distributed the new account as follows:

Federal Government	57%
*States Joint Account	30%
Local Government Fund	10%
Special Grants Account	3%
(to be administered by the Federal	
Government for benefit of mineral	
producing areas)	

*   The States Joint Account, SJA, was the new designation for the Distributable Pool Account.

In addition to the 10 percent from the Center, Local Governments were also to receive an additional 10 percent from each State's total revenue (that is, statutory receipts plus independent revenue). The extra revenue from the States was to commit them to "the survival and flourishing of the newly revised Local Government System."[97]

The Aboyade Committee lived up to its full title in dealing with interstate allocations. It presented its recommendations in the most technical manner, full of complex economic terms and intricate mathematical calculations. The review panel initially carried out a systematic analysis of each and every principle of revenue allocation ever used in Nigeria; and like the Dina Committee, on which Professor Aboyade served, rejected all of them for one major defect or the other, describing them as fissiparous.[98] Some of them were discarded for being "analytically ambiguous and almost technically impossible to operationalize in any meaningful way." Those included in that category were 'Even Development' and 'National Interest'. The principle of 'Need' was regarded as an 'omnibus' concept which could only be useful if it were split into its component parts; 'Equality of States' was seen as a legal and metaphysical concept which did not have budgetary or developmental requirements; and the notion of 'Geographical Peculiarities', in the Committee's opinion, defied any concise definition.[99] As regards 'Population', the panel argued that the use of absolute, raw, unweighted and often dubious figures did not measure the relative fiscal or economic needs of the country; rather, it gave the "erroneous and unhealthy impression that the sharing of the national cake is more important than the baking of it."[100] In the same vein, 'Derivation', the principle that had "evoked more rivalry and bitterness than any other," was rejected outright. In the words of the Committee,

The principle of derivation has little or no place in a cohesive fiscal system for national political and social development.... There is no principle of revenue allocation which has done more to poison inter-governmental relations and hamper a sense of national unity as the principle of derivation. The principle lacks the potency as a tool of fiscal discretion, at least within the context of a dynamic development policy. Besides, it denies the Federal Government the power to effect inter-state redistribution of income.[101]

The Committee then went ahead and recommended a whole new set of criteria — a scheme described by a critic as 'a pursuit of novelty.'[102] They were:

(1)   Equality of Access to Development Opportunities
(2)   National Minimum Standards for National Integration
(3)   Absorptive Capacity
(4)   Independent Revenue and Minimum Tax Effort
(5)   Fiscal Efficiency

In order to quantify and meaningfully understand those criteria, the Committee identified what it termed 'National Norm' and 'State Norm', all within the context of the 1975-80 National Plan allocation. The 'National Norm' measured the relative share of a particular sector in the total plan allocation; while the 'State Norm' was the level of activity in that sector.[103] Mathematically, they can be expressed thus:

Y_f = Total Federal Plan Allocation
Y_s = Total State Plan Allocation
X_{fa} = Total Federal Plan Allocation to Sector A
X_{sa} = Total State Plan Allocation to Sector A

$$State\ Norm\ =\ \frac{X_{sa}}{Y_s}$$

$$Indicator\ for\ Principle\ =\ \frac{X_{sa} + X_{sa}}{Y_s + Y_f}\ -\ \frac{X_{sa}}{Y_s}$$

To measure 'Equality of Access', allocation to economic sector was used, while allocation to social sector was employed to determine score for 'National Minimum Standards'. For the other indicators, the following calculations were used:

Absorptive Capacity Indicator:

$$\frac{\text{State's total actual capital expenditure}}{\text{State's total planned capital expenditure}}$$

Independent Revenue Indicator:

$$\frac{\text{State's Independent Tax Revenue}}{\text{State's recurrent budget}}$$

and Fiscal Efficiency Indicator:

$$\frac{\text{State's estimated personal emolument}[104]}{\text{State's recurrent budget}}$$

The Committee determined that all the principles were not equally important; therefore, weights were assigned to them as follows:

Equality of Access	0.25
National Minimum Standards	0.22
Absorptive Capacity	0.20
Independent Revenue	0.18
Fiscal Efficiency	0.15
Total Weight	1.00

The allocation formula was to be applied only to the incremental changes in the State's Joint Account; that is, whatever was left after allowances had been made for funding existing responsibilities and services, and not to the total absolute sum. Moreover, the weights were to be re-checked and re-calculated on a continual basis.[105]

In its presentation of the new formula, the Aboyade Committee admitted that "there is nothing ultimately scientific about the choice of these weights." But the decision to adopt them was based on "the firm belief that they reflect the qualitative ordering of the various criteria in the contemporary Nigerian setting."[106] How and when that 'qualitative ordering' was established remains to be revealed. Apart from the illogical assignment of weights, the indicators themselves were open to questioning. As a critic saw it, "the primary and fundamental weakness of the Report lies on the fact that the authors based all their measurements on one set of figures — on the Development Plan of 1975-80 and the recurrent budget deriving from the same programme."[107] The Plan was developed before the nineteen states were created, and "the subsequent splitting of a 12-state plan into a 19-state one involves some arbitrariness and cannot be described as a good base for revenue allocation."[108] Moreover, development plans had been known to represent "pious hopes and wide expectations which are unrealistic and unreliable";[109] and are usually products of political compromise.[110] For a review panel that was determined to depoliticize revenue allocation, it was rather unfortunate it had to rely on the development plan which did not have actual performance data but estimates that might have been exaggerated for political expedience.

The dearth of reliable and accurate statistical data in Nigeria is a well known fact, and to devise a formula that was based almost entirely on seemingly endless calculations was foolhardy. As the Raisman Commission (see Chapter V) warned, "In the long run, therefore, it is very desirable to get away from a system under which the distribution of large sums of money rests on calculations that can never be entirely accurate and which, therefore, lend themselves to controversy."[111]

The recommendations of the Aboyade Report were presented to the Federal Military Government which approved them with minor alterations. In the Government's White Paper, the allotted weights were rejected on the grounds that "relative weighing of the five new criteria is a political decision."[112] Otherwise, in spite of the grossly inaccurate statistical data used to derive and calculate those novel criteria, the essence of the Report was accepted, and at the wish of the Supreme Military Council, sent to the Constituent Assembly for a stamp of authenticity. Why the military government, after adopting the Report, decided to forward it to the Constituent Assembly for democratic blessing, remains controversial. It could be that because of the reliance on the new technical criteria, the military authorities felt politics had been removed from revenue allocation, once and for all. That belief was further strengthened when the Aboyade Committee explicitly omitted such vexing and controversial principles as population and derivation — the bane of previous formulas. If the Constituent Assembly had approved of the Report and asserted to the recommendations, then revenue allocation would have been removed from the upcoming electioneering campaigns.[113] The command structure of the military prevented any strong opposition views, especially from the states whose representatives were more committed and obligated to the Center. Whatever final decision the Supreme Military Council made was acquiesced to without much rancor.

The Report, fertilized and nurtured by the military but presented to the civilian Constituent Assembly for final approval, met with disastrous results. What both the experts and the military government forgot was that the political climate in Nigeria then was being recharged with partisan political fervor. There was not enough 'goodwill and national feeling' among the 'assembly of future politicians' to approve the Report.[114] Instead, after a very lengthy and acrimonious debate, they merely noted it. The ostensible reason given was that the Report, with all its esoteric calculations was incomprehensible. Alhaji A. J. Gana, a member from Dambo'okaga, summed it up thus:

> ... it is too technical, too academic, and cannot be clearly understood by the ordinary man. It cannot even be understood by the elites themselves and much less by the ordinary man in the street. Well, it can go to the technicians. Even our economic wizard, Dr. Pius Okigbo, finds it difficult to understand or to explain it to us what the Committee had produced.[115]

Earlier, Dr. Pius Okigbo, an economist and also member of the Constituent Assembly, had enunciated in a very lengthy and lucid monologue, the complicated nature and demerits of the Report.[116] He examined each of the five criteria recommended for inter-state revenue sharing and found all of them unacceptable, the major reason being that they were too technical and it would be almost impossible to operationalize them. Yet, it was precisely for the same reasons of ambiguity and non-operationability that the 'old principles' were discarded. As Dr. Okigbo put it,

> the effort to condemn one criterion in order to introduce another novel criterion seems to me far too tortuous for the layman.[117]

The complex nature of the Report prompted a columnist for the Kaduna-based *New Nigerian* newspaper to lambaste economists. In a diatribe he wrote:

> The most powerful group in our decision-making structure today is that constituted by economists...They are famous for guiding and misguiding the political leadership with their piles of figures, computer printouts, pious assumptions about 'relevant parameters' and passionate appeals to us to believe that 'ceteris' is always 'paribus'...I do not know what they have in their neatly-packaged revenue allocation formula but I already suspect the worst from the quibble in their opening salvo....[118]

The Aboyade Technical committee was in a quandary; though it was appointed by the military, its ultimate client was the politicians. Therefore, it must have been difficult to devise a formula that would have pleased both of them. However, it was in anticipation of a civilian administration that the whole exercise was carried out, so the Committee should have realized that. Even the military government acknowledged it and inserted the 'old principles' in the terms of reference given to the Committee. But they either forgot or chose to ignore the fact that when experts, recruited to help formulate public policy, violate the interests and sentiments of the policy-makers (or potential policy-makers as the case here) by going beyond the parameters set for them, their findings are bound to come under attack.[119] Though the military government did not think the fiscal experts over-stepped their boundaries, the civilians certainly thought so. One of the members of the Assembly, Alhaji Shehu Shagari (who was later elected president of the country) echoed the sentiments of the delegates when he said:

> . . . this Committee had already made up its mind on what to bring, it set aside all the suggestions and it even set aside some of the terms of reference.[120]

And on rejecting the specific principles of allocation explicitly mentioned in the directives, Shagari epitomized the attitude as:

> I would liken this Committee to an arrogant architect who had been commissioned to design a house but would not accept the instructions or wishes of the owner of the house, because he considers them either out-dated, out of fashion, not good enough, or not original. So the architect brings his own ideas.[121]

Therefore, the potential owners of the Nigerian fiscal house refused to accept the product from the architects of what Shagari termed, the 'Professor Aboyade's Technical Committee of Intellectual Arrogance'.[122]

Although the fiscal review bouard came under such assault and verbal barrage for ignoring the 'old principles', a critical examination of the Report showed that they were not completely abandoned, just couched in sophisticated and scientific language so that they would not arouse such passions as they usually did. That is one way policy-makers use experts to obfuscate their political intentions, although the attempt here misfired. The new criteria of, 'Equality of Access' and 'National Minimum Standard' "attempt to respond to a government's 'need' for revenue in both an absolute and a relative sense." Also, those principles would have "operational meaning only when some

151

reference is made to the size of the population within such a government's jurisdiction." Likewise, 'Absorptive Capacity' can be understood in terms of a State's or Local Government's ability to expend revenue wisely, an act that depends partly on the size of its population.[123] Unfortunately for the Aboyade Committee, such deeper and convoluted meaning escaped the Constituent Assembly and the public at large.

The Constituent Assembly, aptly titled 'assembly of future politicians' was composed of members, most of whom were elected in the first 'federal elections' since the army took power twelve years ago. With the anticipation of civilian rule in the very near future, those individuals geared their political behavior toward the goal of becoming part of the on-coming new regime. They saw their future and fortunes being made in the new political system whose framework they were constructing; therefore, they owed no obligation to the present military authority. Being potential politicians, who were already jockeying for position, they had agonizingly scrutinized almost every controversial issue about the political future of the country that came before them. From the tedious debated and fights over those issues, bargains had been struck on matters ranging from creation of more states to a formula for elections. It was into that hot political cauldron brimming with personal and burning ambitions that the Aboyade Report was thrown in. Dr. Omo Omoruyi, a member of both the Constituent Assembly and the fiscal review board, was chosen to present the Report. His selection may have contributed to the rejection of the recommendation. In the first place, when critics attacked the Report, he unwisely and rather arrogantly questioned the competence of the Assembly to produce a better substitute. But more importantly, Dr. Omoruyi was not regarded as a politically neutral person who could convince the Assembly of the Report's objectivity. His political ambitions and biases were shown during earlier debated in the Assembly.[124] As a founding member of a fledgling political organization called Club 19, the precursor of the Nigerian Peoples Party, NNP, his actions and votes were perceived as those sanctioned by his neophyte political party. Though parties were still prohibited, Nigerians had, by 1977, aggregated their interests into several organizations that later metamorphosed into genuine parties when the ban was lifted, and Club 19, to which Omoruyi belonged, was one of the most active.[125] The chairman of the fiscal committee, Professor Aboyade, had earlier rejected an offer to present the Report, but the chances were that he could not have fared better. He, too, would have been suspect because Aboyade was one of those academics who were regarded as pro-military intellectuals. He was a member of the Interim Revenue Allocation Committee, 1969, and had held other positions including a Vice Chancellorship of a university during the military regime (right now, he is engaged in an advisory role to the new military government under General

Ibrahim Babangida). And most of the Assembly's elected members were not sympathetic to the military.[126]

Beyond the presumed arrogance and bias of the Report and its writers, beyond the complexity and technicality of the recommendations, beyond the timing of the presentation (after divisive debates about Sharia courts and Presidential election formula which drove a deep wedge among the members), and beyond the manner of presentation, the Report of the Technical Committee on Revenue Allocation would still have been rejected by the members of the Constituent Assembly on the ground that it was regarded not as a "technical report to be digested, approved and rubber-stamped" as the military wished, but as a political presentation.[127] It was from a political viewpoint that it was analyzed and eventually not accepted. Revenue Allocation has always been a political issue; if not the actual contents of the policy, then the terms of reference were usually products of mutual concessions made by politicians while forging new constitutions. The military, over the last twelve years, had preempted that procedure, and the politicians had bided their time waiting for an opportunity to have their influences felt in the fiscal policy-making arena of the country. Therefore, to those Assembly members, most of whom were poised on becoming actively involved in the upcoming civilian administration, there was the belief that political compromise should form the bed-rock of every public policy, especially one as essential as revenue allocation. For them to accept a report whose terms of reference were decided, not through debate, but by a military command on its way out, went against the grain.

It has been suggested that the group of Assembly members which vehemently opposed the Report represented a clique of intellectuals whose antagonistic economic and political viewpoints were consistent with the opinion of most of the members from the Northern and Eastern States.[128] Looking at the later careers of those people could lend some credence to the allegation. The most outspoken of them, Dr. Pius Okigbo, was later named to chair the next revenue allocation panel. Others like Shagari, became members of the National Party of Nigeria, NPN, which eventually won the national elections in 1979. Shagari himself was then elected President of the Republic and appointed Okigbo to the panel. So the Constituent Assembly was really the preparatory school for the future political leaders of the country.

Notes

1. Lloyd, P.C., 'The Ethnic Background in the Nigerian Crisis', in Panter-Brick, S.K. (ed.), *Nigerian Politics and Military Rule: Prelude to Civil War*. (London: The Althone Press, 1970), pp. 10-11.

2. For details of events during this period, see Chapter II.

3. Whiteman, K., 'Enugu: The Psychology of Secession, 20 July 1966 to 30 May 1967', in S.K. Panter-Brick, op. cit., p. 117.

4. Ibid., p. 111.

5. Cronje, Suzzane, *The World and Nigeria: The Diplomatic History of the Biafran War, 1967-1970*. (London: Sidgwick & Jackson, Ltd., 1972), p. 20.

6. *West Africa*. (January 21, 1967), p. 93.

7. Panter-Brick, S.K., 'From Military Coup to Civil War, January 1966 to May 1967', in S.K. Panter-Brick, op. cit., pp. 47-48.

8. 'Address by Lt. Col. Ojukwu to The Joint Meeting of the Advisory Committee of Chiefs and Elders and the Constituent Assembly 26 May 1967', in S.K. Panter-Brick, op. cit., Appendix C, p. 222.

9. S.K. Panter-Brick, op. cit., p. 48.

10. Ojukwu, C. Odemagwu, *Biafra: Selected Speeches and Random Thoughts*. (New York: Harper & Row, Publishers, 1969), p.130.

11. Ibid.

12. Ibid., p. 131.

13. Dudley, B.J., Instability and Political Order: Politics and Crisis in Nigeria. (Ibadan: Ibadan University Press, 1973), p. 187.

14. S.K. Panter-Brick, op. cit., p. 49.

15. Ibid.

16. Dudley, B.J., op. cit., p. 187.

17. S. Cronje, op. cit., p. 26.

18. Turner, Louis, *Oil Companies in the International System*. (London: George Allen & Unwin, Ltd., 1978), p. 76.

19. Schwab, Peter (ed.), *Biafra*. (New York: Facts on File, Inc., 1971), p. 15.

20. L. Turner, op. cit., p. 76 (see also S. Cronje, op. cit., pp. 26-37 for details).

21. Lindsay, Kennedy, 'How Biafra Pays for the War,' *Venture*. Vol. 21, No. 3 (March 1969), p. 26.

22. *Daily Times* (Nigeria). August 9, 1967.

23. K. Lindsay, op. cit., p. 26.

24. Mackintosh, John, *Nigerian Government and Politics*. (Evanston, IL: Northwestern University Press, 1966), pp. 604-605 from which the whole paragraph was culled.

25. Ibid., p. 605.

26. Bienen, Henry, *Oil Revenues and Policy Choice in Nigeria*. World Bank Staff Working Papers, No. 592, (Washington, D.C.: The World Bank, 1983), p. 4.

27. Phillips, Adedotun, 'Revenue Allocation in Nigeria, 1970-1980,' *Nigerian Journal of Economic and Social Studies*. Vol. 17, No. 2 (July 1975), p. 4.

28. Olalokun, F. Akin, 'Nigerian Federal Finance: Issues and Choices', in Akinyemi, A.B., P.D., Cole and Walter Ofonagoro (eds.), *Readings on Federalism*. (Lagos: Nigerian Institute of International Affairs, 1979), p. 118.

29. Oyovbaire, Samuel E., 'The Politics of Revenue Allocation', in S. Keith Panter-Brick (ed.), *Soldiers and Oil: The Political Transformation of Nigeria*. (London: Frank Cass & Co., Ltd., 1978), pp. 227-28.

30. Phillips, A., 'Nigeria's Federal Financial Experience,' *Journal of Modern African Studies*. Vol. 19, No. 3 (September 1971), pp. 402-3.

31. S. Oyovbaire, op. cit., p. 228.

32. Ibid., pp. 225-26.

33. *Report of the Interim Revenue Allocation Review*. (Lagos: Nigerian National Press, Ltd., 1968), p. 1 (to be referred to as the *Dina Report*).

34. Dudley, Billy, *An Introduction to Nigerian Government and Politics*. (Bloomington, IN: Indiana University Press, 1982), p. 91.

35. *Dina Report*, op. cit., p. 5.

36. Ibid., p. 3.

37. Oyediran, Oyeleye and Olatunji Olagunju, 'The Military and the Politics of Revenue Allocation', in Oyediran, Oyeleye (ed.), *Nigerian Government and Politics Under Military Rule, 1966-79*. (New York: St. Martins Press, 1979), p. 199.

38. S. Oyovbaire, op. cit., p. 240.

39. *Dina Report*, op. cit., p. 2.

40. Ibid.

41. Ibid., chapter 8.

42. *Report of the Presidential Commission on Revenue Allocation*. Vol. 1. (Lagos: Federal Government Press, 1980), p. 20 (to be referred to as the *Okigbo Report*).

43. Billy Dudley, op. cit., p. 258.

44. *Okigbo Report*, op. cit., p. 20.

45. *Daily Times* (Nigeria). April 12, 1969.

46. Rupley, Lawrence A., 'Revenue Sharing in the Nigerian Federation,' *Journal of Modern African Studies*. Vol. 19, No. 2 (June 1981), p. 262.

47. S. Oyovabaire, op. cit., p. 242.

48. Adamolukun, Lapido, *Politics and Administration in Nigeria*. (Ibadan: Spectrum Books, Ltd., 1986), pp. 106-7.

49. Oyeleye and Olagunju, op. cit., p. 200.

50. L. Adamolukun, op. cit., p. 107.

51. Ayida, A., *The Nigerian Revolution, 1966-1976.* Ibadan: (Ibadan University Press, 1978), p. 9.

52. Eisenstadt, S.N., 'Problems of Emerging Bureaucracies in Developing Areas and New States', in Hoselitz, E.F. and W.E. Moore (eds.), *Industrialization and Society.* (Paris: UNESCO-Mouton, 1963), p. 160.

53. L. Adamolekun, op. cit., p. 110.

54. Odetola, Theophilus O., *Military Politics in Nigeria.* (New Brunswick, NJ: Transaction Books, Inc., 1978), p. 78.

55. Smith, Brian, 'Federal-State Relations in Nigeria,' *African Affairs.* Vol. 80, No. 320 (July 1981), pp. 363-65.

56. Ibid., p. 363.

57. S. Oyovbaire, op. cit., pp. 244-45.

58. Benveniste, Guy, *The Politics of Expertise (2nd ed.).* (San Francisco: Boyd & Fraser Publishing Co., 1977), p. 61.

59. T. Odetola, op. cit., p. 59.

60. A. Phillips, op. cit., p. 404.

61. Ibid.

62. *Okigbo Report*, op. cit., p. 21.

63. L. Rupley, op. cit., p. 264.

64. Oyeleye and Olagunju, op. cit., p. 201.

65. Adedotun Phillips, op. cit., p. 2.

66. Gowon, General Yakubu, '14th Independence Anniversary Speech,' *Nigeria Today.* No. 50 (October 1974). This speech laid the foundation for Decree No. 6 of 1975.

67. Adedotun Phillips, op. cit., p. 8.

68. Muhammadu, Turi and Mohammed Haruna, 'The Civil War', in Oyeleye and Olagunju, op. cit., p. 45.

69. Rimer, Douglas, 'Elements of the Political Economy', in S. Keith Panter-Brick, op. cit., pp. 153-54.

70. L. Rupley, op. cit., p. 264.

71. Douglas Rimer, op. cit., p. 153.

72. Panter-Brick, S. Keith, 'Introduction', in S. Keith Panter-Brick, op. cit., p.3.

73. T. Odetola, op. cit., p. 104.

74. Keith Panter-Brick, op. cit., p. 3.

75. Oyeleye and Olagunju, op. cit., p. 196.

76. Ibid., p. 202.

77. For analysis of the civil service during the military era, see Ladipo Adamolekun, op. cit. and A. Ayida, op. cit.

78. Dent, M.J., 'Corrective Government: Military Rule in Perspective', in S. Keith Panter-Brick, op. cit., pp. 111 & 134.

79. *New Nigerian* (Nigeria). March 15, 1975.

80. Offensend, David, 'Centralization and Fiscal Arrangement in Nigeria,' *Journal of Modern African Studies*. Vol. 14, No. 3 (September 1976), p. 510.

81. *Federal Military Government Views on the Report of the Panel on Creation of States*. (Lagos: Federal Government Press, 1976), p. 13.

82. *Guidelines for Local Government*. (Lagos: Federal Government Press, 1976).

83. *Report of the Constitution Drafting Committee Containing the Draft Constitution*. Vol. 1 (Lagos: Federal Ministry of Information, 1976), pp.xxxiii.

84. Oyeleye and Olagunju, op. cit., p. 204.

85. *Report of the Technical Committee on Revenue Allocation*. Vol. 1 (Lagos: Federal Government Press, 1977), pp. i-iii (to be referred to as the *Aboyade Report*).

86. Mazur, Alan, 'Dispute Among Experts,' *Minerva.* Vol. 11, No. 2 (April 1973), pp. 243-62.

87. G. Benveniste, op. cit., p. 55.

88. Adedeji, A., *Nigerian Federal Finance.* (New York: Africana Publishing Co., Inc., 1969), pp. 10-12.

89. Oyeleye and Olagunju, op. cit., p. 203.

90. *Aboyade Report*, op. cit., p. 50.

91. Ibid.

92. A. Rupley, op. cit., p. 266.

93. Fajana, Oladunjoye, 'Inter-Governmental Fiscal Relations in the Report of the Technical Committee on Revenue Allocation,' *Quarterly Journal of Administration* (Ife, Nigeria). Vol. 14, No. 2 (January 1980), pp. 6-8.

94. For a breakdown of the functions, see *Aboyade Report*, op. cit., Chapter IV.

95. O. Fajana, op. cit., p. 16.

96. *Aboyade Report*, op. cit., pp. 85-86.

97. Ibid., p. 87.

98. Ibid., p. 54.

99. Ibid., pp. 50-51.

100. Ibid., p. 33.

101. Ibid., p. 36.

102. *Proceedings of the Constituent Assembly, Monday, May 26, 1978.* (Lagos: Federal Government Press, 1978), p. 5458.

103. *Aboyade Report*, op. cit., pp. 88-89.

104. O. Fajana, op. cit., pp. 25-27.

105. *Aboyade Report*, op. cit., p. 156.

106. Ibid., p. 97.

107. *Proceedings....*, op. cit., p. 5446.

108. O. Fajana, op. cit., p. 24.

109. Ugoh, Sylvester U., 'An Appraisal of the Report of the Technical Committee to Revenue Allocation,' *Daily Times* (Nigeria). June 23, 1978, p. 26.

110. Oyeleye and Olagunju, op. cit., p. 207.

111. *Report of the Fiscal Commission*, cmnd 481. (London: HMSO, 1958), p. 50.

112. *Government Views on the Report of the Technical Committee on Revenue Allocation.* (Lagos: Federal Government Press, 1978), p. 7.

113. Oyeleye and Olagunju, op. cit., pp. 207-08.

114. Ibid., p. 208.

115. *Proceedings....*, op. cit., p. 5466.

116. Ibid., pp. 5435-454.

117. Ibid., p. 5442.

118. *New Nigeria* (Nigeria). May 3, 1978.

119. Merton, Robert, *Social Theory and Social Structure.* (New York: The Free Press, 1968), p. 256.

120. *Proceedings....*, op. cit., p. 5462.

121. Ibid.

122. Ibid., p. 5463.

123. L. Rupley, op. cit., p. 270. (See also O. Fajana, op. cit., pp. 22-23.)

124. Oyeleye and Olagunju, op. cit., p. 209.

125. See Chapter III for details on resurgence of political parties in the 2nd Republic.

126. Informal interview with a member of the Constituent Assembly and a prominent political official under the Shagari Regime.

127. Oyeleye and Olagunju, op. cit., pp. 208-09.

128. Ibid., p. 209.

7 Revenue allocation in the 2nd Republic, 1979-1982

Introduction

The efforts made by the Federal Military Government to give the country a more permanent revenue allocation system came to nothing when the Aboyade Report was rejected by the Constitutent Assembly. Accordingly, on November 23, 1979, one month after his election as the first executive head of post-war Nigeria, President Shehu Shagari set up a fiscal review body under the title of Presidential Commission on Revenue Allocation. The seven-man team selected by the President to serve on the Commission consisted of persons with a wealth of experience, both in academia and public service. As a group and individually, those experts possessed special competence in the field's relevant to the policy issue[1] of revenue allocation — economics, finance and public administration. Three of the members, including the Chairman, Dr. Pius Okigbo, were economists who specialized in Public Finance and had written extensively about revenue allocation; the others had been political scientists, top public officials and civil servants (including former Ministers and Permanent Secretaries who had broad experience in financial administration). In addition, for the first time, one of the members of the panel was from a minority and oil-rich state. His presence must have fulfilled the 'federal character' policy of President Shagari[2] and would also appease the oil producing states.

The presidential commission on revenue allocation

The choice of Dr. Okigbo as chairman of the new commission is significant. He had served on both the Constitution Drafting Committee and the Constituent

Assembly where he led the group of intellectuals that waged the successful assault on the Aboyade Report. His brilliant performance during the debates was praised by a newspaper columnist who had earlier on condemned all economists as being notorious for 'misguiding the nation' and 'botching up the economy'[3] He wrote that:

> Having now read Dr. Okigbo's impressive contribution to this debate, I hasten to restate that there are always exceptions to every rule. Dr. Okigbo, I doff off my hat to you, Sir.[4]

The *New Nigerian* was known to be sympathetic with sentiments expressed in the Northern States, and, later on, with the National Party of Nigeria, NPN. It was more than coincidence that when Alhaji Shehu Shagari, once a member of the Constituent Assembly and active in dumping the Aboyade Report, became president after the NPN won the national elections, he decided to choose Dr. Okigbo to head the new revenue allocation commission. Policy makers have been known to appoint experts who share their point of view[5] and are of the same political persuasion with them. That had led to a kind of camaraderie between the selector and the selected, prompting some scholars to doubt the objectivity of the experts.[6] But, as stated earlier, the notion of the 'castrated intellectual' who has no discretion of his own[7] is extreme. The very cordial relationship between Dr. Okigbo with his team of experts and the President could be considered necessary for the resolution of such a complicated policy problem as Revenue Allocation. As Don Price put it, policy-making is a "process of interaction among the scientists, professional leaders, administrators and politicians,"[8] and for the process to operate smoothly, there had to be a degree of comradeship among the participants. Whether the President 'packed his team' or not is still debatable but that he selected experts who were not antagonistic to him was obvious.

One of the most nagging problems that spelled doom for the Aboyade Report was its incomprehensibility. Therefore, in inaugurating the new Commission, President Shagari emphasized the need for clarity. He said:

> . . . But the situation is not helped where the formula applied, is shrouded in such mystery that the parameters in use cannot be easily comprehended by the greater part of the Nation's citizens...For all these shifts in theme and emphasis, however, a country should opt for a set of principles and concepts for revenue allocation formula which is most capable of being widely understood and accepted as equitable.[9]

Bearing that in mind, the Okigbo Commission set out to deliberate on the issues, guided, in principle, by the specific terms of reference given it. They were:

(a)   The Commission shall in the light of deliberations thereon in the Constituent Assembly and the representations of the Federal, State and Local Governments and other interested parties and the need to ensure that each tier of Government in the Federation has adequate revenue to enable it to discharge its functions as laid down in the Constitution, examine the present Federation has adequate revenue to enable it to discharge its functions as laid down int he Constitution, examine the present formula for revenue allocation having regard to such factors as national interest, derivation, population, even development, equitable distribution and the equality of States.

(b)   Arising from the findings in (a) recommend new proposals considered necessary for revenue allocation between the Federal, State and Local Governments.

(c)   Make whatever recommendations are considered necessary for effective collection and distribution of Federal and State revenues and offer broad guidelines on the distribution of revenue among Local Governments within States.

(d)   Make any other recommendations on any related issues as may be found necessary.

Furthermore, the Commission's attention was drawn to relevant sections of the Constitution that had bearing on the their work. Those provisions stated that:

(1)   The Federation shall maintain a special account to be called 'The Federation Account' into which shall be paid all revenues collected by the Government of the Federation, except the proceeds from the personal tax of the personnel of the armed forces of the Federation, the Nigeria Police Force, the Ministry or department of government charged with responsibility for External Affairs and the residents of the Federal Capital Territory.

(2)   Any amount standing to the credit of the Federation Account shall be distributed among the Federal and State Governments, and the Local Government Councils in each State, on such terms and in such manner as may be prescribed by the National Assembly.

(3)   Any amount standing to the credit of the States in the Federation Account shall be distributed among the States on such terms and in such a manner as may be prescribed by the national Assembly.

(4)   The amount standing to the credit of the Local Government Councils in the Federation Account shall be allocated to the States for the benefit of their local government councils on such terms and in such a manner as may be prescribed by the National Assembly.

(5)   Each State shall maintain a special account to be called 'State Joint Local Government Account' into which shall be paid all allocations to their local government councils of the State from the Federation Account and from the government of the State.

(6)   Each State shall pay to local government councils in its area of jurisdiction such proportion of its total revenue on such terms and in such manner as may be prescribed by the national Assembly.[10]

In addition, the Commission was enjoined to consult as wide and varied opinions as it could in arriving at a revenue allocation formula that "would largely determine the shape of our economic development during and after the Plan period."[11] Therefore, members of the Okigbo Commission felt it was incumbent on them to devise a formula that was, among other things, easy to read and understand, capable of ready application, not easily manipulable, and could be seen as fair and equitable. Those characteristics were important because the resulting report would be used as a basis of legislation by the National Assembly.[12]

In interpreting the terms of reference, the Commission decided to expand the scope of their meaning, that is interpret them broadly. Relevant and sometimes vague items were critically looked at and interpreted to suit the Commission.

The first issue examined and analyzed was that of 'adequately revenue'. According to the terms of reference, the Commission was reminded of the "need to ensure that each tier of Government in the Federation has adequate revenue to enable it to discharge its functions as laid down in the Constitution." It considered the constitutional implications of that requirement and decided that it was beyond its scope and competence to determine the fiscal equivalence of the constitutional functions and responsibilities of each tier of government; instead, it went on to decide the relative weights of their functions and responsibilities. The indicator used for determining those weights was the 1979 expenditure levels.[13] It can be seen that the Commission avoided the constitutional and legal question of determining whether a particular revenue

165

level was adequate for any tier of government. By using levels of expenditure as the yard stick of 'adequacy', the Commission assumed that such levels were in themselves adequate.

Another item that needed clarification was the requirement to "examine the present formula for revenue allocation." It was not clear whether that referred to the Aboyade Technical Committee's formula which was used in the April 1979 budget and in the first supplementary estimates of September 1979. However, Section 272 of the Constitution made some provisions for transitional arrangements between October 1979 and whenever a new revenue allocation bill would be passed. Therefore, the Commission decided to interpret present formula as that contained in Section 272, which shared the revenue in the Distributable Pool Account among States in the following proportion: 50 percent on the basis of derivation, and 50 percent on the basis of equality.[14]

After determining the parameters within which they would work, the parameters within which they would work, the members carried out an extensive and exhaustive study of past revenue allocation formulas as well as a comparative analysis of fiscal arrangements in other federations such as the United States, India, Canada and Australia. Meanwhile, the President had directed them to "engage in the widest consultation of opinion as possible, listen to all points of view and consider all shades of opinion in the country;"[15] all that exercise was to equip the Commission with all available data and information it needed to devise a revenue formula that would be acceptable both to the government and legislature. Unlike the other fiscal panels that gather testimony only form public officials representing the various government, the Okigbo panel elicited opinion from all and sundry. The Commission advertised for written memoranda and oral evidence from a interested persons and institutions — pubic and private; expert advice from experienced Nigerians (including members of past fiscal commissions); and proposals from the various governments.

Several individuals and organizations took time out to send in the views, and, given the salience of the issue and the publicity about it, that was no surprise. The group of interested parties, usually described as the 'attentive public', represented a cross-section of Nigeria. It included State Governors, national and local legislators, professionals in various fields, tradition rulers, religious readers, community organizations, government functionaries, political and ethnic associations, student unions. prominent businessmen and oil companies. What was significant about the group was that about two-thirds (67 percent) of them were made up of individuals and organizations from three States — Bendel, Cross River and Rivers.[16] These States were the so-called oil-rich states which were also composed of minority ethnic groups. The predominance of ethnic associations form those States showed the tremendous grassroots efforts carried out be local leaders who wanted the Okigbo Commission to hear their voices. Since those localities were directly affected by oil production, most of them felt they had been ignored in the decision of how to share the oil revenues. During the military era, they could not express their desires or have any input into any revenue policy; however, with the set up of the new Commission by a civilian government, there was hope that they could play some active role in the policy process. That portrayal of political efficacy, that is, the belief in the ability to effect political change, was in itself significant because it was uncommon. Usually when a community had reason to make their demands known nationally, it was the 'elite' or 'more advanced' representatives who normally resided in Lagos, that pursued the goal. The break up of the regional hegemony, the creation of a Local Government system and the prominence attached to the revenue issue must have contributed to the new phenomenon.

To gather the oral evidence, the Commission embarked on a nationwide tour of the nineteen States, plus the new Federal Capital Territory at Abuja. In each State Capital, the fiscal panel met with those who had sent in the memoranda as well as with government officials and legislators. The sessions were often long and tedious and consisted primarily of speeches and a question-and-answer series between the Commission and the delegates. The main aim of the exercise seemed to be that of debating and analyzing the various memoranda submitted earlier. States that felt they had much grievance against the prevailing revenue allocation system gave the commission the hardest and most difficult time. The panel spent long hours with such delegates, going thorough their many voluminous papers and debating issues an principles which they perceived as fundamental to their cause; with other more satisfied States, the sessions were shorter and less acrimonious.[17] The oral testimonies afford the fiscal board the opportunity to filter and sift through the written materials.

Many critical issues were raised both in the written memoranda and oral evidence given. Looking through the mammoth information presented, three major categories would be isolated. The first dealt with the decision of revenue amount the three tiers of government; the second category involved itself with allocation among the states and the local governments, with emphasis on the principles to be utilized; and lastly, was what could be termed, 'Special Issues' — issues concerned with a plethora of items indirectly related to revenue sharing. (Only the first two categories would be analyzed). In each case, a dichotomy between the positions taken by the state and local governments on one hand and the federal Government on the other hand, appeared.On matters concerning the states alone, the solidarity broke down, and fluid alliances based on shared interest emerged, with each issue demanding a new accord.

Proposals from federal, state and local governments intergovernmental allocation

The Federal Government, in its memorandum and oral testimony, put forward a strong argument to justify its elevated and superior financial position vis-a-vis the other levels of government, and for the maintenance of the status quo. It argued that as the central government, it had the responsibility of promoting national integration. To that end, a rapid development of infra structural facilities was needed to be carried out and unless adequate financial means were put at its disposal, the objective might not be met. In addition to ensuring national economic integration, the federal Government also felt that it has always acted as the paramount authority to control the overall financial policy of the nation; therefore, the Constitution has delegated certain responsibilities to it. Those duties often involved capital expenditure consuming areas like aviation, armed forces, railroads, and power. Furthermore, the country had incurred huge external debts to which the Federal Government remained the guarantor. Also, other international obligations like the United Nations, the Economic Community of West African States (ECOWAS), and aid to other sister African nations, all contributed to the financial responsibility of the central government. Moreover, the Federal Government did not possess any independent sources of revenue on its own, and will depend exclusively on the share it gets from the Federation Account. Therefore, the Federal Government proposed that the Federation Account be shared in the following ratio: Federal Government = 70 percent; States = 20 percent; and Local Government = 10 percent. (See Table 7.1).

Table 7.1
Proposed recommendations for inter-governmental allocation by federal government and the state governments presented to the Okigbo commission

	Federal Government	State Government	Local Government
Federal Govt.	70	20	10
Anambra	40	45	10
Bauchi	45	40	15
Bendel	28	55	15
Benue	45	40	10
Borno	40	50	10
Cross Rivers	50	40	10
Gongola	40	40	15
Imo	40	40	12
Kaduna	40	40	15
Kano	40	40	15
Kwara	50	38	12
Lagos	40	50	10
Niger	40	45	10
Ogun	40	50	10
Ondo	30	60	10
Oyo	30	57	10
Plateau	40	35	10
Rivers	45	45	10
Sokoto	50	40	10

Source: *Report of the Presidential Commission on Revenue Allocation*, Vols. I, II, III, (Lagos: The Federal Government Press, 1980).

The States, on the other hand, resented the concentration of financial resources in the hands of the central government. That trend, which started with the advent of the military government, had continued, and their civilian counterparts seemed bent on carrying on with the tradition. They argued that such a situation had many undesirable consequences. One was the inability of state governments to perform their duties due to financial restraint. The new constitution had further increased the responsibilities of the states and, as such, there was a need for a restructuring of the allocation of the Federation Account, taking into consideration, the changed status of the states.

Depending on the Federal Government for most of their finances had reduced the states to mere vassals, thereby undermining their political autonomy, a situation they wanted to change. They complained of the anomalies in non-statutory grant application, citing the system as unstable and open to political victimization. Rather, they would prefer statutory allocations, adequate to give them the financial wherewithal to discharge their obligations. Being closer to the people, the States reasoned, they were in a better position to assess their basic needs and unlike the prestigious and expensive projects embarked upon by the Federal Government, States provide very necessary aids which should be given higher priority.[18] As the Anambara State memorandum stated:

> We hold that the over concentration of the nation's resources with the Federal Government has led to a national expenditure pattern that encouraged injudicious spending.[19]

Examples of such 'injudicious spending' given included FESTAC and the International Trade Fair. States saw a direct link between having too much revenue and irresponsible spending by the Federal Government. If the financial base of the center were reduced, the taste for 'white elephant' projects would diminish.[20]

With the introduction of uniform personal income tax, the abolition of sales taxes. purchase taxes, export duties, and the harmonization of Marketing Board prices, the much touted independent revenue base of the States has almost vanished or been decreed away. The Federal projects like the Universal primary Education, housing, and basic health care schemes, had been imposed on the States without adequate financing. All that these did was to strip the States financially naked, and therefore the States demanded that only a revenue allocation formula that gave them at least one-half of the Federation Account could rescue them from such a financial plight. Thus of all the nineteen states, only three (Sokoto, Cross Rivers and Kwara) even conceded up to 50 percent to the Federal Government. Most States would prefer giving the center between 40 and 45 percent while one went as low as 28 percent.[21] (See Table 7.1).

Local Government Councils lamented their neglected status as the third tier of government, closest to the grass roots. They, therefore, urged the

170

Okigbo Commission to appropriate to them between 10-15 percent of the Federation Account to enable them to carry out their constitutional functions.[22]

Inter-state allocation

The basis issue involved here was the principles by which revenue could be shared among the States. In the memoranda and oral testimonies, three principles seemed to command the most attention; they were 'Population', 'Derivation', and 'Equality or States'. It was around these that most of the arguments revolved.

The Federal Government in its submissions, suggested that the allocation of revenue among the states as well as among the Local Governments be made on the basis of Population = 60 percent, and Equality of States = 40 percent. (That was the same formula used by the military except that the principles were weighted equally, indicating a tendency of the Federal Government to maintain the status quo). Such a formula was recommended for its simplicity and ease of application. The notion of pure derivation principle was found inadmissible because the Constitution had given the National Assembly the right to legislate on mineral matters and vested ownership of minerals in the Federal Government. However, in order to compensate and develop mineral producing areas, it was suggested that 3 percent of the Federation Account be set aside for that purpose. Such a fund would be managed by a federal agency that would act in close consultation and collaboration with the state governments. The main aim would be to repair some of the degradation caused by mineral extraction in the areas. The Federal Government expressed fear that if the fund were managed by the State or Local Governments themselves, it may be diverted from the affected areas due to political considerations.[23] That apprehension was justified because state governments had been know to deny social and other amenities to communities that did not vote for the party in power. There was no guarantee that such a punitive action would not be taken against a locality that deserved to benefit from the fund by, politically a pariah.

Unlike the formula for inter-governments suggested similar proposals, recommendations for inter-state sharing were as varied as the states. Each state presented its argument mostly in support of those factors that it felt would suit its particular characteristics; with all of them seeing the federation Account sharing as a means of promoting their development.[24]

As state above, the main debate among the states centered on how much weight to give to the three basic principles — Population, Equality of States and Derivation.

Population

All the states agreed to the use of population figure in one form or the other, as a criterion for sharing revenue among them; the difference laid in the form to be used and the wright to be attached.

Table 7.2 shows the various States ranked according the their populations; and the allocation formula each of them proposed. States with large population, like Kano, oyo and Imo (Nos. 1,2,5) suggested the use of the population factor as the main basis for revenue sharing. Their reason for giving such a huge percentage was that expenditure incurred by States to provide social services and other needs for the people was in "direct and positive correlation with the size of their population."[25] Most of them called for the use of the 1963 raw population data but projected forward; others wanted them modified.

Sokoto, the home state of the President declined to put too much weight on population. it was argued that although population was the "most relevant criterion for the rational allocation of national resources" and as the third largest State, it stood to gain by its application, it refused to be bound by "selfish motive of deriving special advantage."[26] Therefore the state recommended only 50 percent for Population.

As expected, states with small populations considered using the factor as taboo and argued that:

It is very unscientific and rather simplistic to assume a linear and highly positive correlation between developmental fiscal needs of a people and their absolute number.[27]

In addition, they questioned the accuracy of the projected 1963 census data and pointed out the controversy of using such unacceptable figures a the basis for resource distribution, and therefore called for a de-emphasizing of population as an allocation principle.

172

Table 7.2

Recommended weights (%) for inter-state revenue allocation proposals by state characteristics

State	Percent by Population	Population Derivation/ Equality	Popl Area/Sq in 1963 KM & Others*	(Mill)	(000)	Party Affil. 1979 Elect.
Kano	75	15	10	5.8	42.6	PRP
Oyo	70	10	20	5.2	18.0	UPN
Sokoto	50	50	30	4.5	36.3	NPN
Kaduna	40	25	35	4.1	68.9	NPN
Imo	70	30	--	3.7	12.9	NPP
Anambra	50	50	--	3.6	17.0	NPP
Cross River	40	40	20(D)	3.5	27.8	NPN
Borno	20	25	50	3.0	116.6	GNPP
Ondo	20	45	35	2.7	14.4	UPN
Gongola	--	50	50	2.6	99.7	GNPP
Bendel	40	60	--	2.5	39.0	UPN
Bauchi	25	75	--	2.43	66.5	NPN
Benue	25	12.5	62.5	2.42	47.8	NPN
Plateau	20	65	15	2.0	20.8	NPP
Rivers	25	25	50(D)	1.72	15.2	NPN
Kwara	40	50	10	1.71	60.4	NPN
Ogun	20	50	30	1.6	16.4	UPN
Lagos	30	30	40	1.4	14.7	UPN
Niger	--	15	75	1.2	75.0	NPN
Federal Gov't	60	40	--	--	--	NPN

*   Other Principles included Need, Geographical Size and Even Development

(D) = % only for Derivation

Source: *Report of the Presidential Commission on Revenue Allocation*, Vol. I, II, and III. (Lagos: Federal Government press, 1980.)

Equality of states

The states in Nigeria are neither equal in population nor in size, but for the basis of resource sharing and distribution, the equality of states as a principle is to demonstrate the equality of political units in the Federation as provided by the country's constitution. This principle, also known as "Minimum Responsibility of States", attested to the legal and constitutional equality of all States. While large states pointed out the inherent inequality, in terms of resources, population and size of states and suggested an average of 15 percent for the factor so that all states could carry out their minimum responsibility of governing, less populous states in 1980 like Bendel, Bauchi and Plateau (Nos. 11, 12, & 14 on the population scale) remind the Commission that:

> We cannot run away from the notion of organic equality of states as social-economic and cultural entities which should be constitutionally entitled to equal sharing of the national revenue. States and Local Governments have been fairly equalized in terms of recurrent expenditures in the sense that they all perform the same functions and services and pay the same salaries.[28]

One of them, Bauchi, demanded a weight as high as 75 percent to the principle (see Table 7.2).

Derivation

Unlike the other principles which all the states, in one way or the other, agreed to adopt, the derivation factor was either passionately advocated for or completely disregarded. The oil producing States of Bendel, Cross River, IMO, Ondo and Rivers, all say derivation as a 'very sound and progressive principle'[29] of revenue allocation and made a very strong plea for its inclusion in the revenue sharing formula. They claimed that each state should receive a proportion of "certain centrally collected revenue indefinitely commensurate with its contribution to the proceeds from such revenues."[30] The reasons were three-fold. First, historically, derivation had been recognized as a valid and essential principle or revenue allocation and it was only in 1977 that the Abayode Committee recommended against it. States had come to regard it as imitable and to jettison it then could lead to a breakdown of unity and stability in the country. They alleged that those states who were opposed to derivation, had acclaimed and benefitted from it when they generated the bulk of the

Federation revenue. Therefore, it would be grossly unfair to deny the same advantages to them that constitute the biggest contributors to the revenue pool.

Another reason enunciated was juridical, that is, based on right and supported by law. Those mineral producing stated argues that as landlords or owners of the land from which the resources were obtained, they ought to, by right, revive payments of rents and royalties from the use of such land. Lastly, the states based their claim for inclusion of the derivation principle on grounds of equity. Since the production of those resources involved destruction of both life and property and "caused general degradation of the environment and of the ecology of the producing areas", those states had to bear the increased cost of rehabilitation and welfare. Therefore, they demanded additional share of the revenue generated from their territories, over and beyond the shares given to each state on other ground.[31]

States who were opposed to the use of the derivation principle in the new revenue allocation scheme based their arguments on the notion that all revenues belonged to all Nigerians regardless of source; therefore, any attempt to treat some part of the general revenue as owned by certain states was indefensible. A sample of their statements will illustrate the vehemence of the disapproval;. Bauchi State called derivation "diabolically against the principle of nation interest"; to Benue, it "negates the basic objectives which a revenue allocation exercise should seek to establish"; the Kano State Governor labeled anyone who suggested its usage as unpatriotic; Oyo State saw derivation in its absolute sense as running 'counter to federal principles'; and the State of Sokoto could see "no justification for its recognition in a cohesive fiscal system which aspires to national political and social development". However, even those states realized that the areas. Therefore, they recommended certain amounts ranging from 2 percent to 10 percent taken from the Federation Account (not the states' share of the Account) to be paid to those areas. The principle of derivation continues, to this day, to be the major source of controversy in the revenue allocation formulation process where it is either embraced wholeheartedly or condemned outright.

Most local governments supported the same criteria for sharing revenue among themselves as the states of which they were part of. In other words, their recommendations almost followed the pattern for inter-state allocation, that is, local governments in large states advocated for a greater emphasis on the use of population while those in smaller states stressed equality. The high degree of congruence between the proposals of states and those of local governments could be attributed to the immaturity of, and lack of competent personnel in the latter. Despite their upgrading to an autonomous tier of government, local government councils still depended on state governments for many services.

Okigbo Commission recommendations and reaction

Inter-Governmental proposals

After reviewing the myriads of memoranda and oral evidence presented by the Federal, State and Local governments, as well as the interested public, the Okigbo Commission decided to make certain recommendation. Its task, as state above, was to devise a formula for sharing central revenues among the three tiers of government; among the states; and among the states for the benefit of their local government councils. And in so doing, the fiscal panel should make sure that each level of government had adequate revenue to enable it discharge its functions.[32]

To translate functions into financial terms, estimates of recurrent and capital expenditures for a four-year pension of 1976/77 to 1979/80 were used, since no accurate data for the real figures were available. Those estimates were then compared and relative weights assigned to the different levels of government. It was found that the Federal Government's weight lay between 60 and 62 percent of total expenditure; states accounted for between 36.2 and 37.1 percent; while local governments were responsible for between 3.2 and 3.3 percent.[33] But the Commission decided not to adhere strictly to the percentages in sharing the revenue because, in the first place, they were estimates, and secondly, there were some policy areas that needed special consideration which neither of the levels of government was constitutionally mandated to take care of.

The panel, therefore, recommended that the Federation Account be shared in the following proportion: Federal Government= 53 percent; State Governments= 30 percent; Local government councils= 10; and the remaining 7 percent; was set aside for a Special Fund.[34] As can be seen, all the levels got below their relative weights of expenditure except the local government councils. The Commission's reasoning was that despite their low expenditure weight, local government council actually carried out most of the functions assigned to States, or if they were not, they should, so as to relive the States of some of the financial burden.[35] Also, it was felt that to make local governments live up to the reform of 1976 which was meant to give them some measure of autonomy and self-government, more funds should be made available to them. Moreover, the Fourth Schedule of the Constitution spelled out specific functions for them and since the councils were ill-equipped to take on those dates, allocation of more revenue was in order.[36]

The Special Fund recommended to receive 7 percent, was to take care of special problems which would have been the responsibility of the federal Government. It was to be shared as follows: Initial Development of the Federal Capital Territory= 2.5; Special Problem of Mineral Producing Areas= 2.0; Continuous Ecological problems= 1.0; and Revenue Equalization Fund= 1.5 percent.

Though the Federal Capital Territory could participate in the general revenue sharing as if it were a State, the Commission felt that its future needs should be a national project.[37] The 2.0 percent provision for Mineral Producing Areas was to take care of the hazards of mining which included environmental pollution and indiscriminate destruction of life and property. The fiscal board believed that the government was obliged to make provision for the restitution and rehabilitation of the people and area. The functions to be covered by the revenue would be the "formulating, developing, and implementing schemes of resettlement and rehabilitation, general development and research into these problems and creating job opportunities in the mineral producing areas."[38]

Areas which were susceptible to continuing ecological problems such as soil erosion, desert encroachment and flood, were to be given 1.0 percent so that they would have ready and available resources to meet with the problems. The Revenue Equalization Fund was meant to "bring up the level of allocation of these state governments that might fall absolutely below the level of allocation they received under the previous formula."[39] The provision was made because some states would have been financially worse off due to the change in the revenge sharing system.

The administration of the Special Fund was to be in hands of Special Agencies which would have the representation of the special interest of the Areas concerned. In addition, they were to work in close collaboration with both the state and local governments of the areas affected. However, it was made clear that the Special Fund was not meant to be a transfer of funds to state governments.[40]

Inter-state proposals

Allocation of funds among the states was more difficult and controversial due to the special interest it revokes as the textimonies presented showed. First,the Commission had to decide which principles of revenue allocation to adopt, and then what weights to assign to them. Of the principles suggested, only four of them were accepted.

Minimum responsibility of governments

This was chosen as a criterion because no matter the size of a state, the Constitution imposed certain responsibilities and functions on it, such as running a government and providing necessary services for its citizens. Moreover, a high weight for the principle would equalize the small with the large states. But the Commission could not think of a scientific way to fix the minimum in financial terms and give it a weight, therefore, it used its best judgment and intuition and assigned it a weight of 40 percent.[41]

Population

Used either in its raw form or in a functional way, population as an allocation factor was accepted by the Okigbo Commission. In its view, the data could not be manipulated by states to their advantage, and it serves as an umbrella factor for other dimensions of need. The figures used were those from the 1963 Census, and population was assigned 40 percent.[42]

Social development factor

This principle was to take care of the disparity in levels of development. of all the indicators of need and development education, health, power and roads — education was the only one with recent figures available, so primary school enrollment was used as a proxy for social development. it was recommended that the principle be applied in two parts — one to vary directly with enrollment; the other to vary inversely in order to provide relatively more assistance to and encourage states with lower figures. Direct enrollment was given a weight of 11.25 percent, and indirect enrollment got 3.75 percent, making a grand total of 15 percent for Social Development Factor.[43]

Internal revenue effort

Introduced to encourage states to raise, collect and use revenues efficiently, the factor was to be represented by the ratio of total internal revenues to the total expenditure, and given a weight of 5 percent.[44] (See Table 7.3)

Table 7.3
Okigbo commission recommendation for inter-government and inter-state allocation

Percentages

Federal Government	53.00
State Governments	30.00
Local Governments	10.00
Special Fund	7.00
Total:	100.00

State Government

Minimum Responsibility	40.00
Population	40.00
Social Development Factor	
Direct Enrolment	11.25
In-Direct Enrolment	3.75
Internal Revenue Effort	5.00
Total:	100.00

Local Government Councils

Same as Among States
> State Governments to pay 5 percent of Total Revenue to State Local Government Joint Account.

Source: *Report of the Presidential Commission on Revenue Allocation*, Vol. 1, (Lagos: The Federal Government Press, 1980).

The most controversial recommendation made by the Commission was its decision not to use derivation as one of the principles of revenue allocation. It was rejected because, according to the review body, the two main arguments put forward by its proponents had been negated. The mineral producing areas had insisted that mineral production created hazards and other problems requiring them to expend extra funds; therefore, they deserved additional revenues. The Special Fund included in the proposed formula was to take care of those problem. The second argument was that as land owners, they were entitled to a portion of the mining rents and royalties. The Commission then recommended that Section 150 of the Constitution be amended so that mining rents could be paid to states as of right. On the issue of royalties, the panel felt that paying them to states would be against existing laws and the Constitution, because at present, only the Federal Government had right to royalties.[45]

To share among the states for the benefit of local government councils, the Commission recommended that each state government contribute five percent of its total revenue to the State Local Government joint Account. It also suggested that local governments use the same scheme proposed for inter-state sharing to allocate revenue among themselves.[46]

Other recommendations made by the Commission include the set up of a permanent Fiscal Commission to study and review the federal fiscal system of the country, and that the system of grants be incorporated into the revenue allocation scheme. As with all the previous bodies, the Okigbo Commission stressed the need for a 'continuous build up of necessary data.'[47]

There had never been any fiscal review commission's report that had not elicited some serious misgivings, protests, and demonstrations from one section of the country or the other, and Okigbo Report was not exempted. However, with the exception of the Dang Report, they had all been accepted, albeit with some adjustments, by the incumbent administration.

The Federal Government, after reviewing the recommendations of the Okigbo Commission accepted the basic premise of the exercise, which was that each tier of government have a share of the Federation Account commensurate with its constitutional function, and that such a formula should be fair and equitable.[48] Having acceded to the underlying principles of the Report, it was not surprising that the Federal Government agreed with almost all the major proposals with some minor amendments. Nevertheless, there were certain areas which the government took exception to.

It rejected the idea of incorporating the system of grants into the revenue allocation scheme, as well as the setting up of a Revenue Equalization Fund. But the major bone of contention between the Commission and the Federal Government lay in the exclusion of the derivation principle in the proposed formula. The Okigbo Commission had rejected the use of the principle based on the reasons given in the earlier paragraphs. The Federal Government, being more aware of and responsive to the political implications of derivation debate, rejected the interpretation of Section 150 of the Constitution about ownership of land, and also refused to accept the matter of indemnity (in the form of the Revenue Equalization Fund) and categorically stipulated of the Federation Account to be shared on the basis of derivation.[49] (See Table 7.4) The formula for inter-state allocation was accepted with very slight modification; so also were the ones for local governments.

Table 7.4
Federal government recommendations for
inter-governmental allocation, 1980

	Percentages
Federal Government	55.00
State Governments	30.00
Local Governments	8.00
Special Fund	7.00
Total:	100.00

Special Fund

Mineral Producing Areas to be shared on the basis of Derivation	3.5
2.0 percent of which should go to the State of Origin	
1.5 percent to a Fund to be managed by a Special Agency for the development of mineral producing areas	
Federal Capital Territory	2.5
Continuing Ecological Problems	1.0
Total:	7.0

Source: *Views of the Government of the Federation on the Report of the Revenue Allocation* (Lagos: The Federal Government Press, 1980).

The stand of the Federal Government as regards the Okigbo Report was at odds with that shown in the original memoranda it submitted to the commissions. For example, earlier, the Federal Government had advocated for 70 percent of the Federation Account, citing numerous constitutional responsibilities; those duties had not disappeared but it was willing to accept only 55 percent (up 2 percent from the Commission's proposal.) For division among the states, it had proposed a simple 60:40 formula using population and equality of states as allocation factors. Yet in its White Paper, it not only approved the Okigbo four-factor formula but it also made provision for the use of derivation as a means of sharing revenue again.

What caused the apparent 'revolt' could be two-fold. One, since it was President Shagari himself who preempted the National Assembly in setting up a fiscal review board, he felt honor bound to accept its proposals. He had promised to use the proceedings of the Commission as a guide to draft a revenue bill. A vote of no confidence in the Report, by rejecting it would have created a credibility gap in the minds of the people and the legislators. It would have also brought into question his competence and sense of judgment in selecting the fiscal commission. Moreover, a reasonable amount of financial resources was utilized by the panel during its heavily publicized national tours; thus a complete abandonment of the products of such an expensive exercise would have given the new civilian administration and ruling party, the NPN, a prodigal reputation.

A more important reason might have been political. If the Federal Government had decided to stick with its original proposals in the memorandum submitted to the Commission, it would have incurred the wrath of the states whose representatives were to pass the revenue bill since all the states had recommended less than 50 percent of revenues for the Federal Government. Their biggest complaint had been that the center was bloated with excess revenue and it was time the states were given access to those resources. Though they might never reach the status of the old regions, in terms of both constitutional and fiscal powers, states, including those won by the NPN, wanted a reduction in the financial status of the central government. And no amount of political maneuvering would have made those legislators vote for a bill that gave 70 percent of the Federation Account to the Federal Government.

On the other hand, if the Shagari Administration had accepted the Okigbo Report, with its exclusion of the Derivation principle, as presented (see Table 7.4), it would have alienated the oil producing states. Those states belong to the minorities; and two of them, Rivers and Cross River were strongholds of the NPN and the third state, Bendel, though not controlled by the NPN, it had a large following there. A complete abandonment of the principle by the government would have been interpreted (and it was, see below) as discriminatory. Also, the NPN could have faced accusations of breach of promise. According to informed NPN sources, there was a tacit agreement between the party and the oil producing minority states that derivation would be used in any forthcoming revenue allocation scheme. That promise was part of the package deal that was offered to those states in order to get their votes. During strategy meetings of the party, prior to the 1979 elections, the concept of 'Direct Compensation for Direct Production', DCDP, was introduced and agreed upon. The slogan was just a cover name for Derivation.[50]

Added to the possible accusation of breach of promise, was the intensive lobbing carried out by the Governors of the oil producing states. Even before the Federal Government made public its views in the White Paper, the Governors of Bendel, Cross River and Rivers States, in a joint conference called for an increased reliance on the derivation principle, and suggested that the entire Special Fund be paid to their states.[51] The same note, but a more stringent one, was sounded by Governor Melford Okilo of the Rivers State, who while addressing a post-graduate seminar at the Command Staff College, predicted dire consequences for the country if the Derivation principle was discarded.[52] Moreover, some influential members of the party like Senators Joseph Wayas (NPN, Cross River), Senate President and David Dafinone (NPN, Bendel) Chairman, Senate NPN Caucus, put pressure on the Executive, citing both personal and party concerns. All those must have weakened the Administration's stance on derivation and finally led to its inclusion in the formula.

As expected, when the Okigbo Report and the Federal Government's White Paper were published, reaction of the states to them was virulent. Giving the Federal Government the lion's share of the Federation Account seemed to be the most irritating and vexing feature. After all, in their memoranda submitted to the Okigbo Commission, a huge majority of the states (about 85 percent) suggested less than 50 percent for the central government. To them, apportioning any amount more than that to the center, represented a reinstating of de facto federal superiority enthroned by the military government. They saw the Okigbo recommendations as "outrageous and unresponsive to the demands of the States". By its action, they argued, the Federal Government had reduced the states to a status of beggary, thereby denying them the financial power to 'wield effectively the political power' constitutionally guaranteed to them.[53] According to a joint communique issued by the Commissioners of Economic Planning and Development in the five states controlled by the Unity Party of Nigeria, UPN, (Lagos, Oyo, Ondo, Ogun and Bendel), the social and economic responsibilities of the country constitutionally lay with the state and local governments; therefore, they should be given sufficient funds to execute those duties, especially as contained in the 4th National Development Plan.[54] And the least amount of revenue that would be adequate for those who perform those functions was 50 percent of the Federation Account; anything less would be disastrous.

The National Association of Local Governments, NALGO, condemned both the Okigbo Report and the White Paper on it as 'unproportionate and unfair' to all local governments by not appreciating their responsibilities, and called for a share of at least 15 percent.[55] Consequently, the *Nigerian Standard* in a editorial, called on the National Assembly to review and revise the revenue allocation formula in favor of states and local governments, and cautioned the legislators not to forget their roots.[56]

The legitimacy of the Okigbo Commission itself was called into question. According to the Ondo State Legislature, setting up the panel was a gross violation of Section 149 of the Constitution, which, in the legislature's interpretation, gave only the National Assembly the power to determine criteria for revenue allocation.[57] The President was accused of usurping the powers of the legislature which had shirked its responsibility.[58] Since the body itself had been deemed unconstitutional, its deliberations and proposals were therefore null and void, so reasoned the legislators.

The other main argument against the Report and the White Paper was based on the issue of derivation, and as such, the oil producing states were in the forefront. Their tiff with the Okigbo Commission and the Federal Government echoed the sentiments presented in their memoranda. First, they believed that using the derivation principle was the most equitable way of sharing the national revenue, therefore, any system that excluded it had to be "politically tainted, prejudiced, insensitive, biased and unacceptable."[59] To them, it was mere common sense that centrally collected revenues should be allocated in proportion to contribution made by the various states into the common pool. For Governor Ambrose Alli of Bendel State, it was ironical that the areas which produced the bulk of the national revenue (oil in that case) should be the least favored in the allocation of revenue.[60] The same reasoning was postulated by Governor Clement Isong of Cross River State who said, "I believe in a policy in which States that have oil should be given a share of the income from the oil drilled."[61] Earlier, the three main 'Oil Governors', Alli of Bendel, Isong of Cross River, and Okilo of Rivers States, had called for the application of the derivation principle to both mineral and agricultural resources, insisting that each state in the Federation had a right to own and be

184

in control of its main resources.[62] Furthermore, they vowed to 'sink or swim together' towards the implementation of what they referred to as the 'non-negotiable' principle of derivation.[63] That belief that revenue derived from oil belonged to the producing states by right was preached from political pulpits by leaders of 'oil states'. President Shagari and Dr. Okigbo were accused of going against natural law and public opinion by ignoring the rights of the 'oil rich minorities' and the "eternal principles of federalism throughout the civilized world." They were indicted or conspiring to "edge the derivation formula into the limbo of federal charity."[64]

A more interesting reason as to why the derivation principle was completely abandoned in the Okigbo Report or given a token representation in the Government's White Paper was rife with hints of political prejudice and ethnic/state bigotry. That sentiment was expressed by Senator Nosike Ikpo (UPN, Bendel) who opined that the conclusions reached by the Okigbo Commission were not based on the numerous evidence (written and oral) submitted before it; rather, they reflected the "position of the politically stronger parities to the bargain."[65] In other words, Senator Ikpo was asserting that because the oil producing states were minority states and therefore 'weaker parties to the bargain', they did not wield enough political influence in the decision-making apparatus of the country; as such, their interests were not taken into consideration, especially by the Okigbo Commission. Following the same line of thought was Chief Eman Etim James, Chairman of the NPN in Cross River State. He regretted that the wishes and fundamental rights of the oil states were "systematically abused or at best ignored because of their minority status which reflected on the weak political position they occupy."[66] People from these states expressed the feeling to this author that if any of the 'majority states' were the source of the bulk of the national revenue, as they were in the hey days of groundnuts and cocoa, derivation would have played a much more important role in revenue allocation. that allegation was not new; certain scholars of Nigeria's fiscal policy had often attributed the fall in importance of derivation to the collapse of the agricultural products from the old powerful regions.[67] There is a number of Nigerians who ascribe to what could be described as the "theory of Double Conspiracy". The theory states that the rest of the country, led by the Northern Region, conspired to wrest away control of oil revenues from the former Eastern Region by splitting it up and isolating the oil producing areas in potentially hostile states. And then, since none of the 'Big Three', that is, North, East and West, had direct control over those resources, they banded together to keep the minority states away from the revenues; and instead vested the fiscal powers in the federal center. The proposition continued that in Nigeria, politics was a game of numbers, and revenue allocation was one of the vital issues of politics as its policy would determine who controlled the revenue generating resources of the country, therefore, minority group interests would always be ignored or given scant attention.[68] Proponents of that position maintained that attitude of the 'majority' groups toward the 'minority' ones was manifested not only on the derivation issue but also on "records of appointments, distribution of largess (especially within the NPN) and artifacts of progress."[69] All in all, they attributed the perceived neglect, ostensibly reflected by the derivation debate, to their minority status in a country which had ignored minority rights and still revolved around the ethno/regional tripartite system.

However, there are others who contend that derivation as a revenue allocation principle lost its status because Nigerians were becoming more politically integrated and thus less attached to the idea of regional security or 'statism' as it was later labeled, which derivation promoted. The united effort to 'keep Nigeria one' during the devastating civil war and the 'no victor, no vanquished' policy pursued by the military government as the country started the rehabilitation process in the post-war era, had brought about an 'emergence of national consciousness'[70] among the peoples and rulers of Nigeria. So they had come to accept that every resource, including oil, "belonged to all Nigeria's citizens, rather than only those resident in the states where the oil wells were located."[71] That was why most of the critics of derivation based their arguments on the idea of national interest, and insisted that no matter where the resources were obtained from, they should be shared by all Nigerians. Moreover, proceeds from oil accounted for more than 80 percent of the federal revenue and its production was concentrated mostly in three states. If derivation were applied as they demanded, that would lead to a gross disparity among the nineteen states. The situation of rich, little states and poor, large ones did not augur well for the political or economic stability of the country.

The use of the derivation principle reached its zenith at the height of regional power. In 1954, Sir Louis Chick, the sole fiscal commissioner was mandated to apply the principle to the fullest degree. However, as earlier shown, its utility declined as regional power ebbed and the federal center assumed ascendancy. By the end of the military regime in 1979, derivation had almost disappeared from the country's fiscal policy system, and the Shagari administration which kept most of the powers at the center, followed suit. The issue now at large is who controlled the federal government and therefore the fiscal policy of the country? Was it the Northern Region who had the most to lose if a derivation-based revenue allocation formula had continued, and therefore downgraded the principle as the Region surged in political power, as many scholars allege? Or was the center truly federal, influenced by none of or equally by all of the regional groups and therefore relegated derivation purely on grounds of national interest?

The answer lies somewhere in between these two positions. In the First Republic, one can safely say that the Northern Region, working through and with its party, the Northern Peoples Congress, NPC, had a "hegemonic control over federal politics."[72] Its position was enhanced by both the numerical advantage the party enjoyed in the federal parliament and the size and population of the region whose peoples were unified by Islam. Though the region was broken up into ten states and the 'authority bulwark' seemed to have disappeared, two-thirds of people in those ten states were still united by their religion which prescribed not only the moral values of the society but also the economic, political, social and cultural values. Thus in the minds of many Nigerians, there still existed a 'Northern Nigeria' or 'Northern States' as they were referred to, and the fact that six out of the eight Nigerian Heads of State (civilian and military) came from the North, seemed to confirm the notion that the federal center was still in the grips of the North. The NPN which won the national elections in 1979 and 1983 and so the presidency was a Northern-based political party. Though it had the most widespread appeal and won votes in more states (coming either first or second in all the states in 1979) than any of the others, it was still basically a political party run by Northerners for the benefit of the country. As Richard Joseph put it:

> What united the party was a willingness to collaborate under the leadership of established northern politicians along with guarantee that power would not only be shared as widely as possible but also that the leading positions in the party would be circulated among individuals from the main regions of the country.[73]

Though one would agree with the anti-derivation group that the principle did indeed promote some sense of separateness in a society that really needed political integration to survive, this author is of the opinion that if any of the larger majority states like Anambra, Kano, Oyo, Sokoto, Ogun, or Borno had been the source of the bulk of the nation's revenues, derivation would certainly have played a bigger role than it did in the new revenue allocation system. The legislative debate on the 1981 Revenue Allocation Bill illustrated, in a subtle way, some of the issues raised here.

The National Assembly debate on the 1981 revenue allocation bill

The fight for an acceptable revenue allocation formula for the country was transferred to the National Assembly when on Monday, November 24, 1980, President Shehu Shagari formally presented the "Allocation of Revenue (Federation Account, etc.) Bill 1980" to a joint session of the House of Representatives and Senate. The Bill was included in the 1981 Budget Message to the legislature was almost identical to that earlier published in the Federal Government's White Paper (a response to the Okigbo Report); the only difference being that the allotments for 'Derivation' and 'Ecological Problems' were added to the States' share of the Account. Here is the text of the Bill:

> This Bill seeks your approval for the distribution of the Federation Account among the various Governments as follows:
>
> (a) Federal Government 55.0%
> (b) State Governments 34.5%
> (c) Local Governments 8.0%
> (d) Fund for the initial development
>   of the Federal Capital Territory 2.5%
>
> The 34.5 percent for the States is to be allocated amongst them as follows:
>
> (1) 30 percent to all the States on the basis of allocative criteria which I will explain shortly;
> (2) 2 percent to be paid directly on the basis of derivation to mineral producing areas;
> (3) 1.5 percent to be specifically used for the development of the mineral producing areas.
>
> It is further recommended that the distribution among the States and Local Government Councils will be on the basis of the following criteria:
>
> (a) Minimum Responsibility of
>   Government (Equality) 40%
> (b) Population 40%

188

(c)   Social Development Factor as
        represented by Primary School
        enrollment 15%
(d)   Internal Revenue Effort as
        represented by the ratio of
        internal revenue to total
        recurrent expenditure 5%

Out of the 15 percent allocated to Social Development Factor, 11.25 percent will be shared on the bias of direct primary school enrollment, while the balance of 3.75 percent shall be shared on the attributive basis of inverse enrollment which will be represented by the number of children of primary school age who are not in school.

In addition to the allocation of 8 percent which will be made direct from the Federation Account to the credit of the Local Government Councils, each State will also pay to the State Joint Government Account a sum of 8 percent of the revenue of the State Government concerned.[74]

After presenting the Bill, the President then went ahead to defend it, especially the need for the Federal Government to take out more than half of the Federation Account. According to him, the proposed 55 percent represented a "trimming of Federal resources to the bare bones in the interest of fiscal federalism;" bearing in mind the host of functions the Federal Government must carry out.[75]

Prior to that time, President Shagari had sent to both legislative chambers a letter containing "A bill for an Act to prescribe the Basis for Distribution of Revenue Account between the Federal and State Governments and the Local Government Councils; and the formula for Distribution amongst the States inter-se; the proportion of the Total Revenue of each State to be contributed to the State Joint Local Government Account, and for other purposes connected therewith."[76] While the Senate did not act on the Bill until the budget speech, the House of Representatives decided to work on it the following week.

In order to give the Bill the thorough and detailed consideration it deserved, the House resolved to dissolve itself into a Committee of the Whole and allocated seventeen working days to deliberate on it. The significance of the Bill on the Representatives, who, one after the other, in their speeches, reiterated the need for them to arrive at a just and equitable revenue allocation system.

Looking through the speeches made during the debate, certain trends could be recognized. Legislators tended to take positions which reflected the interests of their constituencies if the issues were inter-state; on the other hand, the law-makers retreated to the umbrella of their political parties, that is to say, voted the party line, when inter-governmental issues arose. Specifically, while the matter of distribution of revenue among the governmental levels was on the floor, almost all of them, like their counterparts in the State Assemblies, voted for a reduction in the share of the Federal Government. How much to give each level was the question. It was during the lively debate that partisan politics played an important role. Though they all agreed in principle that the central government did indeed have important functions to perform, members of all the parties, with the exception of the ruling NPN, wanted to allocate no more than 50 percent to the Federal Government. Any revenue voted to the center was seen as money to the NPN, and since the other four parties were in opposition, they did not feel like improving the already superior position of the Federal Government. Moreover, they felt more funds were needed to be channeled to the state and local governments in order for them to carry out their development plans. As Representative Faji Fajobi (UPN, Ondo) put it:

> The rationale for the existence of the State Government is the desire to spread development over the country; ...all services connected with the day-to-day life of the citizen came within the ambit of the State Government's responsibilities. The Local Governments are the governments nearest to the people and perform the most vital social services. For lack of funds, the performance of these duties by the Local Governments has been in most cases on a token basis.[77]

Most of the other legislators' speeches echoed the same sentiment and that was evidenced when the House voted 224-144 to allocate 50 percent to the Federal Government, 40 percent to the States, and 10 percent to the Local Governments.

It was during the discussion on the derivation principle that the solidarity portrayed by the non-NPN parties while debating inter-governmental allocation, broke down. Legislators from oil-producing states, irrespective of party affiliation tendered enthusiastic statements in support of the principle. What mattered most was the constituency one represented. For instance, both the Nigerian Peoples' Party, NPP and the NPN representatives from Rivers State supported and voted for inclusion of the derivation principle. Some of the speeches on the issue were fervent. Take Representative Michael Akpabio's (GNPP, Cross River) brusque statement:

Let me say straightaway that anybody who opposes the principle of derivation in the sharing of revenue in this country should see himself as an enemy of the country.[78]

On the other side, one had Representative Mohammed Ne-Rogo (PRP,Kano) saying,

Mr. Chairman, Sir, I would like, with utter vehemence, at least, to condemn in totality that the principle of derivation should be slaughtered butchered and killed on the floor of this House.

Since the NPN was on record as being in favor of the principles, though not all members of the party voted for it, Representative Yunusa Kaltungo (NPN, Bauchi) Leader of the House,[79] put forward an amendment to that effect but it failed to pass by a 133:198 margin.

Other amendments passed by the House included a further reduction of 3.5 percent from the Federal Government's share to be allocated to two areas: Initial Development of the Federal Capital Territory (2.5); and Continuing Ecological Problems (1.0); thereby effectively reducing the federal share to 46.5 percent. The criteria for allocation among the states was accepted. Despite oral testimonies by the Vice President, Dr. Alex Ekweme, the Federal Minister of Finance, Dr. Sylvester Ugoh and Dr. Pius Okigbo himself, on the need for allocating more revenues to the Center, the House stuck to it decision and amended the President's Bill as shown in Table 7.5 below.

Table 7.5
House version of the revenue allocation bill

Federal Government	46.5%
Initial Development of Federal Capital Territory	2.5%
Continuing Ecological Problems	1.0%
	50.0%
State Governments	40.0%
Local Governments	10.0%
Allocation Among States and	
Local Governments	

Source: *National Assembly Debates, House of Representatives*, November-December 1980, (Lagos: The Federal Government Press, 1980).

On partisan grounds, the apparent 'new marriage' between the NPP and the UPN dealt the final blow to any efforts by NPN members to entice their old NPP 'Accord' comrades to join them in voting for more revenue to the Federal Government. The NPN-NPP Accord was at that time nearing its grave, and concerted effort was made by the UPN to convince the NPP in joining the 'Progressives' (a title used by non-NPN political parties). To show its appreciation for the Bill, the nine Progressive Governors met in Benin City and issued a communique praising the House decision and calling it 'patriotic, realistic and sensible' and reminded the members that 'generations of Nigerians will ever be grateful' to them for passing such a Bill.[80]

Before going to examine the Senate's action on the Bill, it will be quite pertinent at this point to look at the NPN-NPP Accord and why it fell apart. After the 1979 elections, the NPN found that it did not have a majority in the Legislature. Below are the figures, as shown in Table 7.6. In order to have a working majority, the NPN decided to enter into a formal agreement with the NPP. In exchange for cooperation with the NPN in the Legislature, the NPP obtained a number of executive and legislative offices,[81] the most prominent being that of the Speaker of the House.

Table 7.6
Composition of National Assembly
House of Representatives

Party	Number of Seats	Percentage
House		
NPN	168	37.4
UPN	111	24.7
NPP	78	17.4
PRP	49	10.9
GNPP	43	9.6
Total:	449	100.0
Senate		
NPN	36	37.9
UPN	28	29.5
NPP	16	16.9
PRP	7	7.3
GNPP	8	8.4
Total:	95	100.0

The NPP was the only party with whom the NPN could have formed the alliance for two basic reasons. One was that the UPN with its leader, Chief Obafemi Awolowo, was bitterly opposed to the NPN as its leadership; years after the election, he still claimed the election was stolen from him, a very misleading statement given the fact that he won only in the five States that made up the old Western Region where he was once a Premier. The other two parties, PRP and GNPP, none had the number needed to form a majority. Secondly, the NPN-NPP Accord echoed of the old NPC-NCNC coalition formed in the First Republic. Dr. Nnamdi Azikiwe, leader of the NCNC and now the NPP, had always made sure that the Ibos which made up the bulk of the NPP, "were not left out in the leadership stakes, a game Azikiwe had played with consummate skill in 1959."[82]

The NPN-NPP Accord worked until twenty months later on July 6, 1981 when the NPP informed its partner that it planned to terminate the partnership; thereupon NPN decided to abrogate the agreement immediately. According to NPP members, they had been denied the opportunity to get involved fully in national policy planning as promised and accused the NPN of having 'fascist tendencies' and of committing 'hideous atrocities'.[83] Thus ended the first and last formal coalition in the Shagari administration.

The Senate debate on the Revenue Allocation Bill, like that of the House of Representatives, was carried out in two stages: first, speeches were made regarding the general principles of the Bill; then, amendments were entertained; The Senate Leader, Olusola Saraki (NPN, Kwara)[84] opened the session with an eloquent defense of the rationale used at arriving at such a Bill. He specifically called attention to the numerous responsibilities of the Federal Government and even suggested increasing its allocation to 60. His views were supported by Senate leaders of Peoples' Redemption Party, PRP, and the Great Nigerian People; Party, GNPP; both, Northern-based parties whose Senators had, in recent past, been giving the NPN "reliable and pivotal support in major legislative confrontations."[85] (That was one of the reasons why the NPN could easily dispense with its accord with the NPP.) As Senator Mahmud Waziri, Senate GNPP leader explained his support for increased allocation to the Center,

The entrance of the Federal Government into new fields has in many cases strengthened the States and helped them improve their services...the Federal Government's functions would continue to expand in response to the national needs.[86]

Senator Suemo Chia (NPN, Benue) concurred about the necessity of a financially strong center when he said:

> I do not dispute the fact that the other levels of government have important roles to play to transform this country, and this fact is recognized in our new constitution. But the new constitution in recognizing the need for a strong center has given enormous responsibilities to the Federal Government. These responsibilities must be backed by sufficient financial provisions.[87]

However, equally intense counter-arguments were also heardspearheaded by the UPN and NPP Senate leaders. In his case against the center, Senator Obi Wali, NPP Senate Leader, called on the Federal Government to "divest itself of most of the revenues that it has appropriated from the States over the past fifteen years",[88] and suggested that it be given only 40 percent. The UPN Leader, Senator Jonathan Odebiyi, on the other had, recommended a 50:40:10 formula, after an exhaustive analysis of revenue allocation systems in the country. Also in support of a reduction of federal funds was Senator Nosike Ikpo (UPN, Bendel) who said:

> This system concentrates an inordinate amount of revenue and consequently power on the Federal Government. It creates an unacceptable political situation in which the component governments of the Federation, which by law are supposed to be equal and coordinate with the Federal Government are starved of vital revenues and therefore became holden to and dependent on the largess of the Federal Government for their survival.[89]

The classical view of federalism as expressed in the statement was the basis of most of the arguments against voting more revenue to the Center. The idea that all the tiers of the government are equal and coordinate is a constitutional fiction that had never been manifested in Nigeria or in any other federal system. The power relationship in a federation is always in a state of flux so that at any given time, one level of government always gains the upper hand in its ability to exploit and control resources in the state.[90] The process of altering the power pattern could be in the form of bargains, compromises or balances, and the adjustments are constantly made at various times. The debate over the Revenue Allocation Bill represented one of those instances when such adjustments were being negotiated.

Members of the ruling NPN political party saw the legislative hearings as an opportunity to hold onto the superior position the Federal Government had assumed since the military era. Led by Senator Uba Ahmed (NPN, Bauchi) and a group of 'young Turks', supporters of a financially stronger center had a field day when an amendment giving the Federal Government a whopping 58.5 percent share passed. It took two divisions, shouting, and an intense lobbying by NPN party stalwarts, Senators and Executive Officials, to help the amendment sail through. Their effort paid off when all the eight GNPP plus five PRP and six NPP Senators closed ranks with their NPN colleagues and voted 46:37:1 for the amendment. An earlier amendment sponsored by the UPN giving the central government only 50 percent failed by a 48:36 margin.[91] On each of those occasions, the NPP vote was split.

The lobbying effort carried out by the NPN was successful for many reasons. Already the NPP had been weakened by its shaky alliance with NPN, which divided it into two camps, as seen in the voting behavior of its Senators. One group led by Senator Nathaniel Anah (NPP, Anambra) believed in the NPN-NPP Accord and always voted with the NPN; the other side, headed by their Senate leader, Obi Wali (NPP, Rivers), adhered strictly to NPP policies and voted against the NPN.[92] The same rift also manifested itself in the PRP, but there it was between the Senators and the State Governors. According to Senator Sabo Zuwo, PRP Senate Leader, there were great personality clashes between the two categories of elected officials; therefore, the Senators did not want to vote for too much money to go the states where the Governors would use it to boost their personal prestige.[93] Moreover, they had not forgiven the Governors for joining with the 'Progressives'. The same arguments could be made to explain the behavior of GNPP Senators.

As it was in the House, the debate on derivation was both poignant and polemical, with supporters of each side often taking extreme views. Senators from oil States often times based their entire speeches on the derivation issue. A vivid example was Senator F.O.M. Atake (UPN, Bendel) who, despite interruptions, pleaded passionately for derivation. Here is an extract from the debate:

> Senator F.O.M Atake: You may say that we did not plant oil as you planted cocoa or groundnut but oil is coming out of somebody's land. It is coming out of my mother's back yard.
>
> Several Senators: No!

Senator Atake: It is true, it is coming out of my mother's back yard. It is coming from Rivers State, from Cross River State, et cetera... Then you say to me: Do not worry; you do not plant oil; you will have nothing on the principle of derivation. Are you being fair to me? Do you think I will go home happy? That was why the President put in something here for us. The only thing we are quarreling with is that the President has not given us enough... All we are saying is that the figure should be increased to at least 6.5 percent.

The wrangling over the derivation issues cut across party lines and even divided Senators from the same State, but representing different constituencies. Charges and countercharges were hurled at each other. At long last, the Senate agreed to allocate 5 percent for derivation.

Most UPN Senators contended that the 5 percent should be taken out of the Federal Government allocation, because Section 149 (2,4,4) of the Constitution specifically stated that the revenue should be shared among three tiers of government, therefore, any other sectoral factor that had to be catered for should be undertaken by the Federal Government from its own account. An amendment to that effect failed, but the Senators succeeded in extracting 2.5 percent for Abuja and 1.0 percent for ecological problems from Federal funds.

Since it had already been agreed that 58.5 percent should go to the central government, 5 percent for derivation, and 10 percent for the Local Governments (this was unopposed), the States were left with only 26.5 percent, a decrease of 3.5 percentage points from the Presidential Bill. It was that apparent loss of revenue to the Federal Government that evoked criticisms or praise from interested parties. State Governors who wanted more money in their coffers were appalled by the outcome of the Senate debate. Governor Jim Nwobodo of Anambra State, castigated renegade NPP Senators who voted with NPN, calling their action, "the greatest tragedy to the nation", and accusing them of carpet crossing.[94] The GNPP National Executive chastised its Senators for abandoning an earlier agreement to vote only 50 percent for the Federal Government.[95] In the House, non-NPN legislators described the Senate version as a betrayal of the development aspirations of the States.[96] But it was not only condemnations that the Senate received. According to Rep. Junaid Mohammad, PRP Chief Whip, passing of the Bill had revealed to the public, the Senate's sensitivity to the socio-economic reality of present day Nigeria.[97] In other words, given the circumstances under which it operated, the Senate was in the right direction in allocating greater revenue to the center.

196

What remained of the Bill was the inter-State allocation formula. During the debate, the principles of Equality of States and Population held sway; all other factors were more or less shelved into the background or fused with these two. However, when amendments were called for, a third principle, Land Area, was introduced. Another name for geographical spread, Land Area had long been advocated by expansive but underpopulated States.[98] In his motion, Senator David Dafinone, who represented small but heavily populated State, Bendel, surprisingly proposed substituting Land Area for Social Development and Internal Revenue, Effort, to be allocated 10 percent. The unexpected turn of events were not lost on a fellow legislator from the same State, Senator E.O. Akpata, who cynically added that:

> I am very glad that it is Senator Dafinone who is making history and who has introduced the question of land area; posterity will judge him.[99]

Some Senators from small coastal states like Bendel and Lagos wondered why Land Area should not be interpreted to include the territorial waters adjoining the states; but a proposal to that order failed to pass. The motive behind Senator Dafinone's move, which incidentally passed, could be the result of behind-the-scene 'horse-trading' between the NPN and Senators from expansive states like Borno and Gongola which were the strongholds of GNPP. The offering of selective incentives to individual states was an age-old technique of lobbying and the NPN used it effectively to achieve its objectives.

Other amendments passed by the Senate include apportioning 10 percent of states' total revenue to the States Local Government Joint Account, and using the same inter-state allocation system for the local governments.

Since the House and Senate versions of the Bill were different, a Joint Finance Committee, JFC,[100] was convened to resolve the differences. Meanwhile, the schisms in the Peoples Redemption Party, PRP, had become so great that two main factions emerged, on supporting the national leader, Alhaji Aminu Kano, and the other one following one of his former lieutenants, Michael Imoundu. The pro-Imoundu faction, which had allied with the 'Progressives', had vowed to support the House version of the Bill; however, the Federal Electoral Commission decided to recognize the pro-Aminu faction as the authentic one.[101] After a credentials snafu, in which each faction tried to present its candidate for the JFC, and thus held up the session for a day, the Chairman of the Committee was able to restore calm and the debate resumed.[102]

Despite all the altercations, the 24-man Joint Finance Committee passed the Senate version of the Bill with no amendments, by a 13:11 margin. The thirteen Senators who voted for the Bill were from the NPN, PRP and GNPP; those against were from UPN, NPP and GNPP (the only party to split its votes).

With what had been described as an undue haste, the Bill was sent to the President the following day, and he signed it into law three days later in a televised ceremony (see Table 7.7). While assenting to the Bill, President Shehu Shagari praised the Joint Finance Committee for demonstrating "in no uncertain terms its belief in the unity and stability of the nation"; and also for realizing that the Federal Government needed to be in a position to discharge its "onerous obligations to Nigerians". He hoped that the Revenue Allocation exercise will be the last for a long time.[103]

The President's hope for a lasting formula was squashed almost as soon as it was expressed. According to Lewis Obi of the *Sunday Concord*, an "unprecedented clamor of protests ever heard in recent history" followed the passage of the Revenue Allocation Bill into law. Those protests took several forms. There were the expected verbal attacks from members of the opposition parties. Ebenezer Babatope, UPN Director of Organization, saw the Bill as relegating the state governments to dignified local councils. His party leader, Chief Obafemi Awolowo, alleged that the clear intention of the Bill was to cripple the UPN-controlled states financially.[104] That was an interesting assertion given the fact that two UPN states, Bendel and Ondo, had cause to rejoice over the inclusion of 5 percent of states revenue for derivation. Although they wanted more, especially Bendel, the House version of the Bill which the UPN favored made no allowances whatsoever for derivation. Maybe what bothered the UPN most was the reduction of States' share to a measly 26.5 percent, while increasing the Federal Government's own to 58.5 percent. Such a cut was bound to be felt deeply by the UPN States because of the party's ambitious programs of free education and health care.

In his condemnation, the then Governor of Kaduna State, Alhaji Balarabe Musa accused the NPN of rigging the proceedings and alleged that the police were used to intimidate some members.[105] In his own submission, Governor Jim Nwobodo of Anambra State vowed to fight to ensure a fair and equitable allocation of revenue to the states, and called on any political party sharing similar views with the NPP on the issue to join hands with him in pursuing it, using all legal and constitutional means available.

In a singular move, the governors of the twelve non-NPN States (Anambra, Bendel, Borno, Gongolo, Imo, Kaduna, Kano, Lagos, Ogun, Ondo, Oyo and Plateau) met and issued a joint statement questioning the legality of the process through which the Bill went before receiving approval from the President. According to their reasoning, it was "unconstitutional and was tantamount to a few people forcing their views on our body politic". The

Table 7.7
Revenue allocation bill passed by the joint finance
committee and assented to by President Shehu Shagari

	Percentages
Federal Government	58.5
State Governments	31.5
Local Governments	10.0
Total:	100.0%

Federal Government

Responsibilities and Duties	55.0
Initial Development of Abuja	2.5
Ecological Problems	1.0
Total:	58.5%

State Governments

All States	26.5
Derivation	5.0
Total:	31.5%

Among States

Minimum Responsibility (Equality of States)	50.0
Population	40.0
Land Area	10.0
Total:	100.0%

Derivation

Direct Proportion of Extraction	2.0
Fund for Mineral Producing Areas	3.0
Total:	5.0%

Local Government Councils
Same as Among States

States to pay 10 percent of their total revenue to Joint Account.
Source: *New Nigeria* (February 26, 1981), p. 2.

Governors felt that the Joint Finance Committee had no authority to enact a Bill on behalf of the National Assembly and accused committee Chairman, Senator Olusola Saraki, of usurping the powers of the Assembly by presenting the Bill to the President for assent. Moreover, they argued that Senator Saraki violated the Constitution by having both an original and a casting vote. Other aspects of the process that came under attack were the recognition of one faction of the PRP by FEDECO (the faction recognized was opposed tot he PRP Governors), the presence of armed police in and around the premises of The National Assembly (necessitated by the PRP fracas when some legislators are forcibly prevented from taking their seats during the Committee hearing). The decision by the Senate to allow Local Governments to get statutory allocations direct from the Federal Government was seen as a deliberate attempt to erode the authority of the State Governments. That enacted by the military and absorbed into the Constitution that level of government was recognized as the third tier of governmental activity. It therefore needed an autonomous source of revenue and had been given one since then. The intention of the military in creating a third tier could be to reduce the political leverage of the states or as they claimed, to bring government closer to the people; but the National Assembly established in 1979, had nothing to do with that decision. Though the states resented the sub-division of their power and sometimes tried to dominate over the local councils, it was fallacious for the Governors to blame the situation on the legislature.

The only legitimate argument those Governors had was with the process the Bill was signed into law. During the JFC debates, the UPN Senate Leader, Jonathan Odebiyi, had hinted that they were dealing with a money bill, and therefore were constitutionally bound to report back to both Houses on the decisions reached. However, Senator Dafinone interjected that "I say authoritatively that it is not a Money Bill", and the legislators did not pursue the matter any further. Nevertheless, in a press conference called by Senator Saraki, Chairman of the JFC, after the vote, he said that a report of the Bill would be sent back to both chambers; and Senate President, Joseph Wayas also implied, when questioned, that the JFC would report to the House and Senate.

Why the normal legislative path was bypassed could be attributed to several reasons. In the first place, since nobody challenged Senator Dafinone's assertion, members of JFC must have been under the impression that they were not dealing with a Money Bill. Secondly, given the mood of the House of Representatives where the NPN had not been very successful in "embellishing its voting power through working alliances," there was little possibility that it would not reject the JFC Bill and set the whole process in motion all over again. The implication of such a repeat exercise was great and would not be too favorable for the President and his NPN. The delay was bound to affect the 1981 Appropriations Bill as well as the 4th National Development Plan. In addition, the constitutional provisions guiding such matters were vague and ambiguous and therefore subject to varying interpretations.[106]

Legal battles over revenue allocation bill

Barely two days after the passage of the Bill, the first series of law suits to contest its constitutionality appeared on the scene. The initial step was taken by Representatives Ralph Obioha and Alhaji Maina Maaji, who wanted a Lagos High Court to declare the decisions of the Joint Finance Committee null and void on the ground that the National Assembly was "incompetent to delegate its power of providing a system of Revenue Allocation under Sections 149 and 272 of the 1979 Constitution to a joint committee to decide whether the Revenue Allocation Bill shall be passed into law."[107] Following them was Senator Franklin Atake who argued that the law was a 'mere recommendation' of the JFC. In the same vein, Governors Nwobodo of Anambra and Onabanjo of Ogun States, also challenged the legality of the Bill.[108] Twelve of the nineteen states of the Federation resolved to seek redress in court, with Bendel State taking the lead.

The main issues involved in the legal tangle were twofold: (1) was the Bill passed a Money Bill and therefore governed by Section 53(3) of the Constitution which says, inter alia:

Where the joint finance committee fails to resolve such differences, then the bill shall be presented to the National Assembly sitting at a joint meeting, and if the bill is passed at such a joint meeting, it shall be presented to the President for assent, or (2) was it under the jurisdiction of Section 58 which stipulates the rules for sitting of committees but adds that:

Nothing in this section shall be construed as authorizing such House to delegate to a committee the power to decide whether a bill shall be passed into law or to determine any matter which it is empowered to determine by resolution under the provisions of this constitution, but the committee may be authorized to make recommendations to the House on any such matter. It was those two seemingly conflicting sections of the Constitution that advocates and opponents of the Bill clung to. Based on that a Lagos High Court threw out the suit brought by Representatives Obioha and Maaji, on the grounds that only the Supreme Court had the last say on issues involving interpretation and application of the Constitution.[109] Thereafter, the Supreme Court decided to hear all the cases relating to the Revenue Allocation Bill at the same time to facilitate proceedings and took the one brought by Bendel State Government as a test case and adjourned all others indefinitely.[110]

By originating summons against the Federal Government, each of the other eighteen state governments, the National Assembly, the President of the Senate, the Speaker of the House of Representatives, and the Clerk of the Assembly, Governor Ambrose Alli, acting on behalf of his Bendel State, expressed in a legal way the dissatisfaction and frustration felt by many interested parties about the way and manner the National Assembly exercised its legislative power in regards to the Revenue Allocation Bill. In his suit, the Governor asked the Supreme Court to determine whether it was the provisions of Section 54 titled, "Mode of Exercising Federal Legislative Power: General" or Section 55 titled, "Mode of Exercising Federal Legislative Power: Money Bills", that applied to the Bill, and also if the Bill was legally enacted, whether it was consistent with Section 149 which dealt with Public Revenue and the Distributable Pool Account.[111]

Based on those clauses, the Court was further requested to make these declarations:

(1)   That it was only Section (I)55 of the Constitution that was applicable to the Bill;

(2)   That the Bill referred to the Joint Committee could not lawfully be enacted into law until it had been passed by a majority of both Houses of the National Assembly;

(3)   That the members who met as a Joint Conference Committee did not constitute a meeting of the Joint Committee of the National Assembly as envisaged by Section 55 of the Constitution;

(4)   That the Revenue Allocation Act was not an Act of the National Assembly, therefore, its provisions were unconstitutional, null and void and of no effect;

(5)   That it would be illegal and unconstitutional for the Federal Government to carry out the provisions of the Revenue Allocation Act;

(6)   That the Supreme Court should issue an injunction restraining all public officials from executing the Act.[112]

The Chief Defense Counsel, the Attorney-General of the Federation, Chief Richard Akinjide started off with a warning about a possible fall out of the case. He told the Court that:

The Consequences of going beyond that legislative proceedings to determine the validity of the Act are very grave and will lead this country to chaos and instability. Replying to him, the Chief Justice answered that the

Supreme Court would not lend its weight to illegality just because of anticipated chaos and instability.

The main text of the defense was threefold. First, the defendants submitted that the Court had no jurisdiction the case because the subject of the complaint concerned power exercised by the Legislature and the Executive. In other words, the Judiciary was not supposed to adjudicate in matters concerning exercise of power by the other two branches of government. Secondly, they argued that there was no dispute between the plaintiff and the defendants, because the claim of the plaintiff which was based on the manner a bill was passed, created no dispute between the states and the Federal Government. Moreover, Section 212(1) of the Constitution stated that the Supreme Court had original jurisdiction in a case only if there is a dispute involving a question, whether of law or fact, on which the existence or extent of a legal right depended. The third line of argument was that since the plaintiff, the Bendel State Government, had benefitted from the Revenue Allocation Act in questions, by collecting its own share of the revenue, it then could not question its validity. By enjoying the provisions of the Act, the plaintiff had waived its right to ask the Court to rule on the Act's legal force. To support the contention, they referred to some similar cases in the United States.

During the trial, counsels for the defendants objected to the admissibility of certain pieces of evidence, the most objectionable being the proceedings of the National Assembly on the said Act. However, the Court overruled the objections on the ground that it could not make any proper ruling concerning the exercise of legislature if its papers could not be examined.

After reviewing the massive legal submissions from both the plaintiff and the defendants, all seven justices of the Supreme Court, in a seven-and-a half hour marathon judgement, agreed that the Revenue Allocation Act, as passed by the JFC was unconstitutional.

In delivering the judgement, the Chief Justice, Atanda Fatayi-Williams, systematically destroyed each of the defense arguments. The initial contention that the Court had no jurisdiction in matters concerning power exercise by the Legislature or Executive was not upheld because Section 4 (8) of the Constitution stated inter alia:

> Save as otherwise provided by this Constitution, the exercise of legislative power by the National Assembly or by a House of Assembly shall be subject to the jurisdiction of courts of law and of judicial tribunals established by law.[113]

The Court held that since the Bill was read, debated and passed, legislative power had been exercised, therefore, it had jurisdiction to hear the case.

On the issue of 'no dispute' between the litigants the Court replied that any state which believed a particular legislative procedure was not in accordance with the Constitution, had a justifiable dispute. Also the contention that Bendel State had forfeited its right to challenge the validity of the Act because it benefitted from its provisions, was dismissed, on the ground that the plaintiff received the said allocation by virtue of the transitional provisions of the Constitution.

Having established the right of the Court to adjudicate and that of the plaintiff to sue, the Chief Justice went ahead to deal with the issue involved. He held that the Joint Finance Committee which agreed on the Bill did constitute a Joint Committee of the National Assembly as provided by Section 55 of the Constitution. Consequently, since the Bill under question was a Money Bill, the Joint Finance Committee had no constitutional power to pass it into law, because Section 58(4) clearly specified that the JFC could not decide for the Assembly whether a bill should be passed into law or not. In addition, the National Assembly had no inherent power of its own to delegate or transfer its exclusive constitutional power to make a valid law, to any joint committee. He did not accept the argument that the JFC Bill represented a resolution of differences between the version passed by the two legislative chambers, holding that "until the two Houses, sitting either separately or jointly as the case may be, pass the bill or the committee's version of it, it is not a bill passed by the National Assembly and cannot, therefore, be assented to the President of the Federal Republic of Nigeria." There upon, the Supreme Court declared that Allocation of Revenue (Federation Account, etc.) Act 1981 (No. 1 of 1981) unconstitutional and therefore invalid, null and void, and of no effect whatsoever. It also constrained all public officers from operating the Act. However, due to the 'nature, complexity, and scope of the claims', no costs were awarded.

The judgement of the Supreme Court was hailed all over the land as historic and commendable. According to some, the verdict signified a "landmark in the history of operation of the Judiciary as far as its independence is concerned." Others saw it as vindicating the impartiality of the Court, thus demonstrating its willingness and capability to always protect and uphold the Constitution of the country.[114] Those accolades, mostly from non-NPN parties, were interesting in that, in 1979, the same Court was vilified and even re-christened the "Nigerian Supreme Court of Injustice" when it issued a ruling against Chief Obafemi Awolowo, leader of the UPN, in his bid to declare President Shagari's election victory as unconstitutional.

The National Party of Nigeria, NPN, was not left out in the sounding of the praise of the Supreme Court. It also extolled the body for manifesting its independence in settling constitutional issues. The NPN had cause to rejoice in the ruling because, by its actions, the Court absolved the Federal Government of the accusation that it controlled the Judiciary. The Attorney-General of Federation, who was the chief defense counsel, exonerated both the President and the National Assembly for their obvious 'illegal' act, on the ground that the "section of the Constitution relevant to the procedure is a very difficult one to interpret."[115]

Final passage of the 1981 revenue allocation bill

Suggestions were made to the Federal Government to revert to the Aboyade allocation formula, or even further back, to that used by the military. State and Local Governments who had already collected their share of federal revenue were threatened by the Attorney-General that they might be made to refund their revenues to the Federal Government. Given that unpleasant situation, legislators started thinking again.

It should be borne in mind that the supreme Court judgment was concerned with a procedural rather than a substantial question. Following that logic, the Senate leaders of the Unity Party of Nigeria, UPN, and the Nigerian Peoples Party, NPP, moved to reconsider the nullified Joint Finance Committee version of the Revenue Allocation Bill. the NPN, on the other hand saw the plan as patently wrong and argued that the whole Act was nullified, therefore, a fresh Bill should be presented for debate. Voting on the motion was tied, giving the President of the Senate, the opportunity to cast the tie-breaker, which he did in favor of those opposed to the motion. Thus the 1981 Revenue Allocation Bill was finally laid to eternal rest.[116]

Once again, the President took the initiative from the Legislature when he sent a somewhat reconditioned Revenue Allocation Bill to the National Assembly. Before sending the new Bill, he consulted with the National Council of States (composed of state governors and former heads of state) as well as with other eminent Nigerians and legislators. The new Bill bore close resemblance to the original one sent; the major difference being an increase in the states' allocation, since that was what led to the doom of the first one.

Lobbying for the Bill was as intensive as before, with the 'oil lobby' in the forefront. They protested against the 5 percent for derivation in the nullified Bill, and asked for a 'more reasonable and equitable' share of the revenue, and vowed to sink their political differences to make sure that their states were not cheated or neglected in the new allocation process about to begin. They were consequently assured by the President, who declared in Port Harcourt, capital of the Rivers State, that his administration still attached importance to the derivation principle and stated that "my stand on the derivation principle in the sharing of the national cake is unshaken."[117] But to their dismay, the derivation share was reduced from the 5 percent to 3.5 percent! That showed that more expedient political considerations took the upper hand at Ribadu House (official residence of the President) between the time that speech was made and the drafting of the new Bill. the President realized that increasing the share to the states would be more beneficial to him and his party by satisfying the other parties who would be inclined to support the Bill. There were only three major oil producing states and they were small states, in size and population, so that their voting strength, especially in the House was minimal. Moreover, in the Senate, two Senators from Rivers State were NPP and belonged to the faction opposed to the Accord and therefore always voted against the NPN and derivation. So in the trade-off between increasing States' allocation and the derivation quota, the former clearly won. In addition, Senators from the GNPP, PRP and NPP who had formed an informal alliance with the NPN were all from non-oil producing states and would rather vote for enhanced states' share. Also, Governor Ambrose Alli who instituted the suit against the old Bill was from Bendel State, the largest producer of oil and thus would have been the biggest beneficiary of the derivation principle; the reduction could be a means of chastising and discrediting him and his party, the UPN.

Discussions on the Bill gathered momentum almost as soon as it was introduced. In the Senate, Senate Leader Saraki opened the debate by calling the Bill the best under the circumstances, and urged his colleagues to pass it. Likewise, both UPN and NPP leaders in the Senate implored their members to attach no amendments in order to ensure a speedy and early passage. The advise, however, fell on deaf ears as Senators decided to stick to their guns and added their own embellishments. In a rather heated but short debate, lasting less than 30 minutes, the Senate passed its version of the new Bill with following amendments: for inter-state allocation, the principles of Equality was to have 50 percent, Population, 40 percent and Land Area given 10 percent. In addition, derivation was raised to 5 percent, out of which 2 percent was to be set aside for the development fund. Party lines were again drawn, with the UPN and N PP voting against the Bill mainly because their states would lose revenue if Land Area was used as criterion; instead, they would rather have the President's Bill that did not include that principle. But they lost by a 45:38 margin. It was not a vote without antics. Senators Dafinone and Akan, both NPN Senators, voted in favor of the amendments and were accused by the UPN of betraying the President. According to Senator Obi Wali, NPP Senate Leader, their action was equivalent to NPN breaking the 'Accord-Concordiale' for the second time, referring to the aborted NPN-NPP Accord.[118]

In the House of Representatives, a different story was heard. After less than two hours debate, the Bill was passed without any amendments, and with a thunderous ovation.

As usual, a 24-man Joint Finance Committee was set up to resolve the differences between the two versions of the Bill. There, all the Senate amendments were rejected in their entirety. It was ironical that it was the President's own party, the NPN which was against his Bill. The rally was led by Senators from the large Northern States who wanted to substitute Land Area for Social Development factor as a criterion for inter-state allocation. If Senator Dafinone had not changed his mind, the President's Bill would have been defeated. Instead of following the lead of his fellow NPN Senators in voting for inclusion of Land Area, the Senator chose state interest over party and voted against the amendments. He realized that his Bendel State had a large growing primary school population, and so would profit if Social Development factor which was based on school enrollment, was used. With the vote tied at 11:11 (one JFC member was absent) the chairman, Senator Ameh Ebute (NPN, Benue) also from a small State, cast the decisive vote against the amendments, thereby giving the non-NPN caucus in the Senate a chance of 'victory'.[119]

Cautious not to make the same mistake twice, the Joint Finance Committee Bill was sent back to both legislative houses. The Senate adopted it with a deafening voice vote despite frantic efforts by Senators Lliya Audu (NPN, Gongola) and Uba Ahmed (NPN, Bauchi) to prevent its passage. It was the same group of Senators that had fought hard for the amendments earlier during the Senate debates. The House of Representatives, often praised for its 'patriotic pragmatism'; came back from a Christmas and New Year recess, and without rancor, passed the Bill. The *New Nigerian*, in an editorial, saw the quick passage of the new Bill as a 'reflection of desperation' rather than a change of attitude.[120] Whatever it really was, the die was cast.

At long last, on January 22, 1982, the Revenue Allocation saga, which began with the setting up on the Presidential Commission under the chairmanship of Dr. Pius Okigbo in November 1981, got to a point of denouement, when the President assented and signed it into law, amidst a very colorful ceremony.

Conclusion

Like his predecessors, President Shehu Shagari envisaged using expert commissions to devise an allocation formula that would be acceptable to the major interested parties. Having been a member of the Constituent Assembly that spearheaded the defeat of the Aboyade Report, he knew the pitfalls any expert advice could face, especially one about revenue allocation — one of most controversial issues in the country. Also, as a politician, he understood that partisan and ethnic considerations play a vital role in the final adoption of any revenue allocation formula. That was why the Bill he presented, which was a modified version of the Okigbo Report he commissioned, had the politically sensitive elements altered to suit his audience; as evidenced by the reinstatement of the Derivation principle. However, as far as the experts were concerned, their duty was to fashion a revenue formula capable of providing a sound foundation for a fiscal policy that would benefit the nation as a whole. They were least worried about producing a Report which would satisfy *ALL* segments of the population. That was the task that proved almost impossible. That was because the NPN itself was a conglomerate of diverse interest groups and could not come to a consensus on the revenue issue.

The long and acrimonious legislative debate over the Revenue Allocation Bill and its aftermath showed that vested interests can nullify some of the results obtained by expert commissions, lending credence to the notion that revenue policy in Nigeria, especially during constitutional periods, is determined through negotiated compromise. And the experts were recruited to translate that 'compromise' into fiscal terms.

The figures in Table 7.8 and the accompanying Graph illustrate how the percentages of revenue retained by the central government varied from regime to regime over the years. The fluctuations correspond to the ups and downs in Nigeria's political history.

Table 7.8
Percentage of centrally collected revenue
retained by federal government

Financial Year	Constitution/ Regime	%.%	Average of Constitutional Period
1948/49	Richards	79.6	
1949/50	Constitution	78.2	
1950/51		75.5	78.8
1951/52		82.2	
1952/53	MacPherson	74.2	75.5
1953/54	Constitution	76.8	
1954/55	Lyttleton	56.2	
1955/56	Constitution	57.0	
1956/57		59.8	58.4
1957/58		59.1	
1958/89		60.0	
1959/60	Independence/	56.8	
1960/61	Republic	64.5	
1961/62	Constitution	59.3	
1962/63		59.3	60.9
1963/64		60.8	
1964/65		64.1	
1965/66		61.4	
1966/67	Military coup	59.9	
1967/68	to end of	59.4	
1968/69	Civil War	69.5	63.1
1969/70	1st phase of	63.2	
1970/71	Military Regime	65.6	

(Continued)

Table 7.8 (Continued)

Financial Year	Constitution/ Regime	%.%	Average of Con- stitutional Period
1971/72	2nd phase of	74.2	
1972/73	Military Regime	75.3	
1973/74		82.9	79.8
1974/75		84.0	
1975/76		82.7	
1976/77	Final phase of	79.5	
1977/78	Military Regime	78.7	76.9
1978/79		75.9	
1979/80		73.7	
1980/81	2nd Republic	55.0	55.0

Source: Figures were taken from several sources used in the body of the text. They include: Adedeji, Adebayo, *Nigerian Federal Finance*, (New York: Africana Publishing Company, 1969); Philips, Adedotun O., 'Nigeria's Federal Financial Experience', *Journal of Modern African Studies*, Vol. 9, No. 3 (October 1971); and *Report of the Presidential Commission on Revenue Allocation*, Vols. I, II, III (Lagos: Federal Government Press, 1980).

Notes

1. Burton, Frank and Pat Carlen, *Official Discourse*. (London: Routledge and Kegan Paul, Ltd., 1979), p. 1.

2. The policy stated that all federal appointments and resources be evenly and fairly distributed across the States. See Chapter II for details on the policy.

3. *New Nigeria*. (May 3, 1978).

4. Ibid., (May 14, 1978).

5. Margolis, Harold, *Technical Advice on Policy Issues*. (Beverly Hills, CA: Sage Publications, 1973), p. 25.

6. Hanser, Charles, *Guide to Decision: The Royal Commission*. (Totowa, NJ: The Bedminister Press, Inc., 1965).

7. Meltsner, Arnold, *Policy Analysts in the Bureaucracy*. (Berkeley, CA: University of California Press, 1976), p. 83.

8. Price, Price, *The Scientific Estate*. (Cambridge, MA: Harvard University Press, 1965), p. 68.

9. Shagari, Alhaji Shehu, 'Inaugural Address', in *Views of the Government of the Federation on the Report of the Presidential Commission of Revenue Allocation*, Vol 1. (Lagos: Federal Government Press, 1980), P. 131. (To be referred to as the *Okigbo Report*).

10. *Constitution of the Federal Republic of Nigeria*. (1979. Chapter VI, Part 1c, Section 149.

11. *Okigbo Report*, Vol. 1 pp. 10-40.

12. Ibid., Vol. I, p. 84.

13. Ibid., Vol. III, pp. 5-21.

14. Ibid., Vol. I, pp. 84-136.

15. *Okigbo Report*, Vols. 11 & 111.

16. Ibid.

17. Informal review with a former top NPN executive who declined to be identified.

18. *Okigbo Report*, Vols. II & III.

19. Ibid.

20. Ibid, pp 9-10.

21. Ibid., p. 84.

22. Ibid.

23. *Daily Sketch (Nigeria)*, op. cit., p. 3.

24. Ibid., p. 90.

25. Ibid., Vol. 3, p. 352.

26. Ibid, p. 454.

27. Ibid.

28. Ibid.

29. Ibid.

30. Ibid.

31. These ideas and sentiments were gathered from conversations with prominent Nigerians such as Dr. Chuba Okadigbo, former political advisor to President Shagari, Dr. Ibrahim Gambari, former Federal Minister of External Affairs, and Dr. Lawrence Ekepbu, former Commissioner of Finance, Rivers State, and a host of others who declined to be identified.

32. Ibid.

33. Ibid.

34. Ibid.

35. Ibid.

36. Ibid.

37. Ibid.

38. Representative Kaltungo's title reflected the fact that the NPN did not have a majority in the House, else he would have been the Majority Leader. However, it was his duty to propose any amendments or motions sponsored by the party.

39. *Daily Sketch* (Nigeria), (January 19, 1981), p. 1.

40. Larry Diamond, "Social Change and Political Conflict" in I. William Zartman, *The Political Economy of Nigeria*. (New York: Praeger Publishers, 1983), p. 48.

41. B. Dudley, op. cit., p. 217.

42. Larry Diamond, op. cit., pp. 48-49.

43. See explanation of title in note 44 above.

44. Larry Diamond, op. cit., p. 48.

45. *Senate Debates*, (November 25, 1980), p. 9.

46. *Senate Debates*, (November 26, 1980), pp. 28-29.

47. A.H. Birch, *Federalism, Finance and Social Legislation*. (Oxford: Clarendon Press, 1957), p. 6.

48. *Daily Times* (Nigeria), (January 15, 1981), p. 32.

49. *Africa Now*, (May 1981), p. 71.

50. *The Punch* (Nigeria), (January 16, 1981), p. 1.

51. *Senate Debates*, (November 25, 1980), p. 11.

52. Melford Okilo, *Derivation: A Criterion of Revenue Allocation*. (Port Harcourt, Nigeria: Rivers State Newspaper Corporation, 1980).

53. Kanu, Chijioke, 'Okigbo Revenue Allocation Formula; A Dispassionate Analysis,' *Nigerian Statesman*. (September 29, 11980), p. 14.

54. *The Punch*, op. cit., p. 1.

55. *Daily Sketch (Nigeria)*, (September 8, 1980), p. 3.

56. *Nigerian Standard*, (September 10, 1980), p. 1.

57. *Nigerian Observer*, (June 21, 1980) p. 1.

58. *Senate Debates*, (December 2, 1980), p. 2.

59. *New Nigeria*, (September 11, 1980), p. 3.

60. *National Concord* (Nigeria), (February 9, 1981), p. 3.

61. *Sunday Sketch (Nigeria)*, (August 31, 1980), p. 1.

62. *Nigerian Chronicle*, (July 5, 1980), p. 1.

63. *Sunday Concord* (Nigeria), (February 15, 11981), p. 5.

65. Jerenton-Mariere, Efe, 'Haba, Mr. President',' *Nigerian Observer*, (September 14, 1980), p. 8.

66. *Daily Star (Nigeria)*, (September 17, 1980), p. 1.

67. *New Nigeria*, op. cit., p. 3.

68. Offensend, David, 'Centralization and Fiscal Arrangement in Nigeria', *Journal of Modern African Studies*, Vol. 14, No. 3, (September 1976), p. 509.

69. For a full text of the statement, see *West Africa*, (February 23, 1981), pp. 357-58.

70. *Nigerian Chronicle*, op. cit., p. 1.

71. Oyovbaire, Sam, 'The Politics of Revenue Allocation', in S.K. Panter-Brick, *Soldiers and Oil: The Political Transformation of Nigeria.* (London: Frank Cass, 1978), p. 224.

72. Larry Diamond, op. cit., p. 50.

73. Dudley, Billy, *An Introduction to Nigerian Government and Politics.* (Bloomington, IN: Indiana University Press, 1982), p. 163.

74. Joseph, Richard, 'The Overthrow of Nigeria's Second Republic', *Current History.* Vol. 83, (March 1984), p. 123.

75. *National Assembly Debates, Senate, (November 24, 1980).* (Lagos: Federal Government Press, 1980), pp.4-5 (to be referred to as *Senate Debates*).

76. *Daily Star* (Nigeria), (March 2, 1981), p. 1.

77. *1979 Nigerian Constitution*, op. cit., Section 55(3).

78. *National Assembly Debates, House of Representatives, (November 3, 1980).* (Lagos: Federal Government Press, 1980), p. 3 (to be referred to as *House Debates*).

79. *House Debates,* (November 1980), p. 7-27.

80. Ibid.

81. *The Punch* (Nigeria), (June 11, 1981), p. 16.

82. SC17/1981, pp. 25-26.

83. *The Punch*, op. cit., p. 16.

84. SC17/1981, p. 48.

85. Ibid., pp. 32-36.

86. *Daily Times* (Nigeria), (October 3, 1981), p. 1.

87. *1979 Nigerian Constitution*, op. cit., Section 4(8).

88. SC17/1981, p. 48.

89. *1979 Nigerian Constitution*, op. cit., Section 4(8) p. 46.

90. *Sunday New Nigerian,* (October 18, 1981), p. 9.

91. Ibid., p. 9.

92. *New Nigerian,* (October 5, 1981), p. 32.

93. Ibid., (October 12, 1981), p. 1.

94. *Sunday New Nigerian*, op. cit., p. 9.

95. *Sunday Observer (Nigeria)*, (January 16, 1981), p. 1.

96. *Daily Sketch (Nigeria)*, (January 31, 1981), p. 1.

97. Boniface Ofoegbu, "History of Revenue Allocation in Nigeria", *Daily Sketch* (Nigeria) (May 20, 1982), p. 7.

98. *New Nigeria*, (January 21, 1981), p. 3.

99. *Nigerian Chronicle*, (November 26, 1981), pp. 1 & 10.

100. Ibid., (January 15, 1981), p.12.

101. *National Concord (Nigeria)*, (February 13, 1981), p. 7.

102. *Daily Times* (Nigeria), (December 10, 1981), p. 5.

103. *West Africa*, (February 9, 1981), p. 261.

104. *New Nigerian*, (February 4, 1981), p. 1.

105. *Nigerian Observer*, (February 19, 1981), pp. 1-3.

106. *Daily Sketch (Nigeria)*, February 6, 1981), p. 9.

107. *Daily Star (Nigeria)*, (February 9, 1981), pp. 3 and 9.

108. *Africa Now*, op. cit., p. 73.

109. *Daily Times (Nigeria)*, (February 14, 1981), p. 1.

110. *Daily Star*, (March 2, 1981) p. 1.

111. *Daily Times (Nigeria)* (March 11, 1981), p. 1.

112. *New Nigeria*, (April 22, 1981), p. 1.

113. *Judgment of the Supreme Court of Nigeria, No. SC17/1981.* (October 2, 1981), pp. 16-17 (to be referred to as *SC17/1981*).

114. *Nigerian Tribune*, (November 6, 1981), p. 16.

115. *Nigerian Herald*, (November 3, 1981), p. 1.

116. *Sunday Punch (Nigeria)*, (December 20, 1981), p. 5.

119. Boniface Ofoegu, op. cit., p. 7.

120. *New Nigeria*, (January 11, 1982), p. 1.

8 Nigeria: Summary of fiscal federalism in retrospect

Nigeria, like any other federation has had to deal with the disparity between the fiscal needs and revenue sources of the different levels of government. This has been done through a system of intergovernmental financial transfers, usually from the higher to the lower tiers. Since most of the nation's revenues are centrally collected, its major form of redistribution is statutorily mandated. The various governments have recruited experts to assist in devising revenue allocation formulas.

Looking through the various revenue allocations systems adopted by policy-makers in Nigeria, one can isolate two major phases. From 1948 to 1954 and from 1966-1979, the country was run as a unitary system, with powers — political and fiscal — concentrated in the central government. The political parties were still basically weak and could not challenge the authoritative colonial government effectively or they did not exist. Hence, fiscal experts who devised allocation schemes saw to it that the bulk of federally collected revenues remained at the center. The central government often retained greater percentages for all revenues collected. This is reflected in colonial and post-colonial governments including the first post-independence military regime which seized power in 1966, (especially after the end of the civil war in 1970). Federal shares of revenues were at their highest during the 1970s, illustrating the stronghold the center had on the country. The states, which had been sub-divided, first into twelve and then, into nineteen and thirty were subordinate to and dominated by a highly hierarchical military administration at the helm in Lagos or Abuja, were in no position to struggle for resources. There were no state representatives at the national level (military governors got their orders from their superiors in Lagos and Abuja, and functioned as central emissaries) to argue the cause for the states, which were more or less treated as vassals.

In inter-state sharing, a similar trend can be observed. During the periods of centralized government, allocation principles which emphasized national integration, such as 'Even Development', 'Need', and 'Minimum Responsibility,' were given more prominence than those like 'Derivation' which stressed separateness. The lack of active participation of regional (state) interests in national fiscal policy making contributed to the feelings of actual or perceived inequities in the operation of Fiscal Federalism.

Unlike other federations like the Indian and the Australian, which have permanent fiscal commissions that meet at prescribed times (India's convenes every five years, while that of Australia is Standing Commission), Nigeria's fiscal panels have been *ad hoc*. The chronic inter-governmental fiscal conflict can be largely attributed to this lack of permanence and durability of revenue systems. As long as revenue sharing was tied to constitutional reviews, each new attempt at fiscal adjustment would bring on either fresh agitations or renew old ones for imagined or real inequalities in the existing formula. The expert commissions would also be subjected to more political influence than would a permanent body. However, despite recommendations by experts, and promises by policy-makers to set up a permanent system in Nigeria has remained *ad hoc*. It seems nobody wants to lose whatever influence he is exerting on the experts and the political benefits obtained by publicly advocating one set of allocation principles or the other. "On all questions of policy the final decisions rest in the hands of the politicians, whose determination will often be dictated by political considerations which bear little or no relation or expertness or impartiality." And Revenue Allocation policy in Nigeria remains one of those that fits the above description perfectly. The importance of the policy, coupled with its controversial nature demanded that vested interests have the final say in formulation of the policy.

Periods of active and sustained regional (state) involvement in every aspect of national politics were from 1954-1960 and 1979-1982. In essence, when the country became federal in 1954, the Constitution granted residual powers to the regions and the consolidation of regional power ensued. Powerful political parties and their representatives fought against each other to obtain access to national resources. Thus regional allocations increased significantly during that period. Fiscal experts understood the new power relationship and acted accordingly. In inter-state allocation, emphasis was placed on the Derivation principle, which was in tandem with the regionalization fever that swept the country — until the first military coup of January 1966. There was 13 year military rule from 1966-1979. When party politics resumed in 1979, state causes were once again in the forefront of political negotiations. Representatives who went to Lagos fought for increased revenues to the states, realizing that their political survival depended on how much, in terms of resources, they could bring home. And as stated earlier, the absence of strong regional parties made the competition more personalized, and so more intensive.

As the country moved away from a unitary system to a more federal one, the proportion of national revenues retained by the center diminished. It reached its lowest point in the 1954-1959 period from the beginning of the federal constitution to independence. That period also saw the height of regionalization of the country, resulting in a much weakened center. The trend reversed, though slowly, due to factors enumerated elsewhere in this study, as the country started functioning as an independent nation.

The end of partisan politics in 1966 that accompanied the onset of military rule brought about an upsurge in central revenues. As the military regime consolidated its power, so did the share of federally retained revenues increase until it reached its zenith during the 1974-76 era, which coincided with the boom in oil prices. As the soldiers prepared to go back to the barracks, the proportion of federally retained revenues started to decrease slightly until they finally left government in 1979. Politicians, once again, resumed control of the country and partisan politics flourished, giving rise to a further and drastic reduction in the share of centrally collected revenues collected revenues retained by the federal government.

From the above, it can be seen that in sharing the revenue between the central and regional (state) governments, attempts were made to correlate formal responsibilities with financial resources. In other words, the more functions a level of government had to perform, the more its allocation of the central revenues. That fulfilled one of the requirements of fiscal federalism — the provision of revenue that corresponds with the division of governmental responsibilities. The regional governments always complained that the revenue allocated to them was never adequate; this was heard more often after the first military takeover. The federal government, on the other hand, had justified its retention of large shares of the revenue on the grounds that its constitutional responsibilities demanded such. Since there can be no strict demarcation of functions between the governments, the central organ in a federation like Nigeria, which has a centralized economy, may be expected to continue to have the upper hand in inter-governmental allocation of revenues.

Most of the literature on fiscal federalism stresses the principles of fiscal economy, equity and efficiency as the goals of federal finance. However, as seen in the analyses of the allocation formulas, these theoretical bases for revenue allocation were not followed. Instead, new sets of principles like Derivation, Need, National Interest and the like, which had little or no bearing to fiscal principles, were employed. As Olaloku (1979) put it:

The development of federal finance in Nigeria is nothing but the history of the various attempts made to contain the financial consequences that

220

accompanied all the constitutional changes which took place in the country since World War II.[1]

These various attempts were actually exercises in public policy-making, and they involved choosing among a variety of possible alternatives. The literature on public policy shows that there is no grand theory on how the choices are made. Public policy-making in Nigeria can best be described as an amalgam of the competing paradigms. While Revenue Allocation policy was indeed a response of the political system to demands, the policy itself had been a result of compromises made by interested groups which struggled to out-maneuver each other. Though leaders of these contending factions could be termed the elite, it cannot be stated categorically that revenue policy in Nigeria represented their own values and preferences. This is because the most effective and significant interest group in the country was the Political Party, and it functioned as a regional/ethnic vehicle. Even during military rule, inter-regional interest aggregation revolved around patterns formed by the old party alliance system. Therefore, the ruling elite, in a sense could be said to have articulated and fought for not interests dictated by the personal values of its individual members, but by the values of the groups they represented. One can thus conclude that revenue allocation policy in Nigeria was a response to the constitutional/political changes in the system by elites who represented the values and preferences of regionally (state)/ethnically defined interest groups through the agencies of semi-institutional fiscal review commissions.

Nigerian political leaders, be they colonial administrators, military officers or indigenous politicians, have called on experts to aid them in formulating public policies. However, although the knowledge possessed by those intellectuals was highly valued and in demand, it could and did serve only as a guide for the policy-makers who used it to help them arrive at politically desirable decisions. The overt reason for using the experts was that they would look at controversial problems from a rational, scientific viewpoint and produce solutions. However, for the policy-maker who would utilize the expert advice, political expediency was paramount in his decisions to adopt the solutions presented.

It is the contention of this study that the various expert bodies set up to formulate revenue allocation policies were well aware that they were dealing with an issue that had a very high political content. Hence, they tried to accommodate the wishes of the interested parties and arrived at solutions which were acceptable to those interests. Experts have been known to underestimate the extent to which they are involved in making political decisions, that does not negate the fact that they usually take positions which have far-reaching political consequences. The very choice of one alternative among many

221

represents a preference that may connote a normative judgement on the part of the expert. Our case study of Revenue Allocation in Nigeria shows that experts had to choose and recommend weights to various criteria of allocation. None of the expert fiscal commissions devised or showed any scientific basis for its choice of revenue principles and their weights. This is because it has so far proved impossible to translate constitutional responsibility and functions into monetary terms and present them as neat statistical packages. The fact that the principles and their weights selected by the fiscal panels were usually accepted with minor modifications by the decision-makers demonstrates that the experts were in tune with the political climate of the Nigerian system — a prerequisite for any expert body that wishes to have its finding used in policy formulation.

The desirability of any particular fiscal system is ultimately a decision made by political leaders through negotiated compromise. Even if the fiscal experts were prepared to be as 'scientific' or 'objective' or 'rational' as possible, they could not have escaped the political influences from the environment. Those influences were exerted directly in two basic ways: (1) via the process of recruitment when policy-makers choose experts who are compatible with them and grateful and willing to serve; and (2) through the politically derived terms of reference given the experts. These directives defined the scope, as well as the degrees of freedom, allowed the experts, and acted as an authoritative advice that steered them toward the goals and objectives of the decision-makers. The particular point of view which prevailed during the constitutional conventions or other high level deliberations that produced the terms of reference usually found its way into them, and the expert panel was, in one way or the other, coerced into adopting and implementing it in the fiscal formula it designed.

The other way influence was exerted on the experts was indirectly, through the political system and their own perceptions and reactions to it. As elaborated in the preceding chapters, politics in Nigeria revolved around the struggle for shares of national revenues by ethnically defined regions (states). In the pre-military era (1954-66), the political parties that developed to articulate and aggregate the interests of the people had what could be described as particularist mentality, strategy and orientation. That was because the credibility of any political party as guardian of the regional interests depended on its access to and ability to make available, the resources needed. And since most of the resources were centralized, the unmitigated struggle, before independence, was one of devolving power to the regions as evidenced in the types of constitutions and consequent revenue allocation systems. After independence, the parties competed for dominance over the federal center — the source of most resources. The purpose of the political parties in the 2nd Republic did not change, but lacking a solid regional base, they concentrated on obtaining resources to satisfy the varied interest groups that made up the parties.

The diminished relevance after the civil war 1967-70 of ethnic/regional political parties meant that legislators became more aware of their own constituencies' needs and desires and fought over acquiring resources to fulfill them. The debate over the 1981 Revenue Allocation Bill showed the trend away form party solidarity and towards more individualized interest aggregation. Even the Unity Party of Nigeria (UPN), a party known for its insistence on party discipline, saw the disintegration of that cohesiveness when the issue became that of sharing revenue among the states. Representatives voted for items that would benefit their particular localities despite whatever stand their parties took on the matter. That pattern of behavior occurred because parties were no more confined to regions/states but instead crossed state and/or ethnic boundaries.

Thus, the pattern of interest aggregation described as ethno-clientelistic in the body of the study can be said to be the main source of the influence on the fiscal commissions. The specific revenue principles, the periods during which they were used and the emphasis placed on them, showed the extreme regional/ethnic self-centeredness which fed the patronage system. One principle that illustrates this phenomenon is the Derivation Principle. Most of the inter-regional squabbles were over the use of this principle and may have aided in precipitating the civil war.

The British colonial administration has often been blamed for creating regions which coincided with ethnic enclaves and publicizing the importance and implication of revenue allocation to the development of these regions. That action ensured that the frontiers of regional political conflict were extended into the revenue area.[2] However, given the ethnic and cultural diversity of the country, together with the ethno-centricity of its leaders, Nigeria as a closely knit unitary nation would have suffocated. Such integrative forces as common language and/or religion did not exist nationwide; what the different peoples of Nigeria had in common was a common colonizer who decided to put together the different pieces of land he grabbed in his imperialistic foray into that part of the West African coast he later named Nigeria. So it was almost impossible to prevent regional competitiveness from finding its way into a vital public issue like revenue allocation which deals with the fiscal needs of the individual regions (states).

Efforts, especially by the military, to focus more on the technical aspects of revenue allocation did not last because the fundamental issues in revenue allocation have their roots in the political infrastructure of the country. Therefore, they can only be resolved by the leaders or representatives of the various interested stakeholders. Nigerians, unfortunately, have not been so fully integrated politically as to abandon their sub-national loyalties, which continue to be expressed in regional (state) or ethnic terms. The absence of groups that articulate pan-Nigerian interests effectively is also a contributor to the politicization of the revenue issue. When national institutions and leaders replace localized ones and policy problems are viewed as national issues, then influences from interest groups would not be so personalized. Then the selection of alternatives during policy formulation may be easier and less acrimonious as it is now.

The 1981 Revenue Allocation Act was one of the few survivors of the two military coups that followed the end of the Shagari administration. The first post-civilian government ushered in by General Mohammadu Buhari on December 30, 1983, was too short-lived to initiate any changes in the fiscal system of the country. On August 27, 1985, that regime was overthrown by General Ibrahim Babangida. The Babangida government resisted pressures from interested parties to reform the existing revenue allocation system. It should be recalled that economic mismanagement by the politicians of the Second Republic was the major rationale given by the military for their decision to intervene again. And when Babangida took office, he was mostly concerned with revamping the economy, laying emphasis on generating new revenues and not on novel ways to share them.

However, as part of the preparations for a return to civilian rule Revenue Allocation was one of the issues discussed by the Political Bureau (an expert advisory group set to study and recommend proposals for the next government). The Bureau noted that revenue allocation "had been one of the most contentious and controversial issues in the nation's political life," and is usually the "first problem every incoming government grapples with".[3] It attributed the problem to the "absence of a permanent body to constantly study the issue and make appropriate recommendations".[4] The government, in its White Paper, agreed with the panel and promised to rectify the situation by setting up a permanent and technical fiscal commission. The new body, to be named the National Revenue Mobilization Commission (NRMC), and was expected to release a new set of fiscal arrangement by 1988.[5]

To carry out its task effectively, the new commission would be periodically assessing the functions of each tier of government and specifically responsible for monitoring accruals from and disbursements of revenue from the Federation Account; and reviewing revenue allocation formula and principles from time to time.[6] It seems that at last Nigeria will have the permanent fiscal panel that almost every previous *ad hoc* revenue allocation commission had recommended.

The military government's plan to set up a permanent fiscal review board was one of the serious attempts being made to mobilize and integrate the population politically. It is hoped that an allocation not tied to constitutional and political changes in the country would go a long way to depoliticize the process of revenue allocation. This may be wishful thinking if the changes enumerated above take place, then the new arrangements should yield results. However, the deep-seated schisms may be difficult to overcome and long held loyalties and identities too established to abandon. The military regime had instructed the revenue board to devise a new allocation formula by 1988. That formula has had strong likelihood to be imposed on the incoming civilian administration, but unless the required societal changes take place, the same perennial intractable problems of ethnicity and statism (the new term for regionalism) will plague the new panel.

In conclusion, policy-makers in Nigeria grappled with the problem of ensuring that there "existed a reasonable balance in power and resources between the various ethnic groups,"[7] and the difficulties were starkly illustrated by the several revenue allocation systems that were used. The fiscal experts, understanding this underlying characteristic of the Nigerian society, in their separate ways, tried to translate that balance into fiscal terms. Some recognized it better and acted accordingly, devising allocation schemes that satisfied the major interests in the country; others tried to ignore the basic premise or wished it were otherwise, and had their findings either rejected or shelved for more opportune times. In the first group of experts, one might include the Hicks, Phillipson, Chick, Raisman, Binns, and Okigbo Commissions; while the Dina and Aboyade fiscal panels belong to the latter category. However, these experts were only advisory and were recruited to work out the technical details, the final decision on what Revenue Allocation system to adopt was ultimately decided by the political leaders themselves. The lack of consensus over major issues, especially fiscal matters meant that the final choices made were products of political bargains and compromises dictated by subjective interest and preferences. And Revenue Allocation policy in Nigeria remains one of those that fits the above description perfectly. The importance of the policy, coupled with its controversial nature demanded that vested interests have the final say in formulation of the policy.

Notes

1. Olaloku, F.A., 'Nigerian Federal Finances: Issues and Choices', in Akinyemi, A.B., P.D. Cole, and Walter Ofonagoro (eds.), *Readings in Federalism*. (Lagos, Nigeria: Institute of International Affairs, 1979), p. 115.

2. Okoli, Ekwueme F., *Institutional Structure and conflict in Nigeria*. (Washington, D.C.: University Press of America, 1980), pp. 74-75.

3. *West Africa*, August 24, 1987, p. 1631.

4. Ibid.

5. *West Africa*, July 13, 1987, p. 1337.

6. Benibo, T.F., 'National Revenue Mobilization and the New Revenue Allocation Formula,' *The Interpreter*. September 1987, p. 9.

7. Diamond, Larry, 'Nigeria: The Coup and the Future,' *Africa Report*. Vol. 29, March/April 1984, p. 9.

9 Nigeria's revenue sharing problem: Perspectives and choices

Tonyesima Furro, Ph.D.

Introduction

Revenue Sharing is an issue with many ambivalent positions in Nigerian politics. It deals with the issue of distribution of federal money to different population groups or subordinate political units with the objective of even or balanced development. Given the degree of difference in resource endowment, level of development as well as revenue-raising capacity which exists among the states in the Nigerian federation,[1] the struggle for the distribution of revenue has been very intense. Since 1946, each region or subordinate unit government in the Nigerian federation has "adhered to various principles of revenue sharing according to whichever was most beneficial to itself."[2] In the words of O. Teriba, revenue allocation was largely "based on the rule of thumb rather than mutually agreed principle."[3] Hence, the methods or indices of revenue sharing and the relative weight to be assigned to each method has been susceptible to the highest level of political manipulation by the larger ethnic groups namely: Hausa-Fulani; Yoruba and Ibo. The manipulation takes the form of "blatant unconstitutional revenue transfers to back-room maneuvers to effect proposed changes in allocation formula."[4] Owing to this sort of manipulation, the allocation formulas have failed to take cognizance of the special needs of the resource producing areas. The crucial issue of economic development needs of the oil producing areas have been barely addressed. These areas continue to lack the basic economic and other social infrastructures in spite of their enormous financial contribution to the national coffers, which in the final

Dr. Furro is an Assistant Professor of Political Science, Voorhees College, South Carolina, U.S.A.

analysis has resulted in the socioeconomic transformation of Nigeria. For over 36 years of oil exploration and production have not lifted the producing communities to a new level of economic activity and development. The material or objective economic conditions of the local population hardly resembles those whose resources have been contributing to a significant socioeconomic transformation of Nigeria.

In this light, this chapter discusses these problems, determine their origin and implications for the oil producing communities, and suggest policy options for the Third Republic and beyond.

Pre-oil economy revenue sharing trend

In the words of Adedotun Phillips, "It is unlikely that in any given federal financial system (allocation of taxing powers and allocation of revenues) will satisfy all the states in a Federation all the time."[5] The distribution of fiscal resources has always remained a volatile issue in Nigeria's political economy from the colonial period to post colonial era. This is more so due largely to the fiscal and structural framework of Nigeria's federalism. In the Nigerian federal system, the national government is the only one empowered, constitutionally to collect or generate all kinds of revenues ranging from corporate to individual taxes, mining rents and royalties, import, export and custom duties. These are also the most lucrative sources of revenue for the government. The national government, in turn, deposits a significant portion of what it collects with the Distributable Pool Account (DPA) in order to be shared among the various unit governments in the federation. The Distributable Pool Account is a central depository for federally collected funds earmarked for the states. The bone of contention is one of devising a 'golden mean' to distribute federally generated revenues between different levels of government so that the principal revenue-producing areas would be adequately compensated without unduly sacrificing the needs of the others. It is due to their ability in devising any acceptable principle of revenue-sharing that has led to a plethora of fiscal review commissions as well as other ad hoc arrangements.

Before oil became very significant in the nation's economic structure, Nigeria was principally an agricultural nation. It generated the bulk of the foreign exchange earnings in cash crops, namely cocoa and groundnut. During this time, revenue distribution had operated more like a zero-sum-game. That is, the resource producing region(s) retained all or a significant portion of the proceeds of its resources. This method of revenue sharing is known as the principle of derivation. "The Derivation principle implies that states should receive allocations from the central pool in strict proportion to their

228

contribution to these revenues."[6] The history of sharing revenue on the basis of derivation began immediately after the amalgamation of Northern and Southern provinces which made up Nigeria in 1914.

The specific Commission's recommendations on the System of Revenue Allocation to the regions/states from 1946-1989 is stated as follows:

Phillipson Commission (1946)

The Phillipson Commission recommended Derivation and Even Progress Principle in the National revenue sharing plan but did not specify system of allocations.

Hicks-Phillipson Commission (1951)

This Commission applied the principle of Derivation, Need based and National Interest factors in resource allocation. The specific system of allocation recommended is as follows:

A 50% of import duties on tobacco; and 100% on motor fuel, was allocated according to consumption. Additionally, capitalization grant on thirteen shillings per head, a 100% grant on education, and police growth, and special grants for equalization were recommended as the basis for revenue allocation amongst tiers of government.

Chick Commission (1953)

This Chick Commission recommended Derivation in principle but the specific system of allocation was such that: a 50% of import and excise duties on tobacco, and 100% of import duties on motor fuel, was based on level of consumption. Also, 50% of other import duties (other than alcohol, tobacco, and motor fuel) was to be distributed by this order: East-30%, West-40%, North-30%, and 100% of income tax (except on companies) was levied according to residence. In the area of mineral revenues 100% mining rents and royalties were allocated according to degree of extraction in that region. Lastly, 50% of export duties were allocated according to origin.

Raisman-Trees Commission (1958)

The Raisman-Trees Commission recommended Derivation, Need, population, minimum responsibility and balanced development as factors to be considered in national revenue sharing. In pursuant of the above principles, the commission recommended that 100% of import and excise duties on tobacco, and 100% of import duties on motor fuel, be

229

allocated according to consumption. 100% export duties be allocated to origination. 50% mining rates and royalties be allocated according to extraction, and also that, 30% of other import duties (other than alcohol, tobacco, and motor fuel) and 50% of mining rents and royalties, be paid into the DPA in this order: North-40/95; West-24/95; and East-31/95.

Binns Commission (1964)

The Binns Commission applied the principle of allocation based on financial conditions of need and even development objectives. The Binns commission recommended that: 100% of import and excise duties on tobacco and motor fuel be allocated according to consumption, and 100% excise duties be allocated according to region of origin. 50% mining rents and royalties be allocated according to extraction; and 35% of other import duties, 34% of mining rents and royalties be paid into Distributable Pool Account in the following order: East-30%; West-20%; Mid-west-8%; North-42%.

Decree No. 15 [Military Administration] (1967)

The Decree stipulated a principle of allocation based on equality of states and population. Thus, the share of the six new states created out of the former Northern region to be divided on the basis of equality of states and the share of the six new states created out of the former Western and Eastern Regions to be divided also on the basis of population.

The Dina Interim Revenue Allocation Commission (1986)

The Dina Commission modified the system of allocation to be based on need, national minimum, Derivation and balanced Development. The Dina Interim Commission recommended that 100% rents on in-shore minerals be allocated to the Federal Government, and 15% royalties on in-shore minerals to the State Government; 10% royalties to the State of origin; 70% to the State Joint Account and 5% to Special Grant Account. The commission also granted 60% rents and royalties on off-shore to the Federal Government: 30% to the State Joint Account and 10% to the Special Grant Account. Additionally, a 50% import duty was allocated to the Federal Government; and the other 50% to the State Joint Account. The other factors recommended were 15% export duty to the Federal Government; 10% to the State of origin; 70% to the State Joint Account and 5% to the Special Grant Account.

The Decree No. 13 [Military Administration] (1970)

The Decree stipulated allocation principles based on population and equality of states. The Decree No.13 specifically stipulated a system of allocation in which: 60% of export duties were allocated to the state of origin and the rest 40% was allocated to the Distributable Pool Account (DPA). Additionally, 50% of excise duty of the DPA and the other 50% was allocated to the Federal Government. However, 50% of import duty on petroleum products went to the state of consumption while 50% went to the Federal Government. The allocation system also specified 45% mining rents and royalties be paid to the state of origin; 50% to the DPA while 5% went to the federal Government. Moreover, 50% of the DPA was shared equally among the states while the other 50% was divided on the basis of population.

Decree No. 9 [Military Administration] (1971)

This Decree applied allocation principles based on population and equality of states. The decree No. 9 of 1971, helped to transfer all mining rents and royalties from the territorial waters and continental shelf to the Federal Government Coffers.

Decree No. 6 [Military Administration] (1975)

This Decree applied principles based on 20% Derivation, population and equality of states. The system of allocation was:

(1) 35% import duty other than petroleum products, tobacco, wine, portable spirits or beer were to be allocated to the DPA, while 65% went to the Federal Government.

(2) 100% import duty on petroleum products and tobacco to the DPA.

(3) 50% excise duty to the DPA while 50% went to the Federal Government.

(4) 100% export duty to the DPA.

(5) 20% mining rents and royalties on in-shore minerals to the state of origin, while 80% went to the DPA.

(6) 100% mining rents and royalties in respect of territorial waters and continental shelf went to DPA and 7.5% of the DPA was shared equally among the states while 50% was divided on the basis of population.

Aboyade Technical Committee (1977)

The committee recommended the following principles of allocation [based on]:

(1) Equality of access to development opportunities.

(2) National Minimum Standards.

231

(3) Absorptive capacity and
(4) Internal Revenue Effort.
The Aboyade Committee recommended of allocation in the following order:

Federal Government	57%
Special Fund	3%
State Government	30%
Local Government Councils	10%
State Governments Councils	30%

The Government accepted an order of 55%, 30%, 10% and 5%.

Presidential commission on revenue allocation-The Okigbo Report (1980)
The Okigbo commission recommended allocation principles based on:
(1) Minimum Responsibilities of Government,
(2) Population and Social Development.
The Okigbo commission allocation system was as follows:

Federal Government	53%	55.0%
Special Fund	7%	4.5%
State Governments	30%	30.5%
Local Government	10%	10.0%

The Government accepted 55%, 4,5%, 30.5%, and 10%.

Decree No. 36 [Military Administration] (1984)
This Decree stipulated an allocation principle based on: Minimum Responsibilities of Government, Population, Social Development, and Internal Revenue Effort. The Military Administration allocated 55% Federal, 2.5% Special Funds, 10% to Local Governments and 32.5% to the States.

National revenue and fiscal mobilization, allocation commission-The Danjuma Commission (1989)
This commission recommended the following allocation principles:
(1) Minimum Responsibilities of Governments
(2) Population (Need) 40%
(3) primary School
(a) Direct-11.255
(b) Inverse-3.75% and
and Internal Revenue Effort-5%

The specific system of Revenue allocation was:

Federal Government	55%
State Governments	30%

Local Government	15%
Special Fund Allotment	10%
Internal Revenue Effort	5%

Sources: (a) and (d) *Report of the Presidential Commission on Revenue Allocation*, Vol. III, (1980), pp.126-130.

(b) Phillips, Adedotun, 'Nigeria's Federal Financial Experience', *The Journal Modern African Studies*, Vol.9, No. 3, (October, 1971), p.394.

(c) *Report of The Presidential Commission On Revenue Allocation*, Vol. 1, (Main Report), (Apapa, Nigeria: The Federal Government Press, 1980), pp.19-22 and 77-104.

(e) Ashwe, Chiichii, *Fiscal Federalism in Nigeria*, (Canberra: Australia: The Australian National University Press, 1986), p.81.

(f) Ashwe, Chiichii, 'The New Revenue Allocation Formula', *The Nigerian Economist*, September, Vol. 2. No. 26, 1989, p.48.

Complaints began to emerge that the resources from one region were being transferred to develop the other. Each of the regions had at one time or another made similar complaints of its resources being used to enhance the development of the other at its own expense. Adebayo Adedeji pointed out the fact that there was little or no relative correspondence between a region's revenue contributions to the total revenue and the relative expenditure or services rendered by the central government in that region. In other words the central government's expenditure within a region was not proportionate to the relative contribution made by that region to the total revenue.[7] Under this scheme, some regions which contributed more to the central revenue received far less expenditures in terms of services, while conversely regions which contributed the least had more government expenditures in services. Hence, there was a gross imbalance between relative regional contribution to total revenue and government expenditure on regional services.[8] Arthur Richards, the architect of the 1946 Constitution summarized the seriousness of the regional imbalances in revenue sharing arrangements this way:

I found that the North, which pays its taxes almost as obediently as people do in England, and which contributes more than any other section of Nigeria to the general revenue, is the part of Nigeria which had the least spent on it by the central Government. The eastern provinces, the part of Nigeria which is the most vocal and which clamors and calls for more education and for more of everything is the part which contributes less than the other two regions to the general revenue, and it is also the part upon which Government has been spending most.[9]

As can be seen in Table 9.1 from 1949-50, the Eastern region which was contributing the least was having the lion's share in inter-regional distributions.

Table 9.1
Revenue allocation to the regions, 1949-50

%Share	Recommended	Actual
Eastern Region	26	37
Northern Region	45	35
Western Region	29	28

Source: Phillips, Adedotun 'Nigeria's Federal Financial Experience,' *The Journal of Modern African Studies*, Vol. 9, No. 3, October 1971, p. 395.

This unfair distribution of resources brought about an avalanche of complaints which called for an overhaul or a restructuring of the inter-regional revenue sharing system whereby each region was to receive according to what it contributed to the central revenue. Therefore, it was largely against this backdrop, among other things, that the first fiscal review commission of 1946 took place. The first fiscal commission recommended derivation as the basis for inter-regional revenue sharing. Since the first fiscal review commission, every successive fiscal commission had recommended derivative principle along with other principles. Hence, from the 1940s through the 1960s, it was the derivative principle that was heavily relied on in sharing inter-regional/state funds in the Distributable Pool Account to the exclusion of all others.

The principle of derivation

At the heart of the debate concerning derivation is the question as to whether or not a significant portion of royalties deriving from any given state or region should belong by right to that state or area. Essentially, what this means is that a substantial portion of the proceeds of any resource, whether petroleum, cocoa, groundnut, or palm kernel "should be returned to the state of origin in recognition of the principle of derivation."[10] This method of revenue sharing is best defined by Melford Okilo in this way:

Derivation in the African cultural context implies that when an individual kills or finds a big fish or animal, the villagers or community expresses their appreciation to that man or woman by first giving him or her the best part of the animal or fish before the rest of the meat or fish is shared. We do not, therefore, have to go far and wide to find a formulae for sharing; as our traditional heritage already teaches us the method of sharing. Derivation is already embedded in the Nigerian culture and is an acceptable method of sharing.[11]

Accordingly, various laws or pieces of legislation have recognized this principle for revenue sharing since 1946. Section 134 of the First Republic Constitution of 1960 endorsed derivation. The Constitution clearly provided that any region which decides to surrender its resources will get back 50 percent of "(a) the proceeds of any royalty received by the Federation in respect of any mineral extracted in that region, and (b) any mining rents derived by the Federation from within that region."[12]

In keeping with above, during the heyday of cash-crop economy as was mentioned earlier the producing regions, notably North and Western Regions, had benefitted immensely from the 50 percent retention scheme provided under the Constitution. "Derivation as applied to export cash-crops lasted effectively for over 22 years (1952-1974)."[13] However, over the years, this instrument for revenue sharing has increasingly come under heavy attack as unfair, discriminatory and, therefore, "likely to lead to greater inter-regional economic disparity and to contribute to the instability of the federation."[14]

The thrust of the argument against derivation centers on the reasoning that given the level of economic unevenness coupled with "uneven stages of development and tax bases,"[15] it is unfair for the resource endowed states or regions to receive the lion's share of funds from the proceeds for their resources, that such huge funds will invariably make these resources blessed areas more developed at the expense of the poorly endowed areas of the country. This principle will accentuate rather than reduce regional economic disparities. The derivation based principle of revenue sharing will result in wide developmental gaps and social welfare disparity among the various component states of the nation. There is very limited geographical spillover or spread of the benefits from derivative based principle. Given the restricted nature of labor mobility which is subject to ethnic and political constraints, it will be difficult to redress such developmental imbalances without fiscal redistribution.[16] Hence, according to this line of reasoning, the derivation based principle will be an impediment to income distribution and, therefore, the principle should be discarded.

Conversely, proponents of the derivative based principle maintain that "what is good for the goose is good for the gander." The issue at stake is not simply as Phillips put it, 'it-is-now our-turn variety.'[17] Revenue allocation by derivation is fair, reasonable and natural whether it is agricultural products or mineral resources. Each of these resources produce negative externalities for the communities in which they are generated. In the case of oil, the negative externalities or byproducts of oil activities are more devastating than in cash-crops production. These byproducts include spillage, blowout, flood, pollution and other forms of environmental degradation. The brunt of these byproducts is borne only by the local communities in which this activity takes place: health hazards, displacement of homes, forced relocation from ancestral home to make room for oil activity; loss of jobs, loss of means of livelihood. Hence, this view maintains that it is not asking too much that a significant portion of the proceeds be returned to the oil producing communities to alleviate their miseries in the form of physical, social, and economic development.[18] This perspective is best stated by A.Y. Aliyu in this way:

> Firstly, agricultural and non-agricultural production are easily distinguishable, as revenue accruing to the former directly benefits the farmer while in the latter case serious damage is sustained by the inhabitants of the areas of production. Secondly, although mining activities are vested in the Federal Government, the land on which such activities are carried out is located in a state which has responsibility for the welfare of its inhabitants. Thirdly, the state government is the primary unit and agency of development. . . it is the best machinery for dealing with the so-called 'developmental' problem of environmental pollution and waste, such that some proportion of revenue derived on this principle should go to the state government.[19]

In light of the above, this view asserts that derivative based principle of revenue sharing has enormous incentives or advantages, namely it creates satisfaction for the producers of the revenue by compensating him for his efforts and or his sufferings, deprivation and ecological damages associated with the generation of the revenue such as in the oil industry. Further, this principle is "revenue-oriented rather than expenditure-oriented as the case of population and equality of state principles."[20] Under this scheme, according to the advocates, derivation can serve as an incentive device for individual states to intensify efforts towards generating more revenue because of the built in enumerations, knowing that the more revenues a state can contribute to the central revenue, the greater its share through his method of revenue sharing in order to adequately meet its social and governmental obligations.[21]

Revenue sharing trend in the oil era

Oil revenue began to form a fairly significant portion of the national export earnings by the end of the 1950s. At this period "only a fraction of the revenue from mineral oil production was a received by the region of production."[22] This was further aggravated by the recommendation of Binns fiscal review commission of 1964. The Binns commission recommended the principle of 'financial compatibility'. This principle was a combination of need and even development. The thinking on this matter by the commission was that revenue allocation should be based or determined on the basis of "the cash position of each region, its tax effort and the standard of service it provides".[23] Bins recommendation was a deviation from the previous fiscal reports which had faithfully recommended the principle of derivation. The fact that the Commission dropped the derivative principle as a means of sharing the inter-regional revenue generated a great deal of controversy and turmoil. Binns report had far reaching implication for the whole of Nigeria although political events overtook its implementation. The outcome of his report laid the foundation for the Nigerian civil war. Binns prescriptions were not acceptable to the Eastern Region, which at this time had become the nerve center of oil production of the nation. Under the Binns fiscal plan as O. Teriba notes:

> The Eastern Region, as the region with the brightest immediate revenue prospects, stands to benefit least from the new arrangement for distributing the Distributive Pool. The Western Region, as the region whose financial position has markedly changed for the worse since 1959, stands to benefit some appreciable extent. It is to the Northern Region that the greatest overall benefit is likely to accrue in line with the views of the commission that the North must be helped to the fullest extent possible to achieve a greater measure of parity with the other regions.[24]

The Eastern Region saw the whole Binns Plan as biased and unjust. In 1964/65 at the time of the Binns' prescriptions, Eastern Region's Gross Domestic Product (GDP) comprised 33.3 percent of Nigeria's total[25] and it felt that its share of revenue distribution should reflect or be proportionate to its contribution to the central coffers. Eastern Region dissatisfaction grew from the fact that all proceeds from agricultural exports were retained by the respective regional marketing boards after 1959, and Eastern agricultural exports had always been negligible.[26] The Western and Northern Regions did not perceive this as a form of reverse discrimination. After all, they maintained that "during the 1940s and early 1950s they were contributing more to the central treasury than they were receiving, with the chief beneficiary being the East."[27]

Lawrence Rupley argues that the politics of revenue allocation largely contributed to the Nigerian civil war. He maintains the 'rules of the game' for sharing revenues were manipulated and changed by the regions notably North and West in terms of their revision of argument about the desirability of the application of the derivation principle. These two regions were the premier advocates of the principle of derivation when the agricultural products were the dominant sources of export revenue. With little prospect of oil being discovered on their soil, they felt that derivation principle which had served them so well was no longer desirable. For Rupley:

> The Governments of Northern and Western Nigeria greatly favored the principle of derivation from 1946 to around 1960, because groundnuts and cocoa were the dominant sources of export revenue. However, after petroleum revenue began to escalate form 1958 onwards, it became clear that there was little prospect of oil being found in these regions. So the two governments then reversed their arguments with respect to the desirability of the principle of derivation.[28]

With the arrival of the military in 1966, one of their first tasks upon assuming power was to declare all existing revenue allocation systems defunct and put in its place a series of ad hoc arrangements for revenue sharing. At the time of the military takeover, the Raisman-Tress fiscal plan was still in operation because the Binns, recommendation had little or no time to be implemented in light of the prevailing political situation in the nation. The first of the military ad hoc schemes was Decree No. 15 of 1967. This Decree accomplished two objectives. It was responsible for the creation of the twelve state structure from the former four regions. Also contained in this Decree was the method of sharing revenue which was essentially an indirect implementation of the Binns recommendation of 1964.[29] The decree had two broad principles of revenue sharing were established: (a) equality of states and (b) population. The share of the six new states created out the former Northern Nigeria were divided on the basis of equality of states. The share of the six new states created out the former Northern Nigeria were divided on the basis of equality of states. The share of the six new states created out the former Western and Eastern Regions were divided on the basis of population. With the creation of twelve states under Decree No. 15, the oil wells came under the territorial jurisdiction or to put it simply in the backyard of the ethnic minority states notably Rivers and Bendel States. By this time the larger ethnic groups saw an opportunity to push for the total elimination of derivative principle as index of revenue sharing and pressed for the case of population principle. The resource producing minority areas see political and ethnic dimensions in the divorce from the original sharing methods which they feel had served the nation so well. Since the above decree, every successive fiscal review commission and ad hoc arrangement have included principally population as the basis of revenue sharing.

The principle of population

The principle of population as an index of revenue-sharing came out of the prescription of the Raisman-Tress Commission in 1958. At that time, population and other variables of revenue-sharing such as continuity in government services, minimum responsibilities and balanced development were subsumed under the principle of need. Population was not a distinct category and hence no significant weight was assigned to it. By 1970, when Decree No. 13 was passed, population as an index for revenue-sharing had become very prominent, and at this time it was applied in the distribution of interstate funds for all of Nigeria. It was given the weight of 50 percent.

The principle of population is taken as a "broad indicator of need, since this determines the scale of the services which each government has to provide"[30] to its people. The population principle simply means that the more people there are in a given state, the greater the share of revenue for that state. Over the years, this principle has become as controversial as that of derivation due largely to lack of accurate population data and the manipulation of figures. The political significance of population began in 1949 with the introduction of the Macpherson constitution when it was used to determine the degree of representation of each of the three regions at the federal legislature.[31] Under this scheme, the more people there were in each region, the greater its representatives in the national leadership structure with all the attendant patronage.

As parliamentary and local council representation came to be determined on the basis of population, what followed next was the application of population as the basis for the distribution of amenities as well as for sharing of federally generated revenues. With this, a great deal of suspicion or controversy began to surround the results of census or head count since 1952. Each region began to inflate, manipulate, or rig census returns in order that it would receive the lion's share in resource allocation or would have greater number of representation in the federal legislature. In this contentious atmosphere, the last officially acceptable head count was that of 1963. In almost 30 years since 1963, Nigeria has had no count that reflects the constantly changing demographic details such as the following; "the number of males and females; age distribution; working or active population; occupational

239

and geographical distribution."[32] The census of 1973 was plagued with so much controversy that it was thrown out due largely to widespread accusation of fraud and rigging as well as differential in growth rate of the regions North and South. Hence, what the government does is to extrapolate the 1963 figures, using an assumed rate of growth which it says is 2.5% for the rural areas and 5 percent for the urban areas.

Over the years, the population principle has been criticized like that of derivation. Notable among the critics of this principle is Adedotun Phillips. He argues that given the lack of population data, "It is at best a poor and an ambiguous criterion of need and hence an unsatisfactory basis for revenue sharing."[33] For Phillips, the bogus application of the government assumed rate of growth of 2.5 percent cannot reflect the actual changes that have taken place in the level of spatial distribution of the nation's population in the last several years since the last acceptable head count.[34] Phillips maintains that population is not total liability. It is also an asset. While it is understandable and without any doubt that a greater number of people in a given geographic area will overtax the existing social services which will inevitably demand higher expenditure, a large population will lay a solid structure of tax base in the form of additional contributions. It can also provide an army of cheap labor for the factories and industries in a given locality or state.[35] Phillips is concerned about the fact that advocates for this principle "ignore the distributional aspects."[36] He states that "a state may receive revenue based on its population size, but the expenditure of the revenue may benefit only a small segment of that population."[37] In spite of the foregoing defects with the population principle coupled with the absence of demographic details, the federal government continues to rely heavily on this principle almost to the exclusion of others in interstate revenue sharing. Under such a formula, as J.K. Onoh notes,

> The most populous states of Nigeria continued to take away the greater portion of the oil revenue ... while the Federal Government's own share of the oil revenue continued to increase to the disadvantage of the oil producing minority areas.[38]

In light of this, in the next section, the implications of this revenue allocation politics on the oil producing areas shall be examined.

Implications for the oil producing areas

The primacy or special contribution of oil in Nigeria's economic development has been widely documented in a large body of scholarly literature. However, what has been given scant attention is the plight of the inhabitants of the oil producing communities in light of the revenue sharing politics. The oil sector has singly determined the dynamics of the Nigerian economic development since the 1960s. While so much of the surplus value created by the oil sector was consumed in corruption, however, its impact on or contribution to the socioeconomic transformation of Nigeria has been profound.

Before oil became significant in the nation's economic structure, Nigeria was one of the poorest countries in Sub-Sahara Africa and was barely sustaining itself on agriculture and foreign aid. The discovery of oil and the boom that followed changed all that. Since the inception of oil activity in 1957, over $200 billion has been generated into the national treasury with average annual revenues well over $7 billion. These funds have enabled Nigeria to undertake enormous capital projects and infrastructure development.[39] Besides the above, one of the great contributions of oil to the nation's economic well-being which is often taken for granted is the regular supply of cheap domestic consumption of energy for factories, industries, commerce, operation of public transportation and private automobiles and the like. The nation consumes about 280,000 barrels a day.

Today, many of the developing countries in Africa, Latin America and Asia are billions of dollars in debt largely due to the external shocks induced in the 1970s by the Organization of Petroleum Exporting nations (otherwise known as the OPEC) of which Nigeria is a member. The impact of the huge oil bill has had a devastating impact on most of the mono-culture economics of these nations, whose governments had to curtail vital social services so as to make savings needed to meet their oil bills. Thanks to energy self-sufficiency, Nigeria was spared this major economic catastrophe.

In spite of the foregoing contributions of oil to the nation's socioeconomic upliftment, the Nigerian revenue sharing arrangement has failed to take cognizance of the physical and economic development needs of the producing areas. Gross imbalances exist in the distribution of benefits. Whether or not the local human consequences of oil exploration are worthy of special compensations has been conspicuously overlooked in the nation's revenue sharing scheme. There have been no major improvements in the living standards of the broad majority of the oil producing communities through housing, electrification, pipe borne water, sewage and drainage, roads and bridges, parks, markets, public transportation and many others. The entire producing communities are stagnant, no job creating opportunities or other self

241

help development projects. More than that, these communities are alone bearing the brunt of the by-products of oil exploration and production, in terms of the unprecedented levels of oil spillage and gas flares. The high levels of oil pollution has degraded the environment, which, in turn, has truncated the traditional occupation of fishing, farming and hunting of the local population.[40] While many of the oil producing communities are infra structurally by-passed, the same is not true of many of the non-producing areas, namely, the impressive skylines of Lagos, and the infra structural developments of Ibadan, Kaduna, Sokoto, Kano, and Enugu to name a few, which are the enclaves of the larger ethnic groups that run the affairs of the nation. Oil revenues have also enabled the national government to construct a new national capital at Abuja to the tune of over $2 billion and the cost still mounting.

The official justification for the blatant neglect of the oil producing areas is the reasoning that the local population of the producing areas have contributed nothing, by way of direct efforts to winning the oil, as it was the case during the cash-crop economy whereby the peasants or farmers labored to produce a bag of groundnut or cocoa. According to this view, the producing areas are not any different from the rest of Nigerians, and therefore, they should be entitled to no special privileges or compensations. This view is largely propagated by the dominant ethnic groups of Yoruba, Ibo, and Hausa-Fulani. Taking together the above group is the mouth piece of the government. They maintain that oil is a free gift of nature. G.B. Leton, one of the critics of the above view challenged the dominate ethnic groups position by saying that if oil is actually a free gift of nature that belongs to no community, then it should be given to the United Nations.[41] So far that has not happened.

The implications of all this on the oil producing areas is that by the time the major oil producing minority areas namely Rivers and Bendel States (renamed Delta and Edo states) received their statehood in 1967, and at the height of the oil boom in the 1970s the derivation principle had been progressively de-emphasized by various laws at different stages over the years in order of 45%, 20%, 3.5%, 1.5%, until it was completely eliminated as an index of revenue sharing.[42] When Rivers, Edo and Delta States began to enjoy some form of revenue allocation on the basis of derivation, the principle was applied only to 20 percent of revenue on inshore mining operations which is the least lucrative part of mining rents and royalties. And this lasted a little over six years until derivation was completely eliminated as an instrument of revenue sharing. The proceeds of their resources have been pillaged to subsidize the rest of the nation at their own expense. Given these areas enormous contributions to the general revenue, not even 1 percent of the petro-billions have been invested back into these communities for their physical and material development. Policy makers should have the following questions in mind; (a) If the entire nation is living off the resources of the oil producing minority areas, why is it that some states which are not self-sustaining are wealthier than the oil producing areas? (b) Regardless of the methods of revenue sharing, is it fair that areas whose resources have been providing the mainstay of the federation should receive less than areas with relatively no income generating potential?

Policy options for the Third Republic and beyond

Robert D. Ebel writes "issues of fiscal federalism are, fundamentally, those of intergovernmental relations and the effects on the achievement of the goals of fairness, equity, efficiency, liberty, and self government"[43] in a democratic society. Nigeria prides itself as practicing federalism particularly of the United States variety since 1954. As a matter of fact "for good reasons the Nigerian constitution, 1979 in particular, is modeled largely after the United States of America's precedent."[44] However, the fiscal aspect of Nigeria's federalism is in sharp contrast with that of the United States which she purportedly emulates. United States fiscal federalism is essentially based on fend-for-yourself variety or otherwise known as competitive federalism. Under the competitive scheme, local, federal, and state governments must compete head on for resources to sustain themselves. The unit governments rely on their internal revenue efforts to meet their governmental obligations. Of course, the federal government gives grants-in-aid to the sub-units only for specific projects or purposes. The base of revenue is within the state structure. Whatever is found within the territorial jurisdiction of the unit governments, whether oil, gold or diamonds, belong to those states. For example, Alaska, Texas, and Louisiana oil are not surrendered to the federal government. The federal government may decide to be a partner if it finds such a venture profitable. The same also holds true of the Canadian fiscal federalism. For example, Alberta's enormous oil resources are not given to Canadian federation.

Conversely, Nigeria's fiscal federalism does not lend itself to the goals of fairness, equity, and efficiency. The national government seizes every conceivable revenue base of the unit governments, thereby making the units dependent on the center for their very existence. Critics have long questioned if Nigerian government practices federalism at all as it purports. In a memorandum presented to the 1988 Constitutional Assembly, Rivers State government, which is the premier oil producing state, made the case that the Nigerian Constitution is only federal in name but very unitary in character. As the memorandum state:

243

This is clearly shown in the distribution of money by the Federal Government. That is a system where Federal Government collects almost all revenues and distributes small fraction to the states on monthly basis is definitely not a Federal System. In a true Federal system, states collect all revenue including oil revenue and the Federal Government merely collects an agreed percentage of the states' revenue for its Federal functions.[45]

As the above indicates, the very nature of Nigerian federalism partly contributes to the states' dependence upon the center. Rivers State is a case in point. Besides its oil revenue which has been faithfully taken by the federal government, the latter also collects the revenues generated from Rivers, harbors and ports. Hence, the state is completely stropped off any independent revenue source other than the federal disbursements. The revenue allocation system between the center and the sub-unit in its present form has created an entitled mentality among the recipient governments. These sub-units have come to view the federal disbursements as a right and with very little financial accountability or efforts for their own independent revenues.

In light of this, Nigeria's future Republic should stress state's internal revenue efforts to meet their respective governmental obligations. The principle of internal revenue effort has been one of the least emphasized principles in Nigeria's revenue sharing scheme. It is given only a weight of 5 percent. In future direction of revenue sharing, greater weight should be attached to a state's ability to generate its own resources. In other words, revenue allocation should be structured in such a manner that a state which contributes more to the general revenue should automatically receive the larger share of allocation. The principle of internal revenue efforts was one of the prescriptions of the Aboyade Technical Committee of 1977. This principle "requires that greater shares of revenues be given to governments which demonstrates greater effort in relieving their fiscal burdens".[46]

According to Phillips, the Nigerian revenue dispensation system as it currently exists:

> Lacks a device for encouraging the states to vigorously exploit the sources of revenue within their jurisdiction. As it is, a state can be indifferent to its internal revenue sources, knowing fully well that the bulk of its current revenue will accrue, regardless from federal sources.[47]

Essentially along the same lines, Teriba and Phillips state:

244

For a federal System to merely take account of state needs without considering their revenue efforts in the allocation of central collected revenues is to encourage financial irresponsibility in state governments.[48]

The unit governments of the older federations, such as the United States, Canada, Germany, and Australia rely on their internal revenue efforts to generate revenues to meet their obligations.

The Third Republic needs to do more to revitalize the oil producing areas. There are grave infra structural underdevelopment issues facing these areas such as lack of running water, sewage and drainage, housing, electricity and abject poverty. The government should pump massive funds to rebuild these communities to bring up to standards with the rest of the nation. The government may give direct fiscal disbursement in the form of lump sum cash compensation to every family of the producing communities to rehabilitate their lives. Due to revenue allocation politics, these areas have not had their share to develop their economic, social and material well-being. Further, the federal government should also create jobs and offer viable self-help development projects and businesses that will continue to sustain the local economy long after the oil wells run dry. The oil companies doing business in these communities should be forced to help improve the lot of the people.

Conclusion

Over the years, more than 15 principles and ad hoc schemes have been used in sharing revenue in Nigeria's fiscal system. Each of these principles have been found to be more controversial than the other. In the pre-oil era, it was the principle of derivation that was heavily relied on. In the oil era, it was the principle of population that was largely used to the exclusion of all others, such as, internal revenue efforts, minimal responsibility, national interest and the equality of states. All these are clouded in politics. What the revenue allocation debates have missed is how best to reward revenue producing areas. The minority oil producing areas strongly feel that revenue allocation is colored by ethnic consideration. They point to the fact that if the country's oil resources were located in the dominate ethnic groups areas, the principle of derivation might have still been used. The answer to Nigeria's fiscal federalism is to apply United States competitive federalism whereby unit governments are on their own to fend for themselves.

Notes

1. Teriba, O. and O.A. Phillips, 'Income Distribution and National Integration', *The Nigerian Journal of Economic and Social Studies.* Vol. 13, No. 1, 1971, p.108.

2. Rupley, Lawrence A., 'Revenue Sharing in the Nigerian Federation', *The Journal of Modern African Studies.* Vol.19, No.2, 1981, p. 260.

3. Teriba, O., 'Nigerian Revenue Allocation Experience 1952-1965; A Study in Inter-Governmental Fiscal and Financial Relations,' *Nigerian Journal of Economic and Social Studies.* Vol. 8, No. 3, 1966, pp. 362-363.

4. Offensend, David G., 'Centralization and Fiscal Arrangements in Nigeria,' *Journal of Modern African Studies.* Vol. 14, No. 3, September 1976, p. 509.

5. Phillips, Adedotun O., 'Reforming Nigeria's Revenue Allocation System,' *Nigeria in Journal of Public Affairs.* Vol. 6, No. 1, May 1976, p. 79.

6. Ashwe, Chiichii, *Fiscal Federalism in Nigeria.* Research Monograph No. 46, (Canberra: The Australian National University Press, 1986), p. 88.

7. Adedeji, Adebayo, *Nigerian Federal Finance: It's Development, Problems and Prospects.* (New York: Africana Publishing Corporation, 1969), pp. 56-57.

8. Ibid, p. 56

9. Quoted in Ibid, p. 63.

10. Okilo, Melford, *Derivation: A Criterion of Revenue Allocation.* (Port Harcourt, Nigeria: Rivers State Newspaper Corporation, 1980), p.13.

11. Ibid.

12. Ibid, p. 10.

13. *Report of the Presidential Commission on Revenue Allocation, Vol IV, Minority Views.* (Lagos, Federal Government Press, 1980), p. 34.

14. Phillips, Adedotun O., 'Nigeria's Federal Financial Experience,' *The Journal of Modern African Studies*. Vol. 9, No. 3, October 1971, p. 390

15. Stolper, Wolfgang F., 'Some Considerations Concerning the Allocation of Fiscal Resource,' *The Quarterly Journal of Administration*. Vol. 4, No. 2, 1970, p. 83.

16. Teriba and Phillips, 'Income Distribution and National Integration', pp. 108-109.

17. *Report of the Presidential Commission on Revenue Allocation, Minority Views*. Vol. IV, p. 34.

18. Okilo, *Derivation: A Criterion of Revenue Allocation*, p. 14.

19. Aliyu, A.Y., 'The New Revenue Allocation Formula: A Critique,' *Nigerian Journal of Public Affairs*. Vol. 7, May/October, 1977, p. 28.

20. For an excellent exposition of this point, see Okilo, *Derivation: A Criterion of Revenue Allocation*, pp. 13-14.

21. Ibid. p. 14.

22. Nafziger, E. Wayne, *The Economics of Political Instability: The Nigerian-Biafran War*. (Boulder: Westview Press, 1983), p. 106.

23. *Report of the Presidential Commission on Revenue Allocation, Vol. I, Main Report*, p. 19.

24. Teriba, 'Nigerian Revenue Allocation Experiences, 1952-1965,' p. 379.

25. Nafziger, *The Economics of Political Instability*, p. 107.

26. Ibid., p. 106.

27. Ibid., p. 107.

28. Rupley, 'Revenue Sharing in the Nigerian Federation', p. 261.

29. Fajana, Oladunjoye, 'Fiscal Centralization Tendencies in the Federal Republic of Nigeria Since 1966,' (Unpublished Monograph, Ile-Ife, University of Ife, 1979), p.10.

30. Adedeji, *Nigerian Federal Finance*. p. 132.

31. Adeniyi, Richard, 'The Politics of Population Census,' *Headlines*. No. 184, August 1988, p. 2.

32. Ibid., p. 2

33. Phillips, 'Reforming Nigeria's Revenue Allocation System,' p. 83.

34. For an excellent critique of some of the revenue allocation principles, see *Report of the Presidential Commission on Revenue Allocation, Vol. IV, Minority Views*, pp. 33-35.

35. Ibid., p. 34. For a similar perspective, see also Ashwe, *Fiscal Federalism in Nigeria*.

36. Ibid., p. 34.

37. Ibid., p. 34.

38. Onoh, J.K., *The Nigerian Oil Economy: From Prosperity to Glut.* (New York, St. Martin's Press, 1983) p. 117.

39. For a detailed explanation of contribution of oil to Nigeria's socioeconomic transformation, see Furro, Tonyesima, *Federalism and the Politics of Revenue Allocation in Nigeria: The Case of the Oil Producing Areas of Rivers State*, (Ph.D. Dissertation, Atlanta, GA., Clark Atlanta University, 1992), pp. 131-176.

40. Ibid., For environmental impact of oil exploration and production on the producing communities, see pp. 249-300.

41. *Report of the Presidential Commission on Revenue Allocation, Vol. IV*, pp.7-8.

42. Okilo, *Derivation: A Criterion of Revenue Allocation*, p. 14.

43. Ebel, Robert D., 'Three Decades of Fiscal Federalism at ACIR,' *Intergovernmental Perspective*. Fall 1989, Vol. 15, No. 4, p. 10.

44. *Report of the Presidential Commission on Revenue Allocation. Vol, III.* p. 379.

45. Makine, Kunle, 'Rivers People Fight On,' *Nigerian Newsweek*. January 2, 1989, p. 11.

46. Ashwe, *Fiscal Federation in Nigeria*. p. 91.

47. Phillips, Adedotun O., 'Revenue Allocation in Nigeria, 1970-80', *The Nigerian Journal of Economic and Social Studies*. Vol. 17, No. 2, July 1975, p. 5.

48. Teriba and Phillips, 'Income Distribution and National Integration', p. 113.

10   Nigeria: Socio-political development and oil

Nigeria as a nation has experienced a number of social, economic and political transformation on her swift road towards modernization. Despite the country's socio political and economic tribulations, the nation has remained one indivisible entity. Modern Nigeria is a British invention which was formed by the amalgamation of North and South Protectorates. Prior to the unification of the North and South Protectorates by the British the diverse ethnic groups in Nigeria existed as a separate and unique tribal kingdoms ruled by chiefs, emirs, kings and obas. Nigeria has a population of nearly 100 million people and therefore established as Africa's most populous nation. It is racially homogenous country but it is socially, religiously and linguistically heterogenous society. Nigerian speak over 300 diverse tongues and divided into many ethnic groups with as many cultural and religious beliefs. The status of Nigerian nationhood, Ken Saro Wiwa (1992),[1] noted that "Nigerian independence in 1960 was to exacerbate all the latent differences and tensions in the multi-ethnic nation. The seeds of destruction had been sown in the political structuring of the nation which established three Regions in a federation while leaving the Regions as unitary states. The country had virtually been handed over to the three major ethnic groups - Hausa-Fulani, Igbo and Yoruba - to do pretty much whatever they liked with it. The interest of the 300-odd other ethnic groups, including the Ogoni was not taken into account. However, there is strong likelihood that the creation of more states and more local government areas in the political Administration of Nigeria has not only minimized the fear of domination but also the existence latent differences and tensions amongst the diverse ethnic groups in Nigeria. Many of the world nation states are multiethnic and Nigeria should not be an exception in building unity in diversity. The ethnic differences should be a source of strength if all the ethnic groups big and small can cooperate to build a viable nation with equity and fairness to all its citizens. Ms. Perham suggested the foundation and responsibilities on part of the majority groups to help build a viable Nigerian nation state. The informing spirit of this arrangement was clearly stated by Margery Perham in a foreword to Obafemi Awolowo's *Path to Nigerian Freedom* (London, Faber & Faber, 1947):

> Each of the three main groups should now be able to develop further its special capacities. The Hausa have their large and historic city-states and their Islamic traditions of law and discipline. The Yoruba have their happy and fertile marriage of aristocratic and democratic principles and of urban and rural societies. The Ibos, lacking in social cohesion, supply their equalitarian outlook and intense individual vitality. If the new Nigerian Constitution can express and develop the special virtues of the main groups, each of these might well make, out of its component societies, a unit sufficient in size, numbers and its unified culture, to rank some day as a nation. If, however, the main groups can come together at the center to pool, and share their traditions and resources, whether through a Federal or a Unitary system, then there may some day be a Nigeria which will be a leading power on the African continent and might make Africa's main contribution in the international sphere.

The Nigerian political units under the 1963 constitution was comprised of the capital territory of Lagos, as well as the Northern Western and Eastern regions. Later Nigeria attained independence in October 1, 1960 and became a Republic in 1962. The Midwest was carved out of the then western Nigeria to become the fourth region. In 1967, the country was carved into twelve state political structure by General Gowon and thereafter emerged into 19 state structure through creations of seven more states by General Mustala Mohammed in 1976. Finally in 1989, the Babangida Administration politically transformed the country into a 30-state structure through further creation of states. (Figure 10.1). Thus, since independence the country has experienced dramatic political and economic transformation.

Nigeria: Political administration 1963-1993

Figure 10.1

Nigeria: Political administration 1993

Figure 10.2

Nigeria: Political administration 1997

Figure 10.3

Ethno diverse politics and the promise of democracy in Nigeria

Nigeria as a nation has the potential to harness and manage its vast human and natural resources effectively to promote growth and development. The proper development and management of its resources remains the focus for its modernization effort to benefit all of its people but inter ethnic rivalry, parochial politics and the inequalities in the national resource distribution system constitute formidable constraint on the country's overall development effort to benefit all its people. Osaghae, Eghosa E. 1995 observed that since the 1950s when they agitated for separate states to deliver them from majority domination both in the former regions and in the federation as a whole, the problem of ethnic minorities has remained central to Nigerian politics. Although the creation of more states in the federation since 1967 has done a lot to redress their disadvantages and, in particular, to expand their access to state power, minorities remain marginalized and subordinate to the big three-- Hausa/Fulani, Yoruba and Igbo--in the country's power matrix. The continued calculations of political balance in the country in terms of the historical 'tripod theory' (The tripod theory involves the belief that political stability can only be maintained in the country by ensuring a balance of power among the three major ethnic groups.) both in military and civilian regimes, as well as the majority domination syndrome which underlies the attitudes of state officials and politicians from the big groups towards the minorities, have ensured that this is so.[2] Thus, beginning from agitations for separate states in the 1950s and 1960s which led to the setting up of the Minorities Commission in 1956, right down to attempts by politicians from the minority groups in the Second Republic to organize to wrest political power from the majority elements, the minorities have been in the forefront focusing on the 'national question' as a problem.[3] Notwithstanding, the Ogoni uprising which lasted between 1990 and 1993 marked a new phase in the interesting interface of oil and minority politics. Not since the rebellion of Isaac Adaka Boro, Sam Owonaro and Nottingham Dick, who declared a short-lived independent Niger Delta Republic in 1967 over oil-related grievances, has any oil-producing community sought redress in ways which involved mobilized mass action and direct confrontation with the state as the Ogonis did between 1990 and 1993. Their action also had a tint of separatist agitation in the assertion of the right to 'national' self-determination though, unlike Isaac Boro and his associates, the demand was for an Ogoni state within federal Nigeria a restructured (con) federal system to be composed of self-governing ethnic states and not separation from Nigeria. (Ogoni leaders promptly denied rumors at the time that they were planning to secede.)[4]

Also, Professor David West portrayed the plight of minorities in the country to have suffered terrible marginalization and deprivation despite controlling the major source of national wealth used to develop other parts of the country. He described the Nigerian Federation as "lopsided and fraudulent adding that a concrete and specific measures and reforms were imperative to safeguard the place of the minorities in the country". What is the real status of minorities in the Nigerian Polity according to Ken Saro Wiwa (1992):

> The Hausa, Yoruba and Ibo politicians took Margery Perham seriously. They got together at the center, not to "pool and share their traditions and resources" but to use their presence to secure for their Regions (for which read "themselves") the resources jointly contributed by all Nigerian groups on a bid, it seems, to each "rank some day as a nation."

> The way to this was, first, the mobilization of each of these majority ethnic groups and the exploitation of the resources and weakness of the minorities whom history had placed at their disposal. A regional community necessarily developed in all Regions; however, the minorities were severely disadvantaged. These minorities were not about to accept this.

> ...In the competition for Federal power, the minarets in each Region began to group against the major ethnic groups, to challenge their dominance and assert their own rights. Thus did the State Movements arise.[5]

Earlier Chief Obafemi Awolowo in Path to Nigerian Freedom, had warned: "Certainly these minority groups are at a considerable disadvantage when they are forced to be in the midst of other peoples who differ from them in language, culture and historical background. And he had added, Under a true Federal Constitution, each group, however small, is entitled to the same treatment as any other group, however large. Opportunity must be afforded to each to evolve its own peculiar political institution." Professor David West also noted that, minorities have been subsumed into the bigger political forces, and insisted that the minorities especially those in the oil producing areas, deserved to be rehabilitated to compensate for the wanton exploitation and devastation of their environment. Professor West cited an alleged typology of the country by Alhaji Maitama Sule which appear to have ignored minorities. The Maitama Sule typology is alleged to have read that the Hausa Fulani have divine right to rule, the Yorubas are destined by God to control commerce and Ibos for technological advancement no other person matters.[6] The Sunday

Tribune 13 August 1995, On the Polity: The Deceit of a Nation, the Tribune quoted this statement credited to former President Shehu Shagari at a meeting where he (Shehu Shagari) condemned the confab as he warned his fellow touch-bearers of northern interest that Ahmadu Bello never told them to "share power."

If these alleged statements are held to be true, it amounts to a discouragement in our concerted effort to build a united Nigeria. In the true spirit of Unity in Diversity and stability of our Federation, we need to learn from J.S. Mill's suggestion that:

> There should not be any one state [in a Federation] so much more powerful than the rest as to be capable of vying in strength with many of them combined. If there be such a one, and only one, it will insist on being master of the joint deliberations; if there be two, they will be irresistible when they agree, and whenever they differ, everything will be decided by a struggle for ascendancy between rival.

In an identical vein, a respected scholar in Federalism, Professor K.C. Wheare, stated that:

> It is undesirable that one or two units [in a Federation] should be so powerful that they can overrule the others and bend the will of the federal government to itself ... there must be some sort of reasonable balance.

It is in the interest of seeking systemic political balance and attaining true unity in our Federation that Chief Obafemi Awolowo enlightened us to take cognizance of the fact that "in a true Federation, each ethnic group no matter how small, is entitled to the same treatment as any other group, no matter how large." The inclusiveness of all elements in the Federation and equality in access and political participation that we can truly build Unity in Diversity that is consistent with the vision of Sir Abubakar Tafawa Balewa, who stated in 1954 that "We must recognize our diversity as a source of great strength, and we must do all in our power to see that this Federal system of government is strengthened and maintained."

We believe all the diverse elements are needed in building a viable entity through economic and political inclusiveness. There is still hope for better days ahead and we cannot be discouraged by any one's myopic views. Minorities have a place in Nigeria and they have contributed immensely to Nigeria's nation building effort. In this regard, there is an encouraging observation and yet a realistic critique of Nigerian ethno-political relationships was made by a former

257

presidential aspirant Alhaji Mahmund Waziri[7]. He stated (inter-alia) that the politicians are tribalists who created barriers among the major ethnic groups while also constantly working towards the marginalization of the minority tribes in the sharing of the spoils of political office and purse of the nation--at the heart of our problem today is to find a constitutional framework and then run it which can contain our extremely complicated mix of political rivalries based on ethnic, regional, cultural, economic, and social functions...that (the) failure to do this will engender recurring military coups and instability, adding that we can only seek unity without division on the principles of ethnic equality and power sharing in our plural society. He further noted that the country is dogged with political instability (because the constitution has not reflected complexity of our plural society nor influenced the nature and orderly development of political ideology of the people. He also observed that although the thirty state structure relocated political activity into smaller units, it had not doused the dominance power of the three major ethnic groups in Nigeria.

Ethno-political orientation in Nigeria's nation building

The origin of ethno-diverse politics and interethnic competition in Nigeria is drawn from analysis provided by Silva Opusunju. According to Silva Opussunju (1994)[8] Before the Nigerian nation was created to realize the corporate needs of imperial Britain, there were other nations in the West African region. When the British left, having sapped the resources of Nigeria, three of these nations — Hausa/Fulani, Igbo, and Yoruba, among others, quickly took the place of Britain and continued the plundering. Collectively, these new landlords battered the intermesh of more than 250 ethnic and linguistic groups under the guise of fostering a sovereign state. As Nigeria's treasury hits zero, the collaboration of these three leading tribal nationalists has turned into intense competition. At the height of these elbowing, these groups are rethinking their partnership and searching for new allies among the minorities of the nation... Opusunju emphasizes, that it is the view of many Nigerians that while the conferees (1994 Constitutional Conference) should focus on the future, they must also seriously dissect the sources of continuing discontent among Nigerians. Drawing from what has been premised above, analysis indicate that Nigeria is presently at the brink of dissolution because of three fundamental reasons, including: (1) Igbo misjudgments and tribal nationalism; (2) Yoruba misadvise and intense tribal nationalism; and (3) Hausa/Fulani misrule. All these factors have a common denominator — the pathological abuse of Nigeria's ethnic minorities who collectively make up more than 50% of its total population.[9] The Igbo modus operandi generated fear among other groups in the country leading to the hurried formation of the 'Egbe Omo Oduduwa' (Association of Children of Oduduwa) by Yorubas, and the 'Jami'yyar Mutanen Arewa' (Congress of People from the North) by the Hausa/Fulanis. These and other cultural organizations became the springboards for the formation of several political parties that locked horns during the period of decolonization. They included Aminu Kano's Northern Elements Progressive Union (NEPU), Ahmadu Bello's conservative Northern Peoples Congress (NPC), Awolowo's Action Group (AG), and Harold Biriye's Niger Delta Congress in Ijawland. The NCNC which was once a national party, was as a result of its relegation to a regional (eastern) party, [the Igbo invention] — the politics of tribe, region and religion had come full cycle.[10]

In the eastern region, minorities often point to what they describe as 'official policy' of Igbo leaders to marginalize them within that region. Igbos, they recalled, diverted federal funds earmarked for minority education, health and other infra structural development to Igbo communities. In addition, when the issue of granting eastern minorities regional autonomy under the then proposed Calabar-Ogoja-Rivers (CORE) region arose, Zik swiftly reached a political understanding with the Balewa government and instead the Midwest region was carved out of the western region. While the denial of a CORE region was a reward for the Igbos compromising on critical issues facing the new nation, the creation of the Midwest was a vendetta against the belligerent Yorubas.[11]

There was a time the Yorubas enjoyed 60 percent of the federal permanent secretary appointments and more than 50 percent of the executive council seats, with this over-representation, they advised the national government to the benefit of their tribe. For example, "the manipulation of the federal executive, the super permanent secretaries and the Supreme Military council, Yoruba elements pushed for the adoption of the indigenization (and Nigerianization) program during the Second National Development Plan (1970-1974) of the Gowon regime." Lobbying effort for the adoption of the program was initiated between 1968 and 1970 when a subgroup of the Yoruba dominated Lagos Chamber of Commerce called 'Group 15' controlled by Chief Henry Fajemirokun (Chairman), Chief Oladotun Okubanjo, Chief J. Akin-George, etc. circulated proposals on indigenization in Nigeria. The groups effort and proposals were met with strong opposition by Federal commissioners Alhaji Shehu Shagari (who later became Nigeria's first Executive President), Chief Anthony Enahoro, and J.S. Tarka, who argued that the proposals be temporarily postponed because the Igbos lacked access to capital as they were recovering from the civil war and the Hausa/Fulanis were not ready. In the council's deliberations, the oil owners were not even mentioned. The

259

harmonized proposals — federal proposals were later rescheduled for voting, deliberately in the absence of many of the Federal commissioners who had opposed them. The proposals were fundamentally adopted in 1971 and what followed was a massive and inequitable transfer of Nigeria's corporate, oil and mineral wealth to the West, which acquired a whopping 56%, compared to the North 27%, East 10%, and Midwest 2% of the shares of the 952 businesses indigenized.[12]

It was also under the Yoruba leadership in the person of General Obasanjo and Prof. Abayode (Chairman of the Technical committee on Oil Revenue) that revenue allocation was reformulated in favor of the current policy of allocation by population. This act of developmental ethnicism erased the last hopes of oil producing minorities as it further perpetuated their peripherization during the economic boom days of Nigeria.

Opusunju further observed that up until the Babangida reign, the north was seen as an ally of southern minorities largely because of its support for the creation of the Rivers State and former South Eastern State, albeit as a scheme for weakening Igbo-Biafran struggle. The North also supported the right of a state government, and the people to the landlordship of the real estate properties on their territory — the 'abandoned property issue'. However, in its race with the Igbos and Yorubas, the Hausa/Fulanis have become the principal actors in carrying out the grand design — the conspiracy to destroy oil producing minorities who they once claimed to have liberated from Ojukwu's policy of 'tribal apartheid'.[13]

In a forum held in New York to discuss minority position at the then proposed national conference (1994), there was anger at a statement credited to Alhaji Tank Yakassai that whenever the Northern oligarchy feels like, it will send Yoruba mercenaries to conquer un-cooperating oil producers and cart away oil resources under armed occupation. They point to the mentality inherent in the statement as responsible for the deliberate fragmentation of the Ijaws who populate the southern coast of Nigeria to as far as Abeokuta. To some, the statement depicted the arrogance of power.

According to the suspicious 1969 census figure, the Ijaw tribe which rank fourth in the nation have only one state — the Rivers State to itself; while the second and third largest groups Igbos and Yorubas — have four and five states respectively. If reason was to prevail, Ijaws would have at least three states. Yet successive governments have ignored this reality in various state creation exercises even though they all have acknowledged that it was the Ijaw group which first advocated the creation of states in Nigeria!

In the whole of Nigeria, the Hausa/Fulanis have found less resistance to access to the beach-head and oil resources of the Ijaws and non-Ijaws of the south east, while they are generally despised and unwelcomed by the Yorubas in the west and the Igbos in the east — along with their cousins in the Midwest. While to some it may be understandable that Northerners would not want to lose this access, it is equally unthinkable that they would want to impose this access by force or coercion.

Unlike the Igbos and Yorubas whose problem with the North is mainly political, oil producers see their problem nationally as both economic and political. They claim that unlike the Igbos, they were not a conquered people. Consequently, they have not at any time in their history surrendered their wealth, territory and right to political self determination to any power in the country. They would always assert their right to control their resources and environment in the Nigerian nation.

A school of thought proffered a solution which it titled 'The Common Ground'. Minorities, they posit should give up the ownership of their oil to the federal government, if the following conditions were met: (1) return to revenue sharing formula based on the principle of derivation, and (2) the oil producers sell the oil themselves. According to the group, these conditions would allow for proper monitoring of native environment and the establishment of much needed Oil/Gas Trust Fund. The Fund, 20% plus all accrued interest of the total cumulative yearly revenue, will be placed in a UN Environmental Program escrow to be reinvested into the oil areas when the wells become 'dry'. The fund — 'disturbance or damage fee' — should be outside the reach of Nigeria's gluttonous corrupt government officials for obvious reasons. Authors Comment: The flood of corruption and mismanagement appeared to pave the way, even suggest to surrender a portion of our Sovereign right to an International agency like the United Nations. The UN is not a nation, it is an International forum where some nations are more politically and economically equal than others. It appears to be the second best to trust our National Trust Funds to evade possible engulfment of our wealth from the unscrupulously corrupt and greedy elements amidst us. It suggests strongly that Nigeria needs to get its house together through proper governance, resource management and equitable National distribution system.

The different resource endowment and regional forms of specializations can be tapped to benefit all the people of the country through interregional cooperative advantage based on interregional resource production, and commodity exchange and equitable national wealth distribution. In building national unity, we must eliminate any mechanisms that contribute divisiveness but cooperate to Foster National Unity and balanced development through care for one another. Participants at the forum unanimously agreed that there was need for such a fund given their disappointment at the gross under-representation of oil producers among the 31 NNPC oil contractors.

As to the question of coalition building with any of the leading tribes, one participant reminded the group that "there may be no permanent friends but permanent interests in politics ... it is paradoxical that our geographic neighbors have been historically hostile and have not in recent memories made fence-mending overtures to us." Meaning that they should pursue their destiny on their own and any alliance in the south should be initiated by the Igbos or Yorubas.[14] Furthermore, an understanding of the intense ethno-diverse politics and the promise of democracy in Nigeria is well demonstrated on the issue of Abiola and June 12, 1993 Elections.

According to Ituah Ighodalo[15] commenting on the Abiola and June 12th, 1993 issue, one thing is abundantly clear from events of the past months (1993). No one is ready to fight anyone! Besides, who is going to fight who and what are we fighting about? Is it a political oppression by the North of the South, by the North of the West and economic oppression by the military of the West, by the Northern military of the West or what? Then who will actually do the fighting? I know that even the Northern foot soldier despite his fierce loyalty to the Emirs and Sultans, is not quite ready or prepared to fire one shot.

I also know that the Northern leaders are not convinced of the need for a fight. As for the Middle Belters, those days are definitely over, none of them is prepared to shed one mosquito full of blood in defense of any oligarchy. And the Ibos. I do not even think they have such a force in the military as to contemplate such a thing.

I believe the Middle Belters, simply want peace and justice. My brothers in the Middle Belt want peace, progress, self expression and an opportunity to be a strong part of main Nigeria rulership.

The Eastern minorities, especially the oil producing areas mainly want to reap the benefits of the produce of their backyards. Some of them are prepared to fight and even kill for the liquid gold as evidenced by the fury in Ogoni land, but to-date they are still settling internal power sharing problems.[16]

Of all the sections of Nigeria, my heart goes out to the West. They are probably collectively the most educated and most outspoken (all the 'activists' seem to come from there) of the lot, but they are also equally the most disunited, the least trustworthy and most selfish of the lot. Personally, I believe they are the microcosm of Nigeria's problems, and have constituted the biggest stumbling block to us being able to take a decision as to moving Nigeria forward.[17]

Why? There are too many fragmented big players with too many personal interests. The westerners are too self oriented and have a cancerous love for money, position, a lot of self recognition perhaps and ego! They always sell out. You can always find a fraction of them that will sell out to the person in power. (Ighodalo, 1993)

Ighodalo continued, "look at the history of politics in the West, Akintola, Awolowo's erstwhile right hand man, for whatever reason good or bad, sold out to the Tafawa Balewa government". The West was divided. When the Easterners were ready to go to war, it was Awolowo's turn to merge and take sides with Gowon. Perhaps the Eastern decision was hasty and unnecessary, but I believed it was the same Western leadership that had said "if the Easterners secede we will follow"?

Nearer home, this same Abiola that we are talking about from the *1970s to Abacha* has always been on the side of the military in power. He was good friends with Murtala, wonderful comrades with Babangida and chummy chum with Abacha. A lot of what he owns personally is because these same people agreed to patronize him. Abiola is today going through his wilderness experience, it is a pity because his cause is just.

Let the truth be told, when Awolowo needed the full Western support in 1979! Abiola sold out. Akinloye, Akinjide and the rest also did. Abiola is just paying his dues. He is still too interested in his personal comfort. Further, concerns on ethno-diverse politics and democratic process in Nigeria (Abike Jaiyeola, 1995) stated that: "Surely everyone in this country knows that we are going through hard times perhaps unprecedented in the history of this country. We must realize however that our present social, political and economic problems are not the fault of any one regime. In the past less this [Abacha administration] regime. The present situation is a culmination of several factors and a result of a gradual but progressive disintegration of social, economic and political stronghold or strata of this great nation."

The truth is that the present hardship and problems faced by the people of this country ... cannot be viewed in isolation and are not unconnected with the ethnic strife and imbalance that have existed long before now, the widespread dissatisfaction with the state of affairs that has been expressed among the various ethnic groups with regard to one inequity or the other. The South-Easterners have persistently complained of discrimination against them in the state power structure, Civil Service, the Military, and in the allocation of national wealth.

The West have always complained of monopoly of the political power by the North, while the North have always felt marginalized in the area of economy and commerce. [Thus], Democracy must never be misconceived. Democracy is not synonymous with civilian rule neither is it antithetical with Military rule. Some civilian rules have been known to be even more undemocratic than military rule. It is doubtful for instance, whether a civilian rule, where people are oppressed and the minority have no say; where people are not free to express their political view, where there is widespread inequality, imbalances and social stratifications; the majority squandering in abject penury in the face of too much in the hands of few, [cannot] be properly called Democratic.

On the military, politics and Nigeria (Okparaolu, K,. 1996)... "noted the sentiments expressed by Mr. Randall Robinson of Trans Africa over 'Nigeria's precarious fate and bleak future'. Particularly, when he said after 35 years of oil exports, valued at $210 billion, Nigeria today has a per capita income of about $250, down from $1000 in 1980, while Haiti, a country bereft of oil resources has a per capita income higher than that of Nigeria.

And his conclusion that the cause of Nigeria's woes is that the Nigerian generals have siphoned off and deposited in dedicated accounts across the world, billions of dollars and so Nigeria that should be great, has been brought to the verge of estruction by these rapacious, greedy corrupt generals'. In other words, the travail of Nigeria since Independence till date, is squarely placed at the door step of the military.

It is the belief of the opponents of the military regime that once the military quits power, all Nigeria's troubles would be over.

I am not an admirer of military governments; I am one of those who believe, and very strongly too, that the military has no business in the politics of any nation, since such involvement negates the military's traditional role which is the security of the nation.

Unfortunately, when people talk of the military in Nigeria, they tend to create the impression that the military is no longer part of the Nigerian polity. The military as a class in any nation, is one of the specialized government services. The Armes Forces of Nigeria is involved in the administration of government just as in any nation and therefore, the Nigerian Armed Forces has a stake in what happens in government.

Dr. Peter Colvert, a military expert in Ohio University one said "Forcible intervention by the military in politics, is, to the Militarist, only a logical method of preserving societal values. It is used relatively sparingly, since involvement in politics corrupts the military for its essential work of preserving the state against outside attack.

I have no doubt in my mind, that the initial military intervention into our body politic , was to save values. And the Nigerian military, is composed of men and women who are burning with patriotic desires to defend this country even at the risk of their personal lives.

264

I disagree entirely, with those who tend to create the erroneous impression that the ills of this nation should be laid on the military, even though I know that the military like any human organization in the 35 years of its involvement in politics, may have made its own mistakes, some of them very costly. Yet the Nigerian Military is made up of respectable and responsible Nigerians with serious commitment to the welfare of this country."

Towards a promise of lasting Democracy in Nigeria, the Head of State General Sanni Abacha said:

Let me emphasize that one commitment to hand over to an elected government stems from our sincere conviction that democracy has a complex and sometimes conflicting definition. That is why various models of democracy necessarily involve compliance with local realities and a socio-cultural and environmental imperatives. What is universal to them all is the common cause of liberty. Democracy and liberty go hand in hand to create the foundations of human excellence which manifest themselves in the development of independent minds in autonomous judgements and in the formation of human reasoning and rationality. These are crucial in the evolution of responsible citizens is to give themselves freely to serve the public interest and good democratic order.[18]

National politics

The complexities, distortions, and undesirable consequences of ethnically diverse politics in Nigeria would require a change in national political orientation, such that the national politics may be stirred through a progressive citizen approach to national integration and unity. Unlike the divisive tribal approach that is inherently detrimental to national unity and balanced development.

Don Eberly (1994) has characterized the citizen (approach) model to mean: public philosophy that seeks to build inclusive coalitions around a broad agenda and prefers persuasion to polarization. The citizen approach begins with an acknowledgment of our pluralism. It is prepared to accept disagreement without denying the humanity and moral worth of those who disagree. Because it eschews the: "Us — against them mentality" in favor of cooperation and community, its victories tend to be long lasting.[19] Because it respects and hears opposing views, it increases the chances that its own views

265

will be respected and heard. The tribes *first* impulse is to repel, the citizens approach include (William Raspberry, 1994).

Hence, Eberly has further enlightened us to know that tribal politics huddles and confronts the hostile world with a hostility that mirrors its antagonists and resist evaluating its own conduct and methods. Tribal politics simply reinforces the sense of fear and anger that many feel over having their dominant space in society invaded by other influences. Tibal politics encourages methods of action that are designed to produce tribal solidarity so as to counter the assault coming from outside...'. Thus the more preferred and compelling model for national integration and unity is the citizen model in which all citizens or political units participate to assimilate and strive to advance a common vision for the common good. The tribal approach in contrast is divisive because it needs enemies to sustain it, would rather split hairs than split the differences. The result says Eberly is to raise disputes to the level of insurmountable disagreement.

Indeed, democracy to be sustained in an ethno-culturally diverse polity like Nigeria would require a sound citizen model as a viable vehicle for 'national integration' through a more inward looking, homegrown-grass root approach to democratic modeling. For democracy in Africa, Emejuaiwe, Stephen 1995[20] stated among other things that:

So far, the development of democracy in Africa has been a story of despondency. Not because the African is any less democratic. In fact, the African society is inherently democratic. This fact is attested to, by the communal African political systems that thrived before the advent of the colonial owners on the African soil coupled with the now almost extinct African extended family system which makes the African his brother's keeper. The main problems which have bedeviled modern democracy in Africa are clearly attributable to certain contradictory endogenous and exogenous factors which are in the main alien to, and have not yet blended fully with the traditional socio-political values within the African society.

Some of these factors could be outlined in the following contexts. Firstly, most African states became politically independent from their colonial metropolis in the early 1960's. Prior to the political independence, the political elite's in those emerging states were supposed to have gone through processes of political orientation on modern political values. If the elite's had received such orientation, the masses of the African population did not, and were consequently, insufficiently prepared for the modern ideas of democracy. The democratic values within the traditional African political system were not identical with the modern concepts of democracy. So, the people could not keep pace with the African elite's in the practice of modern democracy. Therefore political conflicts became the order of the day, the elite's almost seemingly assumed the role of the departing colonial authorities unwittingly.

Secondly, the introduction of new political values into the newly independent African states nipped in the bud and disorientated the growth of the traditional African political systems; resulting in political chaos or anarchy. Thirdly, the newly independent African states were expected to display within a very short span or time, equal political maturity with established democracies which had taken centuries to evolve. Such a situation was similar to trying to make an instant Olympic sprinter out of a toddling baby. Fourthly, the developed world became a little impatient or even hypocritical about the pace of democratic development in Africa and began to push the African states harder than desirable in areas of political, economic and technological performance. For example, although it took all the developed democratic countries centuries to build their systems up to the levels they have attained today; none of the developed countries can understand why the average African state cannot (after just about 30 years of groping), streamline their economies, political systems, science and technology; with contemporary standards.

Fifthly, although the colonial powers eventually granted political independence to the African states after centuries of imposed colonial domination, such political independence was granted with strings which made it impossible for the African leaders to exercise full control of their countries destiny.

Democracy however, would be an expensive system for a developing society if it is totally foreign orientated in its modeling and practice where a major segment of the democratic processing elements are totally alien to the aspiring democratic polity. A developing democratic society like Nigeria ought to be more inward looking to identify the best feasible elements needed for a 'Democratic Concoction' which are likely to induce a viable and unified polity. It is also true that no country in the world today thrives in an entirely closed political and economic system without some vent for external influences. For this reason, a home grown democratic system in Nigeria should have some elements of foreign ideas to shape it towards modernization without losing

267

sight of its indigenous values that can help shape its own democratic Institutions. Therefore, the integration of indigenous values to a viable democratic system is core necessity for sovereign rights to national survival. Hence, the cautionary words of David Heaps (1994) should remind us to note that where foreign statesmen and legislators who tends to insist that a sturdy dose of western democracy is the best cure for the ills of unruly world; where the democracy placebo is prescribed for an epidemic of ethnic racial, tribal and religious conflicts in the worlds most poorest and vulnerable countries ...[21] Notwithstanding, the fact, that prescriber (of Democracy) may not be — familiar with the political quicksand of volatile societies which has the tendency to ill serve the foreign policy interest of restrictive reliance on Eurocentric frame of reference and the impulse to sermonize when the real need is to analyze and understand in the uniqueness and context of the area in conflict with democratic institutionalization. A true democracy cannot be achieved in alien gospel. "Democracy is a difficult kind of Government," said president John. F. Kennedy in 1963. "It requires the highest qualities of self discipline, restraint, willingness to make commitments and sacrifices in the general interest and it also requires knowledge."

Thus, David Heaps (1994) concluded that democracy doesn't arise in pristine conditions or full blown from the ashes of tyranny. It is not nurtured by harsh and prolonged dictatorship nor can it be exported by pleas or arms to societies that have never known the peaceful transfer of political office. Democracy only evolves indigenously over time through a social compact between responsible leadership and a responsive citizenry.

The ethnocentric dominance and national transformation in Nigeria is a complex issue given the ethno-linguistic and cultural diversity in the country. The ethno centric or regional orientation in national wealth distribution and the drive for oil interest is demonstrated by this comment: According to Abubakar Jika (1994):

Historically, since the amalgamation of Nigeria in 1914 to the time oil was exported in commercial quantities after the civil war in 1970, the North virtually sustained the Nigerian Federation through export of groundnut cotton, grains, cows and sheep etc. Contemporary Nigeria also relies almost exclusively in the North for its food needs, grains, cereals, meat, etc. It is true we do not have oil for now, It is also true that the South-West, the most vocal accuser of the North does not have oil as well. In addition it does not feed the rest of Nigeria. While we admire the Yorubas for dominating the economy, education and finance, we recognize that this domination took over 100 years to be perfected through the Federal Government seat in Lagos. We do not envy them and call on others to insist on re-sharing what is obviously our collective heritage. We are prepared to let things gradually evolve. In any case, the North has as much claim on the oil which comes from the East as the Yorubas.[22]

As earlier indicated above, Nigeria is racially homogenous society yet linguistically and ethnically a complex nation such that the influence of counter veiling forces within the socio-political setting (especially the case of political instability, elitism, religion, political factors, incipient classism, ethnicity, the Urban-rural divide, corruption and mis-management) if all are taken together constitute barriers to a successful national integration and unity. However, there are also the inherent Federal integrative potentials toward balanced development through the National Youth Corp Service, Universal Primary Education, infra structural development, Federal Constitution and revenue allocation system. These taken together are a federal comprehensive integrative plan well intentioned to promote unity in diversity but the anomalies inherent in the system appear to prevent comprehensive and effective planning for integration and development. Some of the anomalies can be corrected as seen in the structural inequities in the revenue allocation system, which is the primary interest of this work fostering better fiscal federalism in our Federation.

On the study of fiscal federalism and the growth of national government's influence[23], Ikaba Deeyor (1981) posits that the difference between more developed and less developed countries (if modernization theories are applied) is that developing countries cultural pluralism and tribalism coincide with regions of the country and when regionalism is reinforced by tribalism, governmental regionalization challenges central authority and distracts the central government from modernizing and developing processes. Deeyor further argued that one of the means of minimizing governmental regionalization is adoption of a federal system of government and federalism in both developed and underdeveloped countries has taken on a new meaning because governments seek Riker's old style and Reagan's new style forms of Federalism through the process of integration. That, in many successful Federations, non-ethnic issue politics facilitates the process of integration and in these federations, revenue allocation or fiscal federalism is the lubricating oil that keeps the federal machinery running smoothly. Deeyor's study on Nigeria suggests that the country's historical and Budgetary-data lend to support the revised version of modernization and federalism and that greater national government influence is associated with a more issue based politics as opposed to regional/ethnic based politics. The researcher assumed that the greater the number of states, the more likely issue-politics and the greater the central government's influence.

269

Deeyor Ikaba's study revealed that the states dependency on the center and corresponding widening of the vertical disparity has become an issue in Nigerian politics as well as the increasing trend in national governments influence over the states. The study concluded that the creation of states and the fiscal system in Nigeria confirm a shift from ethnic and regional politics to issue-politics.

There is a certain degree of validity based on the findings of the above referenced study but considering the fact that certain states in Nigeria are inhabited by homogenous ethnicity in major areas of the North, West and the East unlike the minority heterogenous ethnic states in the Middle Belt Areas, Rivers, Southeast and in the former Bendel Areas, the study could not show the possible alternative when minority group or states are concerned over fiscal system in Nigeria. It could be reasoned that issue politics may be ethnically related and become fiercely competitive among the major groups in their dominance of Nigerian Fiscal Scene which in turn normally always produce cleavages and the major groups influence the Federal Center to their fiscal and political advantage [because all state budgets depend on federal pool.]

The influence of minority groups or states has been very minimal hence the call for reform is an attempt to incorporate the real interests and participation of all ethnic groups in the affairs of the nation at the center with feeling of equal citizenship and partnership in Development that benefits all its members. However, when mutual interest factors and differences arise in the politics of revenue allocation where both major and minor ethnic groups or states break from its normal cleavage to specific factor issue then cleavages will be minimized to issue politics. For example Kano may break with Bauchi and joins hands with Oyo and Anambra if population is used as a basis for revenue allocation. Similarly, Ondo, Delta, and Edo may break ranks with Oyo and join hands with Rivers, Akwa Bom, cross rivers Abia and Imo if oil revenues are to be shared on the basis of derivation. In this regard issue politics will minimize the level of ethnic cleavages.

As long as the essentialness of oil and other strategic resources remain viable in the national and international scene, the promise of providing every Nigerian citizen with the greatest good of the greatest number is an attainable option for Nigeria, provided proper use, management and distribution of its National wealth. As Mahatma Ghandi noted many decades ago, that there are enough resources on this earth to meet the needs of all but not enough to justify the greedy. One can liken this statement to Nigeria in that it has enough resources to meet the needs of all its citizens but not enough to satisfy the greedy.

The presence of unscrupulous persons and groups, coupled with the problem of mis management put serious strain on National Development.

270

Nigeria as a nation has the potential to harness and manage its vast human and natural resources effectively to promote growth and development. The proper development and management of its resources remains the focus for its modernization effort to benefit all of its people but inter ethnic rivalry, parochial politics and the inequalities in the national resource distribution system constitute formidable constraint on the country's overall development effort to benefit all its people.

Nigeria: An overview of oil development and producing areas

Nigeria began oil production in 1956 when early discovery was made at Oloibiri in the Niger Delta. Since, then exploration and exploration of oil has expanded to cover many areas in the Niger Delta Basin, (see Appendix) covering Eight States comprising of Rivers, Delta, Akwa Bom, Cross river, Imo, Edo, Abia and Ondo States. The Niger Delta Basin which has an area of 117396 square kilometers remains the main domain of oil production. The area is inhabited by ethnic groups namely Andonis, Annang, Bendes, Ohaji, Ndoni, Etche, Edos, Effiks, Ekpeyes, Engeni, Tai-Eleme, Kalabari's, Ogonis, Ibibios, Isekiri, Isoko, Ilajes, Ijaws, and Urhobos. These are the ethnic groups who make up the indigenous population in the eight major oil producing states of Nigeria. Their combined land size is roughly 12% of Nigeria and their combined population is less than 25 million people. These indigenous people are mainly ethnic minorities in the southern fringes of Nigeria. These are some of the attributes of the indigenous people of the Niger Delta Basin whose land is richly endowed with (The Black Gold) oil.

The rapid expansion oil industry in the country helped Nigeria to obtain a record number of 78 producing oil fields by the 1980s, the largest oil field being at Forcados Yorki. The number of oil producing fields have since increased to more than 158 with well over 2187 oil wells, of which roughly 1563 are producing. The 1993 production location statistics indicate that there are 1,191 offshore producing wells located at Delta, Akwa Ibom, Rivers, Ondo and Lagos. Roughly 18% of total Nigerian oil output comes from off shore locations.

The 1992 NNPC report on inshore oil production by State Shows the following production distribution (%):

Rivers	55.54
Delta	30.54
Edo	7.63
Imo	3.44
Abia	.59
Akwa Ibom	.50
Cross Rivers	.50
	100.00%

In 1993, the Nigerian crude oil production showed a daily output averaging 1.9 mbd. The total percent production distribution by OMPADEC (Oil Mineral Producing Areas Development Commission) member States shows:

Rivers	42.0%	
Delta	32.0%	
Akwa Bom	17.5%	
Other	8.5%	(production unevenly shared by the other producing states)

See Appendix A for oil production and producing areas, oil contracts and a list of oil companies in the Niger Delta Basin.

The evolution of oil in Africa and Nigeria in particular started in 1958 when significant discoveries were made at Oloibiri in the Niger Delta. However, the expansion of oil industry itself took place in the 1970s though historically actual exploration began in 1908 by a German business interest named the Nigerian Bitumen Company. The company stopped operation at the outbreak of the First World War. In 1937 Shell D'Arcy Company reactivated the Nigerian oil operations. Between 1938 and 1941, Shell BP undertook preliminary geological reconnaissance and by 1951, Shell drilled its first wildcat well. In 1956, it made the first commercial discovery at Oloibiri in the present day Rivers State. However, the first exploration well was at Ihuo near Owerri before first commercial discovery was made at Oloibiri. This success was followed by additional discoveries at Afam (1957), Ebubu and Bomu 1958 and thus oil production increased from 1958 through 1964. Other oil fields discovered were Okan (offshore by Gulf Oil 1965) and Ogagi (Ahoada) by Elf 1966 (before the 1967-1969 Civil War period). Following the end of the Nigerian Civil War in 1970, the production of oil reached 560,000 barrels per day and by 1972, Nigeria hit 2 million barrels per day and became a world class oil producer. The development of the petroleum industry in the 1970s transformed the national economy such that the sale of oil accounted for more than 80% of the nation's total export-earnings. Thus, the increased earnings from oil enabled Nigeria to achieve high economic growth and therefore oil displaced agricultural products which had accounted for 66% of the G.D.P in 1960s became less significant in generating national revenues. The oil boom of 1970s which coincided with OPEC power and embargoes of 1973-75 and dramatic upsurge of revenues to N13.86 billion by 1980. According to Terisa Turner[24] revenues from oil exports peaked at $25 billion in 1980 but dropped to under $10 billion in 1983 and to $7 billion in 1986. Though oil prices fell [*Euromoney Magazine*, September 1990:95], Nigeria's oil production capacity increased by 1.9 million barrels per day and earned $5 billion just for the first six months of 1990 on the wake of the Gulf Crisis. Oil still accounts for 95% of foreign earning and 80% of government revenues (See Appendix B for revenues from oil and non-oil sectors, value of Nigerian oil exports, and oil prices for 1972-1994). Oil remains Nigeria's hope in the 1990s and even beyond because the country is also expected to earn $12 billion over a 20 year period from gas, another strategic resource found in large quantities in the same Niger Delta Basin. Nigerian crude oil may be depleted by the year 2018 given the 1988 rate of consumption but gas exports could become Nigeria's main foreign exchange earner in the 21st Century as energy experts estimate the country's gas reserves to last for next 100 years.[25] Nigeria holds a gas reserve of over 100 trillion cubic feet. Thus, oil and gas will continue to influence and sustain the prospect of Nigeria's internal political and economic stability and the prospect for viable external reserves through the 21st century. The production and sale of oil resources give rise to huge national wealth and the existence of large sums of oil revenues gives the impetus to inter ethnic or regional competition to control the national wealth and preside over the distribution and spending of oil revenues. The prospect for national and regional social and economic development depends on the structure of the prevailing revenue sharing formula which is highly influenced by ethnocentric feelings and parochial power politics.

It is our hope that this brief discourse on the development of oil in Nigeria has been helpful in understanding the theme and direction of this discussion on oil and Fiscal Federalism in Nigeria and the conditions necessitating the call for reform on the existing structure of the country's revenue allocation system.

The oil producing areas have been neglected for so many years and suffers from continued under allocation of resources and under development. It is the writers hope that the socioeconomic disparities and the environmental degradation stemming from years of exploitation can be partly remedied

273

through reparation and planned communal compensation for the impoverished masses of the area. The compensation or reparation demand as a result of economic and political exploitation or unintentional spillover cost of victims of mass strife or even into war are nothing new in both global and national terms. A number of reparations have been either made or being called for consideration as a remedy for past wrongs or grave inequities that have been proven to be wrong. Here are examples, Patrick Younge (1991)[26] reported a reparation conference was held in Lagos Nigeria calling for the compensation for the damage wrought on the African Continent by the West. That it's time for the west to repay its debt to Africa. That, Africa has never recovered from the horrors of slavery and colonialism and the continent has been torn apart by poverty, famine and wars — all a result of the west's interference. The conference organizer Chief M.K.O Abiola declared that "For over 500 years we have been the world's favorite victims, exploited by an astonishing number of nations. All that we ask is that these wrongs are officially acknowledged as contributing substantially to the horrendous plight of Africans through out the world and that some gesture of atonement and compensation be made to the survivors of holocaust that has gone on since the 15th century."

In this regard the President of Nigeria General Ibrahim Babangida gave his support and called on Western governments to immediately write off all debts owed by Third World Countries ($1.34 trillion) and to introduce a new marshall plan for Africa along the lines of the fund that helped rebuild Europe after the Second World War. He went further to say that Africa has suffered for a long time. We have now have reached a situation where many countries exist only for the purpose of debt repayment approximately $160,786 million. A Nigerian academic, Chinweizu calculated the total owed for 500 million Africans to be in excess of $2,000 billion without interest!! Also, that North Korea has made a similar claim against Japan of over $5 billion for 35 years of exploitation and occupation.[27] Similarly (Akamu and Adebayo Diran, 1991)[28] reported that identical reparation demands have been made by African Americans for:

(1)   Rents on the lands that were taken from the black people over the last 500 years.
(2)   Compensation for the material and social destruction during the slave trade.
(3)   Payment for the wars and campaigns waged against black people.
(4)   Compensation for all animals vegetable and mineral resources that were stolen including cattle, sheep, cotton, rubber and gold.

(5)   Compensation for the millions of lives lost through slavery, colonialism, conquest and pacification and in the wars of de-colonialization...etc.

In light of the above, Congressman John Conyers of Michigan introduced a bill in U.S. Congress (HR 1684) to establish a seven member commission to study the impact of slavery on racial segregation and make policy recommendation including reparations to Congress. This call might have been motivated by the decision of the Congress of the United States in actually making $1.25 billion payment in reparations to Japanese-Americans deprived of their civil rights during World War II which is seen as establishing an important precedent. It is further reasoned that slaves were long deprived of 'life, liberty and the pursuit of happiness' and have yet to be reparated.[29] In *Reparations Yes!*, Prof. Imar Obadele (1993)[30] affirmed the following reparations payments be made by the American government that "the United States government accepts the obligation of the United states to pay reparations to the descendants of Afrikans held as slaves in the United States and undertakes to make such payments to the New Afrikan nation as political unit, to compensate in part for the destruction and/or damage to Afrikan political units and for the abortion and the destruction of New Afrikan political units in the United States during the era of slavery, and payments to New Afrikan organizations to compensate in part for the deliberate subversion of the New Afrikan social structure, and obligation to pay directly to each New Afrikan, descendant of Afrikans held as slaves in the United States and born on or before the date of ratification of this Act, and still living on the date of each appropriation, the total sum of ? dollars. Congress is authorized to appropriate and pay annually sums of money and credit to discharge this obligation over a period of years, not less than three-billion annually..."

There are conceptual views on compensation for environmental damage. These views are (1) the full cost principle which states that all users of environmental resources should pay there full cost, the principle is based on the notion that humanity has a right to a reasonable safe and healthy environment. (2) The property rights principle which assume that the lost of efficiency in modern environmental problems involve mis-specified property rights which has the tendency to create perverse incentives therefore local communities should have property rights over there flora and fauna and other species within their community. (3) The Sustainability principle states that all resources should be used in a manner that respects future generations as such restoration of inter-generational fairness in the use of depletable resources is desirable. (4) Lastly there is also debt-Nature Swaps which involves strategy reducing pressure on forest caused by international debt owed by developing countries. Strategy involves offers to a holder of debt to council the debt in return for environmentally related actions on part of the debtor nation. This is an option Nigeria can consider as part of its conservation policy since part of the oil revenues are used to service external debt.[31]

Though, there are a number of secular values and guidelines for compensation but there are also both Christian and Islamic religious guidelines for Reparation and restitution when a justifiable rationale exists to enforce restitution as a remedy.

Ecclesiastical thoughts on restitution

Here are some examples of ecclesiastical thoughts on restitution. An example of Islamic thoughts on restitution is "the relationship between talamidah units in Mauritania and the shaikh is well illustrated in the following excerpt from a letter to Muhammad Lhabib, in which he was instructed to make restitution to a certain group of talamidh, the Ahl Ahmad wuld Haiba. Following an introduction, in which the Trarza amir is reminded of his obligations to follow the sunna of the Prophet, Sidiyya informs him that he is to return all that was taken:

> . . . of wealth to our talamidh and brothers, who are among those protected blood brothers and among a section of the talamidh at our side, the Ahl Ahmad ibn Habiba, and all their tribe ... in such a manner that there will be no desire [on their part] for more of this wealth ... and provide the bearer of this note with hospitality ... This [matter] concerns those who were distressed among us. Give to the Ahl Ahmad ibn Habiba the necessities of life in order that they may be the same as the [others] of the beloved with us ... for what is prosperity for us is prosperity for them, and what is equality for us is equality for them, and that which is kindness to them is kindness for us, and what is charitable to them is charitable to us.[32]

The Christian Holy Bible recorded the following examples on Restitution:

> Now the men were watching for an omen, and they quickly took it up from him and said, "Yes, your brother Benhadad." Then he said, "Go and bring him." "Then Benhadad came forth with him." Then Benhadad came forth to him and he caused him to come up into the chariot. And Benhadad said to him." [...] "The cities which my father took from your

father I will restore; and you may establish bazaars for yourself in Damascus as my father did in Samaria." [I King 20:33-34]

Now Elisha had said to the woman whose son he had restored to life, "Arise, and depart with your household, and sojourn wherever you can; for the LORD had called for a famine, [...] upon the land for seven years." [...] she went with her household and sojourned in the land of the Philistines seven years. [...] she went forth to appeal to the king for her house and her land. [...] So the king appointed an official for her, saying, "Restore all that was hers, together with all the produce of her fields from the day that she left the land until now." [II King 8:1-6.] The ecclesiastical thoughts on restitution has encouraging insights to fairness and social justice. Additionally, a notable Islamic scholar M. Ali Fekrat points to a pattern of pervasive underdevelopment side by side with extreme and highly concentrated wealth which resulted from the oil boom. Such a disparity between the rich and poor is in his view, diametrically opposed to the fundamental precepts of Islam and thus leads to a widening gap between the Islamic socioeconomic ideals on the one hand and the actual state of economic affairs on the other...[33]

With regard to compensation for oil areas, Peter Nijkamp contends that energy extractions has catastrophical effects, hence, firms that cause damage to the oil areas should be obliged to pay for it through adequate compensations.[34] In Nigeria, the operating oil firms are in partnerships with the Federal Government and thus the corporate social responsibility to the oil areas including compensations should be undertaken by both the Federal Government and the oil companies. It is worthwhile here to briefly account for specific benefits and cost of oil to Nigeria. The increase in government revenues from oil enabled the government of Nigeria to make increased expenditures in various supporting sectors of the economy particularly the development of social and economic infrastructures. In essence, revenues from oil afforded Nigeria the budgeting flexibility with respect to its development programs.

Prior to the oil, the country's economy was dependent on cash crops (cotton, cocoa, groundnut and palm oil) for foreign exchange but the development of oil industry transformed the economy. The politburo in 1986 revealed that by mid 1960s only a few years after independence. when indigenous sourcing of revenue effectively began, the export of cash crops "had collapsed in the world economy." And even at that *The African Guardian* newspaper's findings show that between 1956-58, the years immediately preceding independence, groundnut, produce exclusively by the North earned Nigeria so £30 million annually. Palm produce from the east and west netted

£33 million. Cotton from the north earned £8 million. Cocoa from the west earned £25 million. Rubber from the west later from the Midwest earned £7 million. Cumulatively therefore, revenue from the east and west amounted to about £65 million per annum during that period. That from the North hovered at about £38 pounds (Ango Abduulahi, 1994). Also, it should be noted that before the advent of the military, resources were never fully exploited for the benefit of all. By the derivation formula, regions kept 50 percent of the proceeds from their resources and contributed only 50 percent to the center. At the time of this writing, the mineral producing areas get only 3 percent, and even then, it has to be administered by a government agency. The increased export earnings from oil enabled Nigeria to attain high level economic growth. The GDP expanded to 9.7% per year between 1965 and 1973 and enhanced annual growth rate of 3.9% between 1973 to 1979, but declined to about 1.9% by 1983. With oil wealth, Nigeria was about to carry out major capital projects such as building major refineries at Warri, Kaduna and Port Harcourt. Also a $300 million petrochemical plant, Murtala Mohammed International Airport, a steel complex and even new capital territory Abuja including a network of oil pipe lines from the south to the North of the country. The increase in oil wealth not only afforded Nigeria in financing impressive huge development projects domestically but also enhanced its assertive power in Africa and international diplomacy. Olaniyan, Omotayo 1988 noted that:

> As Nigeria's oil output increase, so too did the foreign exchange earnings of the country and her image. There was an increased inclination to use this as leverage in certain global issues. Nigeria split with the United States over the latter's Angola policy. She also took a strong position against great power intervention in the Horn Of Africa in 1976-77. Also, Henry Kissinger's request to visit Nigeria was refused more than once. But when the U.S. was perceived to be committed to majority rule in independent Zimbabwe, relations were rapidly restored even though the US did not recognize the MPLA government in Angola. Also, Nigeria's arbitrary sequestration of British Petroleum's assets on the eve of the Commonwealth Heads of Government conference at Lusaka in August 1979 represented another important instance of the use of oil power. The move jolted the ambivalent position of the British government and precipitated the Lancaster House Conference which confirmed the independence of Zimbabwe.[35]

In this regard Kayode Soremekun, 1988 also noted that:

> Nigeria interactions with a super-power [like the United States of America], Nigeria has used its oil as a leverage. Bassey Ate points out, for instance, that largely because of oil revenues, Nigeria made vigorous bids to the United States as regards African affairs from a position of relative economic independence in the bilateral sphere. He goes on to specifics by contending that the comparative dynamism of Nigeria's foreign policy in this period with particular reference to its diplomacy with the United States in Africa, reached its high points with Gowon's unyielding resistance to the Nixon Administration, Mohammed's historic challenge to President Ford over Angola, and Obasanjo's progressive partnership with Jimmy Carter in liquidating Ian Smith's settler colonialism in Zimbabwe. Similarly, an American writer, William Foltz, has pointed out that on the basis of America's dependence on Nigeria's oil imports, Pretoria's influence on the United States's policy has declined substantially in favor of Nigeria.[36]

The incidence referred above is with respect to Nigeria-American relationship in the 1970s. Nigeria also helped a number of African countries:

a.   In 1975, General Mohammed gave 13 million to the MPLA in Angola to facilitate its fight against reactionary parties in the civil war. The federal government did not ascertain how to benefit The Angolan government on her own initiative requested for the establishment of a Nigerian embassy in Launda, Nigeria also proceeded further to establish a N20 million Southern African Relief Fund to assist freedom fighters and cater for refugees of liberation wars in Africa.

b.   But in spite of the dramatic decline of the Nigerian economy in the early 1980s the above aims continue to be governments's central interest. Hence, at Zimbabwe's independence in 1980, the federal government donated N10 million towards her economic recovery. The grant was to be used for the establishment of an institute for manpower development to train Zimbabweans to take over the administration of their country.

c.   The drought victims on the continent, in 1985, received N5 million. For the same reason in the following year, Cape Verde alone received US$100,000 together with 100 tonnes of maize, 100 tonnes of millet and 50 tonnes of sorghum. Also, in 1986. the federal government assisted Botswana and Zambia with a grant of N10 million for the rebuilding of houses destroyed after invasions by South Africa. And this was further complemented with a pledge of N50 million aid to assist all embattled frontline states under the constant attack of South Africa.

d.   In 1987, bilateral aid evolved into a new scheme, the Technical Aid Corps. Under this scheme young Nigerian professionals in agriculture, veterinary medicine, etc, were to be sent to work in other African countries requesting for them. In the first instance, they would be required to serve for two years. Each participant will receive US$500 per month as salary from the federal government while the host country will provide accommodation.[37]

The oil wealth made the country so credit worthy that its debt grew from a modest $80 million in 1968 to $33 billion by the late 1980s with huge debt service. However, the drastic decline in oil prices in the 1980s threw the country to severe economic dislocation and eventually the austerity, structural adjustment program (SAP) and turned to the IMF for rescue.

The official estimates of debt service obligations before the debt rescheduling - itself a major part of SAP - were $4.5 bn in 1986, $5.5bn in 1987 and $6.0bn in 1988. With the major rescheduling efforts led by the Finance Minister, Dr. Chu Okongwu, the 1987 debt service obligations were reduced to an estimated $2.8bn - still a huge sum for the CBN's lean purse but, a far cry from the former estimate of $5.4 bn.[38]

The 1980s have turned out to be a trying period for Nigeria. The slide in oil prices from about $40,00(U.S) in 1981 to less than $10.00 in 1986 led to massive balance-of-payments deficits which were largely financed by a net outflow of foreign exchange amounting to N2,993.0 million in 1981, N1,539.4 million in 1982 and N244.8 million in 1983 and by an embarrassingly uncontrolled mountain of short-term un-refinanced trade arrears which rose to N1,981.7 million in 1982 (representing 22.46 percent of Nigeria's external total debt) outstanding, N5,443.4 million in 1984 (37.4 per cent of total external debt), and N6, 164.3 million (35.6 per cent of total external debt) in 1985.

In essence, the economic and the political viability of Nigeria have been largely supported by oil revenues derived from minority wealth and thus it is inconceivable that the minority areas where the major wealth of the nation is produced should suffer any form of deprivation. It is a matter of compulsion that Nigeria cares for its wealth producing areas through adequate compensation and effective development planning for the mineral producing areas. The disparities in development might be linked to this statement credited to Phillip Asiodu who said in a public lecture in 1980 that "Like (sic) in many other areas of the world, the regions where oil is found in this country are very inhospitable. They are mainly in swamps and creeks. They require a massive injection of money if their conditions and standards of living are to compare with that elsewhere in the country where possibilities of agriculture and diversified industry are much greater. There is a nudging acceptance of the special needs of the areas in the latest proposals being discussed by the government but I believe there is a long way to go to meet the claims of the oil producing areas which see themselves losing irreplaceable resources while replaceable and permanent resources of agriculture and industry are being developed elsewhere largely with oil revenue. Given, however, the small size and population of the oil producing areas, it is not cynical to observe that even if the resentments of oil producing states continue they cannot threaten the stability of the country nor affect its continued economic development."[39] Oil exploration and the hazards of oil spillage has degraded oil communities environments and have left their communities desolate. In addition, the oil communities farmlands and fishing areas within the riverain areas of the Niger Delta Basin have been polluted and they also lack basic infrastructure and amenities such as electricity, roads, schools, hospitals, portable water and so on. The minorities have directed their grievances to both the oil companies and the producer government to use some of the huge oil profits for the improvement of their respective communities.

It seems unjust to care for non oil producing areas in distant lands nationally and internationally to the detriment of the oil producing minority communities. Hence, a policy change is required to correct past and present socioeconomic and environmental imbalances suffered by the people of the oil producing areas. It is also inconceivable that the mineral producing areas that sustains the country's national and international political and economic power should be subjected to insurmountable neglect and impoverishment while the revenues derived from their resource (oil) are used to better the socioeconomic and political welfare of others.

A policy change is necessary to correct the observed disparities and proper development planning for the mineral producing areas.

However, it still a correctable system through a proper progressive and integrative approach to a National democratic process that includes all its diverse elements as a unique source of strength in building a viable Nation. The recognition and the pragmatic approach to understanding unity in diversity is consistent with the vision of Sir Abubakar Tafawa Balewa, the first prime Minister of Nigeria who stated that:

To me the most important result of the constitutional changes in 1954 was the introduction of a federal form of government for Nigeria is a system which I had advocated as far back as 1948 in the old Legislative Council. I am pleased to see that were are now all agreed that the federal system is, under present conditions, the only sure basis on which Nigeria can remain united. We must recognize our diversity is a source of great strength, and we must do all in our power to see that this federal system of government is   strengthened and maintained. [40]

Notes

1. Wiwa, Saro Ken. Genocide in Nigeria: The Ogoni Tragedy. Saro Publishers. Port Harcourt, Nigeria. 1992. p. 25

2. Osaghae, Eghosa E. The Osoni Uprising: Oil, Politics, Minority Agitation, and the Future of the Nigerian State. Journal of African Affairs. 1995. Volume 94. p. 325-344.

3. Ekpu, U. Ethnic Minority Problems in Nigerian Politics (Acta Universitatis Uppsaliensis, Uppsala, 1977).

4. Ibid.

5. Ibid. p. 26.

6. *The Guardian*, February 28, 1994.

7. Waziri, Alhaji Mahund. Sunday Vanguard. September 18, 1994. p. 1-2.

8. *Nigerian Times*, New York, March/April 1994, p. 24.

9. Ibid.

10. Ibid.

11. Ibid.

12. Ibid.

13. Ibid.

14. Ibid.

15. Ibid.

16. Ighodalo, Ituah. 'Yoruba, Abiola, and June 12 in Vanguard', January 5, 1995, p. 5.

17. Ibid.

19. 'Budget of Renewal', *The U.S. — Nigerian Voice*, February/ March, 1995, p. 13.

20. 'Demonizing Opponents', *Washington Post*, October 28, 1994, p. A27.

21. Emejuaiwe, Stephen. "Democracy in Africa: What hopes?". Daily Sunray. July 19, 1995. p. 12.

22. Heaps, David, 'The Democracy Placebo,' *The Washington Post*, October 28, 1994, p. A27.

23. *Nigerian Times (New York)*, March/April, 1995, p. 13.

24. Ikaba, Deeyor and Baridoo Yereba, 'Fiscal Federation and The Growth of National Governments Influence: The Case of Nigeria', Doctoral Dissertation, Arizona State University, 1981, UMI, Ann Arbor, Mich.

25. Turner, Terisa, 'Oil Workers and Oil Burst in Nigeria', *Africa Today*, Vol. 33, No. 4, October, 1986, p.36.

26. *West Africa*, March 28, 1988, p.561.

27. Younge, Patrick. 'Reparations: Africa Demands Damages for Horrors of Slavery', *Global Africa*, Vol. 2, February-March, 1991.

28. Ibid, p. 4.

29. Obadele, Imari A., 'Reparation Yes!', *Lecture Saturday*, March 13, 1993, Oakland, CA. Also, *Reparation Yes in the Legal and Political Reasons Why New Afrikans — Black People in the United States Should Be Paid Now for the Enslavement of our Ancestors and for War Against Us after Slavery.* Third Edition, (Baton Rouge, LA: Shonghay House, 1993), pp. 67-80.

30. Ibid, p.4.

31. Ibid.

32. Tietenberg, Tom, *Environmental Economics and Policy*. (New York: Harper Collins, 1994), pp. 186-89 & 406-08.

33. Stewart, C.C. and E.T.C. Stewart, *Economic Power and Religious influence in Islam and social order in Mauritania*, (UK: Clarendon Press, 1973), p. 713.

34. *Holy Bible*, Thomas Nelson, New York 1972
   (ii) M. ALI FEKRAT "STRESS IN THE ISLAMIC WORLD" JOURNAL OF SOUTH ASIAN AND MIDDLE EASTERN STUDIES 4 (1981) P.7.

35. Nijkamp, Peter, 'Theory and Application of Environmental Economics', (New York: North Holland Press, 1971), p.41.

36. *Economic Development and Foreign Policy in Nigeria*, Edited by Olusanyaga, O., p.105, et al 1988.

37. Ibid.

38. Ibid.

39. Ibid.

40. As quoted in the book titled "Genocide in Nigeria" by Ken Saro Wiwa, 1992. p. 87.

11   Oil, fiscal federalism, and Nigeria's destiny

A federal solution has often been sought as a way to integrate diverse elements or groups in a heterogenous society into a single political entity while maintaining their independent ethnic identities at the same time. A number of attempts, at bringing about unity in diversity have been made in many diverse societies as in the United States, India, Brazil and a host of other former colonies in the Third World and Nigeria is not an exception.

The development of unity in diversity in a nation state through political cohesiveness is not an easy task and the degree of success differs from one polity to another depending on the uniqueness of its internal power structure, economic status, state of development and the nature of political relationship amongst the diverse groups within the polity.

Even in the most successful federal systems, the power boundaries between political units are hardly clearly delineated. Since the political units share certain functions and responsibilities, the struggle for influence over crucial policy areas is a regular source of friction in any federation and, one area where the struggle is highly intensified is the financial area where the ultimate goals of fiscal policy are decided.

In Nigeria and other developing federal systems, the historical mixture of economic and political circumstances empowers the federal government to collect the bulk of the nations revenues and share it among and between different tiers of government [local, state and federal]. The process of carrying out the inter governmental transfer of revenues in the Nigerian Federal System forms the unit of this inquiry given the complex political and economic changes particularly the impact of oil revenues on inter governmental transfers and ethnic power politics within the context of fiscal federalism. In Nigeria given the practical interest along with ethnocentric cleavages in the political arena which has culminated into gross disparities in its constituents parts, the need to satisfy all interested parties and at the same time, engage in economic growth and development still remain a serious challenge for policy makers in effective formulation and implementations of fiscal policies.

The Nigeria constituent parts or states are more or less ethnically defined and are locked in a fierce competition over the sharing of national revenues and other resources. Each successor government has made efforts to establish regular and institutionalized mode of revenue allocation as practiced in developed federations but the issue has generated more conflict rather than success.

The major bulk of national revenue is derived from the parts of the country populated by ethnic minorities who bemoan what they perceive as a lack of access to the federal policy making machinery and if in fact they did their influence is so minimal to impact federal decision in their favor.

Though minority oil producing areas or groups lack a strong influence on the national political apparatus yet they aggregate into a sort of political buffer state by their political behavior to seek benefit from a greater portion of the revenue derived from their mineral wealth through the derivation principle which presumes that oil mineral producing states should have a greater share of the revenues derived from their resource. The minority groups in the pursuit of this principle and with the view to achieve fair share of oil revenues simply throw their political weight behind any one of the major ethnic groups. The minorities try to ally with a major group to gain attention in the bid to meet their demand although not necessarily with one collective voice. Thus, Nigeria's complex inter ethnic relationships in the nations political arena have not been able to strike balance between the demands and needs of ethnic minorities and the self interest of majority ethnic groups who control the processes and distribution of wealth and resource allocation at the federal center. In essence, the politics of revenue allocation in the Nigerian Federal System has failed to take full cognizance of the special needs of the minority oil producing areas in the Federal Revenue allocation system and thus requires structural reform in the nation's resource allocation system. The conditions necessitating the call for structural changes in Fiscal Federalism in Nigeria would not be sufficient without understanding the Nations Socio political Development and the history of oil production and producing areas, the trend in oil revenues (from oil growth through boom and bust) for over a 38 year period. Hence, Chapter Ten was devoted to in-depth analyses of the Socio-Political Development and the development of oil industry in the country.

Nigeria oil based economic growth creates a glaring fiscal gaps between oil producing and non producing areas where the nation bestows its revenue bounties on the federal government whose responsiveness to growth and development imposes major burdens on the minority oil areas who must support that development without adequate benefit or care for them. It is essential to understand that the enduring needs of mankind [be it ethnic minority or majority within a given political system like Nigeria] can never be satisfied by a national wealth distributive philosophy based on group (ethnic) or regional inequalities [where there is portrayal of unequal citizenship within the ethnic composition in the national political order]. The minority groups have never ceased to be aware that the national power structure in Nigeria is contrary to their real interest and well-being as it concerns revenue allocation since independence (1960) hence conflict and controversy has often dominated all patterns of resource allocation systems in the country. It is worthwhile for Nigeria and its policy makers to harness their energies toward encouragement of national unity and that the unity of the ethnic groups while allowing for differences must also consider care for one another which rests upon the feeling in each member that they all belong together in an entity named Nigeria.

Furthermore, Federalism in Nigeria will suffer (even unto grave concern for disintegration) if the fiscal dividends derived from oil or any resource continually favors majority groups self interests without sensitivity to minority group interests and concerns for justice, fairness and better balance in our federation. It is imperative for federal policy makers in Nigeria to balance the inherent allocational inequities between the major federal revenue eaters [non-oil producing areas and the federal revenue producers], the [minority oil producing areas] if equity and fairness is to be achieved. The minority oil producing states who contribute the bulk of revenues to the federal coffers have been squeezed dry by structural inequities of the federal revenue allocation system and the system appears insensitive to the adverse environmental, and socio-economic conditions of the oil mineral producing areas. A number of studies have shown that the Nigerian State that benefits from oil royalties by permitting an exploitation of oil mineral resources that clearly results in pollution, disruption and degradation of the ecosystem has neither instituted adequate compensation planning nor a comprehensive mitigation policy for the affected areas. On the study of environmental and socioeconomic impact of oil spillage in riverain areas of Nigeria (Angaye et al., 1983) stated that "although the petroleum has created an economic boom for the entire nation, it has also led to environmental and socio economic problems for the entire nation and, that the inhabitants of the ecological zones of the riverain areas of Nigeria where petroleum is produced are the most obvious victims of environmental and socio economic hardships that oil mining and spillage have produced in the country."[1]

In another study Paul Collier (1978) noted that the oil industry and the inequalities it has created in Nigeria do paint a picture of economic growth without progressive change. From 1960-1978, the country recorded a growth rate of 3.6% per year. It was considered Africa's success story. However, the

288

dream wealth from oil was unequally distributed — that, the socio economic status of the people was determined by access to land, and oil had displaced part of the vast land on which rural people depend. The rapid export of oil actually reinforced income reduction in rural areas; naively one would have expected their income to have risen

In the recognition of the repressive conditions for the poor and the concern over the plight of the rural masses the International Labor Organization in 1981 sponsored a mission to Nigeria. The chief of the mission, Dudley Seers observed among other things that more people are living in poverty than before the oil boom. In spite of the enormous revenues accrued to the national government, the vast majority of the population, particularly those in the rural areas have benefitted little if at all that, oil derived growth has made possible a very opulent life style for a small minority, where as large sections of the population have remained as poor as ever.[2]

Indeed, one has no choice than to concur with a notable Nigerian social critic, Yusufu Bala Usman that the petronaira has not blessed (Nigerian producers) with the essentials of existence, rather its abundance is part of the process of denying them the benefits of what they produce. They continue in their poverty.[3]

Arising from inequities and inequalities in the current system calls for structural reform. The new deal fiscal federalism in Nigeria is to redefine the national fiscal contours in both philosophical and pragmatic terms, if equity and fairness is to be attained to satisfy all constituent parts of the federation. It may even require each state to pursue for its own independent revenue policies where the responsibility shifts from the center to states so as to reduce regional disparities as a consequent of inequities inherent in federally centered revenue allocation system. It will be an insurance against the asymmetric adverse shocks induced by political manipulation of revenue allocation formula by the powers that control the federal central government.

The central government marriage of political convenience or a system of state creation as political complement of regional or ethnic interest without strong foreseeable foundation for self reliance fiscal capacity constitutes an unintentional indirect economic burden for mineral producing areas. In essence the wealth derived from mineral producing areas must support itself and other states through the influence of the federal government revenue allocation system. That, state creation on the back of minority oil producing areas of the country and the heavy reliance on oil without economic diversification has generated undue excess burden for minority oil states except some structural changes are made in national distributive formulae. The federal policies appear to have displaced non-oil producing areas incentive to generate alternative sources to enhance their respective fiscal capacity and also make a fair and equitable contribution to the national treasury. The current federal system stifles each state fiscal initiative and seems to be a policy that requires serious revision requiring a fiscal policy coordination with enhancement of fiscal capacity utilization that will induce better balance between revenue generation capacity and equitable distribution. The weakness of the federal government in encouraging under-utilization of non-oil producing areas revenue potential imposes undue economic burden for minority oil producing states.

The writers propose a unique system of functional federalism while recognizing for states to organize themselves in the federal pattern of government with overlapping political units yet should not be engaged in prioritization of ranking national wealth distribution based on population, central power politics and wealth consumption tendencies instead each state should work to have limited autonomy with responsibility to control its naturally endowed resources and generate the necessary funds for its own development. No state should solely depend on the central government but must make constitutionally agreed financial contribution to the federal center.

In changing the face of fiscal federalism in Nigeria, each state government should be replaced by a competitive fiscal federalism in which state government be made to finance their own activities without having excessive reliance on federal Government. The federal government should take steps to level up if need be merge certain states that do not have the wherewithal to provide adequate public infrastructure for their own development or alternatively help non-oil producing states develop their resource base to induce self sustained development. This will give way to some limited and significant 'fend for yourself' fiscal federalism to ease off excess burden for minority oil producing states. The federal government should also take corrective steps in the form of reparation and restitutions for oil areas that have suffered for long in terms of disparities in development, deprivation, environmental degradation and the cumulative depletion of non renewable oil resources which have been exploited for over many decades.

This compensational plan is justifiable since it is the same government that is in partnership with private interest in putting pressure for oil exploitation without comparative adequate care for oil producing minority states since independence. Moreover, it is also conceivable that the increasing international market linkages among oil producing countries may result in adverse economic conditions that would limit the power of oil wealth to the disadvantage of oil producing areas who must then fend for themselves (probably without alternative viable economic resources) in the post oil era.

At that time the non-oil producing states may not succumb to sharing the burden of the disadvantages of oil outcome in a competitive and fend for yourself federalism, even though the non oil producing states benefitted during the viable oil era. However, this scenario could be avoided if other strategic resources in the country are developed to meet national and international demand and a proper national distributive system is enforced to benefit all political units as oil revenue benefitted all the political units in the country.

Again, an increase in international competition in a weak oil market scenario may amount to reduced revenue allocation and wealth redistribution system under taken by the central government would be weakened by reduction in oil revenues; Consequently, both the fiscal capacity of the federal government and the oil producing states will be weakened and the development budgetary outlook will also become deficient, except serious steps are taken to plan for a viable economic alternative in the future if the essentialness of oil in the global market is weakened.

One of the desirable planning for economic alternative is the establishment of Oil Heritage Saving Fund to secure a better future in the post oil era. Also, if there is economic diversification without mono-commodity reliance there can be a better prospect for sharing the national fiscal burden in a fair and equitable manner in a competitive federalism, (with no excess burden to any sector of the federation in contributing into central government treasury). Any system of fiscal federalism in Nigeria that is characterized by increased dependency of a state or local government on the federal revenue distributive pool will have a de-stabilizing effect on the national or regional economic conditions and probably the oil producing states fiscal potentials may be made continually worse off for the very burden to generate oil revenues to support both federal and local needs in the Nigerian Federation.

It is also important to take cognizance to the fact that under a competitive 'Fiscal' Federalism, each state government will be better informed than the central federal government about the developmental needs of the people within each locality within each state jurisdiction.

Nigeria became independent in 1960, since then the political manipulation vested in the self interest actions of heavily populated regions or states have not only created excess burden for minority oil areas in generating revenues for the federal government but also embarked on lopsided and unbalanced development strategies to the disadvantage of the minority oil areas [who remain largely under developed.] The oil areas have continually suffered from the pangs of impoverishment and environmental degradation.

Thus, the unbalanced development priorities of the federal government have generated patterns of wide disparities in national and regional socio economic development (with a feeling of neglect and lack of care for the minority oil areas who generate the most funds for the federal coffers through their endowed natural resource oil). The resulting effect has been cycles of adverse socio economic conditions for the oil mineral producing areas and in

291

turn constrains oil areas to weakened fiscal interactions among local public and private service providers. The oil companies [which operate in the areas] that could have minimized the fiscal stress and enhanced the development needs of the communities do not render adequate corporate social responsibility to the host communities. In essence, the minority oil producing states lack the fiscal equity that is proportional to the level of contribution to the national revenue base since their revenue situation is also made worse by inability of each oil state to tax oil companies fairly on their own to increase its revenue. It is the writers view that any national wealth distribution in Nigeria that creates welfare inequities will be deemed unjust.

The growth and development of Nigeria's oil wealth has been derived from mostly rural areas inhabited by minority groups yet the per capita development expenditures on the minority oil producing states appear relatively low if compared with majority and heavily populated non-oil producing states. This unfortunate scenario can be linked to the structural inequities in the country's revenue sharing system in addition to the federal government unbalanced development planning and implementation.

The observed disparities and gaps in development is not necessarily the fault of the people in the non-oil producing areas rather it is an ineffective national revenue distributive system that requires serious revision if fairness and balanced development is to be achieved.

Nigeria is in dire need of federalism with fiscal equity if it is to survive as a nation state. The concept of fiscal equity (Ana Bela Santos, 1989)[4] as the equal fiscal treatment of equals who live in different local jurisdictions. The social economic understanding of fiscal equity in the context of fiscal federalism demands horizontal equity as the equal treatment of equal such that the approach to fairness would be envy free distribution [within the context of horizontal equity]. If all Nigerians are equal in citizenship then the use or mis-use of population based national wealth distributive system or changing the national distributive formula at will to better the self interest of majority powerful groups has the tendency to suppress and exploit the feelings of minorities who produce a major bulk of national wealth embedded in oil.

Prior to the growth of the oil industry, the revenue distributive systems operated in a manner where the resource producing region retained all or a major portion of the revenues derived from its own regional resources, not until oil became a significant national revenue resource that the system of revenue distribution changed. This change scenario is well stated by Wayne Nafziger, 1983. He stated that before 1959, all revenues from mineral and agricultural products had been retained by the producing regions. However, this picture changed after 1959 as oil revenues began to form a fairly significant portion of the national export earnings. At this period only a fraction from the mineral oil production was received by the regions/state of production[5]. Therefore, it became apparent that the groundwork of conflict over resource allocation might have been firmly laid by reversing the pre-1959 system of resource distribution. The scholarly interpretation of the causes of the Nigerian Civil War[6] are linked to some historically deep-rooted socio-political and economic imbalances in the country such as: In 1964/65, the Eastern region saw the Binns plan as biased and unjust. The Eastern region had a gross domestic product of roughly 33% of the Nigeria's total and thus felt that its share of revenue distribution should reflect or be proportionate to its contribution to the central coffers. The dissatisfaction of the Eastern region grew from the fact that prior to 1959, all revenues from mineral and agricultural products had been retained by the producing region. However, after 1959 only a fraction of the revenue from mineral to mineral oil products was received by the region of production. In contrast, all proceeds from agricultural exports were retained by the respective regional marketing boards after 1959 and Eastern agricultural exports had always been negligible. The western and northern regions did not perceive this as a form of reverse discrimination. After all they maintained that during the 1940s and early 1950s they were contributing more to the central treasury than they were receiving, with the chief beneficiary being the East. Thus, the politics of revenue allocation was an apparent smoldering factor that contributed to the civil war particularly concerning the division (of proceeds from oil resources) was highly influencing factor in the secessionist interest. However, there was other historical factors of smoldering discontentment from regional crisis (or problems of national concern that contributed to the civil war. For example, Larry Diamond, Turi Muhammadu and Mohammed Haruna, 1988. (They all) noted that other historically specific precipitating events leading to the such as the 1963 the highly controversial or disputed census figures; ethnically defined political parties; Western region election crisis of 1965, the 1964-65 federal election crisis; the military takeover which resulted in the selected killing of some of the key political actors in the First Republic which was widely believed to be ethnically motivated, all these factors cannot be underestimated. However, the straw that finally broke the camel's back concerning the war, was the distribution of oil revenues.

On the other hand, a notable scholar L. A. Rupley pointed out that: The Governments of Northern and Western Nigeria greatly favored the principle of derivation from 1946 to around 1960, because groundnuts and cocoa were the dominant sources of export revenue. However, after petroleum revenue began to escalate from 1958 onwards, it became clear that there was little prospect of oil being found in these regions. So the two governments then reversed their arguments with respect to the desirability of the principle derivation. When it became apparent that they wished to change the rules of the game, Eastern

Nigeria moved towards secession. Such history is vital to an understanding of the events leading to civil war in 1967.

In the same vein, on March 24 1969, Alhaji Yahaya, the then Federal Commissioner for Economic Development stated that:

The root cause of the present civil war is really an economic one. For example, I am convinced that if there were no petroleum discovered in large quantities in parts of the former Eastern region, the secessionist leaders would not have tried to break up Nigeria. Thus, there was a clear linkage between oil, revenue allocation and the civil war. In 1970, Decree 13 was enacted in which the principles of interstate revenue sharing was enforced which was principally based on two approved formulas (Population and Equality of States). The Decree 13 stipulated a 45% mining rents and royalties be paid to state of origin and 50% to the Distributive Pool Account of the Federal Government. However, 50% of the Distributive Pool Account was shared equally among the states while the other 50% was divided on the basis of population.

In 1971, Decree no. 9 was passed with the view of transforming all mining rents and royalties from the territorial waters and continental shelf to the Federal Government. The promulgation of the Decree and its policy interest meant that the Federal Government will have absolute rights and control over both inshore and offshore mining rents and royalties. The 1971 Decree (9) did not change the interstate sharing formula rather it was in all likelihood a preemptive move by the Federal Government to prevent the possibility that the major and fast growing source of petroleum revenue might be allocated to states on the basis of the derivation principle.[7]

According to Tonyesima Furro (1992), the promulgation of Decree No. 9 brought about a great deal of resentment by the oil producing minority states. The minority oil states expressed great disappointment and displeasure with the decree and saw it as an oppression by the dominant ethnic groups against minority oil producing areas by denying them their due derivative rights. That, their protests and grievances centered on the fact that the decree did not take cognizance of their special needs as well as the negative externalities of oil production. The minority oil producing areas felt betrayed. On the outbreak of the Nigerian Civil War, the minority oil producing areas were assured by the Federal Government to stay in the cause of one Nigeria and that after the cessation of the war, according to Onoh (1983), "Oil revenues arising from rents and royalties were to be paid directly to their state treasuries."[8]

Further reflections on post civil war interstate revenue sharing formula varied from period to period with continued disproportionate shares accorded to minority oil states. For example in 1975 Decree No. 6 stipulated revenue sharing which accorded 20% mining rents and royalties on inshore minerals to the state of origin while 80% went to the Federal Distributive Pool Account.

294

On the other hand, 100% mining rents and royalties in respect of territorial waters and continental shelf went to Distributive Pool account. However, 7.5% of the Distributive Pool account was shared equally among the states while 50% was divided on the basis of population. By 1977 the Aboyade Technical Committee recommended different components into the revenue sharing formula, among them: (1) Equality of access to development opportunities, (2) National minimum standards (3) absorptive capacity, (4) Internal revenue and tax effort, and (5) finally fiscal efficiency.

On the basis this recommendation, the Aboyade Committee allotted 57% of the revenues to the Federal Government, 30% to State governments, 10% to local governments and 3% to a special fund.

In 1980, the Okigbo Commission came up with four basic elements of interstate revenue sharing. They are:

(1) Minimum responsibilities of governments.
(2) Population
(3) Social Development factor
(4) Internal revenue effort

The Okigbo Commission recommended 53% to the Federal Government, 7% Special Fund, 30% State Government and 10% local government.

In 1986 Decree No. 36 reversed the interstate revenue sharing formula to read:

55.0% Federal Government
2.5% Special Fund
32.5% State Governments
10.0% Local Governments

It is interesting to note that though the Decree No.36 did not alter the revenue sharing arrangement significantly with some slight increase for the states yet there was remarkable reduction of the special funds from previous 4.5% to 2.5%, whereas, in the Revenue Allocation Act of 1981, the oil producing areas had 3.5% on the basis of derivation, Decree No.36 did allocate insignificant 1.5% to the oil producing areas. The oil producing areas resented it and spurred strong feeling of discontentment.

The Federal Government was asked to repeal Decree No.36 or at least maintain the Special Fund at the same level or be increased from 10% to 15%. The government of Rivers State expressing the plight of Oil areas, sent an official memorandum to the Federal Government. The Rivers State Memorandum stated:

We wish to appeal to the Head of State and Commander-in-Chief of Armed Forces to take a compassionate consideration of the feelings of the people of the oil producing Rivers State. While in the various laws, the emphasis on population as a factor for revenue allocation continues to be pronounced and new factors introduced, the peculiar circumstances and needs of the poverty stricken people occupying the oil producing Deltaic areas are ignored. Every piece of legislation reduces or eliminates any provision in the law immediately preceding it that is beneficial to the oil producing areas ...we oppose the orchestrated elimination of the Derivation Principle, particularly in view of our peculiar environment and circumstances. We appeal to the present leadership to reconsider the Revenue Allocation Laws and give some significant prominence to the principle of derivation.[9]

The effort made by the Rivers State Government did not convince the Federal Government to repeal Decree No.36 and remained enforce until 1989.

The continued discontentment by oil states and the intense conditions culminated by Decree no. 36 greatly influenced the Babangida Administration to set a National Revenue Mobilization Commission. The Commission was headed by retired General Theophilus Danjuma. The commission was empowered to evolve a rational, fair, equitable and generally acceptable fiscal arrangement. The Danjuma Commission responsibility was to devise an effective process for the mobilization of resources of public revenue, periodic review of revenue allocation principles and formula to reduce political pressures on allocations of national resources[10]. Given the contentious nature of the revenue issue in the nations politics, the overall objective of the Danjuma Commission was two fold: to put in place a sound, less contentions revenue sharing scheme before re-civilization of government and to accommodate the interest of the oil producing areas so as to have a sense of belonging. Regrettably this objective is still far fetched and in fact the Danjuma Commission did not come close to achieving the worthy objective though the intentions were good. The Danjuma Commission final report did not change the previous interstate sharing formula except there was upsurge of local governments share from the previous 10% to 15% and the Special Fund from 2.5% to 5%. The 1.5% allotted to mineral producing areas was not changed and thus the disproportionate scenario in revenue allocation between oil producing and non-producing states remained intact until Babangida left office.

Against this background of covert socio-political undernourishment of minority oil areas and the existing overt economic disparities, calls for questions whether minority groups have a real sense of belonging in Nigeria's nation building process and the benefits there of. The minority oil producing areas deserve special attention since they have suffered so long from the problems and deficiencies made worse by ineffective national resource distributive system. It is commonly observed fact that the huge national wealth generated in the minority oil states has not resulted in better quality of life or in the overall improvement of oil areas socioeconomic development. The oil producing areas that have generated vast sum of money from oil wealth into the national coffers for decades continue to experience a great marginalization and under development particularly by the sheer neglect in the allocation of infra-structural facilities. No Federalism will thrive well in a system of inequalities where one group progresses at the expense of other group(s). As Claude Ake puts it:

> ...In so far as there is economic inequality in a society, that society cannot have political democracy because political power will tend to polarize economic power. Also a society where a high degree of economic inequality exists just necessarily be repressive. This repression comes from the need to curb the inevitable demand of the have nots for redistribution.[11]

The nature of economic and distributive policies pursued by each successive administration has not resulted in a sustainable development for minority oil producing areas instead there has been constant disruption of economic and political life of the people of oil areas. The extraction oil has brought remarkable comfort and unprecedented wealth to a few but it seems to have cast a spell of doom to the masses and other inhabitants resident in the oil producing areas.

The oil boom created in Nigeria a ready attitude to public spending, government and governed alike were intoxicated with the power of wealth. The oil boom made it possible for the government and the new plutocrats to make millions of Naira fortunes without seeming to work at all (Okigbo, 1992)[12].

The oil wealth suppose to improve the quality of life for all Nigerians considering the objectives of national development as stated in the Third Plan, that (a) the primary objective of economic planning in Nigeria is to achieve a rapid increase in the standard of living of the average Nigerian, (b) a second central objective of the plan is not only to improve the overall income levels in Nigeria, but to improve the distribution of income so that the average Nigerian would experience a marked improvement in the standard of living.

Regrettably, Nigeria's oil wealth did not trickle down enough to benefit all its citizens and to truly make the national planning objective realizable throughout the country. In fact, the quality of life of the masses was made worse off by oil mining as demonstrated by P. Collier (1978) and Dudley Seers (ILO Mission) studies on the socio-economic conditions in the oil producing areas. In essence, what minority oil producing areas are asking for is the provision of essential socioeconomic infra structural facilities commensurate with the level of financial contribution into the National Wealth through a fair and just resource distributive system.

The absence of fair and just distributive systems makes fiscal federalism to appear regressive and repressive. The problem is not only the lack of equitable allocation of public funds and infra structural facilities but also the feeling of inadequate inclusiveness of minority people in the national political machinery where decisions that affect them are made.

The expression of minority concerns over these political and socioeconomic inequalities seem to have fueled the rise of minority regional or ethnic nationalism since independence. One cannot but recall some of the old and renewed ethnic nationalism with the view to correcting inter-regional or inter-ethnic socioeconomic and political imbalances. A notable activist for minority interest in early 1960s Isaac Boro lamented during his treasonable felony while fighting for the interest of ethnic minorities in the Niger Delta stated that:

> Let us examine with some latitude whether the state of development is to any extent commensurate with a tint of the bulk of the already tapped mineral and agricultural resources. First, we may run our eyes through the health services. From the area concerned, covering a territory of 10,000 square miles and about two million inhabitants, there are just a few hospitals of ordinary health center status. One is at Degema, the second at Yenagoa, and the other at Okrika. It takes two days to travel by canoe from most of the remote villages to any of the hospitals . . . In the educational field, the areas is infested with many missionary elementary schools whose buildings are mainly thatch-huts or sandy half-walled block buildings, a majority of which are under water during the floods especially those on the fresh water banks . . . Of all parts of the country, the Niger Delta is the richest in water and so the governments have not found it necessary to give the inhabitants pipe borne water . . . People drink from the most squalid wells and so dysentery and worm diseases are rife . . .[13]

Isaac Boro reacted to the Nation and particularly the economic development policies of the then eastern Nigeria where ethnic minorities in the Niger Delta areas were systematically denied adequate distribution of social amenities. The minority groups lacked equal status under the government of the former Eastern Nigeria such that minority groups continually experienced tremendous degree of neglect and poverty.

As Ugbana Okpu pointed out the minorities were denied provision of research and advisory services in their area, the allotment of the various grants, loans, and subsidies to fishermen and farmers, provision of public services, supplies, construction and repairs of roads and improvement of the network of natural creeks.[14]

The concerns for minority interest is furthered re-echoed by a new wave of ethnic nationalism in the 1990s, seeking integration or autonomy.

According to (Remi Oyelegbin, C. Ilozue and A. Ben Akpan 1994) a resolution was adopted in Calabar by leaders of Southern minorities comprising Akwa Ibom, Cross River, Rivers, Edo and Delta states in which they noted that "Nigeria today is a federation in name; in practice, it is structurally unbalanced with a very strong central government in which the ethnic majority groups oppress the minority, depriving them of political and economic recovery. The southern minority leaders emphasized that Nigeria has given these [Oil] states no sense of belongings, no love and no brotherhood and since we are not wanted, we now demand our true independence from Nigeria ... Where we can control our resources and destiny and enjoy a sense of belonging and brotherhood so we move from the shackle of Marginalization."[15]

They argued that since Nigeria gained independence in 1960, the real ethnic nationalities comprising at least 450 groups particularly, the ethnic groups found in the five minority states have not enjoyed what should be the inalienable right of a true citizen despite their abundant economic resources.

Thus,... "the oil producing communities of the southern minority states, according to them, have continued to bear the burden of generating the national wealth and prosperity from oil mineral operations and the communities are not given any satisfactory treatment for their onerous contribution except abject poverty and neglect."[16]

Furthermore, Dr. Monima Briggs (1994) in lamenting over the plight and agony of minorities in the oil producing areas stated [inter alia] that "while it is true that for the vast majority of us any solution to the Nigerian problem will be in the context of 'ONE NIGERIA', this should not preclude the right of people to advocate other solutions especially when time and again their pleas for equality and fairness have fallen in deaf ears. I should stress that, for avoidance of doubt, I remain committed to the concept of a strong united Nigeria. However, it will only be fair to point out that since the amalgamation of the north and south by Lord Lugard questions have been asked about the nature of this federation. What we got in 1960 was a constitution arrived at after a number of constitutional conferences (Richard Constitution,... among others). Since then several attempts have been made with varying degree of success to alter or improve on the concept of ONE NIGERIA: creation of the Mid-west state, Unitary Government, Biafran secession, creation of 12 states, revision of the revenue allocation formula, creation of 19 states and the Abuja Federal Territory, introduction of the Land Use decree, creation of 21 states, creation of 30 states and numerous local government areas. The majority of these acts- some of which are laudable in themselves- were established by military decrees without the benefit of a constitutional conference or a referendum. The point I wish to make is that the sum total of these far reaching decisions is to affect the position of the center via-a-vis the component parts. This has contributed to the mentality of Nigerians being divided along ethnic lines and regarding the center as a price to be captured for their particular ethnic region, the sad culmination of which we are now witnessing.

When cocoa was the mainstay of the Nigerian economy, the Yorubas did not agitate to have a separate country. I may venture to suggest that this was probably because they were quite satisfied with the revenue allocation formula. It is again very unfortunate that since the discovery of oil in commercial quantity in Nigeria, the pleas of the oil producing areas have been ignored. It has taken the threat of secession or confederation from the Ogonis to make the policy makers in Lagos and Abuja to sit up. But this is not the first instance of protest. In 1991, a village in Umuchem River State, was razed to the ground and scores of people including the traditional ruler were killed by the security forces because they dared to protest to the oil companies about inadequate compensation for their land and environmental damage. As much as any act of secession cannot be condoned, but good governance demand that justice and fairness must be properly administered to all members of Nigerian society because the unity of the country rests on the political and economic inclusiveness for all ethnic groups big or small.

It is true that wealth from oil revenues is in the pockets of some of our leaders. But at the risk of sounding ethnocentric - are any of these leaders from the oil producing states? Probably not. Such arrogance was not even exhibited by the colonial masters! We are even told that the owners of the land on which the oil is found do not contribute anything (or is it value-added?) to the exploitation of this resource, no doubt because of this the derivation formula for revenue allocation should not apply! Using the same logic, perhaps we should allow the foreign oil companies to enjoy this wealth, since they alone invested in the exploration and marketing of the crude oil. Even the Federal Government was not involved in the exploration or any of the technical process that produces the crude oil. (see the *Economist* of August 21, 1993: 'Easy Money' - A survey of Nigeria').

We are told that oil as a commodity will not last, and what happens when the oil runs out? Indeed, we are told that the oil will run out by the year

2018. My argument is that this is all the more reason why the oil producing states should fight to have a greater say in the way this revenue is used. I for one would not like to wake up to the nightmare that by the year 2018 the oil revenue has died out, and the ecosystem of the oil areas would have been thoroughly devastated; without adequate development, and all the oil revenues would have either been used to set up industries in other parts of the country or are in the pockets of the ruling class who are now using it to industrialize their regions; and horror of horrors, making the argument that value-added economic activity revives the old derivation formula! I didn't know how much of the oil wealth of Kuwait is in the hands of their ruling elites, but I am sure that not even the author will compare the living conditions of the average Kuwaiti to those of the Ogonis or indeed any of the people on whose land, creeks, and mangrove forest the oil is found. No doubt he is aware that 'Kuwait, Inc.' has such a large investment at home and abroad that it is estimated that in a few years from now they will make more money from these investments than from oil. At least they have the foresight to realize that the oil will not last and are taking actions to maintain the standard of living of their people even when the oil runs out.

This writing would not be complete if the comments and observations made by the Former Head of State, General Olusegun Obasanjo was not included in this analysis with reference to the political events in Nigeria between 1993 and 1994.

General Obasanjo stated among other things in his state of the nation address on February 2, 1994 that "Many Bosnians would be created in many parts of Nigeria if the country breaks up. This is too frightening a possibility to contemplate. The inter-wovenness and complementarity of the various aspects of our national life make a break up totally undesirable and almost impossible. It may be assumed, therefore, that the recent agitations from some minority sections are not unconnected with the mis-management of our resources, particularly those resources emanating from the minority areas and the apparent continuous destabilization by the competition among the majority groups.

I have often heard that poverty is our problem and not political administration. I beg to disagree. If those who manage our politics and hence our economy impoverish us in the process, we cannot blame our inadequacy on material poverty, but on poverty of leadership. Other nations whose level of material poverty were similar to ours at independence and which are less endowed in resources have made greater strides because they are better led politically.

For quite some time now, there has been, sadly, a serious contraction of the focal point of some of our so-called national leaders. Some have slipped from their high national pedestal to the pedestal of regionalism and regional mentality. Today, we hear of Northern Forum, Western Elders and Eastern Caucus, Middle Belt Group and so on. Some of the members are known national figures. These responsible leaders are no doubt desirous of making effective contribution to nation-building and of being taken seriously. I will want to see them promote only one forum, the Nigerian Forum. If they do otherwise, their conduct is bound to be disorienting and divisive. I am not against state forums and I am against any idea, organization or arrangement that tends to preserve regional hegemony.

It was the economic costs of non-democratic practice in Nigeria in the past eight years, the group self-aggrandizement and the webs of patron client relations and politics of distribution which led to the clamor for a National Conference as a means of redressing the past and preventing a reoccurrence. The government is offering a Constitutional Conference instead.

Some expect to emerge from the National Conference with new local governments, while others expect new states and yet others expect to lift oil for expected new Ogoni State. Ogoni is symbolic of most minorities' plight and thinking all over the country. No matter how we perceive their claim it is an issue that must be put on the table. There are many Ogonis. Our dispensation must allow for the right of minorities, including the enjoyment of part of the God-given resources in their area and there must be a delicate balance between the rights and interests of the minorities and the rights of common interests of all Nigerians. We must listen to them. We must respond warmly and imaginatively to their special demands.

Policy alternatives for better federalism in Nigeria

In this chapter we have attempted to provide the reader with obstacles to effective Federalism in the country and here we have identified some desirable alternatives for better Federalism in Nigeria. Here, we will attempt to offer prospect for better Fiscal Federalism in Nigeria with the view to correcting past mistakes and the needed care for the mineral producing areas. All federal systems are a compromise between national and regional interests. The compromise is constructed of countervailing forces or tensions generated by the conflicting demands of national unity versus local diversity and national sovereignty versus local autonomy.

The dynamics of diverse ethnocentric forces competing to share National wealth within a Federal system is bound to undergo structural changes and such changes may be needed from time to time in order to correct imbalances in the system. In a study of formal and informal authority and Federalism in Nigeria,

Joseph Ndu (1983)[17] pointed out that from time to time the federal structure of a country undergoes a revolutionary change. In the United States, an example of such a fiscal change was the community development block grant. In Nigeria, a far reaching revolution has been the formal recognition of 299 units of local governments by the Federal Government in 1976 and the channeling and earmarking of funds specifically for local governments. This revolutionary change is known as the local government reform movement. Ndu suggested that the effects of intergovernmental grants are similar for both and industrialized nations, like the USA, and for a developing nations like Nigeria and also the inter-governmental changes affected the decision making structures of both countries. He therefore concluded that the cooperation between the three levels of government in Nigeria was attained despite the scars of the civil war and the problems of the reinstitution of democracy in country. He explained that high degree of fiscal cooperation under a democratic federal system can be attained in most third world nations characterized by the existence of informal and formal governments. If there is no alternative, federalism remains the viable option.

For a democratic Nigeria, federalism as an option demands fairness to all its diverse elements. In balancing the needs of all sectors of the federations, Nigeria must take positive steps to address interests of minorities. A Federal system must have the same standards to sort out those functions that are national including balancing the need of all interest groups along with identification of responsibilities that are national and those that are state or local but excessive federal control and resource centralization is no longer desirable a viable option for Nigeria; because it tends to stifle state and local fiscal capacity initiative. It makes all states to be on Federal Welfare with little or no responsibility to revenue sources for which each development depends; each state should be accorded some limited autonomy with planned local initiative for generating its own funding sources. In the United States, L.D. White (1993) stated that those standards have been set in constitutional law and refined by congressional action and judicial decision and they are powerfully shaped by the relative fiscal strength of the national government and the state-local sector and the prevailing attitudes of the citizens about the respective roles of the three tiers of government. In modeling new federalism in America[18] Rivlin (1992) posits that state governments would be responsible for accomplishing a productivity agenda of reforms designed to revitalize their economy and raise incomes. Furthermore, states would strengthen their revenue base by developing one or more common taxes and sharing the proceeds. This would better enable poorer states to finance needed programs.

The lesson learned from the American example is the limited fend for yourself and self reliant federalism without excessive dependency on Federal

Government. Over the years, majority groups through political power have accorded themselves a major bulk of national wealth and this practice must give way to a more progressive means of resource distribution. Otherwise, Federalism in Nigeria will suffer if Fiscal dividends continually favor majority groups self interest without sensitivity to minority interests and concerns for equity and fairness.

The first system of fairness should be adopted from the African traditional system of derivation and secondly, the reinstatement constitutionally adopted derivation system of revenue allocation practiced in the pre oil era. In recognition of the African concept of derivation, it is better to reiterate Chief Melford Okilo who stated that:[19]

> Derivation in the African cultural context implies that when an individual kills or finds a big fish or animal, the villagers or community expresses their appreciation to that man or woman by first giving him or her the best part of the animal or fish before the rest of the meat or fish is shared.

In compliance of this derivation principle a substantial portion of proceeds from sales of cash crops or minerals were returned to the region state of origin. And, further to buttress this interest the constitution guaranteed that the "proceeds of any royalty received by the federation is respect of any mineral extracted in that region and any mining rents derived by the federation from within that region, the region get back 50% of the proceeds."[20] Again, in recognition of the derivation principle, both the North and the Western regions benefitted immensely from the 50% retention scheme constitutionally guaranteed by the Federal Government. How then could the oil mineral producing areas be denied and the revenue sharing formula be revised to their disadvantage? In the oil era, the derivation concept as a rule became a national controversy for national wealth distribution. The proponents of derivation principle maintain that 'what is good for the goose is good for the gander'. The issue at stake is not simply as Phillips stated 'it is now our turn variety'[21] Revenue Allocation by derivation is fair, reasonable and natural whether it is agricultural products or mineral resources.[22]. The use of the principle of derivation as basis for revenue allocation stands to reason because the respective oil producing states directly bear the brunt of spillover costs of oil extraction as such derivation basis for revenue allocation will enable oil states to tackle extraneous problems caused by the oil industry operation in their environment in addition to the normal developmental needs of their respective states through enhanced fiscal capacity from derivation. In emphasizing the negative externalities of oil industry operation in the country, Ikporukpo noted that oil spillages, environmental pollution and the other related hazards have begun to constitute very serious danger to the safety and security of life and property of the inhabitants of oil producing areas (in Nigeria). There has also been serious disruption of economic life in some cases, especially in erstwhile agricultural and fishing areas as a direct result of oil production activities.[23]

Furthermore, in recognition of the unique differences in agricultural benefits as opposed mineral extraction and the implications for the host communities. A.Y. Aliyu argued that firstly, agricultural and non-agricultural production are easily distinguishable, as revenue according to the former directly benefits the farmer while in the latter case serious damage is sustained by the inhabitants of the areas of production. Secondly, although mining activities are vested in the Federal Government, the land on which such activities are carried out is located in a state which has responsibility for the welfare of its inhabitants. Thirdly, the state government is the primary unit and agency of development...it is the best machinery for dealing with the so called developmental problem if environmental pollution and waste, such that some proportion of revenue derived on this principle should go to the state government.[24]

It appears that the application of derivation principle could offer sentiments for satisfaction in compensating the inhabitants for deprivation of land and ecological degradation in its effort to generate national wealth imbedded in oil. In contrast, those who oppose the derivation principle argue that given the uneven conditions of development, it is unfair for the resource endowed states to receive a larger share of the resource proceeds and that such huge funds will invariably make these resource blessed areas more developed at the expense of the poorly endowed areas of the country. The derivation based principle of revenue sharing will results in wide developmental gaps and social welfare disparity among the various component states of the nation. There is very limited geographical spillover or spread of the benefits from derivative based principle given the restricted nature of labor mobility which is subject to ethnic and political constraints, it will be difficult to redress such developmental imbalances without fiscal redistribution.[25]

Those who oppose the derivative principle may have seen oil production in myopic terms as seen by Kole Omotoso. Ken Saro Wiwa noted that after Kole Omotoso reviewed his book titled, On A Darkling Plain: An Account of the Nigerian Civil War, Omotoso asked the question in his review of the book which read, "How true is it to say that the riverain areas produce oil? Are we to assume that the people of the riverain areas produce oil in the same way that the Ondo people produce cocoa or Kano produce cotton?" If this were the way of thinking of what comes out of the soil of the riverain areas, the distribution of the resultant revenue would have been different. To this end, Ken Saro

Wiwa offered a counterview to Omotoso's position in which he said, "Dr. Omotoso did not ask if the Ondo farmers had been deprived of their land nor did he ask if the planting of cocoa had poisoned the air of the Yoruba people in the Ondo area or whether Yoruba farmers had been denied the ownership of the fruits of their farms. Thus, even the purest minds in Nigeria are marked by their greed for oil money and their insensitivity of the suffering of the minorities."[26] Ironically by the 1970's Ondo also became an oil producing state. Any state in the country has the potential to produce a strategic mineral. Therefore, it behooves us to care for all mineral producing areas fairly and equitably in the sharing of wealth derived from strategic minerals.

The fact of the matter is that the non-derivation based revenue allocation system have accentuated regional economic disparities for those who argued against derivation principle wish to avoid. No one can argue against the fact that economic disparities and developmental gaps exit between oil producing areas and non producing areas. Ironically, developmental gaps or disparities exist to the disadvantage of minority oil producing states who produce a major bulk of the national revenues from oil. When tin, coal and cash crops were essential commodities in their hey days did the argument against derivation principle emanate to show the possible interregional disparities it could cause when derivation principle was adopted as a basis for the national resource allocation? Should the oil areas of the nation (the goose that lays the golden egg) be ignored? It is just fair and reasonable that (if total derivation principle cannot be accorded to oil states because of imbalances of political bargaining power) at least 15-20% of revenues derived from oil be set aside for the producing states to care for their suffering masses and to restore and rehabilitate the inhabitant and their environment. The 3% allotted to oil producing states if far too small and inconsequential to the degree of extractive activities, environmental pollution and the huge profits made by the oil companies and the national government.

A prominent Nigerian politician from Kano Alhaji Tanko Yakassai put it this way in response to this question in an interview:[27]

If Nigeria depends so much on oil, even for her unity as you have analyzed, why are oil producing communities being neglected?

Yakassai's response:

...I have even suggested it to the new administration that if there is going to be a constitutional conference, we must have a technical look at the questions of oil producing communities. Nobody is saying that other Nigerians should not have their own share of the oil but that oil producing communities should be fairly treated. I know what happened when the British were taking minerals from the Jos plateau and some parts of Kano state. There was a policy that where the land was disturbed, the people would be re-settled and compensated for the damage. If you go to the Plateau today, there are so many areas that cannot be inhabited in the next 1000 years...it is only natural that if you are benefiting from somebody, you should give him something in return....what has happened in Nigeria is that there has never been a deliberate attempt on the part of the government to address the problem. One is not saying that the oil must go back to the communities that produce it. No!, no!, no!. What I am saying is that in the process of getting this oil, you are destroying the lives of these people. What do you do to rehabilitate these people to make them live again? If you take away the oil and one day it gets finished and they have no means of livelihood how do you expect them to survive? Honestly, between me and my God, I believe something must be done.

The necessity to care for the oil producing areas is something the nation and its elements cannot ignore, and it must be made integral to national and regional development planning at all phases of nation building.

In continuation of the discussion on revenue allocation principles for equitable distribution of resources in the principle of internal revenue effort. This principle is particularly as appealing suitable to us because it emphasis that states within a federation intensify independent efforts to generate greater portion of their own revenues to meet their financial obligations. Every nation that practices true federalism, for example, U.S. and Canada adopt this method. In the U.S. in particular, the sub-units generate their own revenue for the state obligations.

The relative utility of internal revenue effort is best put forward by Phillips, that:

Indeed, the system should encourage and reward the internal revenue effort of the beneficiary governments. It can do so by setting aside an amount which will be shared among the beneficiary governments in indirect proportion to their internal revenue efforts, so that the state government with the highest effort will receive the largest share and the state government with the lowest effort will receive the smallest share. That way it will reduce the state governments' dependence on revenue from federal sources and, importantly, increase the total financial resources mobilized by the overall government sector.[28]

The revenue allocation system between the center and the sub-units in its present form has created an entitlement mentality among the recipient governments. These sub-units have come to view the federal disbursements as a right and with very little financial accountability or efforts for their own independent revenues. The future direction of revenue sharing, greater weight should be attached to a state's ability to generate its own resources or as we put it, 'spend as you earn.' In other works, revenue allocation should be structured in such a manner that a state which contributes more to the general revenue should automatically receive the largest share of allocation. The present welfare method of revenue dispensation where by the recipient governments make no effort to look for alternative ways of generating resources other than the ones given to them by the federal sources should be discouraged.

Critics have long questioned if Nigerian government practices federalism at all as it purports. In a memorandum presented to the 1988 constitutional Assembly, the Rivers State Government made the case that the Nigerian Constitution in only Federal in name but very unitary in character. As the memorandum states:

> This is clearly shown in the distribution of money by the Federal Government. That in a system where Federal Government collects almost all revenues and distributes small fractions to the states on monthly basis is definitely not a Federal system. In a true Federal system, states collect all revenue including oil revenue and the Federal Government merely collects an agreed percentage of the states' revenues for its Federal functions.[29]

As the above indicates, the very nature of Nigerian federalism partly contributes to the states' dependence upon the center. The Federal Government seizes every conceivable viable resource of the states thereby making these sub-units absolutely dependent upon federal hand-outs.[30]

Another step forward influencing structural changes in the nations revenue allocation system is to adopt and modify some elements of the political bureau report of 1987. The content and character of the report would require further political compromises and negotiations to correct perceived or actual imbalances within the report or the national revenue allocation practice. Here is a summary and analysis of the political bureau report. The Political Bureau report (1987), among other things, stated that (1) the government will rectify the discrepancy in revenue allocation by setting up a technical revenue mobilization commission which will in the future emphasize revenue sharing and not revenue allocation; (2) the Technical Revenue Mobilization

Commission will review from time to time revenue allocation formulae and principles in operation to ensure that they conform to changing realities, thereby avoiding unnecessary political pressures; and (3) the fiscal responsibilities shared between the federal and other levels of government should be reviewed to give local governments greater latitude to collect revenue from more sources, enabling them to meet their expanded roles in the new political order proposed for the country. Furthermore, the innovative revenue-sharing plan has proposed that the federal government should get 40 percent, the state 40 percent and local government 20 percent. And, specific to oil producing areas, the following recommendations are made:

1. that the dichotomy between onshore and offshore production in the allocation of revenue to the oil producing states should be abolished, as it fails to reflect the tremendous hazards faced by the inhabitants of the areas where oil is produced offshore.

2. that there is a need to revise upward to at least 2 percent the present 1.5 percent allocation from the federal account for the development of mineral producing areas. The political bureau further recommends that the 2 percent from the distributive pool that is given to oil producing states be sent directly to the local governments of the areas concerned. Comment: by 1992/93 the Federal government upgraded the 1.5 percent allotted to oil producing areas to 3 percent and also established the oil mineral producing areas development commission. However, the authors view this change as a step in the right direction but the 3 percent allotted for the mineral producing areas is far to insignificant relative to decades of deprivation, impoverishment and underdevelopment suffered by the oil producing areas. For this reason and the continual negative externalities borne by the oil producing areas as a result of oil activities in the environment requires an upgrade of at least 20 percent of total revenue derived from oil to be allocated for the development of oil producing areas.

Furthermore, the bureau appreciated the fact that any meaningful revenue allocation formula must take into account the allocation of constitutional responsibilities among the different tiers of government. Also, while the bureau appreciated the zeal and the interest the issue generated in the course of the debate, it pointed out that in its view, some of the proposals put forward were clearly self-serving and selfish, and reflect the desire by some sections of the country to get a larger share of the so-called 'national cake.' Be that as it may, the bureau recommends the following principles:

a.   A higher percentage of revenue for the Federation Account than the current 10% should be allocated to the local government. The bureau recommends at least 20%. This reflects its conception of the local government as the basic unit for the administration and development of the country to which more constitutional responsibilities should be assigned in the new dispensation.
b.   There is need to create a Local Government Joing Account to be opened at the nearest Central Bank of Nigeria branch in each state into which all funds, including state contribution of not less than 10% of internally generated revenue, meant for the local governments in that state should be put and disbursed to them directly.
c.   Fiscal responsibilities between the Federal and other levels of government should be reviewed to give local governments greater latitude to collect revenue from more sources to enable them to meet their expanded roles in the new political order hereby proposed for the country.
d.   Revenue from the Federation Account should continue to be allocated to the states based on the existing principles.
e.   A permanent national revenue and fiscal commission should be established. The commission which should have an autonomous status comparable to that recommended for the national commission on political parties and elections should draw its membership. From economist, political scientist, accountants, geographers, the military, and the labor unions. It should be charged with the following responsibilities:

1. Monitoring the accruals from and disbursements of revenue from the federation account.
2. Reviewing from time to time revenue allocation formulae and principles in operation to ensure that they conform to the changing realities, thereby disconnecting the exercise from the unnecessary political pressures.

Finally the bureau recommended the insertion of a constitutional provision barring the creation of new states for at least twenty-five (25) years, to enable the country use that period to settle down politically and tackle more fundamental issues of national development. In a commentary on the draft constitution on Revenue Allocations, the Nigerian Tribune 11 August 1995 stated that:

... In recognition of the historical fact that the basis of Federal Statutory Revenue Allocation has always been one of the "most contentious and destabilising factors in the Nigerian Polity", the draft constitution opts for an "efficient" revenue allocation formula with an inherent capability to accomplish the five objectives of national unity, economic growth, balanced development, self-sufficiency and a high standard of living for Nigerians.

While assuring that the proposed revenue allocation formula was based on equity, justice, and an ability to induce the federal unity to "achieve self-generating growth and a healthy development competition", the Constitution proceeds to prescribe that funds from the Federation Account shall be disbursed on the basis of the principle of derivation (a minimum of 13 per cent), population, equality of the federating states/Local Governments, land masses and terrain, population density and internal revenue effort.

FINALLY, on the modality for enacting a revenue allocation formula, the draft constitution recommends that the National Revenue Mobilization Allocation and Fiscal Commission (NRMAFC) shall forward a recommended formula to the President of the Federal Republic of Nigeria, who shall forward a proposal based on the NRMAFC recommendations, to the National Assembly for debate and approval. When passed into law, a revenue Allocation formula shall subsist for a 5-year period in the first instance.

No one can quarrel with the set goals and objectives of the revenue allocation formula. Moreover, we find very plausible and democratic the prescribed modality for legalizing a specific revenue allocation formula.

OF course, given the competing demands of the federating units out of the Distributable Pool, a consensus on a revenue-sharing ratio may never be reached in Nigeria. For instance, while a few will disagree with the principle of derivation as a basis of revenue-sharing, loud protests have already greeted the stipulated minimum of 13 per cent of the Federation Account being shared out on the basis of this principle.

WE consider that there is some merit in the argument that the presented minimum of 13 per cent is too high in view of the facts that oil based revenues shall, for the next decade or more, continue to dominate the Federation Account and that Nigeria's oil money represents more of an economic rent than income earned by Nigerian capital and labor. Considering these facts, the higher the percentage earmarked for distribution on the basis of derivation, the higher the likelihood that some parts of the Federation may be receiving, out of the Federation Account, statutory allocation far in excess of their absorptive capacities with the attendant negative socio-economic consequences for growth and development in the affected areas, in particular and, Nigeria, in general.

NEXT to derivation, another contentious basis of revenue-sharing is population. Using population as a criterion for revenue-sharing is clearly a contradiction in a country where considerable resources are allocated to a vigorous campaign on population control. Besides, the fact of the linkage between population and Federal Statutory allocations has been the bane of a reasonably accurate population census in Nigeria as each federating unit, almost without an exception, routinely seeks to inflate its population figures in order to receive higher statutory allocation from the federation account.

The enhancement of the Fiscal Capacity of mineral producing areas is highly desirable, hence some creative means of strengthening the fiscal potential of oil producing should be instituted and be made into law. One such desirable way to enhance the fiscal capacity of oil producing states is through equity participation in all oil companies operating in their environment. This option may require both the Federal Government and the foreign oil companies to allow a limited share of equity participation by the host oil state. Alternatively, state governments be allowed to enter joint venture arrangement in certain phases of oil industry operation. This arrangement proved to be fair in that the country will benefit from greater indigenous participation in oil industry and the oil companies will also feel better about their corporate social responsibility increased indigenous participation and the ultimate minimization risk and conflict in oil activities. This concept of state participating was already proposed by a non-oil producing state of Oyo (but has other mineral resources). The Oyo benefit plan for its resource areas (1990) stated that to ensure that the people of the state derive maximum benefit from the exploitation of these resources, this administration has adopted guidelines which include allocation of 10% equity participation to the state government on mineral resources development venture(s) and an undertaking by the mining companies to provide social and economic benefits for the area to be affected by their operations.[31] It is preferred that this policy interest be made integral to all mineral interests in the producing areas.

312

The non-mineral producing states should be allowed to participate in joint ventures if conditions for mutual benefit exist in the partnership venture. This strategy if it becomes operational, will also step up oil multinational socioeconomic responsibility to improving the quality of life in the host communities, this way the success of oil companies in Nigeria will be made to match the cultural demands as well as the economic advantages of their operational environment.[32]

For sub-Saharan Africa,[33] Cornelius Pratt (1991) suggests that multinational corporations involved in sub Saharan Africa should use a value-based corporate social policy process as the basis for a corporation-formulated regional code of conduct. This process should embody utilitarian and situation ethics in the responsibilities to society. For the African normative environment, this approach is substantiated by the notion that both utilitarian and situation ethics are consistent with the region's investment codes, development interests, and value systems. Moreover, utilitarian and situation ethics can help MNCs effectively meet their social responsibilities by helping them reverse the economic stagnation of most of Africa. MNCs should de-emphasize ethics that stress autonomous actions that satisfy individual goals because they are largely at odds with sub-Saharan African value systems that typically stress the ethnic group.

One of the intractable features of Federalism Nigeria is the ethno-clientelistic patterns of interest aggregations within the Federal Policy making machinery so that revenue allocation is not viewed as an economic undertaking but as a battle over who get how much of the nation's resources. This special competitive feature in the Nigerian resource allocation system has worked to the disadvantage of oil producing areas, notwithstanding their major contribution to the national wealth. Hence, the nation's revenue sharing system should reconsider given higher weight to the principle of internal revenue effort. In the past the proportionate weight accorded to this principle as basis for revenue allocation has been very minimal. Therefore, the principle of internal revenue effort should be reintroduced with the view of compensating the states that contribute the most revenue to the Federal coffers are rewarded proportionately. For instance, if a state contributes more than 50% of the total federal revenues for any given year, that state should receive 15-20% of the total automatically before any national revenue allocation or sharing is under taken. This premise can be a motivating factor for other states to develop potential revenue sources and resource development within their jurisdiction to enhance their fiscal capacity and contribute proportionately to the national revenues. The high revenue producing states will also be encouraged to do more because it seems fair, equitable and rational in the nation's fiscal approach to federalism.

313

Ashwe[34] posits that the internal revenue effort principle requires that greater shares of revenues be given to government which demonstrate greater effort on relieving their fiscal burdens. Furtherance of the principle of internal revenue effort, the financial relations between the states and the federal government should require that all fiscal and taxing powers be vested in the states, with Federal Government relying on equal or proportionate contributions from the states to carry out its responsibilities. The internal revenue effort can improve each state capacity to generate its own income without excessive federal dependency. The prevailing revenue dispensation system according to Phillips[35] lacks a device for encouraging the states to vigorously exploit the sources of revenue within their jurisdiction. As it is, a state can be indifferent to its internal revenue sources, knowing fully well that the bulk of its revenue will accrue, regardless from federal sources. Phillips further argued that "it is appropriate that the revenue allocation scheme should give explicit recognition to state tax effort by sharing some of the relevant revenues on the basis of tax effort."[36]

In support of the internal revenue effort principle, (Teriba and Phillips) maintains that for a fiscal system to merely by taking account of state needs without considering their revenue efforts in the allocations of centrally collected revenues is to encourage financial irresponsibility instate governments. It is therefore reasonable to conclude that centrally collected revenues can be shared proportionately in accordance with proportionate level of contributions into the centrally collected revenues of the nation. Nigeria is endowed with a significant number of national resources which are either underdeveloped or under utilized in terms of their potential contribution to national wealth. Since oil became an essential commodity in the world market, Nigeria has laid excessive emphasis on the economic significance of oil to the extent that other potentially viable commodity production which would have added additional revenues for the nation have been either ignored or displaced (partly through misguided national policies). Nigeria is rich in nature resources and other raw materials that are unevenly distributed throughout the country. (Figure 11.1) For example, while oil and gas deposits are found in the states covering major parts of the Niger Delta Basin, there are also mineral such as gold deposits are found (in Sokoto, Kwara, Kaduna, Bauchi, Akwa Bom and Oyo states). The other mineral deposits are phosphate, limestone, tin, columbite, zinc, lead, iron ore, coal, and silver.[37] This list is by no means exhaustive and there are many other minerals. The deposits of these minerals are found in both northern and southern states. There is still also potential to encourage development of cash crops such as cocoa, cotton, palm oil, tobacco, groundnut and coffee. These cash crops were the major revenue sources for the nation but were abandoned in the wake of the oil boom thus, the country should encourage the development all other potential sources of fund in each state of the federation through diversification of the economy. There is high risk in mono commodity (oil) reliance which is very vulnerable international oil market fluctuation and geopolitics Nigeria should learn from the oil market slump of 1986. The non-oil natural resources are available throughout the country and they have not been fully tapped to reap the potential benefits imbedded in them.

It has been pointed out earlier in this discourse that oil was discovered in the country since 1958 in the Niger Delta Basin and Nigeria became internationally recognized as a major oil producing nation. Nigeria has paid inadequate attention to the socio-economic and environmental problems of the oil producing areas from which the country has benefitted immensely from the natural endowment of oil resource. The Vanguard Paper reported that it has long been recognized that (oil) areas need special attention to alleviate their suffering hence the independence constitution of 1960 had provision for a Niger Delta Development Board (NDDB) with the main aim of addressing the depressed areas of the Niger Delta Region of the country, which even in colonial times suffered neglect. The NDDB was entrenched in the constitution because of the special attention political determination and huge resources needed to undertake any meaningful development in these areas of the country. But the NDDB was easily smoldered by political subterfuge and killed.[38]

In 1981, the Revenue Act tried to resurrect the idea behind the NDDB, and thereby allocated 1.5 percent of the Federation Account towards centering to peculiar needs of the Niger Delta from where the nation gets over 80% of federally collected revenue failed to meet the needs of the areas. For decades, this region was milked and neglected. It rivers were polluted, its land laid bare and rendered infertile. Daily the people watch their land and rivers churn oil billion dollar revenue to the government and prospecting oil companies while they languish in the most in human squalor. Lite for them was near the Hobsian ideal.[39] Are there theoretical, theological and moral foundations for the Nigerian Society and its government in the care for all its citizens? There may be no ready made theology of revenue allocation which would provide Christians, Muslims and animists in Nigeria with prefabricated solution ideas to the problems of inter ethnic competition in the politics of revenue allocation and the minority question. However, if there are religious values for Christians, Moslems and others they are very likely to be concerned for social justice, equitable allocation of public wealth and the right of minority people to have greater access and inclusiveness in the national decision making apparatus. Nevertheless, if there are no socio political and religions ideas in effecting better public funds allocation system in the country, we can still invoke major religious, socioeconomic and political inspirations, examples and guidelines for implementing fairness and equity in the nations revenue allocation system and better compensation planning for the minority oil producing areas. An equitable principle in contending for the rights and claims of minority oil producing areas for better compensational disposition is none other than call for enforceable planned reparation for the oil producing areas. We have already provided in our earlier discussion on reparation with some examples of actual reparations or call for reparation stemming from past economic exploitation or victims of socio political wrong doing.

We have demonstrated in this writ that the oil producing minority areas have suffered decades of neglect, economic exploitation, impoverishment ecological degradation and underdevelopment while their endowed resource oil enriches others nationally and internationally, against this background necessitates the call for reparation.

For many decades, the oil producing areas directly or indirectly yielded its natural resource oil to the multinational corporations and the producer government by being a constitutional part of Nigerian Federation. This implied that the Federal Government has the responsibility in balancing the developmental needs of oil areas alongside with the rest of the country but this expectation remained deficient for decades in its negligence of developmental needs of oil areas hence the call for reparation as a form of restitution is to restore hope and proper development and fully integrate the oil areas into the mainstream of Nigerian society.

Though there are seemingly no religious guides to fabricating a National Revenue Allocation System but there are religious guides to restitution or reparation when a wrong is identified. The inspirational guiding light for restitution can be drawn from both Christian and Islamic teachings as earlier noted. The Christian enlightenment on restitution is provided in the Biblical teachings in the *Book of Exodus 22:5* which states that "if a man shall cause a field or vineyard to be eaten and shall put his beast and shall feed in another of mans field; of the best of his own vineyard he shall make restitution."[40] (One may liken today's corporate/business organization engaged in exploitation of a resource for profit in other people's land, should require compensation for the people for the exploitation of their oil resource in their vineyard). Similarly, to deal with economic problems (among many), Islamic laws have addressed them very rigorously. We can see that Islamic law is structured so that it can address every issue. For example: (1) The Qurán (2) The Sunna of the Prophets (3) The Ijma (Consensus) and (4) Qiyas (Analogical) reasoning.[41]

Interesting enough, these laws predict the fact that life presents new problems. We can learn a lot from these laws and we think the solutions of our national wealth distributional problems can be found implicitly if not explicitly in these four foundations of Islamic thought specifically done to the uniqueness of our problems. The last two (Qiyas and Ijma) have lots to offer. Though the

316

authors' understanding of Islamic Teaching is very limited yet given the principles of fairness and common understanding which drive the great minds and hearts of Muslims which the inner light and the guidance of ALLAH (God Almighty) there is a possibility to find solutions that are in line with ALLAH's will of fairness and to care for all members of our Republic. The Islam's teachings on wealth distribution is further noted as follows.

On wealth and distribution, Khan (1986) stated that:

> All sources of wealth, the earth, its capacities and treasures, the sun, the moon, the planets, the winds that drive the clouds, rain, sub-soil water, rivers and oceans are all God's gift to mankind. They are not anyone's property. Wealth is produced by the application of human skill, capital and labor to these sources. According to Islam, produced wealth should be distributed not only between skill, capital and labor but a portion of it should be set aside for the community as a whole, as the beneficiary of the basic sources of wealth. In the Quran this portion is designated Zakat, meaning that which purifies and fosters such that all beneficent methods of acquiring property are permitted; trade, commerce, industry, mining, agriculture, etc, may be purses intensively, by individuals, alone or in partnership, and by co-operatives and corporations. Non-beneficent methods are forbidden ... The purpose of the Islamic economic system is that wealth should be in constant circulation, should be widely distributed and should be so employed as to yield the maximum beneficence for the largest number of people. It should not circulate only among the well-to-do (59:8).[42]

The Christian view on social justice, stewardship and equitable distribution of resources as expressed by the United Methodist Church states:

> We believe in God, Creator of the world; and in Jesus Christ the redeemer of creation. We believe in the Holy Spirit, through whom we acknowledge God's gifts, and we repent of our sin in misusing these gifts to idolatrous ends.

> We, as stewards, affirm the goodness of life. We rejoice in accepting the abundance with which God has endowed the earth. We commit ourselves to participate in God's redemptive intention for the world; that all people should be able to live in peace and to enjoy the days of their lives free from hunger, disease, hopelessness and oppression.

317

As stewards, we commit ourselves to love and justice among persons and nations in the equitable distribution of income and wealth. We affirm the ownership of property as a trust from God. We acknowledge the responsibility to share the abundance of creation. We regard the conditions created by poverty to be demeaning to the human spirit.

As stewards, we insist on the efficient management of human and natural resources in the production of the goods and services needed by the human community. We insist on conserving resources in order to sustain permanently the fruitfulness of the earth.

As stewards, we acknowledge the necessity of civil government. We encourage all people to participate in the activities of responsible citizenship.

We believe that Christian stewardship is a joyful, response to God's gifts; it is a spiritual understanding of the practical and economic aspects of all of life.

Nigeria: Major mineral deposits

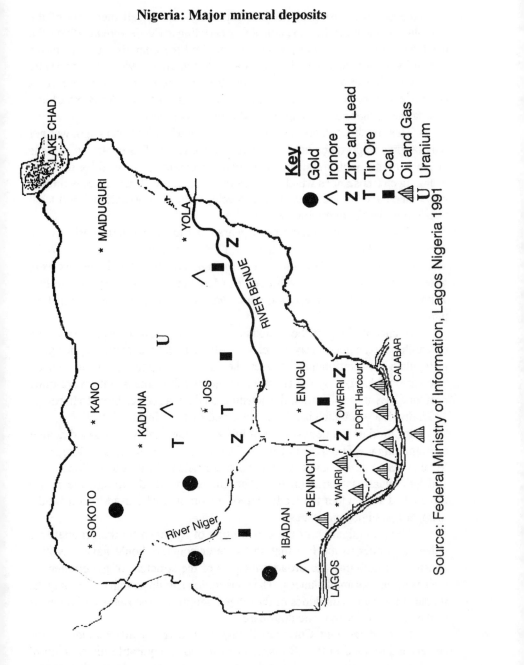

Figure 11.1

Islamic constitution of Medina stipulates care for all members of the republic and the minorities in particular: According to (M.O. Junaid, 1994), the need for evolving a viable political system and the administration to move forward was earnestly felt when the State was founded in Medinah. The state itself was diverse and complex judging from the heterogenous nature of its component parts. This brought into prominence the institution of Brotherhood among the Emigrants (Muhajirun) and their hosts (Ansars).

This constitution promulgated over fourteen hundred years ago, was not only of great importance but also a relevant document of recent times. This is because of its application to the prevailing condition as well as the ever changing circumstances which its authors had in mind. Thus, the constitution was indeed a vital document in the development of constitutional and legal freedom in the contemporary world.

What was said to have been guaranteed to the modern world by the American Declaration of Independence (1776), the French Revolution (1789), and the Universal Declaration of Human Rights of the United Nations were already embodied in the constitution of Medinah. It is regarded as the first written constitution of the world which has been preserved by the Muslims intact.

A cursory look at the various articles of the said constitution would reveal that it was not merely a Treaty of Alliance, but a constitution designed to regulate the relationship between the various components of the society. The various changes by the constitution on the life of the people were quite profound. By its application, the constitution dealt a serious blow to tribalism and individualism which has been preserved by the Muslims intact.

It introduced a new system of life where nationality was based neither on common race, language or tribe.... The center of gravity was no longer the tribal system but the new Ummah which consisted of tribes as political units and individuals as its members. The Ummah worked through the newly established state under the leadership of the prophet who used to consult the members on important issues.

The promulgation of the constitution of Medinah by the prophet was indeed a pointer to the fact that any state or country should have a written constitution outlining the broad principles of the structure of government as well as its checks and balances. The constitution should guarantee not only the fundamental rights and duties of the citizen but protect the rights and interests of the minorities with meticulous care.[43]

In identical light Christian thoughts on care for all members of the society is provided in the affirmation of care, love, equitable distribution of resources and justice for all people, the Christian United Methodist church social creed reads:

320

We believe in God, creator of the world and all people and in Jesus, Incarnate among us ... and in the holy spirit present with us to guide, strengthen and comfort.

We rejoice in every sign of God's kingdom in the upholding of human dignity and community in every expression of love, justice and reconciliation in each act of self-giving on behalf of others in the abundance of Gods gifts entrusted to us that all may have enough; in all responsible use of earth's resources.

Glory be to God on high and on earth peace.
We confess our sins, individual and collective by silence or actions through the violation of human dignity based on race, class, sex, nation or faith; through the misuse of power in personal, communal, national and international life; through the search for security by those military and economic forces that threaten human existence (pollution of mineral areas) through the abuse of technology which endangers the earth and all life upon it -We commit ourselves to take up the cross--- To seek abundant for all humanity struggle for peace with justice and freedom----

There should be a responsible social, political and economic behavior without threat to any unit of mankind; God's creation or species of the ecosystem.
The authors feel that it would be appropriate to institute an enforceable restitution or reparation policy as a form of compensation for the oil producing areas. The compensation planning can take the form of:

(1) Cash compensation to individuals and communities if the parties mutually agree to it as a useful remedy for damage done. However, cash benefits are sometimes too ephemeral to sustaining a long term benefit effect. Cash benefit as only remedy to environmental pollution should not be encouraged since ecological damage cannot be easily corrected by cash payment. Therefore, other technical alternatives must be sought for clean ups and other mechanisms for ecological restoration.

(2) A carefully orchestrated planned development specially for oil producing areas through provisions of socio economic and public infrastructures should be established. The role of Oil Mineral Producing Areas Commission can be expanded to accommodate this interest including planned restoration for the damaged environment resulting from oil activities.

321

(3) The reparation and restitution process also calls for establishment of Oil Heritage Fund for each oil producing state or community in order to save for the future and protect the socio economic viability of the oil communities today and also in the post oil era. The Oil Heritage Savings Plan can also cater for the succeeding generation to benefit from the current exploitation and revenues from oil which is not guaranteed to last forever.

(4) The reparation plan should also include a community reinvestment programs in addition to oil fueled special Marshall plan to divert some of the oil revenues to rehabilitate the peoples traditional agricultural scenario in order to assure food security.

Though the writers are not legal luminaries but it is worth drawing lessons from the law that while the oil areas suffered neglect and underdevelopment for decades, the national government in partnership with the multinational corporations bountifully reaped billions of dollars in revenues at the expense of or to the disadvantage of minority oil producing areas without rendering adequate compensation or socio economic responsibility for the affected areas constituted a form of unjust enrichment. The doctrine of unjust enrichment holds that people should not be allowed to profit or enrich themselves inequitably at the expense of others. The doctrine reflects the ethical conviction that justice should be done, even in the absence of a contractual cause of action.[44]

Therefore planned enforceable reparation as part of compensation planning would be a useful means of restoration of hope, and meaningful development for the oil communities after many decades of neglect, impoverishment and ecological degradation. Thus, socio-economic responsibility for the oil areas cannot be ignored since the national government and the oil companies benefited to the disadvantage of oil areas.

The stepping stone to reparation and restitution has already begun with the establishment of Oil Mineral Producing Areas Development Commission (OMPADEC) but requires further improvement to enhance its capacity to develop oil areas. The objectives of 'OMPADEC' are aimed at:

(a) the rehabilitation and development of oil producing areas.
(b) a tackling ecological problems that have arisen from the exploitation of oil minerals.

The oil mineral producing areas commission was established in 1992 (under Decree No. 23) to address the difficulties and suffering of the inhabitants of the oil producing areas resulting from the effects of oil exploration

322

and exploitation. The primary responsibility of the OMPADEC is to embark upon physical and human development in the oil producing areas with the objective of (inter alia):

(1) compensating materially, the oil communities which have suffered environmental damage or deprivation as a result of mineral prosection in their areas.

(2) Open up the affected areas and effectively link them up socially and economically with the rest of the country by establishing various physical and infra structural development to liaise with the various oil companies on matters of pollution control and to obtain from the Nigeria National Petroleum Corporation the proper formula for actual oil mineral production of each state, local government area and community and to ensure the fair and equitable distribution of projects, services and employment of personnel in accordance with recognized percentage of production etc.

The OMPADEC objectives are plausible but the allotment of mere 3% is too minimal to accomplish a meaningful development and comprehensive mitigation policy considering the intensity of devastation, neglect and the decades of socioeconomic undernourishment of oil producing areas. If meaningful development and restitution is to be achieved, the policies, functions and funding of OMPADEC must be improved to fulfill its mandate. The funding of OMPADEC should be improved from 3% to 20% if derivation principle is not totally applied in the Federal Revenue Allocation System. Again, in planning for compensation and restitution in oil producing areas is for the establishment of the Oil Heritage Fund. The purpose of the Heritage Fund is to save for the future and encourage diversification of oil areas economy such that their can be an improvement in the quality of life of the people today and in the post oil era (particularly the fate of the succeeding generation).

The pragmatic usefulness of the Heritage Saving Funds have been established in the oil producing areas of Alberta (Canada), Alaska (USA) and the state of Kuwait. The establishment of the Heritage Fund is both moral and long-term economic responsibility for the care of the oil producing areas. The Federal Government should set aside 15 percent annually of oil proceeds from each producing state as contribution to the Heritage Fund for that oil producing state or an amount proportionate to the level of production and derived revenues. In addition, the oil companies should contribute 10 percent of their annual profits to each oil State and Heritage Fund as part of their corporate responsibility to the mineral oil producing areas.

A comprehensive planned care for mineral producing areas should be expanded to cover better government and oil company coordinated and cooperative responsibility to environmental stewardship. The government should exercise its sovereign rights to assure that oil companies adhere to better clean up practices in event of any level of environmental pollution. It is also the responsibility of the government at all levels to assure that oil companies minimize hazards in their operation through application of appropriate state of art technology that would reduce the overall social cost to the barest minimum for those inhabitants who are vulnerably exposed to oil industry operations.

In essence, the government must take direct responsibility to assure that extractive industries in the country adhere to environmental protection guidelines so that pollution can be controlled in order to protect the indigenous people and their ecology.

Furthermore, the federal government should seriously reconsider the application of derivation principle in revenue allocation if fairness and social justice is to be achieved. The application of the 'derivation' system in Nigeria has been systematically revised in a declining order since 1954.

In the interest of concerned southern minorities, mineral producing areas and for the overall peace, unity, and stability of Nigeria Joseph Awani, (TSM, Sunday Magazine, August 20, 1995, Vol. 26) stated in part in his article that the derivation principle as basis for revenue allocation should be maintained and included in the constitution. Awani recalled the order in which the derivation principle has been used for revenue sharing over the years 1953-1992 and he also noted the declining order in which the derivation principle has been used to the disadvantage of minority oil producing states from 1972-1992. According to Awani the Percentage accorded to the derivation declined in the following order:

Year	% Derivation in revenue sharing	Head of government
1953	100%	Chicks Constitution
1960 Reduced to	50%	Independence Constitution under Alhaji Tafawa Balewa
1972 Reduced to	45%	Military Rule - General Gowon
1975 Reduced to	20%	Murtala/Obasanjo
1982 Reduced to	2%	Democratically elected Alhaji Shehu Shagari

| 1984 Reduced to | 1.5% | Military regime - General Buhari |
| 1992 Increased to | 3% | Military Regime - General Babangida |

The declining order was a reflection of the each political era. In 1953 100% derivation principle was based on non crude oil products controlled by major tribes (100% revenue allocation for each region based on the derivation).

1960   Independence Constitution was drawn in collaboration in with the British and derivation principle was fairly applied where 80% of the revenues from non-crude oil products from major tribe regions benefitted and 20% crude oil went to southern minorities.

1972   The rise of crude oil accounted for greatest proportion of national income and thus the principle of derivation was revised under General Gowon's rule. General Gowon northern minority had considerable understanding and reduced it by only 5% from 50%.

1975   Majority tribes influence reduced revenue allocation by derivation to mere 2%.

1982   This era was the greatest in consideration during Shagari Regime. Derivation was reduced to negligible 2%. The minority oil mineral producing states protested over the reduction.

In light of the reduction to the disadvantage of minority oil states Awani quotes Chief Obafemi Awolowo on the book *Tactics and Strategies of the Peoples Republic of Nigeria*, Awolowo wrote:

Where the opponents of the principle of derivation believe that they have the advantage of numbers, they insist on all the revenues being collected into a common pool and then shared out on the basis of population where this advantage is absent, they still insist on a common purse from which allocation to all concerned should be made on the basis of equality... In the capitalist society, whether it is a federation or not, it is untenable and dishonest in the extreme to insist on sharing another state's wealth on any basis rather than that which the rules of the capitalist game allow. In this kind of society, every state is perfectly entitled to keep any wealth that accrues to it either by the sweat of its brow, by cunning or by unaided bounty of nature. And to accuse a rich state of lack of fellow feeling or patriotism because it insists on keeping practically all that comes to it by whatsoever means is unreasonable and unrealistic.

In 1984 the Buhari/Idiagbon regime continued with 2 percent derivation. Awani emphasized that the Buhari/Idiagbon regime poured further scorn and contempt to the minority states by not only reducing the 2 percent to 1.5 percent but also utilized all the accrued amount on the fund to grant non - refundable loans to all states governments for the payment of arrears of salaries which were inherited from the Shagari Administration.

In 1992 the 1.5 percent was controlled and managed by a presidential committee until Babangida created OMPADEC (Oil mineral producing areas development commission) and increased the derivation to 3 percent.

The derivation principle application and relative revenue allocation in declining order shows:

1954	100%	
1958	50%	(Raison Commission)
1970	45%	
1974/75	20%	
1981	2%	
1992	1.5%	
1992/93	3%	(Later upgraded 3%)
1994	3%	

The 1994-95 draft constitution recommended the following criteria for revenue allocation in the country. The constitutional Committee on Revenue Allocation recommended the following formula:

A. **Vertical Allocation**

Percentages:

Federal Government	33.0
State Governments	32.5
Local Governments	20.0

326

Special funds:

- FCT (Federal Capital Territory)	2.0
- OMPADEC (Oil Mineral Producing Areas Commission)	6.0
- Ecological Fund	2.5
- Stabilization Fund	0.5
- Special Projects	3.5
- SOMPADEC (Solid Mineral Producing Areas Commission)	0.5

B. Horizontal allocation to states

	Percentages:
Population	40.0
Equality of States	30.0
Internal Revenue Efforts	10.0
Land Mass and Terrain	10.0
Population Density	10.0

C. Horizontal allocation to local governments

	Percentages
Population	40.0
Equality of Local Governments	30.0
Internal Revenue Efforts	10.0
Land Mass and Terrain	10.0
Population Density	10.0

The Constitution of the Federal Republic of Nigeria 1995 [Article C-Public Finance Section 163 (2)] stipulates that:

The President, upon the receipt of the advice from the National Revenue Mobilization, Allocation and Fiscal Commission, shall table before the National Assembly proposals for Revenue Allocation from the Federation Account. In determining the formula, the National Assembly shall take into account allocation principles especially those of population, equality of states, internal revenue generation, land mass, terrain as well as population density provided that the principle of derivation shall be constantly reflected in any approved formula as being not less than 13 percent of the revenue accruing to the Federation Account directly from any natural resources, so however, that the figure of the allocation for derivation shall be deemed to include any amount that may be set aside for funding any special authority or agency for the development of the state or states of the derivation.

The constitutional assembly criteria for recommendation on revenue allocation is with the hope of accomplishing following national goals:

The goals of the revenue allocation system are:

- Fiscal Efficiency

- Price Stability

- Viable Budgetary Positions

- Equity

- Justice

- Fairness

- Peace

- Unity

- Self-generating Growth of Government Tiers

- Sustainable Growth

- Egalitarian Society

- Restoration of Economic Growth

- Competitiveness in Productivity

328

- Full Employment

- High Standards of Living

The Federal sources of Petroleum Revenues are as follows:

1. Petroleum profit tax, Royalties and Rents
2. Oil Pipeline License Fees and Signature Bonus
3. NNPC Nigerian National Petroleum Corporation] Earnings from direct sales and proceeds from sale of Domestics crude to NNPC
4. Proceeds from equity and profit crude oil export
5. Penalty from gas flare.

Petroleum Profit Tax (PPT)

Petroleum Profit Tax is now cited and based on PPTA 1959 Cap 354, Laws of the Federation of Nigeria, 1990 which encompassed all amendment made in 1967, 1970, 1973, and in 1979 (3 Acts). The PPT imposes tax upon profit from the winning of petroleum in the country and provides for assessment and collection thereof. The assessable tax for any accounting period of a company to which the Act applies is 8.5%. A reduced rate of 65.75% is payable within the first 5 years until all pre-production capitalized expenses have been fully amortized.

Royalty

In the Oil Industry, the terminology, royalty means the country's share at Official Service Price fiscalization of the oil and produced from the concession under OPL and OML completely free of the producers' production expenses. The percentage rates applicable are:

1. Onshore Production   20%
2. Production in Territorial waters and
   continental shelf areas up to 100m   18.5%
3. Production in Territorial waters and
   continental shelf areas beyond 100m   16.6%

Rents and fees

Small statutory fees are required for various licenses and lease applications and renewals of OPL, OML etc.

329

Memorandum of understanding (MOU)

The decline in the pace of exploration and development of oil resources in the 1970s imposed on oil producing companies operating in the country undue burden of the PPT (85%), high royalty rates that eroded their profit margin, thus led to an unfavorable climate of further investment. In response, the Federal Government continually adjusted the margins allowed oil Companies to offset their notional technical cost of production per barrel. The 1986-1990 MOU and the amendments effective from 1st January, 1991 labeled MOU 1991-1995. The highlight of the current MOU contains the following.

1. A minimum granted notional margin of $2.30 per barrel, after tax and royalty on equity crude, and minimum $4.50 per barrel after tax and royalty on NNPC equity and previous rates were $2.00 and $1.00 respectively.

2. Notional fiscal Technical Cost was set $2.30 per barrel. Previously $2.00 per barrel.

3. Where Capital Investment cost per barrel equals or exceeds $1.50 per barrel, then the minimum guarantee notional margin specified in (1) above is increased to $2.50 in respect of NNPC crude lifted by the oil Company. In such event, the notational fiscal technical cost is increased to $3.50 per barrel.

4. The guaranteed notional margin granted to oil Companies is decreased when realizable prices fall below $12.50 per barrel.

5. Two new tax offsets are introduced.

   (a)   CITO Capital Investment Tax Offsets
   (b)   Reserve Addition Bonus except for these changes
         all other provisions of the 1986-1990 MOU remain basically
         the same.

The complex computation can be summarized as follows:

   (i)   MOU Technical Cost of production at $4.20 per barrel.
   (ii)   MOU notional margin allowed at $2.30 per barrel.

The federal government also receives 100% of royalty payments. This regressive and lopsided trend in revenue collection should be revised to a more progressive mode of applying derivation principle such that the revenue generation structure of every state in the federation can be improved to reflect proportionate contribution to the center with corresponding proportionate receipt of allotment from the central government coffers. In the furtherance of equity and fairness, the oil royalty payments should be revised preferably to read: 50% royalty payment to federal government and 30% royalty should be retained by the producing state and 20% of the royalty be paid to the local government. Additionally, 20% of all annually produced mineral revenues should be given to the state of origin. Each state should pay 5% of the total mineral value produced in its jurisdiction to landowners and communities who are directly impacted by mineral extraction.

Finally, all mineral rental fees should be paid directly to landowners as part of the compensation planning and for the interest of human settlement. The state should collect mineral tax directly from the operating companies and also encourage indigenous equity participation in all mineral companies operating in their environment. The afore-mentioned conditions are amendable through negotiated compromise agreements relevant to foster harmony and development that is acceptable to the people and their government.

Also, there should be planned reforestation of oil areas vegetation and regeneration mechanism with the view to restore the natural ecological balance of the oil areas unique ecosystem. In addition, both the government and the oil companies should cooperate to render direct assistance to local farmers to upgrade and restore community food security systems. The government and oil companies should further cooperative to improve oil areas, waterways, and other natural linkage systems which may have been blocked, polluted or damaged in the course of oil exploration and exploitation.

In order to further alleviate the problems of inequalities and distributive imbalances which suffered the oil producing areas for decades, Nigeria should adopt the Malaysian example where there is the establishment of economic, agriculture and industrialization research units aimed at seeking to maintain balance between agriculture and industrial development. The Malaysian oil policy has planned orderly exploitation and involve the petroleum industry in development of the agro-based section of its economy designed to benefit the vast majority of its people. Unlike Nigeria which 'neglected' its agricultural sector in the face of growth and development of oil. Also, Malaysia has conservation policy through the country's depletion policy. In addition, though the oil producing states of Malaysia ceded all oil rights to the National Government, the States receive half of the oil revenues or royalties and free to spend the money as they see fit to boost development and still receive federal allocation for development projects.[45]

In a similar stance, Venezuela has a policy of 'sow the petrol' which translates to mean "use the oil revenues for the systematic development of the internal economic structure of Venezuela with emphasis on the oil producing areas." Under this policy, according to Wolfgang Hein[46] there have been an appreciable improvement in the situation of the poor such that oil revenues enhanced real benefits to the people including agrarian reform. In a similar vein, Laura Randell (1987) noted:

> that the role of the oil industry was expected not only to maximize revenues for the government but also to boost the country's overall economic development through the development of the production of goods and services used by the oil industry and the economic development of the areas in which the oil industry operates....[47]

These are worthy examples Nigeria can adopt to reform its National Oil Policy to benefit all its citizenry. With all the aforementioned factors taken together including community reinvestment programs would in effect be a oil fueled special Marshall plan for the development of oil producing areas.

Lastly, Nigeria's lasting economic and social well-being cannot be guaranteed by long run extraction and export of a non-renewable resource oil except serious policy steps are taken to diversify the economy to promote a wider base for enhancing national revenue sources. Also, the heavy reliance on oil to boost national revenues cannot possibly sustain Nigeria's economic future for the obvious reason that oil is too vulnerable to the vagaries of international trade and geopolitics (and in fact always subject to external demand and price instability). The future of oil producing areas partly depends on the essentialness of oil in the global economy which is not guaranteed to last for ever, hence a planned orderly exploitation along with proper compensation planning and conservation policy in the interest of the Nation [and the oil producing areas in particular] are important to the wholesome economic and social well being of the nation and its succeeding generations.

Notes

1. Angaye, et al. 'Proceeding of the 1983 International Seminar' (Lagos, Nigeria: NNPC, 1983). (ii) P. Colliers, Oil and Inequalities in Rural Nigeria. Geneva, Switzerland: Labor Office, 1978, p. 191.

2. Seers, Dudley, 'What needs are really basic in Nigeria. Some thoughts prompted by an ILO Missions.' *International Labor Review*, Vol. 120, No. 6, November/December 1981, pp. 739,742.

3. Quoted by Michael Watts in *Political Economy of Nigeria* by I. William Zartman (New York: Praeger), p. 105.

4. Santo, Ana Bella. Horizontal Fiscal Equity: A Theoretical Contribution with an Application to the Portuguese Municipalities (Fiscal Equity) University of New York, United Kingdom, Doctoral Dissertation, 1989.

5. Nafziger, Wayne E., 'The Economics of Political Instability: The Nigerian Biafran War', *Westview Press*, Boulder Colorado, 1983, p.103.

6. For the cause of the Nigerian Civil War from 1967-70, see Diamond, Larry, *Class, Ethnicity, and Democracy in Nigeria: The Failure of the First Republic.* (Syracuse, NY: Syracuse University Press, 1988), pp. 2-329.
    Muhammadu, Turi and Mohammed Haruna, 'The Civil War', in Oyediran, Oyeleye (ed.), *Nigerian Government and Politics Under Military Rule, 1966-79.* (New York: St. Martins Press, 1979), p. 1-24.
    Rupley, Lawrence, 'Revenue Sharing in the Nigerian Federation', p. 261. For a similar view of this perspective, see Onoh, *The Nigerian Oil Economy*, (New York: St. Martins Press, 1983), pp. 112-116.
    Nafziger, E. Wayne, *The Economics of Political Instability: the Nigerian Biafran War*, (Boulder, Colorado: West View Press, 1983), pp. 106-108.

7. Rupley, Lawrence R., 'Revenue Sharing in the Nigerian Federation', *Journal of Modern African Studies*, Vol. 19, No. 2, 1981, p.264.

8. Onoh, J.K., *Nigerian Oil Economy: From Prosperity to Glut*, (New York: St Martins Press), p. 115.

9. *Rivers State Government Official Letter to the Federal Government*, 1984.

10. *Danjuma commission Appointed by General Babangida Administration,* 1989.

11. Ake, Claude, *A Political Economy of Africa,* (New York. Longman Publishers, 1986), p. 2.

12. Okigbo, P., 'National Development Planning in Nigeria', p.174.

13. Adaka, Boro, As quoted in Nigerian *Newsweek,* December 19, 1988, p. 12.

14. Okpu, Ugbana, *Ethnic Minority Problems in Nigerian Politics: 1960-65.* (Stockholm: Uppsala University Press, 1977), p. 11.

15. Oyelegbin, R., C. Illuzue and Ben Apkan, 'Southern Minorities Demand Autonomy or Integration', *The Guardian Newspaper,* February 28, 1994. p. 40.

16. Ibid. Also, Briggs, Monima. Nigerian Electronic Network News. Naijanet @ athena.MIT.edu. August 30, 1993.

17. Ndu, Ovi Joseph, 'Formal and Informal Authority and Federalism: Fiscal Federalism in Nigeria', Doctoral Dissertation, University of Texas, Arlington, Texas, 1983.

18. Rivlin, A.M. 'A New Vision of American Federalism', *Public Administration Review,* 52(4). p. 315.

19. Okilo, Melford, 'Derivation: A Criterion of Revenue Allocation', (Port Harcourt River Newspaper Corporation, 1980), p.13.

20. Ibid, p.10.

21. Phillips, 'Nigeria's Fiscal Financial Experience', p.390.

22. Tony Furro, 1992, p.233.

23. Ikpurukpo, C., 'Petroleum Exploration and the Socioeconomic Environment in Nigeria', p.202.

24. Aliyu, A.Y., 'The New Revenue Allocation Formula A Critique,' *Nigerian Journal of Public Affairs,* Vol. 7, October, 1977, p.120.

25. Teriba and Phillips, *Income Distribution and National Integration,* p.108-109.

26. Wiwa, Saro Ken. 1992. p. 100.

27. Yakasai, Tanko, Special Interview by Ademola Oyinlola of *Tell Magazine*, January, 1994, pp.21-24.

28. *Report of the Presidential Commission on Revenue Allocation. Okigbo Report*, 1980.

29. Makinde, Kunle, 'Rivers People Fight On,' *Nigerian Newsweek*, January 2, 1989, p.11.

30. Furro, 1992, p.339.

31. State, Oyo, 'Turning the Industrial Wheel', *The African Guardian*, Vol. 5, No. 35, September 10, 1990, p.24.

32. Seth, S. Parkash, 'Opportunities and Pitfalls for Multinational Corporations in a Changed Political Environment Longrange Planning', Vol. 20, No. 6, 1987, p.45.

33. Pratt, Cornelius C., 'Multinational Corporate Social Policy Process for Ethical Responsibility in Sub-Saharan Africa,' *Journal of Business Ethics*, Vol. 10, No. 7, 1991, pp.527-541.

34. Ashwe, Chiichii, 'The New Revenue Allocation Formula', *Nigerian Economist*, Vol. 2, No. 26, September 1989, p.91.

35. Phillips, Adedotum O, 'Revenue Allocation in Nigeria 1970-1980', *The Nigerian Journal of Economic and Social Studies*, Vol. 017, No. 2, July 1975, p.5.

36. Phillips, 'Reforming Nigeria's Revenue Allocations System', *Nigerian Journal of Public Affairs*, Vol. 6, No. 1, May 1976, p.83.

37. Map of Nigeria showing natural resources and raw materials, Federal Ministry of Information, Lagos, 1991.

38. *Vanguard*, December 22, 1993, p.11.

39. Ibid, p. 11-12.

40. *Holy Bible*, Standard Revised Version, 2nd Edition. (New York: Thomas Nelson, 1972).

41. Rahman, Fazlur, *Islam*. (New York: Holt, Rinehart and Winston, 1966).

42. Khan, Muhammed Zafrulla, 'Wealth and Charity,' *The Review of Religion*, Vol. LXXXI, No.5, May 1986, p. 5-6.

43. *Daily Champion*, July 1,1994, p. 5.

44. Cross, Frank. B., et al. (1992), *West's Business Law*, 5th Edition. (St. Paul, MN: West Publishing), pp.195-197.

45. Hills, Peter and Paddy Bowie, 'China and Malaysia: Social and Economic Effects of Petroleum Development', (Geneva, Switzerland: International Labor Organization, 1987) pp.70-80.

46. Hein, Wolfgang and Terisa Turner, 'Oil and the Venezuela State in Petter Nore', *Oil and Class Struggle*, (London: Zed Press, 1980), p. 36-243.

47. Randell, Laura, 'Political Economy of Venezuelan Oil', (New York, Praeger, 1987), p.22.

AppendixA

Nigeria: Oil production and producing areas

Name of field, discovery date	Depth, ft	No. of wells Producing	Production 1993 average	b/d
AGIP				
Agbara, 1981	7,500-12,000	13	15,568	36.2
Agwe, 1975	10,800	2	2,714	44.0
Akri, 1967	9,600-10,600	8	6,331	40.8
Akri W., 1972	9,900-10,200	0	0	43.0
Ashaka, 1968	9,700-12,000		1,157	37.4
Azuauama, 1975	9,700-14,900	3	3,650	34.1
Beniboye, 1978	9,000-10,000	9	5,176	28.6
Beniku, 1974	12,000	0	40	28.0
Clough Creek, 1976	10,000-12,400	8	5,261	25.5
Ebegoro, 1975	11,500-12,000	7	7,952	37.1
Ebegoro S., 1975	14,100	0	1,028	36.0
Ebocha, 1965	8,000-10,900	5	6,085	36.3
Idu, 1967	7,750-10,700	0	0	30.0
Kwafe, 1967	10,000-11,500	6	6,796	37.1
Mbede, 1966	7,300- 9,400	12	11,054	43.1
Obama, 1973	11,600-14,300	8	12,883	30.7
Obiafu, 1967	9,300-12,200	17	20,282	41.6
Obrikom, 1967	8,000-10,000	9	7,035	43.4
Odugri, 1972	12,500	1	2,508	45.9
Ogbogene, 1972	10,000	1	614	33.0
Ogbogene W., 1982	13,000	0	0	45.0
Okpai, 1968	10,000-12,000	6	4,342	42.8
Omoku W., 1974	11,000	1	916	40.0
Oshi, 1972	9,600-11,300	10	12,914	35.2
Pirigbene, 1987	13,700	0	4,045	43.0
Taylor Creek, 1985	9,300-10,400	1	1,718	37.3
Tebidaba, 1972	10,300-11,300	8	10,704	30.4
Umuoru, 1977	14,100	3	3,178	40.3
ASHLAND				
Adanga,1980	8,500	8	5,385	31.9
Akam, 1980	6,700	8	3,817	34.0
Bogi 1989	7,500	3	945	28.7
Ebughu, 1983	7,250	3	855	23.8
Izombe, 1974	8,000	10	7,350	34.3
Mimbo, 1984	7,500	3	1,470	31.1
Ossu, 1974	8,000	3	209	31.6
Ukpam, 1989	5,500	1	627	40.6

CHEVRON

Abiteye, 1970	5,750- 9,400	23	8,036	39.7
Belema N., 1989	6,573-12,130	0	352	34.0
Delta, 1965	5,600- 9,500	34	19,635	37.3
DeltaS., 1965	7,100-10,179	22	21,883	38.4
Idama, 1974	8,100-11,250	6	1,928	33.4
Inda, 1982	7,250-11,030	8	764	44.8
Isan, 1970	5,900- 9,000	7	3,136	40.4
Jisike, 1975	6,300- 7,600	6	9,242	41.1
Makaraba, 1973	7,100-12,005	27	22,870	27.7
Malu, 1969	4,800- 6,300	15	13,265	40.4
Mefa, 1965	8,570-12,030	19	20,713	38.1
Meji, 1965	5,200-10,900	35	21,747	31.9
Meren, 1965	5,000- 7,500	60	2,402	31.9
Mina, 1985	6,700- 9,300	5	2,996	40.3
Okan, 1964	5,500- 9,245	77	50,509	38.1
Opuekeba, 1975	6,000-10,200	10	3,341	36.7
Parabe/Eko, 1968	4,500- 8,200	33	9,895	40.4
RobertkiRI, 1964	11,484-13,19	20	22,991	40.2
Tapa, 1978	8,150-10,842	11	12,181	39.5
Utonana, 1971	7,400- 9,165	3	877	20.4
W. Isan, 1971	7,825-10,229	8	5,283	40.4
Yorla South,1974	11,389-12,635	3	658	41.0

ELF

Aghigho, 1972	7,303	29	7,800	24.8
Erema, 1972	11,211	6	3,800	24.6
Obagi, 1964	8,377	74	50,750	24.6
Obodo-Jatumi, 1966	7,656	17	10,700	24.8
Ukpoko, 1967	6,745	20	8,650	24.8
Upomani, 1965	6,256	18	5,600	24.8
Afia, 1982	3,780	5	9,000	26.0
Odudu, 1977	4,930	8	6,000	35.0

SHELL

Adibawa, 1966	11,950	14	10,400	26.4
Afisere, 1966	8,500	24	11,500	19.6
Afremo, 1972	9,263	8	23,300	36.8
Agbada, 1960	10,000	32	26,000	23.9
Akaso, 1979	13,122	6	24,900	37.1
Awoba, 1981	....	..	21,900	....
Benisede, 1973	8,941	13	29,000	21.9
Cawthorne Chan, 1963	11,000	21	41,900	36.9
Egwa, 1967	9,350	17	19,500	34.1
Ekulama, 1958	10,483	23	42,200	31.6

338

Elelenwa, 1960	11,000	6	11,500	35.8
EscravosBeach, 1969	8,176	7	11,500	31.2
Etelebou, 1971	12,000	8	14,000	31.3
Forcados Yorki, 1968	10,859	55	70,400	24.4
Imo River, 1959	7,900	37	25,500	30.3
Jones Creek, 1967	80,000	29	46,800	29.7
Kalaekule, 1972	9,236	7	20,000	40.5
Kolo Creek, 1971	12,000	18	17,300	39.1
Nembe Crk,1973	12,213	39	82,200	31.0
Nun-River, 1960	14,200	5	12,900	32.7
Oben, 1972	12,036	18	15,300	37.6
Obigbo N., 1963	8,250	30	14,000	23.2
Odeama Crk, 1981	12,897	5	23,000	35.5
Odidi, 1967	10,980	30	30,700	36.2
Oguta, 1967	10,300	13	14,000	43.2
Olomoro, 1963	8,500	24	18,100	21.5
Opukushi, 1962	7,823	11	17,300	28.3
Otumara, 1969	8,176	23	45,800	24.9
Sapele, 1969	12,788	8	10,400	42.9
Soku, 1958	11,500	15	13,400	27.7

TEXCO-CHEVRON-NNPC

Funiwa, 1978	8,000	19	35.5
Middleton, 1972	9,000	6	33.3
North Apori, 1973	8,500	26	35.5
Pennington, 1965	11,000	2	38.5
Sengana, 1987	12,000	..	....

MOBIL

Auda, 1967	6,970	4	38.4
Asabo, 1966	5,600	5	34.6
Asabo 'D', 1979	7,621	..	34.6
Ata,1964	8,823	..	....
Edop, 1988	9,215	8	37.4
Ekpe, 1966	8,200	7	34.9
Ekpe-WW, 1977	6,810	6	31.9
Eku, 1966	5,420	2	30.4
Enang, 1968	6,600	6	37.4
Etim, 1968	6,200	5	37.1
Idoho, 1966	9,020	1	30.5
Inim, 1966	5,850	5	37.5
Isobo, 1968	7,345	2	30.4
Iyak	....	1	...
Iyak S.E., 1979	7,441	10	38.6
Mfem, 1968	5,200	2	36.1
Ubit. 1968	5,400	18	36.1

Unam, 1967	5,180	4	33.3
Usari, 1965	8,431	..	538,887 ...
Utue, 1966	5,700	5	36.8

PAN OCEAN

Ogharefe, 1973	9,900	5	46.6

DUBRIL

Gilli-Gilli, 1967	9,357	2	47.1

TENNECO

Abura, 1979	13,471	3	44.7

OTHER OPERATIONS

All Fields	....	310	....
Total Nigeria	1,797	1,905,200	

Source: *Oil and Gas Journal*, December 1994

Nigeria: Oil contracts, 1994
NNPC Contracts as per March 1,1994

Crude oil	bbl/day
1. Ferrostal, Spain	40,000
2. Total S.A. France	40,000
3. Reposol, Spain	40,000
4. NNPC/Calson, Nigeria	30,000
5. Erik Emborg A/S, Denmark	30,000
6. Incomed, Spain	30,000
7. Vitol, UK	30,000
8. Clarendon	30,000
9. Wintershall, Germany	30,000
10. Tomeni Corporation, Japan	30,000
11. Petrogaz Distribn. SA Switzer.ld.	30,000
12. VIT Vulcan, Switzerland	30,000
13. H-Oil, Spain	30,000
14. Windpemij N.V, Holland	30,000
15. Statoil, Norway	30,000
16. Arcadia Petroleum, UK	20,000
17. Oranto Petroleum, Nigeria	20,000
18. Summit Oil, Nigeria	20,000
19. Amni International Petroleum	20,000
20. Queen Petroleum, Nigeria	20,000
21. Navacor	20,000
22. OK Petroleum Sweden	20,000
23. Scandinavian	20,000
24. Nova Petroleum, Intl. Canada	20,000
25. Itochu Cop., Japan	20,000
26. Raqma Oil, Nigeria	20,000
27. Basic Resource Serv. Swiz.	20,000
28. Vermont Petroleum, US	20,000
29. Ghana National Pet Co., Ghana	20,000
30. Moncref, Nigeria	20,000
31. Republic of Togo	10,000

Nigeria:Oil companies(1993)

- List of Rightholders -

Group Abbr.	Partners (*=operator)	Interests
AGIP 1	*Nigerian Agip Oil Co Ltd(NAOC)	20.000%
	Nigerian National Petroleum Co.	60.000%
	Phillips Oil Co (Nigeria) Ltd	20.000%
AGIP 2	*Nigerian Agip Oil Co Ltd(NAOC)	
	Amoco Corp	
	Esso E & P Nigeria Ltd (EEPN)	
AGIPEN 1	*Agip Energy & Natural Resource	0.000%
	Nigerian National Petroleum Co	100.000%
ALLIED 1	*Allied Energy Resources	57.500%
	Dupont E & P No. 13 B.V.	40.000%
	Camac Int'l (Nigeria)Ltd	2.500%
ASHLAN 1	*Ashland Oil (Nigeria) Co	0.000%
	Nigerian National Petroleum Co	100.000%
ASHLAND	*Ashland Oil (Nigeria) Co	100.000%
CAVEN 1	*Cavendish Petrol. Nigeria Ltd	57.500%
	Du Pont	40.000%
	Camac Int'l (Nigeria) Ltd	2.500%
CHEV 1	*Chevron (Nigeria) Ltd	40.000%
	Nigerian National Petroleum Co	60.000%
CONOCO	*Conoco Inc	100.000%
CONS OIL	*Consolidated Oil Ltd	100.000%
DUBRI	*Dubri Oil Ltd	100.000%
ELF	*Elf Petroleum Nigeria Ltd	100.000%
ELF 1	*Elf Petroleum Nigeria Ltd	40.000%
	Nigerian National Petroleum Co	60.000%
ESSO	*Esso E & P Nigeria Ltd (EEPN)	100.000%

342

EXPRES 1	*Express Petroleum & Gas Ltd	57.500%
	Du Pont	40.000%
	Camac Int'l (Nigeria) Ltd	2.500%
IPEC	*Int'l Petro-Energy Co Ltd	100.000%
JAMES PT	*Alfred James Petroleum Co Ltd	100.000%
MOBIL 1	*Mobil Producing Nigeria	40.000%
	Nigerian National Petroleum Co.	60.000%
MONCRIEF	*Moncrief Oil International Ltd	100.000%
NAPIMS	*Nat. Pet. Invest. Management Serv	100.000%
NPDC	*Nigerian Petroleum Develop. Co	100.000%
NPDC 1	*Nigerian Petroleum Develop. Co	80.000%
	Tenneco Oil of Nigeria	15.000%
	Sun DX Nigeria	5.000%
ORIENT 1	*Oriental Energy Resources	57.500%
	Du Pont	40.000%
	Camac Int'l (Nigeria) Ltd	2.500%
PACLAN 1	*Paclantic Oil Co Nigeria Ltd	97.500%
	Camac Int'l (Nigeria) Ltd	2.500%
PAN 1	*Pan Ocean Oil Co (Nigeria) Ltd	40.000%
	Nigerian National Petroleum Co	60.000%
QUEEN PC	*Queens Petr Co Nigeria Ltd	100.000%
SHELL 1	*Shell Pet. Dev. Co of Nigeria	30.000%
	Nigerian National Petroleum Co	60.000%
	Elf Nigeria Ltd	5.000%
	Nigerian Agip Oil Co Ltd(NAOC)	5.000%
SHELL NI	*Shell Nigeria E&P Co Ltd(Snepco)	100.000%
STATOIL 1	*Den Norske Stats Oljeselskap	50.000%
	British Petroleum Co	50.000%
SUMMIT O	*Summit Oil International Ltd	100.000%
SUNL 1	*Sunlink Petroleum Ltd	40.000%
	Nigerian Petroleum Develop. Co	60.000%

SUPRA	*Supra Oil & Chemical Co Ltd	100.000%
TEXACO 1	*Texaco Overseas (Nigeria) Pet.Co	20.000%
	Nigerian National Petroleum Co	60.000%
	Chevron Oil Co (Nigeria)	20.000%
UNION SQ	*Union Square Petrogas Ltd	100.00%
YINKA	*Yinka Folawiyo Ltd	100.00%

Source: Petro Consultants, Geneva Switzerland 93.

Nigeria : Oil producing states

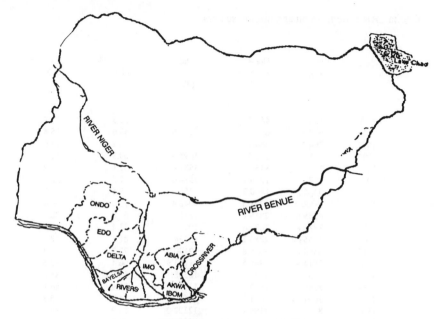

OIL PRODUCING AREAS

Size: 117,396 Square Kilometers
12.8% of the size of Nigeria

Population: 241,694 Million or 25% of Nigerian Population

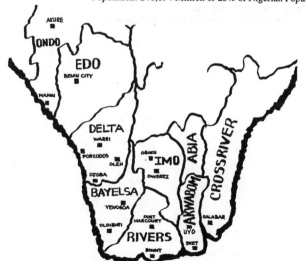

Source: Adopted from the administration map of Nigeria
Federal Ministry of Information, Lagos, Nigeria,
N.N.P.C.

345

Appendix B

Nigeria : Revenue from oil and non-oil sectors

Year	Oil Revenue (1)	Non-Oil Revenue (2)	Total (3)	1 as a % of 3	2 as a % of 3
1970	166.5	467.4	634	26.3	73.7
1971	510.1	658.7	1168.8	43.6	56.4
1972	764.3	640.8	1405.1	54.4	45.6
1973	1016.0	679.3	1695.3	59.9	40.1
1974	3724.0	813.4	4537.4	82.1	17.9
1975	4271.5	1243.1	5514.6	77.5	22.5
1976	5365.2	1400.7	6765.9	79.5	20.7
1977	6080.6	1961.8	8042.4	75.6	24.4
1978	4555.8	2815.2	7310	61.8	38.2
1979	8880.8	2031.6	10912.4	81.4	18.6
1980	12353.8	2880.2	15234	81.1	18.9
1981	8564.4	3615.8	12180.2	70.3	29.7
1982	7814.4	3949.5	11763.9	66.4	33.6
1983	7253.0	3255.7	10508.7	69.0	31.0
1984	8269.2	2922.0	11191.2	73.9	26.1
1985	10915.1	3691.0	14606.1	74.7	25.3
1986	8107.3	4194.7	12302.0	65.9	34.1
1987	19027.0	6027.0	25054.0	75.9	24.1
1988	20933.8	6377.0	27310.8	76.7	23.3
1989	41334.4	8937.7	50272.1	82.2	18.8
1990	54713.2	12182.2	66895.44	81.8	18.2

Sources: CBN, Statistical Bulletin, Nos. 1&2, vol. 1, 1990
Sources: David B. Ekpenyong
The Nigerian Banker April/June, 1992 (page 13).

Value of Nigerian oil exports

COUNTRY	1970	1980	1985	1987	1988	1989	1990	1991	1992
Nigeria	716	25290	12353	7161	6267	7500	13200	12150	11500

Source: OPEC Annual Statistical Bulletin, Various issues.
WORLD ECONOMIC SURVEY 1993 (Page 256)

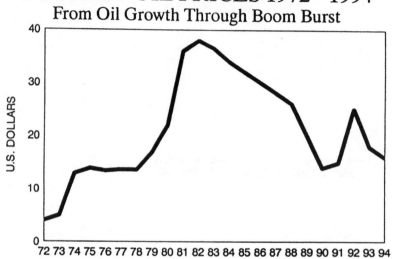

NIGERIA OIL PRICES 1972 - 1994
From Oil Growth Through Boom Burst

Sources: Ministry Petroleum Resources, Lagos, Nigeria British Petroleum, Statistical Review of World Energy London (1986) 5, Petroleum Encyclopedia 1988, p.248. Platts Oil Gram Price Report, New York McGraw Hill Energy Information Administration. Washington DC.

Bibliography

Adamolukun Ladipo. *Politics and Administration in Nigeria.* (Ibadan, Nigeria: Spectrum Books, Ltd., 1986).

Adarkar, B.P. *The Principles and Problems of Federal Finance.* (London: King & Son, 1933).

Address by His Excellency, Sir Arthur Richards, CGMG, Governor and Commander-in-Chief of Nigeria at a meeting of the Colonial Affairs Study Group of the Empire Parliamentary Association. (January 28, 1947).

Adedeji, Adebayo. *Nigerian Federal Finance.* (London: Hutchinson Educational Ltd., 1971).

Ademoyega, Wale. *The Federation of Nigeria: From Earliest Times to Independence.* (London: George G. Harrap & Co., Ltd., 1962).

Administrative and Financial Procedures Under the New Constitution: Financial Relations Between the Government of Nigeria and the Native Administration, 1994, *Nigerian Journal of Public Affairs. Vol. VII* 6 (Lagos: Government Printer, 1946).

Africa Now (May 1981), p. 71.

African Contemporary Record, Vol. XI (1978-79).

African Research Bulletin (Political, Social and Cultural Series), Vol. 15, No. 1 (January 1979).

Aliyu, A.Y. *"The New Revenue Allocation Formula: A Critique".* (May/October 1977).

Aluko, Sam A., "Nigerian Federal Finance: A General Overview", *Quarterly Journal of Administration (Ife), Vol, IV, No. 2* (January 1970).

Aluko, Sam A., The Trends in Public Expenditure in Nigeria Since 1960". *The Economic Insight, Vol. 2, No. 1* (June 1978).

Ayoade, J.A., "Intergovernmental Relations in Nigeria". *Quarterly Journal of Administration (Ife), Vol, XIV, No. 2* (January 1980).

Ake, Claude. *A Theory of Political Integration.* (Homewood, IL: The Dorsey Press, 1967).

Akinyemi, A.B., Cole, P.D., & Ofonagoro, Walter (eds). *Readings in Federalism.* (Lagos: Nigerian Institute of International Affairs, 1979).

Almond, Gabriel & Verba, Sidney. *The Civic Culture.* (Boston: Little Brown & Company, 1965).

Aluko, Sam. *Recent Trends in Federal Finance.* (Lagos: Nigerian Institute of International Affairs, 14979).

Anderson, James E. *Public Policy Making 2ed.* (New York: John Wiley & Sons, 1965).

Anderson, James E., Brady, David W., & Bullock, Charles, III. *Public Policy and Politics in America.* (North Scitutate, MA: Duxbury Press, 1978).

Arikpo, Okoi. *Development of Modern Nigeria.* (Middlesex, England: Penguin Books, 1967).

Austin, Dennis. *Politics in Africa 2ed.* (Hanover, RI: University Press of New England, 1984).

Awa, Eme O. *Federal Government in Nigeria.* (Berkeley & Los Angeles: (University of California Press, 1964).

350

Awolowo, Obafemi. *Path to Nigerian Freedom.* (London: Faber & Faber 1947).

Awolowo, Obafemi, Awo: *The Autobiography of Chief Obafemi Awolowo.* (Cambridge: Cambridge University Press, 1960).

Ayandele, E.A. *The Educated Elite in the Nigerian Society.* (Ibadan: Ibadan University Press, 1974).

Ayida, A. *The Nigerian Revolution*: 1966-1967. (Ibadan University Press, 1978).

Azikiwe, Nnamdi. *Political Blueprint for Nigeria.* (London: Longmans, Ltd., 1943).

Baeun, Raymond A. & Gergen, Kenneth (eds). *The Study of Policy Formation.* (New York: The Free Press, 1957).

Ballard, J.A. *Policy Making in a New State.* (St. Lucia, Australia: University of Queensland Press, 1981).

Ballard, J.A. "Administrative Origins of Nigerian Federalism", *African Affairs,* Vol. 70, No. 281 (October 1971).

Beckett, Paul & O'Connell, James. *Education and Power in Nigeria.* (New York: African Publishing Company, 1977).

Bennet, W.H. *American Theories of Federalism.* (Birmingham: University of Alabama Press, 1966).

Benveniste, Guy. *The Politics of Expertise 2ed.* (San Francisco: Boyd & Fraser Publishing Company, 1977).

Bienen, Henry and Diejomaoh, V.P. (eds). *The Political Economy of Income Distribution in Nigeria.* (New York: Homes & Meier, 1981).

Birch, A.H. *Federalism Finance and Social Legislation.* (Oxford: Clarendon Press, 1957).

Bird, Richard & Head, John. *Modern Fiscal Issues.* (Toronto: University of Toronto Press, 1972).

Blitz, L. Franklin (ed). *The Politics and Administration of Nigeria.* (London: Sweet & Maxwell, 1965).

Blume, Stuart S. *Towards A Political Sociology of Science.* (New York: The Free Press, 1974).

Bowie, R.T. and Friedrich, Carl (eds). *Studies in Federalism.* (Boston: Little Brown & Company, 1954).

Break, George F. *Intergovernmental Fiscal Relations in the United States.* (Washington, D.C.: The Brookings Institution, 1967).

Burton, Frank and Carlen, Pat. *Official Discourse.* (London: Routledge & Kegan Paul, Ltd., 1979).

Chaba, Patric (ed). *Political Domination in Africa: Reflections on the Limits of Power.* (Cambridge: Cambridge University Press, 1968).

Chapman, Richard (ed). *The Role of Commissions in Policy Making.* (London: George Allen & Unwin, Ltd., 1973).

Clokie, Hugh and Robinson, J. William. *Royal Commissions of Inquiry: The Significance of Investigations in British Politics.* (Stanford: Stanford University Press, 1937).

Coleman, James. *Nigeria: Background to Nationalism.* (Berkeley & Los Angeles: University of California Press, 1958).

Cronje, Suzanne. *The World and Nigeria: The Diplomatic History of the Biafran War, 1967-1970.*(London: Sidgwick & Jackson, 1972).

Currie, David. *Federalism and the New Nations in Africa.* (Chicago: University of Chicago Press, 1964).

Daily Sketch (Ibandan), (September 8, 1980) p. 3.

Daily Sketch (January 19, 1981), p. 1.

Daily Sketch   (January 31, 1981) p. 1.

Daily Sketch   (February 6, 1981), p. 9.

Daily Sketch   (May 20, 1982), p. 7.

Daily Star (Enugu), (September 17, 1981) p. 1.

Daily Star   (February 9, 1981), pp. 3 & 9.

Daily Star   (March 2, 1981), p. 1.

Daily Times (Lagos), (January 29, 1966), p. 4.

Daily Times (August 9, 1967), p. 2.

Daily Times (April 12, 1969), p. 1.

Daily Times (June 23, 1978), p. 1.

Daily Times (January 15, 1981), p. 32.

Daily Times (February 14, 1981), p. 1.

Daily Times (March 11, 1981), p. 1.

Daily Times (October 3, 1981), p. 1.

Daily Times (December 10, 1981), p. 5.

Diamond, Larry. "Nigeria in Search of Democracy", *Foreign Affairs, Vol, 62.* (Spring 1983).

Diamond, Larry. "Cleavage, Conflict and Anxiety in the Second Nigerian Republic", *Journal of Modern African Studies, Vol. 20* (December 1983).

Dibelius, Whilhelm. *England.* (New York: Harper Bros., 1930).

Dror, Yehezkel. *Public Policy Making Reexamined.* (Scranton, PA: Chandler Publishing Company, 1968).

Dudley, Billy J. "Federalism and the Balance of Power in Nigeria", *Journal of Commonwealth Political Studies, Vol. IV.* No. 1 (March 1966).

Dudley, Billy J. *Parties and Politics in Northern Nigeria.* (London: Frank Cass & Company, 1968).

Dudley, Billy J. *Instability and Political order; Politics and Crisis in Nigeria.* (Ibadan: Ibadan University Press, 1973).

Dudley, Billy J. *An Introduction to Nigerian Government and Politics.* (Bloomington, IN: Indiana University Press, 1982).

Dunn, John (ed). *West African States: Failures and Promises.* (Cambridge: Cambridge University Press, 1978).

Dye, Thomas & Zeighler, Harman. *The Irony of Democracy.* (Belmont, CA: Wadsworth, 1970).

Earle, Valerie (ed). *Federalism: Infinite Variety in Theory and Practice.* (Itasca, IL: F.E. Peacock Publishing, Inc., 1968).

Easton, David. *The Political System.* (New York: Knopf, 1953).

Easton, David. *The Framework for Political Analysis.* (Englewood, NJ: Prentice Hall, 1965).

Easton, David. *A System Analysis of Political Life.* (New York: John Wiley & Sons, 1965).

Eicher, C.K., and Liedholm, C. (eds). *Growth and Development of the Nigerian Economy.* (Lansing, MI: Michigan State University Press, 1970).

Eleazu, Uma. *Federalism and Nation Building: The Nigerian Experience, 1954-1964.* (Great Britain: Arthur Stockwell, Ltd., 1977).

Elias, Taslimi O. *Government and Politics in Africa.* (New York: Asia Publishing House, 1963).

Episoto, John. *Islam and Development.* (Syracuse University Press, Syracuse, New York, 1980).

Eulau, Heinz & Prewitt, Kenneth. *Labyrinths of Democracy.* (Indianapolis: Bobbs-Merrill, 1973).

Eyestone, Robert. *Political Economy.* (Chicago: Markham Publishing Company, 1972).

Eston, Robert, (ed). Public Policy Formation Public Policy Studies, Vol. 2, (Greenwich, CT: JAI Press, Inc., 1984).

Ezera, Kalu. *Constitutional Development in Nigeria.* (Cambridge: Cambridge University Press, 1964).

Fajana, Oladunjoye. *"Fiscal Centralization Tendencies in the Federal Republic of Nigeria Since 1966".* (unpublished monograph, 1979).

Fajana, Olandunjoye. "Intergovernmental Fiscal Relations in the Report of the Technical Committee on Revenue Allocation", *Quarterly Journal of Administration.* (Ife), Vol. XIV, No. 2 (January 1980).

Federal Military Government Views of the Report of the Panel on Creation of States (Lagos: Federal Government Press, 1976).

Federal Republic of Nigeria:, The Struggle for One Nigeria. (Lagos: Federal Ministry of Information, 1967).

Finer, Herman. "The British Style", *University of Chicago Law Review.* (Spring 1951),

Forsyth, Frederick. *The Biafran Story.* (Hammonsworth, Great Britain: Penguin Books, 1969).

Frankel, Charles (ed). *Controversies and Scholarship.* (New York: Russell Sage Foundation, 1976).

Friedrich, Carl. *Federalism: National and International.* (Oxford: Oxford University Press, 1963).

Friedrich, Carl. *Trends of Federalism in Theory and Practice.* (New York: Fredrich Praeger, 1968).

Goertz, Clifford (ed). *Old Societies and New States: The Quest for Modernity in Asia and Africa.* (New York: The Free Press, 1963).

Government Views on the Report of the Technical Committee on Revenue Allocation. (Lagos: Federal Government Press, 1978).

Greenstein, Fred & Polsby, Nelson W. (eds). *Governmental Institutions and Processes.* (Reading, MA: Addison-Wesley Publishing Company, 1975).

Guidelines for local Government. (Lagos: Federal Government Press, 1976).

Haines, C. Grove (ed). *Africa Today.* (Baltimore: The Johns Hopkin University Press, 1955).

Hammond, Kenneth R. (ed). *Judgment and Decision in Public Policy Formation.* (Boulder, CO: Westview Press, 1978).

Hanser, Charles J. *Guide to Decision: The Royal Commission.* (Totowa, NJ: The Bedminster Press, Inc., 1965).

Helleiner, G.H. "The Fiscal Role of the Marketing Boards in Nigerian Economic Development, 1947-61", *The Economic Journal, Vol, 74.* No. 265 (September 1964).

Herskovits, Jean. "Democracy in Nigeria", *Foreign Affairs.* (Winter 1978- 80).

Hirschman, A. "Policy Making and Policy Analysis in Latin America-Return Journey", *Policy Sciences, Vol. 6* (1975).

Hicks, Ursula K., et. al. (eds). *Federalism and Economic Growth in Underdeveloped Countries.* (London: George Allen & Unwin, Ltd., 1961).

Hodgkin, Thomas. *African Parties.* (London: Penguin African Series, 1961).

Holy Bible (Thomas Nelson Publishers, New York, 1972).

Hoselitz, E.F. & Moore, W.E. (eds). *Industrialization and Society.*(Paris: UNESCO-Mouton, 1963).

Hurwick J. *Religion and National Integration.* (Northwestern University Press, Evanston, IL, 1992).

Ikein, Augustine A. *The Impact of Oil on a Developing Country: The Case of Nigeria.* (New York: Praeger Publishers, 1990).

Jones, Charles O. *An Introduction to the Study of Public Policy 2ed.* (North Scituate, MA: Duxbury Press, 1977).

Jones, Charles O., & Thomas, Robert D., (eds). *Public Policy Making in a Federal System.* (Beverly Hills, CA: Sage Publications, Inc., 1976)

Joseph, Richard A. *Democracy and Prebendel Politics in Nigeria: The Rise and Fall of the Second Republic.* (Cambrigeshire, NY: Cambridge University Press, 1987).

Joseph, Richard A. "Class, State and Prebendal Politics in Nigeria", *Journal of Commonwealth & Comparative Studies, Vol, 21.* No. 3 (November 1983).

Joseph, Richard. "The Overthrow of Nigeria's Second Republic", *Current History, Vol. 83* (March 1984).

Judgement of the Supreme Court of Nigeria, No. SC17/1981 (October 2, 1981) (Lagos: Federal Government Press, 1981).

Junaid, Mo. *The First Islamic Constitution.* (Daily Champion, July 1, 1994), p. 5.

Kash, Don E. and Roycroft, Robert W. *U.S. Energy Policy: Crisis and Complacency.* (Norman, OK: University of Oklahoma Press, 1984).

Kelly, George A. "The Expert as a Historical Actor", *Deadalus, Vol. 92.* No. 3 (Summer 1963).

Key, V.O. Jr. *Public Opinion and American Democracy.* (New York: Knopf, 1961).

Kirk-Greene, Anthony H. (ed). *Crisis and Conflict in Nigeria: A Documentary Source Book, 1966-1967, Vols., I & II.* (London: Oxford University Press, 1967).

Kirkwood, Kenneth (ed). *African Affairs No. 2, St. Andrews Papers No. 15* (London: Chatto & Windus, 1963).

Kraus, Jon. "Return of Civil Rule in Nigeria and Ghana", *Current History, Vol. 79* (March 1980).

Kumo Suleiman & Aliyu Abubakar (eds). *Issues in the Nigerian Draft Constitution.* (Zaria, Nigeria: Institute of Administration, Ahmadu Bello University, 1977).

Kuri, Ahmadu. *The Nigerian General Elections, 1959 and 1979 and the Aftermath.* (Lagos: MacMillian, Nigeria, Ltd., 1981).

Laffin, Martin. *Professionalism and Policy: The Role of the Professional in the Center-Local Government Relationships.* (Aldershot, England: Gower Publishing Company, Ltd., 1986.)

LaPalombara, Joseph. *Politics Within Nations.* (Englewood Cliffs, NJ: Prentice Hall, 1974).

LaPalombara, Joseph & Weiner, Myron (eds). *Political Parties and Political Development.* (Princeton: Princeton University Press, 1969).

Laswell, Harold. *The Decision Process.* (College Park, MD: Bureau of Governmental Research, University of Maryland, 1956).

Latham, Earl. *The Group Basis of Politics.* (New York: Octagon Press, 1965).

LeMarchand, Rene. "Political Clientelism and Ethnicity in Tropical Africa: Competing Solidarities in Nation-Building", *American Political Science Review, Vol. 66.* No. 1 (March 1972).

LeMarchand, Rene & Legg, Keith.   "Political Clientelism and Development",   *Comparative Politics, Vol., 14.* No. 2 (January 1972).

Lerner, Allan W. *The Politics of Decision Making.* (Beverly Hills, CA: Sage Publications, 1976).

Lindblom, Charles E. *The Policy Making Process.* (Englewood Cliffs, NJ: Prentice Hall, 1968).

Lindsay, Kennedy. "How Biafra Pays for the War", *Venture, Vol 21.* No. 3 (March 1969).

Luckham, Robin. *The Nigerian Military: A Sociological Analysis of Authority and Revolt, 1960-67.* (Cambridge: Cambridge University Press, 1971).

Lugard, Frederick, Lord. Report of North and South Nigeria and Administration, 1912-1919, *Command Paper 46.*, (London: HMSO, 1920).

MacDonald, Neil A. *The Study of Political Parties.* (New York: Random House, 1961).

Mackenzie, W.J.M. & Robinson, Kenneth. *Five Elections in Africa.* (Oxford: Clarendon Press, 1960).

Macintosh, John P. *Nigerian Government and Politics.* (Evanston, IL: Northwestern University Press, 1966).

Margolis, Harold. *Technical Advice on Policy Issues.* (Beverly Hills, CA: Sage Publications, 1973).

Maxwell, James. *Financing State and Local Governments.* (Washington, D.C.: The Brookings Institution, 1969).

May, R.J. *Federalism and Fiscal Adjustment.* (London: Clarendon Press, 1969).

McIlwain, Charles H. *Constitutionalism: Ancient and Modern.* (Ithaca, NY: Cornell University Press, 1947).

359

McWhinney, E. *Federal Constitution-Making For A Multinational World.* Leyden, Sweden: Stijhoff, 1966).

Mackintosh, John P. "Federalism in Nigeria", *Political Studies, Vol. X.* No. 3 (October 1962),

Mackintosh, John P. "Politics in Nigeria: The Action Group Crisis of 1962", *Political Studies, Vol, XI.* No. 2 (June 1963).

May, R.J. "Intergovernmental Finance", Public Administration (Sidney), Vol. 28, No. 1 (March 1969).

Mazur, Allen. "Dispute Between Experts", *Minerva* (April 1973).

Meekinson, J.P. (ed.). *Canadian Federalism: Myth or Reality* (Toronto: Methuen Publications, 1968).

Meltsner, Arnold J. *Policy Analysts in the Bureaucracy.* (Berkely, CA: University of California Press, 1976).

Merton, Robert K. *Social Theory and Social Structure.* (New York: The Free Press, 1968).

Milnor, Andrew (ed.), Comparative Political Parties: Selected Readings (New York: Thomas Y., Cromwell Company, 1969).

Mogi, Sobei. *The Problems of Federalism.* (London: George Allen & Unwin, Ltd., 1931).

Morning Post (Lagos), January 3, 1966, p. 3.

National Assembly Debates: House of Representatives (Lagos: Federal Government Press, 1980-1982).

National Assembly Debates: Senate (Lagos: Federal Government Press, 1980-1982).

National Concord (Lagos), (February 9, 1981), p. 3.

National Concord (February 13, 1981), p. 7.

National Concord (December 19, 1981), p. 3.

Nelkin, Dorothy (ed.). *Controversy: Politics of Technical Decision.* (Beverly Hills, CA: Sage Publications, 1979).

Nelkin, Dorothy. "The Political Impact of Technical Expertise" *Social Studies of Science, Vol. 1.,* No. 1 (February 1975).

New Nigeria (Kaduna), (February 23, 1966), p. 5.

New Nigeria (April 24, 1967), p. 2.

New Nigeria (May 21, 1974), p. 1.

New Nigeria (March 15, 1975), p. 5.

New Nigeria (May 3, 1978), p. 2.

New Nigeria (May 14, 1978), p. 3.

New Nigeria (September 16, 1980), p. 3.

New Nigeria (January 331, 1981), p. 3.

New Nigeria (February 4, 1981), p. 1.

New Nigeria (April 22, 1981), p. 1

New Nigeria (October 5, 1981), p. 32.

New Nigeria (October 12, 1981), p. 1.

New Nigeria (January 11, 1982), p. 1.

Nigerian Chronicle (Calabar), (July 5, 1980), p. 1.

Nigerian Chronicle (November 26, 1981), pp. 1 & 10.

Nigerian Herald (Ilorin), (November 3, 1981), p. 1.

Nigerian Observer (Benin-City), (June 21, 1980), p. 1.

Nigerian Observer (September 14, 1980), p. 8.

Nigerian Observer (February 19, 1981), pp. 1-3.

Nigerian Standard (Jos), (September 10, 1981), p. 1.

Nigerian Statesman (Owerri), (September 29, 1980), p. 14.

Nigerian Tribune (Ibadan), (November 6, 1981), p. 16.

Nigerian (Constitution) Order-in-Council, 1951 (London: HMSO, 1951).

Nigerian Sessional Paper, No. 4, *Command Paper 6599 (1945)*, (London: HMSO, 1945).

Nicholson, I.E. *The Administration of Nigeria, 1900-1960.* (Oxford: Oxford University Press, 1969).

Nowotny, Helga. "Experts and Their Expertise: On the Changing Relationship Between Experts and Their Public", *Bulletin of Science, Technology and Society, Vol. 1.* No. 3 (1981).

Nwabueze, Benjamin O. *The Presidential Constitution of Nigeria.* (New York: St. Martins Press, 1982).

Obadele, Iman. *Reparation.* Tes Shanghay House Baton Rouge, LA, 1993.

Odetola, Theophilus O. *Military Politics in Nigeria.* (New Brunswick, NJ: Transaction Books, Inc., 1980).

Offensend, David. "Centralization and Fiscal Arrangement in Nigeria", *Journal of Modern African Studies, Vol. 14.* No. 3 (October 1976).

Ojigbo, Okion. *Nigeria Returns to Civilian Rule.* (Lagos: Tokion (Nigeria) Company, 1980).

Ojukwu, Odumegwu C. *Biafra: Selected Speeches and Random Thoughts.* (New York: Harper & Row, Publishers, 1969).

Okigbo, Pius N.C. *Nigerian Public Finance* (Harlow, Essex: Longmans, Ltd., 1965).

Okilo, Melford. *Derivation: A Criterion of Revenue Allocation.* (Port Harcourt, Nigeria: Rivers State Newspaper Corporation, 1980).

Okwudiba, Nnoli. *Ethnic Politics in Nigeria.* (Enugu, Nigeria: Fourth Dimension Publishers, 1978).

Olorunsola, Victor (ed.). *The Politics of Cultural Sub-Nationalism in Africa.* (New York: Anchor Books, Doubleday & Company, 1972).

Opusunju, Silva, Isbo. *Yoruba and Housa Oppression of Minorities.* (Nigerian Times, March/April 1994), p. 24.

Ostheimer, John. *Nigerian Politics.* (New York: Harper & Row, 1973).

Oyovbaire, Samuel E. "The Theory of Federalism: A Critical Approach", *Nigerian Journal of Political Science, Vol. 1.* No. 1 (1979).

Oyediran, Oyeley (ed,). *Nigerian Government and Politics Under Military Rule, 1966-1979.* (New York: St. Martins Press, 1979).

Oyediran, Oyeleye (ed.). *Nigerian Government and Politics Under Military Rule, 1966-1979.* (New York: St. Martins Press, 1979).

Panter-Brick, S. Keith (ed.). *Nigerian Politics and Military Rule: Prelude to the Civil War.* (London: University of London, Althone Press, 1970).

Panter-Brick, S. Keth (ed.). *Soldiers and Oil: The Political Transformation of Nigeria.* (London: Frank Cass, 1978).

Parliamentary Debates: House of Commons Official Report, 5th Session, Vol, 515 (May 1953), (London: HMSO, 1953).

Phillips, Adedotun. "Nigeria's Federal Finance Experience", *Journal of Modern African Studies, Vol.9.* No. 3 (October 1971).

Phillips Adedotun. "Revenue Allocation in Nigeria, 1970-80", *Nigerian Journal of Economic and Social Studies, Vol. 17.* No. 2 (July 1975).

Phillips, Adedotun. "Three Decades of Intergovernmental Financial Relationship in the Federation of Nigeria", *Nigerian Journal of Public Affairs, Vol. 6.* No. 1 (May 1976).

Political and Constitutional Future of Nigeria, Governor of Nigeria Despatch to the Secretary of State for the Colonies Dated December 19, 1944. (Lagos: Federal Government Press, 1945).

Post, Kenneth W.M. *The Nigerian Federal Election of 1959.* (London: Oxford University Press, 1963).

Post, Kenneth & Vickers, Michael. *Structure and Conflict in Nigeria, 1960-1966.* (Madison, WI: The University of Wisconsin Press, 1973).

Prest, Alan R. *Public Finance in Theory and Practice.* (London: Weidenfeld & Nicholson, 1960).

Prest, Alan R. & Stewart, I.G. *The National Income of Nigeria, 1950-51 Colonial Research Studies,* No. 11 (London: HMSO, 1953).

Price, Don K. *The Scientific Estate.* (Cambridge, MA: Harvard University Press, 1965).

Proceedings of the Constituent Assembly (Lagos: Federal Government Press, 1978).

Proceedings of the General Conference on the Review of the Constitution, 1950 (Lagos: Federal Government Press, 1950).

Ranney, Austin (ed.). *Political Science and Public Policy* (Chicago: Makham Publishing company, 1968).

Ransome, Patrick (ed.). *Studies in Federal Planning* (London: Mamillan & Company, Ltd., 1943).

Ray, Amal. *Intergovernmental Relations in India.* (Bombay, India: Asia Publishing House, 1966).

Reagan, Michael. *The New Federalism.* (New York: Oxford University Press, 1972).

Report by the Conference on the Nigerian Constitution Held in London in July and August, 1953, Command Paper 8934 (London: HMSO, 1953).

Report by the Resumed Conference on the Nigerian Constitution, Command Paper 9056 (London: HMSO, 1954).

Report by the Resumed Nigerian Constitutional Conference Held in London in July and August, 1953, Command Paper 8934 (London: HMSO, 1953).

Report by the Resumed Conference on the Nigerian Constitution, Command Paper 9056 (London: HMSO, 1954).

Report by the Resumed Nigerian Constitutional Conference (Lagos: Federal Government Printer, 1958).

Report of the Commission on Revenue Allocation (Lagos: Government Printer, 1951).

Report of the Constitution Drafting Committee Containing the Draft Constitution (Lagos: Federal Government Press, 1976).

Report of the Fiscal Commission, Command Paper 481 (London: HMSO, 1958).

Report of the Fiscal Commissioner on Financial Effects of Proposed New Constitutional Arrangements, Command Paper 9026 (London: HMSO, 1953).

Report of the Fiscal Review Commission (Lagos: Federal Ministry of Information, Printing Division, 1965).

Report of the Interim Revenue Allocation Commission (Lagos: Nigerian National Press, Ltd., 1969).

Report of the Nigerian Constitutional Conference, Command Paper 207 (London: HMSO, 1957).

Report of the Presidential Commission on Revenue Allocation, Vols. I,II & III (Lagos: Federal Government Press, 1980).

Report of the Technical Committee on Revenue Allocation (Lagos: Federal Government Press, 1977).

Review of the Constitution: Regional Recommendations (Lagos: Government Printer, 1949).

Riker, William. *Federalism: Origin, Operation, Significance.* (Boston: Little, Brown & Company, 1964).

Rothchild, Donald S. *Toward Unity in Africa: A Study of Federalism in British Africa.* (Washington, D.C. Public Affairs Press, 1960).

Rupley, Lawrence A. "Revenue Sharing in the Nigerian Federation". *Journal of Modern African Studies, Vol, 19.* No. 2 (June 1981).

Sartori, Giovanni. *Parties and Party Systems.* (Cambridge: Cambridge University Press, 1970).

Schultze, Charles L. *The Politics and Economics of Public Spending.* (Washington, D.C.: The Brookings Institution, 1968).

Schwab, Peter (ed.). *Biafra.* (New York: Facts of File, Inc., 1971).

Schwartz, Frederick A.O. Jr. *Nigeria: The Tribes, the Nation or the Race–The Politics of Independence.* (Cambridge, MA: MIT Press, 1965).

Scott, Anthony. "The Evaluation of Federal Grants", *Economica, Vol. 14* (1947).

Scott, Anthony. "The Economic goals of Public Finance", *Public Finance, Vol. 29.* No. 3 (1964).

Scott, James. "Corruption, Machine Politics and Political Change", *American Political Science Review, Vol. 63.* No. 4 (December 1969).

Simon, Herbert. *Administrative Behavior 2ed.* (New York: The Free Press, 1957).

Sklar, Richard. "Contradictions in the Nigerian Political System", *Journal of Modern African Studies, Vol. 3.* No. 2 (August 1965).

366

Sklar, Richard L. *Nigerian Political Parties: Power in an Emergent African Nation.* (Princeton: Princeton University Press, 1963).

Smiley, D.V. *Conditional Grants and Canadian Federalism.* (Toronto: Canadian Tax Foundation, 1963).

Smith, Brian. *Policy-making in the British Government: An Analysis of Power and Rationality.* (Totowa, NJ: Rowman and Littlefield, 1976).

Smith, Brian. "Federal-State Relations in Nigeria", *African Affairs, Vol. 80.* No. 320 (July 1981).

Sunday Concord (Lagos), (February 15, 1981), p. 5.

Sunday New Nigeria (Kaduna), (October 18, 1981), p. 9.

Sunday Punch (Lagos), (December 20, 1981), p. 5.

Sunday Sketch (Ibadan), (August 30, 1980), p. 1.

Sunday Times (Lagos), (February 13, 1966), p. 4.

Tamuno, T.N.T. "Separatist Agitations in Nigeria Since 1914", *American Political Science Review, Vol, 63.* No. 4 (December 1969).

Teich, Albert H. (ed.). *Scientists and Public Affairs.* (Cambridge, MA: MIT Press, 1974).

Teriba, O. "Nigerian Revenue Allocation Experience, 1952-1965: A Study in Intergovernmental Fiscal and Financial Relations", *Nigerian Journal of Economic and Social Studies, Vol. 8.* No. 3 (July 1966).

The Constitution of the Federal Republic of Nigeria (With the Amendments) (Lagos: Daily Times Publications, 1979).

The Constitution of the Federation of Nigeria (Act No. 2 of 1963), (Lagos: Government Printer, 1963).

The Punch (Lagos), (January 16, 1981), p. 1.

The Punch (June 11, 1981), p.16.

Tilman, Robert O. & Cole, Taylor (eds.). *The Nigerian Political Scene.* (Durham, NC: Duke University Press, 1962).

Tom, Tietenberg. *Environmental Economics and Policy.* (Harper Collins, 1994).

Tordoff, William. *Government and Politics in Africa.* (Bloomington, IN: Indiana University Press, 1984).

Tripathy, R.M. *Federal Finance in A Developing Economy.* (Calcutta, 1960).

Truman, David. *The Governmental Process.* (New York: Knopf, 1965).

Turner, Louis. *Oil Companies in the International System.* (London: George Allen & Unwin, Ltd., 1978).

Views of the Government of the Federation on the Report of the Revenue Allocation Commission (Lagos: Federal Government Press, 1980).

Watson, M.M. "Federalism and Finance in the Modern Commonwealth", *Journal of Commonwealth Political Studies, Vol. 3.* (1965).

West Africa (January 21, 1967), p. 93.

West Africa (September 1, 1980), pp. 1641-42.

West Africa (February 9, 1981), p. 261.

West Africa (February 23, 1981), pp. 357-58

West Africa (May 26, 1981), pp.1641-42.

West Africa (July 13, 1987), p. 1337.

West Africa (August 24, 1987), p. 1631.

Whitaker, C.S. Jr. "Second Beginnings: The New Political Framework", *Issue, Vol, XI.* No. 1/2 (Spring/Summer 1981).

Wilensky, H. "The Professionalization of Everyone?", *American Journal of Sociology, Vol, 70*. (1964).

Watts, R.L. *New Federations: Experiments in the Commonwealth.* (Oxford: Oxford University Press, 1966).

Wheare, Joan. *The Nigerian Legislative Council* (London: Faber & Faber, Ltd., 1949).

Wheare, Kenneth C. *Modern Constitutions.* (London: Oxford University Press, 1956).

Wheare, Kenneth C. *Federal Government.* (Oxford: Oxford University Press, 1968).

Whitaker, C.S. Jr. *The Politics of Tradition.* (Princeton: Princeton University Press, 1970).

Williams, Walter. *Social Policy Research and Analysis: The Experience in the Federal Social Agencies.* (New York: American Elsevier Publishing Company, 1977).

Wilson, Harold. *The Government of Britain.* (New York: Harper & Row, 1976).

Wong, Dennis H. *Power: Its Forms, Bases and Uses.* (New York: Harper & Row, Publishers, 1978)

Wright, Deil S. *Federal Grants-in-Aid: Perspectives and Alternatives.* (Washington, D.C.: American Enterprise Institute for Public Policy Research, 1968).

Zartman, I. William. *The Political Economy of Nigeria.* (New York: Praeger Publishers, 1983).

Zolberg, Aristide R. *Creating Political Order: The One-Party State of West Africa.* (Chicago: Rand McNally & Co., 1963).